TERRORISM

TERRORISM

Patterns of Internationalization

Edited by

JAIDEEP SAIKIA
EKATERINA STEPANOVA

⑤SAGE www.sagepublications.com
Los Angeles • London • New Delhi • Singapore • Washington DC

First published in 2009 by

SAGE Publications India Pvt Ltd
B 1/I-1 Mohan Cooperative Industrial Area
Mathura Road, New Delhi 110044, India
www.sagepub.in

SAGE Publications Inc
2455 Teller Road
Thousand Oaks, California 91320, USA

SAGE Publications Ltd
1 Oliver's Yard, 55 City Road
London EC1Y 1SP, United Kingdom

SAGE Publications Asia-Pacific Pte Ltd
33 Pekin Street
#02-01 Far East Square
Singapore 048763

Published by Vivek Mehra for SAGE Publications India Pvt Ltd, typeset in 10/12 pt. Calisto MT by Star Compugraphics Private Limited, Delhi and printed at Chaman Enterprises, New Delhi.

Library of Congress Cataloging-in-Publication Data

Terrorism: patterns of internationalization/edited by Jaideep Saikia, Ekaterina Stepanova.
    p. cm.
  Includes bibliographical references and index.
    1. Terrorism—Case studies. I. Saikia, Jaideep. II. Stepanova, Ekaterina.

HV6431.T4865   363.325—dc22   2009   2009007165

ISBN: 978-81-7829-951-8 (Hb)

The SAGE Team: Elina Majumdar, Pranab Jyoti Sarma, Mathew. P.J. and Trinankur Banerjee

CONTENTS

Disclaimer   *vii*

List of Abbreviations   *ix*

Introduction   *xiii*
  Ekaterina Stepanova and *Jaideep Saikia*

PART ONE
EXTERNAL LINKS OF HOMEGROWN TERRORIST ORGANIZATIONS

1. **The IRA and ETA: The International Connections of
   Ethno-Nationalist Terrorism in Europe**   3
   Rogelio Alonso and *Florencio Domínguez Iribarren*

2. **Transnational Links and 'Local Connection':
   Latin America and Global Terrorism**   18
   Khatchik DerGhougassian

3. **Transnational Tigers: Liberation Tigers of Tamil
   Eelam's Paw across the Globe**   47
   Ramani Hariharan

4. **Jihad or Joi Bangla: Bangladesh in Peril**   71
   Subir Bhaumik

5. **External Links of the Maoist Insurgency in Nepal**   93
   Bishnu Raj Upreti

6. **Transformation of Kashmir's Insurgency:
   Azaadi to Global *Salafi***   118
   Jennifer Lynn Oetken

PART TWO
INTERNATIONALIZATION OF TERRORISM: REGIONAL AND GLOBAL THEATRE

7. **Circle of Design: 'Proxy Wars' in North East India**   141
   Jaideep Saikia

8. **Internationalization of Terrorism and its Limits in the Middle East**   161
   Amos N. Guiora

9. **Regionalization of Terrorism: Jemaah Islamiyah in South East Asia**   175
   Mohamed Nawab Bin Mohamed Osman

10. **Al-Qaeda Inspired Transnational Terrorism: Ideology and Organizational Forms**   191
   Ekaterina Stepanova

11. **Transnational Terrorism: Unlimited Means?**   210
   Adam Dolnik

Appendix: The Attack on Mumbai   231
   Subir Bhaumik and *Jaideep Saikia*

Consolidated Bibliography   234
About the Editors and Contributors   257
Index   263

DISCLAIMER

Views expressed in the various chapters are those of the contributors and not necessarily that of the editors

LIST OF ABBREVIATIONS

AHAB	Ahle Hadith Andolan Bangladesh
AMIA	Argentine Jewish Community Center
ARNO	Arakanese Rohingya Nationalist Organization
ATTF	All Tripura Tiger Force
AUC	Autodefensa Unida de Colombia
BBC	British Broadcasting Corporation
BNP	Bangladesh Nationalist Party
CBRN	Chemical, Biological, Radiological and Nuclear Materials
CCOMPOSA	Co-ordination Committee of Maoist Parties and Organisations of South Asia
CIA	Central Intelligence Agency
CNN	Cable News Network
CPA	Comprehensive Peace Agreement (Nepal, 2006)
CPI (M-L)	Communist Party of India (Marxist-Leninist)
CPI	Communist Party of India
CPN (M)	Communist Party of Nepal (Maoist)
CRPF	Central Reserve Police Force
CSA	Covenant, Sword, and Arm of the Lord
DDII	Dewan Dakwah Islamiyah Indonesia
DGFI	Directorate General of Forces Intelligence
DIN	Avenging Israel's Blood
DMK	Dravida Munnetra Kazhagam
ELN	Ejército de Liberación National
EROS	Eelam Revolutionary Organization of Students
ERP	Ejército Revolucionario del Pueblo
ETA	Euskadi ta Askatasuna
Europol	European Police Office
FAC	Fast Attack Craft
FAL	Fuerzas Armadas de Liberación
FARC	Fuerzas Armadas Revolucionarias de Colombia
FBI	Federal Bureau of Investigation

FLN	Front de Libération Nationale
FSB	Federal Security Bureau
FTO	Foreign Terrorist Organization
FUI	Muslim Ummah Forum
GAM	Free Aceh Movement
GMIP	Mujaheedin Movement of Pattani
Hamas	Harakat al-Mukawama al-Islamiya
Harkat	Harkat-ul-Mujaheedin
HEU	Highly Enriched Uranium
HRW	Human Rights Watch
HT	Hizb-ut-Tahrir
HTI	Hizbut Tahrir Indonesia
HUJI	Harkat-ul-Jihad-al-Islami
HuM	Hizb-ul-Mujaheedin
IBBL	Islami Bank Bangladesh Limited
ICG	International Crisis Group
ICNA	Islamic Circle of North America
ICS	Islami Chatra Shibir
IDF	Israel Defence Forces
IDL	Islamic Democratic League
IHL	International Humanitarian Law
IICO	International Islamic Charitable Organization
IIF	International Islamic Front
IISS	International Institute of Strategic Studies
IIU	International Islamic Universities
IPKF	Indian Peace Keeping Force
IRA	Irish Republican Army
ISI	Inter Services Intelligence
JeI	Jamaat-e-Islami
JeM	Jaish-e-Mohammed
JI	Jemaah Islamiyah
JIJK	Jamaat-e-Islami Jammu and Kashmir
JKLF	Jammu Kashmir Liberation Front
JMB	Jama'atul Mujahideen Bangladesh
JMJB	Jagrata Muslim Janata Bangladesh
KMM	Malaysian Mujaheedin Group
LeT	Lashkar-e-Toiba
LoC	Line of Control
LTTE	Liberation Tigers of Tamil Eelam

MDI	Markaz-ud-Dawa-wal-Irshad
MI 5	Directorate of Military Intelligence, Section 5
MILF	Moro Islamic Liberation Front
MIPT	Memorial Institute for the Prevention of Terrorism
MIR	Movimiento de Izquierda Revolucionaria
MMI	Majlis Mujaheedin Indonesia
MPC	Minnesota Patriots Council
MUF	Muslim United Front
MWL	Muslim World League
NATO	North Atlantic Treaty Organization
NORAID	Irish Northern Aid Committee
NSI	National Security Intelligence
PA	Palestinian Authority
PFLP	Popular Front for the Liberation of Palestine
PLO	Palestine Liberation Organization
PoK	Pakistan-occupied Kashmir
PULO	Pattani United Liberation Organization
PUPJI	Pedoman Umum Perjuangan Al-Jamaah Al-Islamiyah
RCMP	Royal Canadian Mounted Police
RDD	Radiological Dispersal Device
RIHS	Revival of Islamic Heritage Society
RIM	Revolutionary Internationalist Movement
RPG	Rocket-propelled Grenade
RSO	Rohingya Solidarity Organization
RU	Rabitatul Mujaheedin
SIMI	Students' Islamic Movement of India
SPA	Seven-Party Alliance
SPIN	Segmented Polycentric Ideologically Integrated Network
TELO	Tamil Eelam Liberation Organization
TII	Tentera Islam Indonesia
Triple A	Argentine Anticommunist Alliance
TRO	Tamil Rehabilitation Organization
TTN	Tamil Television Network
TULF	Tamil United Liberation Front
TWEED	Terrorism in Western Europe Events Dataset
UK	United Kingdom
ULFA	United Liberation Front of Asom

WAMY	World Assembly of Muslim Youth
WPRM	World People's Resistance Movement
WTCC	World Tamil Coordinating Committee
YCL	Young Communists League

INTRODUCTION[1]

Ekaterina Stepanova and Jaideep Saikia

Terrorism must be held to be wrong in every case.

—Mahatma Gandhi

Greater the sensitivity of security threat that international terrorism begets, the greater is the political and public confusion and speculation it generates. Also, pressing is the need to clarify its key patterns and trends. Poor and politically speculative analysis of this complex phenomenon leads to inaccurate threat assessment, misguided policy decisions and public perception.

In an era marked by conflicting tendencies of globalization and localization, the processes, forms, stages and degrees of internationalization, and even transnationalization, of modern terrorism, have not been addressed comprehensively and systematically. So far, only certain aspects of the problem, such as the nature and extent of state support to terrorism and the financing of transnational terrorism (Murphy 1989; Byman 2005; Napoleoni 2003), have received some attention from academic, political analysts and certain state actors.

Terrorism is diverse in its manifestations and is spread across different political and regional dimensions and at different levels—from local to global. The notion of 'international terrorism' is particularly blurred and misleading. As this confusion is partly generated by a lack of clarity about the definition of terrorism and understanding of how it is different from other forms of violence, a sound way to begin the quest is to attempt to provide a definition. Unlike most sceptics, who argue that terrorism as a term is so politically contested that it is almost impossible to come up with a clear definition, the editors of the book have a different point of view.

The editors' understanding of terrorism is, first and foremost, that it is a tactic that involves the threat and use of violence in order to achieve a political goal. This goal may be formulated in ideological or religious terms, but it invariably retains a political element. However, while the political motivation of terrorism can by no means justify the violence it perpetrates, it does help to distinguish it from—and, in fact, makes it more dangerous than—plain crime, motivated solely or primarily by material gain. To put it simply, if there is no political motivation behind an attack or threat of force, it can be stated that there is no terrorism involved.[2]

Second, terrorism is different from the classic guerrilla warfare in that it directly and explicitly targets non-combatants, or is intentionally indiscriminate in its method, causing civilian casualties. In contrast, rebel attacks against armed combatants—for instance, government forces—should be distinguished from terrorism and should be referred to as insurgency, or 'guerrilla warfare'. However, the same militant group can both target civilians in terrorist attacks and attack government forces. One of the editors, Jaideep Saikia, had earlier questioned whether countries such as India have deliberately kept a flexible anti-terrorism policy? According to him, the dilemma that India is faced with also stems from the fact that there exists a non-articulated perception in policy-making circles that there is an inherent distinction between insurgencies, such as the National Socialist Council of Nagalim (NSCN) and the United Liberation Front of Asom (ULFA) on the one hand, and terrorist groups such as the Jaish-e-Mohammad (JeM) and the Lashkar-e-Toiba on the other. Indeed, this is so despite the fact that (at times) the activities of the ULFA approximate to that of groups like the Lashkar-e-Toiba. If such features of Indian officialdom are any indication, then policy planners of the country do not seem to be suffering from a crisis of definition. It is quite clear in its understanding of the meaning of terrorism. Indeed, in the opinion of Saikia, it is in fact such an understanding that has led not only to the ambivalence that characterises India's response to terrorism, but the non-articulated perception of what constitutes terrorism (Saikia 2005).

While terrorist and guerrilla tactics may well be employed by the same armed group or movement, the use of one or the other tactic has different implications from the point of International Humanitarian Law (IHL). While the IHL explicitly warns against attacks against civilians in the course of the armed conflict—either intentionally or otherwise—it does not apply to attacks against government forces.

Third, what distinguishes terrorists from other non-state actors—as well as states—who may use other forms of politically motivated violence against civilians, such as genocide, ethnic cleansing, etc., is that, for terrorists, civilians are the immediate victims, but never the ultimate targets of violence. Terrorism is specifically designed to create a broader political and psychological effect that goes beyond its direct 'affect' and human costs among civilians. One of the facets of terrorism is also that it needs to be visible: it has to showcase itself—it is aimed at an audience. Civilians are terrorists' cannon fodder, but not their main addressees. Terrorists' core message is always directed at someone far more important than their innocent, unarmed victims—elements that the terrorists cannot normally effectively challenge by using conventional military tactics. It is also important that terrorism, as noted by one of the editors, Dr Ekaterina Stepanova, in her works on the subject, is an asymmetrical tactic employed by a conventionally and politically weaker party that also lack formal status—usually, an oppositional non-state actor—against a more powerful status 'enemy'—the state or a group of states. A transnational non-state actor who seeks to advance political goals that go beyond its national context may see the entire international system—state-based order—as its ultimate enemy. To put it simply, terrorism is a specifically oriented violent tactic of the 'weak' that is employed against the 'strong' by pressurising the conventionally stronger side of a higher formal status by killing or threatening civilian population. While the state as a 'stronger' side may also engage in mass violence against its own civilians, these criminal actions are not defined as 'terrorism' in this context, as they are not used as an asymmetrical tactic of the 'weak'. Moreover, most of such crimes committed in the course of an armed conflict are already categorized by the IHL as either 'war crimes' or 'crimes against humanity'. In other words, the notion of 'terrorism' as defined here is *politically motivated violence against civilians carried out or threatened in an asymmetrical manner, that is, in order to create a disproportionately high political effect to exercise pressure on a more powerful opponent that is usually the state.*[3]

The clearer the definition of terrorism as a certain tactic of political violence, the less space it leaves for political deception and blackmail on the part of terrorists themselves and for political speculations on the part of any other actors, including governments that may tend to interpret terrorism too broadly, on the basis of their political or counter-insurgency priorities. To say, for instance, that 'one man's terrorist is another man's freedom fighter' is to allow oneself to be dragged into a political maze. No matter how common this aphorism is or how well it underscores the highly politicized and politically speculative nature of terrorism, the fact of the matter is that it is quite misleading. To begin with, it tries to juxtapose two aspects that do not in principle make up a dichotomy: *freedom-fighting*—against foreign occupation, colonial dominance, real or perceived social, political, ethnic, religious or other oppression or injustice—which is a political goal—and *terrorism* which is not a goal at all, but a specific violent method to achieve a political goal. A militant–political group can advance political goal(s) that can be interpreted as 'freedom fighting'—whether just by the group itself and its supporters or even by much of the international community—as it has often been the case with anti-colonial struggle or resistance against foreign occupation. Sometimes, such political goal—for instance, the end of the occupation of the Palestinian territories—may be even recognized as legitimate by the international law and codified by resolution of the UN Security Council. Whether or not a group that pursues such a goal qualifies as a group engaged in terrorist activities depends, however, not on the nature of its political goal, but solely on whether or not it actually uses or threatens a certain violent tactic—politically motivated, intentional, asymmetrical use or threat of violence against civilians and non-combatants designed to create a broader destabilizing and intimidating effect, namely terrorism. The same ultimate political goal—for instance, the independence of India from British rule—can be shared by different groups who use different tactics: some of the more radical ones would employ terrorism, while others, as in the case of India's struggle for independence led by Mahatma Gandhi, may even opt for mass non-violent resistance. In other words, *freedom fighting as a goal*—whether it implies anti-colonial struggle, resistance against occupation, or the fight for greater autonomy—and *terrorism as a tactic* are not mutually exclusive; terrorism may and has been used to augment freedom fighting in certain cases, and in the name of freedom fighting.

***

Apart from subjective political interpretations and the high level of politicization of the notion of 'terrorism,' the main reason for the lack of agreement on its definition is the wide diversity and multiplicity of forms and manifestations of terrorism. To achieve the broadest destabilizing political effect, terrorists seek to tailor, and time their actions as closely as possible to a certain political context, which makes the phenomenon extremely context-dependent and context-specific. It is hardly surprising, therefore, that, given the range of political contexts, terrorism can take various forms. This complicates the task of trying to fit all these different forms and manifestations of terrorism under one single, all-encompassing definition without running the risk of leaving some important aspect of terrorism aside. This also explains why the definition of terrorism is closely connected to its typology, and vice versa. In other words, while there are some general criteria that apply to all types of terrorism, as has been elucidated above, there may also be significant specifics of and variations between different types of terrorism.

One of the most traditional and common typologies of terrorism—and the one most relevant to this study—involves a basic distinction between international and domestic, internal or homegrown, terrorism. In demarcating one from the other, international terrorism has usually been defined, both in legal and political documents, and in academic literature and datasets, in a rather simplistic, technical way—as any terrorist activity carried out on the territory of more than one state or involving citizens of more than one state. This is precisely how international terrorism, for instance, is defined in the US legislation,[4] as well as in many other national anti-terrorism laws. For practical reasons of data collection and categorization, the world's largest database on terrorism since the late 1960s—Terrorism Knowledge Base operated by the US-based Memorial Institute for the Prevention of Terrorism (MIPT)—sticks to this traditional mechanical demarcation. It defines international terrorist incidents as those 'in which terrorists go abroad to strike their targets, select domestic targets associated with a foreign state, or create an international incident by attacking airline passengers, personnel or equipment' and domestic ones as 'incidents perpetrated by local nationals against a purely domestic target'.[5]

In the past, this distinction had never been too strict in practice. Leaving more distant times aside, since modern terrorism emerged as a specific asymmetrical tactic of political violence in the second half of the 19th century, terrorist activity, especially when it was perpetrated systematically, often went beyond state borders. It was often internationalized in terms of logistics—bases, funding, arms and materials supply—or/and could be guided by some form of internationalist ideology. Well into the 20th century, when terrorism peaked again since the late 1950s and the 1960s, the newly reinforced distinction between 'international' and 'domestic' terrorism was integrated to—and partly dictated by—the broader security context of the Cold War. Even as terrorism emerged as one of the main forms of political violence in the 1960s–1980s for many western and third world countries, in a situation when external threats stood higher than internal ones on leading nations' security agenda, 'domestic' terrorism took a backseat.

The turn of a number of separatist movements to terrorist tactics in the 1980s and the1990s, coupled with the end of the Cold War and the relative decline of ideological terrorism, stimulated greater attention to 'domestic' terrorism, including the first systematic efforts to collect relevant data. However, the dramatic and symbolically staged terrorist attacks of 11 September 2001 in the United States, unprecedented in their lethality, have had the most significant international repercussion yet, and shifted the political, public and security focus back to 'international terrorism'.

Yet, despite the growing post-9/11 emphasis placed by some of the world's leading states and international organizations on 'international' terrorism as the main terrorist threat, traditionally defined 'international' terrorism still comprises a smaller part of the global terrorist activity, compared to domestic terrorism. The data systematically collected by MIPT for a decade since 1998 on a global scale explicitly shows that measurable indicators such as incidents and casualties for 'international' terrorism—both prior to and following the 11 September attacks—were significantly outmatched in absolute terms by the same indicators for 'domestic' terrorism. In other words, even in the post-9/11 world, *international terrorism lags behind terrorist activity carried out in domestic context* in terms of incidence and direct human costs. Why are then international terrorism and the process of internationalization of terrorism considered to be such grave threats to global security? Why does international terrorism rank so high on the lists of major security concerns of most states and most international political and security organizations, from the regional to the global ones? Of all the possible responses, it would suffice to list at least three reasons here.

First, in the modern age of 'global village'—the advance of the global media and other modern information and communication technologies—the immediate direct damage caused by armed violence in terms of human and material costs is not necessarily of primary importance as a destabilizing factor. Depending on a political context, there is no longer the need to cause hundreds of thousands of human deaths to advance and publicize a radical political agenda and to affect political and security agenda of states and international organizations. Of greater, and growing, significance is often the potential of armed violence to cause broader destabilizing political effect and to be tailored to a certain political context in a way that could maximize the desired political effect. Of all forms of modern armed violence, terrorism is the one best suited to serve this purpose. At the global level, the terrorist attacks of 11 September 2001 evidently demonstrated how a series of terrorist attacks carried out against highly symbolic targets and staged in a global straitjacketed-media-way can lead to major changes in international politics despite the fact that the total death toll of 9/11 was comparably lower than that of most of the world's major armed conflicts. In contrast to quantifiable parameters of terrorist attacks, such as the number of incidents and casualties, this broader destabilizing political effect of terrorist attacks can hardly be measured. Quantitative indicators of terrorism may be useful, especially for comparative purposes, but they cannot capture the scale of the main public danger posed by terrorism. In other words, in the context of quantitative data, annual totals for domestic terrorism may well exceed the indicators for international terrorism; they are unable to accurately measure or reflect the much broader destabilizing political and security effect of international attacks, as compared to the ones limited to any specific local or national context. The more internationalized is terrorism, the greater are its broader destabilizing effect on international politics and security.

Second, despite the fact that the overall indicators for 'domestic' terrorism—in the late 20th and early 21st century—have outmatched the indicators for 'international' terrorism, the trend towards further internationalization of terrorist activity is evident. This drift has taken many forms and has developed rather unevenly, with repeated peak periods followed by relative declines. In absolute terms, at the time of writing in March 2008, the primary peak of international terrorist incidents have taken place in the early to mid-2000s and international fatality rates peaked in the early 2000s at a level incomparably higher than the previous peak of international terrorism-related deaths in the late 1980s.

Third, while the traditional distinction between domestic and international terrorism may still be relevant in certain cases, this distinction is increasingly becoming inaccurate. Today, the strict demarcation between narrowly defined 'international' and 'domestic' terrorism has further blurred, as even those terrorist groups whose political agenda is confined to local (or national) context, that is, *localized*, tend to *internationalize* some or most of their logistics, fund-raising, propaganda, and planning activities. They may extend these activities to regions far from their areas of operation, and may have bases of operations outside such areas. This phenomenon also reflects the broader trend that can be traced in the dynamics of global security—the slow, gradual, but steady erosion of the borderline between domestic (homeland) and international security. Furthermore, the process of internationalization of terrorism itself takes new forms. Among other factors, the post-Cold War decline in state support to terrorist activity by non-state groups contributed to a shift towards more active cooperation between autonomous, increasingly self-sufficient groups and to the formation of truly transnational networks.

Several attempts have been made by scholars to at least partially address the eroding boundaries between 'international' and 'domestic' terrorism and come up with more satisfactory definitions. However, so far such attempts have mostly been confined to defining 'domestic', rather than 'international', terrorism. For instance, in compiling Terrorism in Western Europe Events Dataset (TWEED), Jan Engene of the University of Bergen, Norway, defines terrorism as 'internal' when 'terrorists act within their own political systems'. Terrorists originating from outside western Europe, but committing acts of terrorism inside the region, are excluded from TWEED. In summation, TWEED defines 'internal terrorism' as terrorism that originates and takes place within the political systems of particular states, in this case, within the western European countries (Engene 2007). Following this logic and extending it to 'international terrorism,' one may end up with two interpretations—one limited and another broader one. The limited interpretation builds upon a more traditional definition of 'international terrorism' and defines it as terrorism that takes place outside the political/national system within which it originated. The broader interpretation would be a more ambitious one: if 'internal terrorism' is the one that originates, takes place in and targets domestic political systems at a local or national level, then the most developed and advanced form of 'international terrorism' is the one that takes place within—and is directed against—the international system as a whole.

A possible way to make sense out of the growing confusion between domestic and international terrorism and the multiplicity of forms that the internationalization process can take is to go beyond the pure 'domestic–international' dichotomy. As would be clear from the above, a strict demarcation between domestic, or internal, and international terrorism in their traditional interpretation (based on terrorist activity crossing the borders of one state or involving and/or targeting citizens of more than one state) is no longer adequate. However, distinctions between terrorism employed by groups confining their goals primarily to national politics and terrorist activity by organizations with a much broader internationalized agenda not only remain valid, but become more evident. That is why, instead of rejecting this typology altogether, one should rather upgrade, reinforce and update it by adding other typological criteria. The book is an attempt to offer such a solution and test it against a wide range of empirical cases culled from different political contexts and regions, and by experts from five continents.

The first step to address the problem of inadequacy of one typology of terrorism is to combine it with criteria employed by other traditional typologies of terrorism, such as the other most common categorization of types of terrorism—*typology by motivation*. By their main motivation and ultimate goals, terrorist groups are usually categorized under three broad categories: socio-political (secular-ideological); nationalist; and religious. Apparently, the level of internationalization may significantly vary from one motivational type of terrorism to another. For much of the 19th–20th century, it was the secular socio-political (ideological), especially left-wing terrorism that showed the greatest propensity for internationalization, in both practical/logistical and ideological terms. In terms of incidents, international activity by left-wing terrorists reached its peak at the end of the Cold War—in the 1980s and the early 1990s. However, left-wing terrorism has shown lower international fatalities than nationalist and especially religious terrorism since then.

Nationalist terrorists—ranging from radical anti-colonial and other national liberation groups to armed separatists—also often tended to internationalize their activities, both for the purpose of gaining broader international attention to their cause (as in the case of the Algerian anti-colonial struggle or the Palestinian resistance) and to raise logistical and especially financial and technical support from abroad.[6] However, internationalization of terrorism driven and dominated by a nationalist agenda is limited by definition and is confined to the technical, rather than the ideological level. Needless to say that nationalist terrorists, with their central focus on—and, in fact, obsession with—the nation-state, in principle cannot advance a transnational agenda aimed at challenging and changing the international system and the world order as a whole.

This limitation does not apply to religious terrorism that has been on the rise in the recent decades in terms of all indicators, but especially in terms of fatalities. In fact, at the transnational level, the relative post-Cold War decline of secular, left-wing internationalist ideology in general and as an ideology of radical militant groups employing terrorist means in particular, has created a vacuum that started to be quickly filled by religious extremism.[7] While religious extremism also made serious gains as an ideology of terrorism at the national level where it is usually combined with some form of radical nationalism, it is at the transnational, even global level that it had its largest and the most destabilizing effect in the post-Cold War period. This is demonstrated both by the 9/11 events and by the post-9/11 emergence of a broader transnational Islamist movement inspired by the al-Qaeda, pursuing the same ideology, but far more flexible, elusive and fragmented in organizational terms. Of all 'motivational' types of terrorism, religious terrorism is best tailored—especially in ideological terms—to generate the most advanced patterns of internationalization, up to the level of achieving fully transnational goals, agenda, activities and organizational forms.

A simple merger of the two traditional typologies of terrorism may provide a somewhat more accurate picture of the prevailing forms of international terrorism. However, what it does not reflect is the qualitatively different forms and stages of internationalization of modern terrorism. A new typology may be needed to adequately meet this task. Of the non-traditional typologies of terrorism, the *functional typology* developed by one of the editors, Ekaterina Stepanova is perhaps the only one that integrates the level of a group's ultimate goals, interests and agenda.[8] According to this typology, of critical importance is not so much—and no longer—the demarcation between purely 'internal' and 'international' terrorism—terrorist activity may be internationalized to some extent even at the local level—but the distinction in overall level of a group's goals and agenda—transnational (global) or more localized. This distinction is seen as one of the main criteria for the functional typology of terrorism (along with the relation of terrorism to a broader armed conflict as a second criterion), and provides the basis for identification of the three main types of modern terrorism. The first two types are: (*a*) classic terrorism of the peacetime, and (*b*) terrorism employed as a tactic in ongoing local and regional armed conflicts—that may be internationalized to a varying degree, in terms of both logistics and ideology, but are used by groups whose goals are limited by local and regional context and whose agenda do not challenge the international system as such. The third, more recent type of terrorism is the so-called super terrorism (macro-terrorism, mega-terrorism or global/transnational terrorism), which is used in the name of unlimited goals by radical groups with transnational, global agenda, playing the role of the world's 'anti-system' actors.

In summation, today it is more relevant to distinguish between *local/regional terrorism* employed to pursue an agenda confined to a particular armed conflict, national borders or regional context and internationalized to some extent—and the truly *transnational terrorism* employed by networks pursuing unlimited goals in a transregional or even global context. While these are two ends of the spectrum, as shown by several case studies in this book, a range of groups and movements involved in terrorist activities may fall somewhere in between internationalized terrorism at the local level and transnational super terrorism with a global outreach.

Still, the editors' basic preliminary assumption is that all parallels and links between the 9/11-type, the al-Qaeda inspired transnational terrorism with a global outreach and more traditional forms of terrorism that may be internationalized to some degree, do not make the latter fully dependent or conditional on the former. As with other forms and levels of terrorism, transnational terrorism with a global outreach and agenda retains a significant degree of autonomy and has its own logic and dynamics. Therefore, rather than confronting an integrated, universal terrorist network that is spreading from local to global levels, the international community and individual nations face a far more difficult challenge: coping with terrorism that serves different functions, operates and cerebrates at different levels and displays different degrees of internal and transnationalization manifestations, and with complex, elusive, and increasingly disturbing relationship between the two.

Finally, while the book's primary focus is on the patterns of internationalization of terrorism, it does not ignore the new, post-9/11 phenomenon of international 'war on terrorism'; the way it relates to armed conflicts and its role as a factor of internationalization of some of these conflicts. Against the more general trend of the growing internationalization of local armed conflicts, the 'war on terrorism' in some local and regional contexts had an effect—deliberate or unintentional—of contributing to the large-scale internationalization of the more localized tensions and of terrorism tactics employed by local non-state actors tying them closely to the international security agenda. This problem may, for instance, be illustrated by the fact that all four internationalized major armed conflicts in 2006–07 were linked to the US-led 'war on terrorism' in one way or another.[9]

But even as the manuscript of the book that attempted to knit together case studies, description and analyses of the new terrorism reached the publishers in June 2008, and the book was bring readied for publication, the subject that made up the book's core—that of the internationalization of terrorism—began manifesting itself in India in a series of well-coordinated terrorist strikes. On 26 July 2008, Ahmedabad felt it. Delhi witnessed it on 13 September 2008, and the North East Indian states of Tripura (Agartala) and Manipur (Imphal) faced the scourge on 1 October 2008 and 21 October 2008 respectively, as did four different places in Assam, including its capital city Guwahati, on 30 October 2008. Although investigations into the various attacks are still continuing, the needle of suspicion in almost all the above terrorist strikes pointed to agendas in India's near abroad. India was experiencing the heavy hand of urban terrorism. But, India was subjected to one of the unkindest cuts when a group of heavily armed and rabidly motivated terror actors sneaked into the country's financial capital, Mumbai, and held a 'billion' people to ransom. The group had only one objective: draw global attention to the systematic massacre that it was perpetrating in the doorway of India and showcase India's vulnerability to the world, which was beginning to respect the nation's strength. They were able to achieve this—for 62 hours—inside a warren of carpeted corridors, opulent suites and blood stained five-star hotel boardrooms, until India's professional and apolitical counter terrorist apparatus (bulk of which were culled from the Indian army) brought the macabre drama to a close. It was clear that the *fidayeen* (suicide squad) attack was 'aimed at the people watching' and in somewhat of a departure from other earlier targets of attack, the victims were from the affluent class, a tribe whose anger can cause tectonic shifts in political circles. It is this reality—at least in India—that proved that terrorism is a tool of politics, and not religion. Indeed, with the internationalization of terrorism, the internationalization of politics aided by terrorism was manifested.

The Mumbai incident, the editors felt, necessitated an account. This is primarily so not only because of the internationalization of terrorism that it exhibited, but also because of the unique military-militant nexus that it showcased. A brief analytical narrative by Subir Bhaumik and Jaideep Saikia has been placed in the appendix.

***

The book's main focus is on the stages, levels and forms of internationalization and transnationalization of modern terrorism. One of the main research tasks that drive the editors and the contributors is to study a variety of such stages and to explore whether they may—or may not—constitute a continuum. The task required an examination of selected case studies that exemplify different stages of internationalization and transnationalization of terrorist groups, as well as the main cross-cutting functional issues, such as the structures, ideologies, and means employed by such groups.

It has been deemed useful to start with the more traditional cases of internationalization of some activities of homegrown armed opposition groups that may use terrorist means, but *whose goals do not go beyond local or national context*. At this level, internationalization may, for instance, take the form of attacks against foreign targets, efforts to build up financial, logistics and propaganda networks abroad or support from foreign states to non-state groups involved in terrorist activities. A group may also be guided by an internationalist ideology, but limit its agenda and activities to a certain country or area and have minimal external logistical links. The variety of patterns of internationalization displayed by groups primarily active at the local or national level in different political contexts while pursuing political goals that do not quite go beyond national level are analyzed in Chapters 1–6 of the book.

Chapter 1, by Rogelio Alonso and Florencio Domínguez Iribarren, analyzes external connections of the more traditional type—those of the two best-known ethno-nationalist terrorist groups in Europe—the Irish Republican Army (IRA) and the Euskadi ta Askatasuna (Basque Homeland and Freedom, or ETA). While the nationalist goals of both groups have never acquired a broad international dimension, and in the new century the IRA had entered into a peace process and the ETA is in decline, for more than three decades both the IRA and the ETA had been very active in their search for external political, financial and other support and were involved in both violent and non-violent activities outside the United Kingdom (UK) and Spain respectively, and had established links with a number of other terrorist groups, including links between themselves. Overall, these groups present classic cases of limited internationalization of homegrown nationalist terrorism as some of their activities were planned and perpetrated beyond the territory in which the terrorist groups emerged and both groups' goals had serious cross-border implications in the UK—Irish and Spanish-French context. Putting these classic cases in the modern, post-9/11 context, the contributors argue that the very rise of a new type of terrorism in the early 21st century—the more lethal Islamist terrorism, with its more destabilizing and far-reaching political effects—and the rigid counter terrorist measures taken in response to this phenomenon became a major factor of deterrence for the use of terrorist tactics by the older, more localized nationalist groups, such as the ETA or the various post-IRA splinter groups.

In Chapter 2, Khatchik DerGhougassian applies the same approach to localized terrorist groups of socio-political, left-wing type in South America. He points out that these groups, especially in Colombia and Peru, failed to secure large-scale support from foreign states or diasporas at the time of the Cold War and were only involved in limited logistics and training cooperation with terrorist groups beyond their region. Rather, they have managed to develop external links mainly at the cross-border or, at most, regional level, while any broader dimension and more advanced level of internationalization of their terrorist activity have been primarily related to their participation in the illicit drug business. Noting that, due to the almost total absence of terrorism of Islamist bent, with a few rare exceptions, the region has not become a hot spot in the US-led 'war on terrorism', the contributor manages to showcase how this anti-terrorism campaign has nevertheless affected the perceptions of internationalization of terrorism in Latin America.

Ramani Hariharan's exposition of the Liberation Tigers of Tamil Eelam (LTTE) in Chapter 3 provides a systematic and detailed trans-national, country-wise connection of the Tamil terrorist organization in Sri Lanka. The LTTE reportedly carries out action and has a *modus operandi* in as many as 52 countries. Hariharan's examination is extensive and exposes the international character of the LTTE, its widespread political, military, criminal, financial, and transport linkages—the anchorages that has enabled it to operate in Sri Lanka with impunity. It is quite clear from the contributor's analysis and description that the support and financial contribution of the Tamil diaspora are important factors that sustain the Tigers. Despite sanctions by 'frontline states', especially after the breakdown of the ceasefire agreement with Colombo in 2002, the LTTE's transnational human resources and propaganda machinery has remained by and large intact. Indeed, proscription of the organization in 32 countries has not witnessed a visible waning of the diaspora support. One reason for this is the interpretation of laws relating to proscribed organizations in different countries—an aspect that concerns the book. However, the latent sympathy for the Tamil struggle for autonomy among sections of the diaspora is considered—as aforesaid—to be one of the most important reasons for the LTTE's survival. The organization has skilfully used the historical grievances of the Tamils and their feeling of alienation from mainstream Sri Lanka, and has been able to create a unique status for itself as the 'saviour' of Tamils from Sinhala chauvinism. The transformation of the LTTE from a local militant group into a full-blown insurgency and terrorist movement with tentacles throughout the world is intimately connected with the exodus of Tamil population from Sri Lanka in order to escape the repressive measures of the Sri Lankan state. The continuing quest for their rights among Tamils, both at home and abroad, constitutes the basis of the LTTE's international support network.

Hariharan also analyzes the losses that the LTTE has incurred, most of which is due to the expulsion of the Tamil group by the Sri Lankan armed forces from the Jaffna peninsula in 1995; the restraining effects on its activities generated by the global tide of hostility towards terrorism following the al-Qaeda attack on the United States of 9/11; and the revolt inside the LTTE led by Karuna in March 2004. The impression conveyed by the experiences in each of these episodes, however, is that the LTTE possesses the inner resilience and the external support required for recovery, and to carry on the war against the government forces.

An interesting aspect that Hariharan states is about the withdrawal of the Indian Peace Keeping Force (IPKF) from Sri Lanka. The contributor is of the view that LTTE's political links in the Indian state of Tamil Nadu resulted in the pull out of Indian troops from Sri Lanka. This may indeed be the case, but the fact of the matter is that the then Sri Lankan president, Ranasinghe Premadasa had quite categorically sought the withdrawal of the IPKF from the island nation. In a letter (30 June 1989) to then Indian prime minister, Rajiv Gandhi, Premadasa had written:

> The Indian Peace Keeping Force came to Sri Lanka at the request of the President of Sri Lanka. Due to the circumstances that arose thereafter the IPKF was requested by the President to afford military assistance to ensure the cessation of hostilities. The only condition that should be satisfied for the withdrawal of the Indian armed forces is a decision by the President of Sri Lanka that they should be withdrawn. The request made by me to withdraw the Indian armed forces has satisfied this condition. It is therefore incumbent on the Government of India to withdraw its forces from Sri Lanka. (Dixit 1998)

Premadasa also wrote 'far from being of any assistance in the complete resolution of the ethnic problem, the presence of the Indian forces are now a serious impediment' (Dixit 1998). It is wondered whether the tide of the war would have changed were the IPKF been allowed to complete its unfinished task.

In Chapter 4, the classic case of internationalization of terrorism amid domestic tussle between religion and culture, receives vivid description. Tracing the growth of Islamist terrorism in Bangladesh and its internationalization, Subir Bhaumik begins by informing the reader about the imperatives that closely link military dictatorships in South Asia to Islam, and the manner in which the 'barrack politics' of Dhaka—betraying the secular and nationalist sentiments that liberated Bangladesh from Pakistan—began to not only systematically rehabilitate pro-Pakistan forces and enshrined Islam as the state religion, but also paved the way for the current Islamist upheaval.

Bangladesh's geo-location is an important factor in the furtherance of the global *Salafi* movement. It is a key mid-point between the troubled spots of South East Asia and West Asia: its socio-cultural mosaic is an ideal safe haven and a regrouping zone for armed Islamist activity in Asia Therefore, even as Islamist groups such as the Jemaah Islamiyah, the al-Qaeda and the Lashkar-e-Toiba has engineered close links with homegrown groups such as the Harkat-ul-Jihad-al-Islami (HUJI)—much of it as compatriots during the Afghan war against Soviet occupation—the erstwhile East Pakistan has emerged as the 'cocoon of terror,' recruiting, training and launching terrorist attacks in the region, including cities in India. The HUJI has also emerged as the crucial link between the national and the global pan-Islamist terror project, and the Jemaah Islamiyah and HUJI trade fighters and utilize each other's bases, training facilities and safe houses to evade western intelligence. Indeed, Bangladesh has become the critical post-operation pullout area for Islamist groups in South East Asia, India, Kashmir, Pakistan and Afghanistan. The financial links that it has engineered with the al-Qaeda and Saudi and Kuwait-based financial fronts sustains not only the home-grown terrorist groups, but Islamist groups in southern Myanmar and India's northeast. The financial reach and range of the HUJI and the Jamaat-e-Islami (JeI) can be gauged from an isolated, but interesting instance. According to Bhaumik, in the year 2004, sleuths belonging to Russia's Federal Security Bureau assassinated Zelimkhan Yanderbiyev, the former vice president of Chechnya, in a car bomb attack in Doha, Qatar. The Russians believe that Yanderbiyev was meeting with wealthy Middle Eastern personalities to collect funds for a *jihad*. Yanderbiyev was reportedly a recipient of Jamaat funds to wage war on Russia.

Another important aspect that Bhaumik reveals in the chapter is the role of the JeI and the manner in which it has combined legitimate political activity with covert support for violent Islamist groups that it nurtures. The contributor is of the opinion that the JeI works through the democratic system, but does not believe in it. Its constitution makes it clear that it wants to establish the 'Islamic way of life for the well being of mankind' through Dawa and Islamic finance. Indeed, it was during the five years between 2001 and 2006, when the JeI was in government, that Bangladesh witnessed the most violent phase of Islamist terror, the height of which was the more than 450 serial explosions during the course of a single day throughout Bangladesh on 17 August 2005.

The military leadership that is purportedly guiding Bangladesh's interim government has taken some cosmetic action against certain homegrown terrorist groups, but the real culprits that constitute the 'fountainhead of terrorism in South Asia,' namely the JeI and the HUJI, have not yet come under any pressure. This aspect underscores the sort of clout both these groups wield in Dhaka, with JeI's external linkages being billeted as crucial for the establishment of *Nizam-e-Mustafa* in the country. Subir Bhaumik's position as the BBC's East India bureau chief provides him a unique ringside view of Bangladesh, incidentally the country from where his ancestors entered India. It is not a matter of surprise, therefore, that he has been able to penetrate a group such as the HUJI. Much of what he describes about the organization comes, therefore, from first-hand source. When he states that 30 per cent of HUJI activists play a 'sleeper role' in Bangladesh, India and elsewhere in South and South East Asia and they are only activated for special operations, it can be certain that his arithmetic is correct. So, would it be when his source inside the HUJI states that another 20 per cent of the trained activists have left Bangladesh for other battlegrounds of the world as far as Chechnya and the Philippines.

In Chapter 5, Bishnu Raj Upreti shows that even in the case of Nepal, where the Maoist movement seems more 'domestically' oriented compared to other insurgencies covered in the book, some degree of internationalization has taken place. While terrorism has not been the Maoist insurgency's main tactic, and the movement has been primarily confined to the national context, it did establish some cross-border links and some aspects of its activity, such as logistical support and arms channels, have been internationalized, albeit to a limited extent. The contributor shows that even in cases when the militant movement's external logistical links or support from diaspora are quite limited, it may develop an international profile and interact with like-minded groups abroad through its internationalist—in this case, Maoist—ideology. The chapter also addresses broader international dimensions of the Maoists insurgency in Nepal, including the policies of interested states and international organizations, as well as the moral and political support to insurgency by some human rights groups. Finally, Upreti draws—for what could be of particular interest to readers in India and South Asia—a brief comparison between the Maoist insurgency in Nepal and the left-wing movement in India. He notes some parallels in the respective movements' motivation to turn to armed struggle, examines their social roots and military strategies and tactics as have been influenced by Maoism, and such movements' attempts to build quasi-governance structures, as well as the terrorist means they sometimes resort to. After all, most Maoist action in both Nepal and India have been against government forces, and in the case of India, the movement has a clear proletariat bearing, with a unambiguous ideology at its core, that of struggle against social and economic injustice. At the same time, even as the two respective Maoist movements in Nepal and India are guided by the same type of ideology, Upreti estimates that the actual inter-organizational links and cooperation between the two are limited and emphasizes they are primarily homegrown in nature.

Jennifer Lynn Oetken's examination of the insurrection in Kashmir in Chapter 6 provides a unique progression of a homegrown movement's transformation to a full-bodied international one. However, the peculiarities in this case are startling. The movement is guided by an internationalist ideology; its agenda and activities are confined to a particular area, but the external links that engender the movement is maximum. In other words, it is a classic case of a movement that has been internationalized by the ingress of international or outside actors into a localized region (namely India-administered Kashmir), which is quite different from certain other cases that are being studied in the book.

Among the reasons that Oetken cites for the above, the effect that collapse of regimes elsewhere and the proliferation of Islamist militant groups in reaction to the Iranian Revolution and the Soviet invasion of Afghanistan in 1979 had on the Kashmir scenario are novel. Furthermore, the contributor is quite categorical about the involvement of Pakistan in Kashmir, and the 'failed state' debris spill over into the valley, especially after the partial 'detalibanization' of Afghanistan and the shift of focus of theatre of the 'war on terror' to Pakistan. The instability in Pakistan, characterized at the time of writing in March 2008 by the assassination of Benazir Bhutto, the Islamization of the armed forces in the country, the growing violence and belligerence of the Islamists inside Pakistan (despite a decidedly fair election) and the role of the United States are also called in for questioning. Commenting on the growing 'guest militant'-led agenda in Kashmir, Oetken wonders whether Pakistan is actually committed to permanently stopping its support for terrorist groups that are willing to fight its proxy war with India? She also states that the ideological orientation of terrorism in the Valley received a fillip and began to get internationalized as Pakistan began to actively sponsor a plethora of Islamist organizations with international links. The transformation was complete when such groups began to adopt a pan-Islamist agenda—the liberation of all Muslims for the creation of a single, united Islamic state—as opposed to their earlier sole agenda of support to Pakistan's cause for Kashmiri accession. However, Oetken also apportions blame to India. She states, '(Indian) counterinsurgency policies that are too coercive or too moderate may provoke terrorist organizations to internationalize their activities, recruitment, funding and operations.'

She evokes the Indian Kashmir watcher and noted journalist, Praveen Swami to reiterate the aspect, when she quotes that: 'the failure of successive Indian governments to vigorously defend its secular culture had tragically contributed to the nightmare it now confronts.'

The next, more advanced stage implies upgraded forms of internationalization and even some elements of transnationalization of a terrorist network's agenda and activities at a broader regional or cross-regional level. The latter may range from steady patterns of cross-border and region-wide violence, including terrorist activity, to cooperation between distinct groups in different countries and parts of the world or even more or less stable inter-organizational associations. These patterns of internationalization of terrorism at the regional level are explored in Chapters 7–9.

In the examination of the 'Proxy Wars in North East India' in Chapter 7, Jaideep Saikia opines that it is a phenomenon that characterizes the post-colonial policy of South Asia and constitutes the grey area between war and peace. Nations in the region have either fought only 'limited' or short-scale wars, choosing instead to settle scores by embarking on a war of attrition. Such a methodology, the contributor states, permits the warring nations of South Asia to engage in low-cost offensive postures.

A description of North East India reveals that it is a perfect playfield for South Asia's 'proxy war'. Determined to a considerable extent by the 'strategic encirclement' that the region is heir to, as well as the emotional distance from New Delhi, anti-India forces have not allowed an opportunity of subterfuge to go by—awaiting dissonance in the region that erupt with almost predictable regularity. But, North East India constitutes a special case and while it is the case that the various insurgencies in the region have sought and received support from countries like China, Bangladesh and Pakistan, almost all such movements have remained loyal to their founding principles. Therefore, if there has been internationalization of the movements in North East India, it has only been by way of insurgent groups looking for aid in their war against India. Whereas, in certain cases, the methodologies of war have been adopted—for instance when the ULFA began to be pressurized by the ISI to target non-combatants—ideologies of the inimical forces have not attracted them. But, the situation is changing, with Islamist organizations from Bangladesh, the ISI and the Bangladesh intelligence outfit, the Directorate General of Forces Intelligence (DGFI) and the illegal Bangladeshi migrant population in North East India creating a volatile mix. A concerted effort is also underway to carve out a 'Greater Bangladesh' from the region. But the battle for lebensraum in the northeast (which both Pakistani and Bangladeshi ideologues have been advocating for decades) is being fought by engineering a demographic invasion, and not by the conventional methods that the Islamists and their sponsors are perpetrating in the rest of South Asia. Indeed, North East India is not being operationally activated only because it serves as a gateway for the entry and exit of groups such as HUJI into the Indian heartland from Bangladesh, as also because the growing illegal Bangladeshi migrant population in the region provides such groups an ideal safe haven. The contributor is also of the opinion that agencies such as the ISI are 'creating prairie fires' in the northeast primarily to pin down the Indian army in the area and from their primary duties in Kashmir. Whereas the People's Republic of China has stopped its policy of aid to the northeast insurgents, Pakistan—in close concert with its surrogate, Bangladesh—has begun to (at the time of writing in March 2008) activate the area, and reports state that there are as many as 16 trained Islamist groups in the region that are being directly supported by the ISI–DGFI. Such groups have travelled to places such as Batrasi in Pakistan-occupied Kashmir for training alongside other Islamist groups, as have certain ethnic insurgent organizations such as the ULFA. However, as aforesaid, apart from a few instances when the ethnic insurgent groups have fallen prey to the nefarious designs of their alien masters, most outfits have continued to remain steadfast to their ideals and local considerations. This aspect is, however, true for only the ethnic insurgent groups, and not the ones that are beginning to surface on religious lines, and with both clear origin and loyalty to Bangladesh.

In Chapter 9, Mohamed Nawab Bin Mohamed Osman argues that the Afghan war played a significant role in the transformation of the Jemaah Islamiyah (JI) from a group with local aspirations to one that aligned itself with a larger Islamist discourse of forming a supra-national Islamic state or Caliphate. Although the JI's genesis can be traced to the Dar-ul-Islam movement that came into existence to fight against Dutch colonialism, at a more ideological level, the 'handbooks' used by the JI is similar to that of groups such as the al-Qaeda, Hamas and the Egyptian Muslim Brotherhood. This, Osman analyzes, is the result of the cross-fertilization of ideas and practices that occurred during the Afghan war. The JI grew from Indonesia and spread to rest of South East Asia, including Malaysia, Thailand and Singapore, with organized chapters in each country, heralding a truly international organizational concept. Its footprints have been found in Bangladesh as well, which Subir Bhaumik examines in Chapter 4. This, as Jaideep Saikia stated above, is because of Bangladesh's unique geographical location: it stands as an important pullout area for both the JI and Islamist groups such as Lashkar-e-Toiba, after say the respective groups violent actions in Bali and Mumbai. An interesting point of difference in methodology between the JI and the al-Qaeda that has been noted is the JI's intense attack on some 38 churches across five provinces, an Islamist methodology that seems to be peculiar to South and South East Asia. Although the contributor to the chapter is of the opinion that the present status of the JI has weakened, with its international linkages becoming more or less defunct, it is opined that these are yet early days to make such a prognosis. Linkages once engendered can be easily revived, and Islamist action has only just begun in South Asia. As Saikia had stated in one of his books, the Islamists in parts of South Asia 'are silent, not by the absence of activity; but by the presence of non-activity' (Saikia 2004). The commonality of agenda that groups such as the JI had found with Indian, Bangladeshi and Pakistani Islamist groups during the Afghan War could well see commonality of future action as well, if not in the areas of their origin in South East Asia, in other parts of the world where Islam is perceived to be experiencing 'Dar-ul-Harb'.

Clearly, even as Mohamed Nawab Bin Mohamed Osman, Jennifer Lynn Oetken and Subir Bhaumik—who are examining Islamist militancies in South and South East Asia in the book and have un-ravelled unambiguous international links with global terror groups like the al-Qaeda—Amos Neuser Guiora, has, at the very outset, in Chapter 8, stated that, in his not-so-short career as a prosecutor and legal adviser in Israel, he has not come across any al-Qaeda trace in the Palestine uprising. Indeed, this makes the case of the Hamas and the Palestine Liberation Organization (PLO), that Guiora is examining in the book, rather different from some of the other case studies included in the book, and indeed, intriguing as well, given that the al-Qaeda is waging a full-fledged war in Iraq, a country that abuts Israel and the Palestine Authority so closely. Instead Guiora describes the PLO as a secular terrorist organization with focused local goals. The contributor does, however, state that the PLO openly sought assistance and support within a global context from the USSR and other international secular terrorist organizations. But that, Guiora states, is quite different from the internationalization pattern that engenders the JI, the HUJI or the JeM. In some sense, despite the awkwardness of the comparison, the case study that Guiora brings to the book is similar to the insurgency situation in North East India that Jaideep Saikia examines in Chapter 7. Hamas is a locally focused terrorist organization, with even suicide as methodology—driven at times even by religious fanaticism. But Guiora is quite emphatic about the fact that the essence of Palestinian terrorism is the creation of a Palestinian state and it has no connection with international Islamist terrorism. The contributor invokes the Hamas' rejection of offer of support from the al-Qaeda leader, Ayman-al-Zawahiri as proof. As a matter of fact, Guiora also queries whether international Islamist terrorism actually exists, or whether it a product of the media or states anxious about threat of attacks. He also questions whether Samuel Huntington's thesis about clash of civilizations has any basis. Guiora does propose, however, that the west is confronted by a determined foe whose actions are driven by a particular interpretation of the Koran. In this context it might be of some pertinence to inform that the celebrated South Asia watcher, Stephen Philip Cohen, had told Jaideep Saikia during a television conversation that Huntington's 'Clash of Civilizations' thesis is a 'profoundly wrong statement', as Cohen perceives clashes even within civilizations.[10]

At this stage, it is also crucial to make a distinction between Islam and terrorism. One of the editors, Jaideep Saikia, had earlier written:

> ...the US-led War on Terror has not been an objective one, and either by devise or ignorance, the conflict is being given the colour of a civilizational clash...Islam is submission, a faith whose sacred duty is to construct a just society where everyone, including the weakest and the most vulnerable, is treated with absolute respect. However, recent years—particularly after 9/11—have witnessed an understanding of Islam, and consequently Islamist terrorism, that has been marred with confusion. In large measure, the misunderstanding has been in part also due to 'the western media often (giving) the impression that the embattled and occasionally violent form of religiosity known as fundamentalism is a purely Islamic phenomenon'. (Saikia 2006)

While, the term *jihad* has been grossly misunderstood,[11] the fact of the matter is that fundamentalism is a phenomenon that has characterized almost all religions of the world, and Hinduism, Buddhism,

Christianity, and even Confucianism have exhibited shades of this experience. As an Islamic scholar states, fundamentalism appeared for the first time *in* the United States, 'the showcase of modernity,' and among the 'three monotheistic religions, Islam was in fact the last to develop a fundamentalist strain' (Armstrong 2002). In fact, if a strict interpretation of the term 'fundamentalism' is made, then it would be noted that the word is 'ill-fitted for the Islamic context because in Arabic the word becomes *usuli*, which means 'one who relies on the fundamentals or basics.''[12] In this context, it must also be noted that the Koran enjoins Muslims to be a moderate people. Indeed, the traditions of Prophet Mohammed state that when two extremes are confronted, the prophet would invariably choose the middle path. Moreover, the prophet is always described as a moderate man who shunned extremes (Saikia 2006b). It is, therefore, appropriate that Islamist scholars congregated in Deoband (the seat of Darul Uloom, some 475 km from the famous Indian city of Lucknow) on 25 February 2008 to 'denounce all acts of terror as unislamic, severing (thereby) its umbilical cord with the jihadi brand of Islam' (*The Telegraph* 2008).

Finally, the most recent phenomenon of the globalization of terrorism in the form of loose, but fully transnationalized networks is addressed in Chapters 10 and 11. While these networks comprises semi or fully autonomous cells, they view themselves as parts of the same movement and employ terrorist means for the same ultimate goal. Special attention should be paid to the most advanced transnational network of our times with a truly global agenda, that is, to the cells of the transnational violent Islamist movement inspired by the al-Qaeda, with an emphasis on its ideological and organizational forms.

This broad post-al-Qaeda transnational movement that displays the most advanced stage of transnationalization of terrorism is the subject of Chapter 10 by Ekaterina Stepanova. The chapter analyzes the role played by the extremist ideology of the al-Qaeda and the al-Qaeda inspired cells and networks in shaping their unlimited, global goals—centred on establishing Islamic rule worldwide—its transnational agenda, activities and organizational forms. Stepanova argues that this ideology gives a radical, quasi-religious response to the challenges of the modern, globalizing world. She examines the characteristics that help distinguish cells of transnational violent Islamist networks with global goals and agenda not limited to any specific national context or armed conflict from the more localized militant groups who combine Islamism with radical nationalism and for whom Islamism is only part of their identity, ideology, socio-political goals and programmes. Stepanova also analyzes how the al-Qaeda-style quasi-religious ideology of transnational violent Islamism with a global agenda is different from radical, secular left-wing revolutionary ideologies that dominated international terrorist activity in the past. Finally, the chapter challenges the conventional view of the al-Qaeda inspired transnational violent Islamist movement organizational form as a standard horizontal network. It suggests that its organizational forms are closer to a more complex, hybrid multi-level network. Furthermore, this movement, comprised fully or semi-autonomous cells, displays a combination of effective coordination through generally formulated strategic guidelines (untypical for the main known organizational forms and increasingly transmitted through modern means of communication) with close social bonds and cohesion at the micro-level of individual cells. This type of organization, combined with the movement's global goals and agenda, allows autonomous cells emerging in different political and regional contexts to see themselves and operate as parts of one movement.

Whether the unlimited goals of the al-Qaeda and the broader transnational violent Islamist movement require or are matched by unlimited means to advance these goals, such as the chemical, biological, radiological, and nuclear (CBRN) weapons and materials, is the main subject of the final chapter by Adam Dolnik. Noting that in the modern world even small radical groups of individuals are increasingly gaining the capacity to inflict considerable damage, Dolnik critically explores the prospects of mass-casualty CBRN terrorism at the technological, motivational and organizational levels. Providing a brief overview of the past cases of CBRN terrorism, the chapter looks at its motivational aspects, with special attention to the impact of the level of transnationalization of the respective perpetrators on their interest in CBRN. This is followed by a thorough analysis of technological problems and difficulties involved in the use of CBRN materials and of the possible scenarios of 'super terrorist' unconventional attacks. While Dolnik acknowledges the long-term possibility of the rise of the threat of smaller-scale operations with the use of some CBRN agents that are unlikely to cause large-scale death and destruction, but could have destabilizing political and psychological impact, he also argues that at present super terrorism's unlimited goals do not necessarily require unlimited (CBRN) means. In his opinion, in the long term, transnationalization of terrorism, and the associated rise of global decentralized networks of small cells, operating independently of any central command, may well reduce motivational constraints for the individual cells to resort to unconventional means. However, not only terrorists' technological capacities to launch mass-casualty unconventional attacks are generally quite limited at present, but also the upcoming trend of terrorist operations by Islamist cells around the world is likely to be one of *decreasing,* rather than increasing in technological sophistication.

***

As is clear from the broad range of patterns and forms of internationalization of terrorism that is being examined in the book, one of the main objectives of the project is to enhance the general understanding of the processes, degrees and stages of internationalization and transnationalization of modern terrorism from the local to the global level. This would hopefully promote more active international cooperation on anti-terrorism. The editors and the contributors also seek to introduce policy-makers, the media and the wider public to the lessons from—as well as inadequacies of—various national and international approaches to preventing and combating terrorism with regard to various degrees of its internationalization and transnationalization. The book is, therefore, addressing both the policy-making community, international affairs, anti-terrorism and other security professionals, journalists, the students of international affairs, security and political science, and the wider public that may have an interest in the highly debated and politically and socially relevant issue of internationalization and transnationalization of terrorism in all its forms and manifestations. Finally, the book's composition and the list of contributors also stand in contrast to the standard work on terrorism-related issues, still dominated by authors representing mainly western-centric geographical, cultural and civilizational perspective and discourse. The book hopes to introduce the reader to a selection of broader, more culturally and geographically balanced, perspectives on patterns of internationalization of terrorism. Indeed, the book's analytical, policy and public contribution would lie not only in its quest to anvil an acceptable definition of terrorism and the distinction between its different manifestations, but also in the hope that it would lead practitioners and theoreticians, studying the phenomenon, to comprehend the menace in a holistic manner so that combat procedures receive more precision-guided application, and are enforced more comprehensively and without prejudice.

NOTES

1. A co-edited book invariably involves a division of labour. The editors accordingly divided the selection and commissioning of the contributors, and the editing of the chapters. Therefore, even as Jaideep Saikia brought together the five contributors who examine the situation in Sri Lanka, Bangladesh, Kashmir, the Middle East and South East Asia, Ekaterina Stepanova was responsible for the experts who have written on Ireland-Spain, South America, Nepal and the one pertaining to the means of transnational terrorism. The chapters by the editors for the book have been researched and written by the editors themselves.

2. For more detailed discussion on the definitional issues and on terrorism as an asymmetrical tactic of non-state actors, see also Stepanova 2008.

3. One of the acceptable terms to denote mass repressive actions by states themselves against civilian population is the term 'terror' (for instance, Nazi terror, Stalin terror, Pol Pot terror, Jacobin terror) which should be distinguished from 'terrorism' by non-state actors.

4. That is, 'terrorism involving citizens or the territory of more than one country'. US Code, Title 22, Section 2656f (d).

5. For more detail, see MIPT Terrorism Knowledge Base, <http://www.tkb.org>.

6. International terrorist incidents by nationalist groups peaked in the 1980s, while fatalities first peaked in the early 1980s and reached an even higher peak in the first half of the 2000s (based on data from the MIPT Terrorism Knowledge database—see endnote 5).

7. International incidents by religious groups showed first a moderate increase in the mid-1990s and then a major and sharp rise since 1999 until the mid-2000s. While the first significant peak of international fatalities by religious groups dates back to the early 1980s, the second and far more significant peak can be observed in the first half of the 2000s (based on data from the MIPT Terrorism Knowledge database—see endnote 5).

8. For more detail on the 'functional' typology of terrorism and on how it is different from traditional typologies, see Stepanova 2008: 5–11; also Stepanova 2003: 3–5.

9. Of the 14 major armed conflicts identified by Stockholm International Peace Research Institute/Uppsala University Conflict Data Programme as active in 2007; four conflicts were categorized as internationalized (i.e. they included troops from a state that was external to the conflict itself fighting on behalf of one of the parties). All the internationalized major armed conflicts in 2007 (as in the previous year) were linked to the US-led 'war on terrorism': the conflict between the US government and the al-Qaeda; the conflict between the Afghan government and the Taliban; the conflict between the Iraqi government/US-led Multinational Force and the various insurgency groups in Iraq and, to a lesser extent, the conflict between the government and the Supreme Islamic Council in Somalia (where the US air strikes against the al-Qaeda, allegedly hiding among the Somali Islamists, were carried out in the context of the ongoing armed conflict). See L. Harbom and P. Wallensteen 2008.

10. In response to a direct question by Jaideep Saikia during a television discussion recorded on 30 October 2003 for and later aired over Doordarshan.

11. The word *jihad* is a derivative of *juhd*, which means, 'to make substantial effort.' It has also been defined as 'to strive to attain something loved or to save one from something disliked.' Islamic scholars have argued that were the word *jihad* meant to have merely signified 'holy war', then there are plenty of other words in Arabic which convey it unambiguously. *Harb* (war), *sira's* (combat), *Ma'araka* (battle) and *qutal* (killing) are some of the words, which the Holy Koran could have used were war to be the principal manner in which a Muslim engages in the effort (*jihad*). The Holy Koran chooses a vaguer, richer word with a wide range of connotations. The tendency to translate *jihad* as 'holy war' could also be due to the influence of the Christian usage of the term 'holy war' which refers to the Crusades of a thousand years ago. The *jihad* is not the central prop of Islam, but it is a duty for Muslims to commit themselves to a struggle on all fronts—moral, spiritual and political—to create a just and decent society, where the poor and vulnerable are not exploited, in the way that God had intended man to live. See Noorani 2002: 39.
12. See Khaled Abou El Fadl 2006: 18.

Part One

EXTERNAL LINKS OF HOMEGROWN TERRORIST ORGANIZATIONS

1

THE IRA AND ETA: THE INTERNATIONAL CONNECTIONS OF ETHNO-NATIONALIST TERRORISM IN EUROPE

Rogelio Alonso and Florencio Domínguez Iribarren

INTRODUCTION

At the turn of the 21st century, a new wave of international terrorism with very distinctive characteristics—such as religious inspiration, search for global objectives, as well as very high levels of lethality—was surfacing. This occurred parallelly with the decline of the Irish Republican Army (IRA) and Euskadi ta Askatasuna (ETA, or Basque Homeland and Freedom), two terrorist organizations that were part of what has been referred to as the third wave of modern terrorism (Rapoport 2004). Both terrorist groups have espoused an ethno-nationalist ideology, on the basis of which they have justified intense campaigns of killing while in pursuit of their territorial claims against European liberal democracies like the United Kingdom and Spain. The protracted campaigns of violence perpetrated by the IRA and ETA have also been marked by an international dimension, whose main patterns will be analyzed in this chapter.

Contrary to the type of terrorism that is presently being perpetrated by Islamist militanta, the goals of the kind of violence pursued by those ethno-nationalist terrorist groups that have operated in Spain and the United Kingdom cannot be defined as global. Nonetheless, the search for international support and the involvement in different activities beyond the borders, within which their violence was waged, constituted a main objective of both terrorist organizations. Therefore, as this chapter will analyze, both organizations did regard the international sphere as a key element of their terrorist strategy. By the end of the 1960s, at a time when both terrorist groups resumed their violence, the international political scenario did provide inspiration for many ETA and IRA activists.[1] Furthermore, the concern about the way in which their violence would be perceived internationally has decisively influenced their campaigns along with the evolution of the most recent wave of international terrorism.

Terrorism, inflicted by ETA and the IRA as well as that of Unionist terrorist groups in Northern Ireland, such as the Ulster Volunteer Force and the Ulster Freedom Fighters, has challenged democracy in Spain and the United Kingdom for more than three decades,[2] the gradual decrease in their campaigns having been influenced by the emergence of a more indiscriminate type of terrorism like the one perpetrated by Islamist militanta. In the aftermath of 11 September 2001, at a time when the IRA and ETA were already aware of the limitations and the counterproductive effects of their violence, as demonstrated by the ceasefires called by each organization in 1994 and 1998, respectively, terrorism increased its political cost for these groups.

The disadvantageous comparison that would stem from the association with the brutality of Islamist terrorism, should the IRA and ETA have maintained their traditional levels of violence, constituted an importance deterrence for these organizations, encouraging them to alter their strategy. The 11 September 2001 events and the subsequent terrorist attacks in Madrid and London made it less profitable for the IRA and ETA to continue resorting to sustained campaigns of murder since such a course of action would have damaged the efforts of their political representatives in Sinn Fein and Batasuna while they were attempting to reverse the pattern of delegitimization derived from their prolonged involvement in violence. This factor, complemented with others, such as the normal waning of a protracted cycle of violence and the effectiveness of state counter terrorist measures, help to explain the tactical shift of these terrorist organizations.[3]

TERRORIST ALLIANCES
AND INTERNATIONAL CONTACTS

ETA's Network of Contacts

Since the 1970s, the Basque terrorist group has included within its organizational structure what has been termed as an 'international department'. This body has been in charge of the development of contacts with other terrorist organizations and international institutions.[4] It was at that time that the terrorist group reached international notoriety as a result of the death penalties that had been imposed on several ETA activists by the Spanish ruling dictator General Francisco Franco. Intense contacts were maintained between 1971 and 1974 to exchange experiences, knowledge and weapons, and to enhance relationship with other terrorist groups, on some occasions, by signing joint declarations.

In 1971, ETA, the IRA and The Liberation Front of Brittany (Front de Libération de la Bretagne) signed a joint communiqué coinciding with the celebrations of 1 May (*Documentos Y* 1971a). One year later, the same groups expressed their joint opposition to the European Common Market (*Documentos Y* 1971b). Also in 1972, ETA signed with 12 different groups, including the Palestinian Liberation Organization (PLO), a statement lending support to the IRA. In September 1973, a new declaration was signed by ETA and the IRA reaffirming their determination to strengthen their bonds (*Hautsi* 1973, *Documentos Y* 1973). Public declarations became less common after the split in the IRA between the Officials and the Provisionals. Nonetheless, contacts between the Irish and Basque terrorist groups were maintained, gradually increasing the contacts between their respective political wings.[5]

Over the years, the relationship between ETA and the IRA has gone through different stages, at one point even leading to members of the IRA on the run being sheltered by sympathisers of the Basque terrorist group.[6] In 2002, it was claimed that out of the 28 members of Jarrai, ETA's youth wing, who had previously visited Sinn Fein in Derry, 23 had been subsequently arrested on terrorist charges, several of them in France (Walker 2002). Throughout the 1990s, political advice from Sinn Fein and the IRA was sought by the leadership of

ETA and Batasuna.[7] Prior to this, the IRA's historical experience had also helped ETA to elaborate on one of the group's first manuals on security procedures. As early as 1971, Sean McStiofain met ETA representatives who offered the IRA leader some guns in return for training in the use of explosives (Mcguire 1973). At the end of the 1970s, ETA activists went to Kerry, in the South of Ireland, where they were trained in the use of mortars.[8]

Despite the obvious differences between the root causes and consequences of the conflicts in Northern Ireland and the Basque Country, both ETA and the IRA have fostered some ideological and operational affinity. To that extent, José Antonio Urrutikoetxea, one of the main leaders of ETA, defined the IRA as 'a reference' for the Basque terrorist group: 'For me it is normal that the movements of national liberation, wherever they are, in Ireland, Colombia or Corsica, should work together, put their experience in common and help each other–why not?' (Fitzgerald 2002). In a similar vein, throughout the years ETA has also set up contacts with left wing terrorist organizations like the German Baader-Meinhof, the Italian Red Brigades, the Chilean MIR (Movimiento de Izquierda Revolucionaria, or Revolutionary Left Movement) and the Tupac Amaru Revolutionary Movement in Uruguay. In 2007, the trial of terrorist Ilich Ramírez Sánchez, known internationally as 'Carlos', confirmed that he had maintained 'regular operational' connections with one of ETA's factions (ETA *politiko-militarra*, or ETA pm) in the beginning of the 1980s. This relationship was endorsed by the Communist secret services of East Germany, Hungary and Romania (Iturribarría 2007).

ETA's international dimension also manifested itself in the presence of the activists in training camps located in Algeria, Lebanon and Yemen during the 1970s. The Algerian War of Independence constituted a colonial model that ETA used in order to place its terrorist campaign against a democratic regime in a different and more legitimate framework. The way in which the Algerian Front de Libératon Nationale (FLN, or National Liberation Front) conducted negotiations with the French authorities was also inspirational to ETA. This appeal was complemented by the aid provided to ETA by the Algerian government as a response to the Spanish authorities' attitude towards the Sahara conflict between the North African country and its Moroccan neighbour. In 1976, over 60 members of ETA received military, physical and communications training at the police academy in Souma. More training was provided in 1984 at an Algerian military base.

Despite the generous support received throughout this period, the Algerian regime would finally expel ETA's activists from the country following the failure of the negotiations in 1989 between the terrorist group and representatives of the Spanish government (Domínguez 1998a).

Lebanon and Yemen were also favourite destinations for the training of ETA militants who travelled to these countries on several occasions between 1979 and 1980. Some of the training was arranged by various Palestinian factions such as Fatah and the Popular Front for the Liberation of Palestine (PFLP). The relevance of these experiences was summed up as follows by a former Head of the Spanish intelligence service: 'Rather than in the operational knowledge acquired the main importance of these courses lay in the psychological motivation and international contacts they provide to the organisation' (Casinello 1984).

South America has been another area where ETA has developed a support network. Mexico (Bedoya 2007), Venezuela, Cuba, El Salvador, Nicaragua, Uruguay, Panama and the Dominican Republic have hosted activists of the Basque terrorist group since the mid-1980s.[9] Although some of those who settled in those countries did so after moving away from the terrorist group, others were hiding from the Spanish authorities. During the 1990s, the Mexican government changed its position on ETA's activists and started to extradite some of them to Spain. Nonetheless, ETA has continued to finance itself through business set up in Latin American countries (Dios Colmenero 2004). Police operations have intercepted several documents in ETA's possession that have confirmed that the Basque terrorist group have met the FARC terrorists on several occasions. The Columbian terrorists offered ETA some assistance in providing hide-outs to ETA activists if needed. In return, FARC asked for medical assistance as well as for SAM 7 missiles. The Columbian terrorist group also asked ETA if Basque terrorists could carry attacks in Europe against targets identified by FARC.

THE IRA'S INTERNATIONAL CONNECTIONS

The IRA was particularly successful in developing contacts abroad. Since the early 1970s, the Irish terrorist group acquired weapons from America and Libya. The support provided by the regime of Colonel

Muammar Qaddafi was extremely profitable and by 1972 a leading IRA figure, Brian Keenan, had already managed to import RPG-7 rockets and missiles from Libya (Moloney 2002). The contacts had been initiated that same year through the mediation of the Breton nationalist movement in France and the initiative of the then Sinn Fein president, Ruari O'Bradaigh (Moloney 2002). However, in 1973 the Irish Navy arrested IRA member Joe Cahill off the coast of County Waterford on board a Cyprus-registered boat, the Claudia. The consignment of Libyan weaponry found in the boat included over two hundred rifles and several hundred small weapons as well as anti-tank mines and explosives (Taylor 1997). Despite such a serious setback, four shipments from Libya would reach its destination in Ireland during the 1980s before a major delivery was caught again by security services, in November 1987, on board the Eksund, a Panamanian-registered vessel.[10]

America was also going to prove a very lucrative source of weapons and money for the IRA, which took advantage of the sizeable Irish community in the United States. Although successive US administrations rejected and condemned IRA violence,[11] a certain amount of support for the terrorist campaign existed among some sections of the Irish American community in the United States. The Irish Northern Aid Committee (NORAID) was set up in April 1970 and was able to channel important financial aid to the republican movement, also initiating publicity campaigns, which denounced the alleged discriminatory and repressive British policy against the nationalist community in Northern Ireland.[12] In 1984, as a result of the pressure exerted by the Justice Department, NORAID was obliged to register under the Foreign Agents Registration Act as an agent of the IRA, albeit with certain qualifications. The group argued that the money collected was not destined for the IRA campaign but for the support of the families of imprisoned IRA recruits. By the 1990s, Friends of Sinn Fein, formed following the IRA ceasefire in 1994, became the major fund-raiser and lobbying group in the US.

Lobbying by sympathisers of Irish republicans also aimed at benefiting from the criticism aimed at the British policy in Northern Ireland that was aired during the 1970s by influential political figures such as Senator Edward Kennedy and Hugh Carey, later governor of New York. In fact, their demands for the withdrawal of the British troops and the unification of the island of Ireland were two of the main IRA objectives, thus providing useful arguments in favour of the supporters of the terrorist group in America. In 1976, presidential candidate Jimmy Carter had asked for an international commission on Human Rights to be sent to Northern Ireland, also stating that his party supported the unification of the North and the South of Ireland. This type of criticism directed toward the British government alerted the representatives of constitutional and non-violent nationalism in Northern Ireland as represented by the Social Democratic and Labour Party. Its leader, John Hume, together with the Irish government, set upon a diplomatic initiative aimed at countering the IRA propaganda that the terrorist group could have derived from the criticism referred to. Hume's lobbying proved successful and the criticism of British policy articulated by some American politicians was immediately complemented with a strong and explicit condemnation of IRA terrorism.

Arms smuggling from America continued until the last stage of the IRA campaign. In July 1999, four people were arrested while they were attempting to illegally ship weapons from Florida through the US mail. More than 90 weapons had been mailed from Fort Lauderdale in packages that had been disguised as toys and electronic equipment. This was the last in a series of failures and successes for the IRA, which, according to some estimates, during the 1970s, was able to smuggle to Ireland from the US over 2,500 weapons and a million rounds of ammunitions (Taylor 1997).

The reversals suffered by the IRA meant that throughout the conflict the terrorist group was in constant search for new sources of supply to the extent that at one point the organization's activists visited North Korea looking for contacts that could facilitate more innovative weaponry.[13] In July 2001, three members of the Real IRA, a splinter group from the main IRA, were arrested by Slovakian police after receiving intelligence that the group was looking for a 'rogue' state that would provide it with arms. It is believed that officers from the British counter-intelligence service, MI5, posed as Iraqis willing to supply weapons and explosives to the three men while others pretended to be European arms dealers (Hopkins 2001). One year earlier a massive arms shipment had been seized in Croatia before it could reach the Real IRA in Northern Ireland. Jorge Dezcallar, Head of Spain's intelligence service from 2001 to 2004, has confirmed the existence of links between the IRA and ETA, pointing out that the Basque terrorist group also turned to the former Yugoslavia for weapons and explosives (*El Correo* 2002).

International connections were also established with the Colombian main terrorist organization, Fuerzas Armadas Revolucionarias de Colombia (FARC, or Revolutionary Armed Forces of Colombia), as it emerged in August 2001, when three IRA members were arrested by the country's police at Bogota airport. They were subsequently accused and convicted of training Colombian terrorists in return for a considerable amount of money. It is believed that IRA members trained the FARC in the use of mortars and other technology as the mainly rural terrorist organization wanted to step up its campaign in urban areas (Smyth 2002). In return, the IRA may have received as much as two million USD for its assistance. According to a RAND Corporation Report, this would have been a profitable business for the Irish terrorist organization, since 'the costs of running a nationwide organization such as Sinn Fein, which boasts of 1500 election workers, is expensive, and the group's criminal operations may not be enough to sustain it militarily and politically' (Cragin et al. 2007).

The revelation of the Colombian connection proved to be very damaging for Sinn Fein's reputation in the United States where the FARC is designated as a terrorist organization that is being combated by the Colombian government with great financial and logistic support from the American administration (Holland 2001). Gerry Adams, president of Sinn Fein, refused to attend a hearing by the Committee on International Relations of the US Congress that held hearings on the links between the IRA and FARC. The decision came as Henry J. Hyde, senior US Congressman and Chairman of the Committee, argued that it was in 'American national interests' to investigate links between the IRA and Colombian 'narco-terrorists', since Americans could be killed or injured by the 'advanced terrorist tactics' FARC may have learned from the IRA (Thornton 2002).

The investigation conducted by the Congressional Committee concluded that the IRA 'had well-established links with the FARC narco-terrorists in Colombia since at least 1998'. In the view of the Committee, 'more Irish nationals than just the three arrested in Colombia in August, 2001 may have been involved in visiting Colombia for possible terrorist activities'[14], a point corroborated by other sources that were able to establish the fact that other senior IRA leaders had travelled to the Latin American country to meet the terrorists who were being trained by the IRA (Harnden 2002). The Committee also believed that they had 'been training in the FARC safe haven in explosives management, including mortar and possibly car-bomb urban terrorist techniques, and possibly the use of the rural jungles safe haven as a location to test and improve the IRA's own terrorist weapons and techniques'. The findings also pointed out that 'explosives management training for the FARC by the IRA, and possibly by other foreign-based terrorists suspected by the Colombians, such as Cubans, Iranians, ETA', had 'markedly improved the FARC's proficiency in urban terrorism in the last few years'. Press reports backed up the links between the IRA, ETA and the FARC, quoting security sources that believed in the exchange of weapons and technology by the three terrorist groups (Morris 2001).

The US National Strategy for Combating Terrorism constituted in 2003 used the arrest of the IRA members in Colombia as an example of the interconnection between different terrorist organizations across the world:

> The terrorist threat is a flexible, transnational network structure, enabled by modern technology and characterized by loose inter-connectivity both within and between groups. In this environment, terrorists work together in funding, sharing intelligence, training, logistics, planning, and executing attacks. Terrorist groups with objectives in one country or region can draw strength and support from groups in other countries or regions. For example, in 2001, three IRA members were arrested in Colombia, suspected of training the FARC in how to conduct an urban bombing campaign. The connections between al-Qaeda and terrorist groups throughout Southeast Asia further highlight this reality. The terrorist threat is both resilient and diffuse because of this mutually reinforcing, dynamic network structure. (*National Strategy for Combating Terrorism* 2003)

THE INTERNATIONALIZATION OF THE CONFLICTS

LOOKING FOR EXTERNAL LEGITIMIZATION

The activities of ETA's so called 'international department' have overlapped with those of the political party that has developed under the shadow of the armed wing of the terrorist movement. It has been judicially demonstrated that the party constitutes a part within the network of organizations ultimately led by ETA, which complemented terrorist actions, conforming all of them within a movement that has shared objectives as well as membership.[15] The Spanish state awareness of the terrorist movement's multifaceted structure led to the banning of the organization's political wing in 2002.[16] Under these circumstances, a great deal of the external actions of ETA and Batasuna during the last years have been aimed at gathering international support against an anti-terrorist initiative that has considerably damaged the terrorist group's efficiency. Previously, ETA had already devoted a significant amount of efforts in the search for the 'internationalization of the conflict'. To that extent, the terrorist group has been constantly looking for the support of international figures by portraying a biased and manipulated interpretation of the conflict.[17] ETA has done so by denouncing the alleged denial of political and civil rights in the Basque Country, the systematic practice of torture, and the lack of democracy in Spain.

Therefore, ETA's propaganda has also been oriented towards the garnering of an international public opinion in an attempt to disguise the reality of the terrorist threat. As the 2001 Report produced by the Council of Europe Commissioner for Human Rights puts it, ETA systematically violates human rights through their campaign of assassination, kidnapping, threat, harassment, and extortion activities (Office of the Commissioner for Human Rights 2001). Accusations of torture allegedly committed by state agents on detainees held on suspicion of terrorist offences have continued over the years. Most of these accusations have proved to be unfounded, originating in ETA's own instructions on their activists to systematically claim torture when arrested, as it was revealed in internal documents elaborated by the terrorist group.[18] The United Nations Special Rapporteur concluded in 2004 that torture or maltreatment of prisoners in Spain was not a systematic practice. He also observed that the system made torture possible, particularly in incommunicado detention, and recommended the recording of the interrogation of detainees to prevent any infringement of their rights (Commission on Human Rights 2004). However, police trade unions have frequently rejected such a practice, as the disclosure of their identity would seriously endanger their work, putting at risk their lives.[19]

In the search for an 'internationalization' of the conflict, ETA has also demanded the involvement of international mediators that could put the terrorist campaign in the same level as the legitimate actions of a democratic State like Spain. The Spanish authorities have accepted on several occasions the engagement of international mediators. In 1995, following ETA's requests, Argentinean Adolfo Pérez Esquivel, winner of the 1980 Nobel Prize for Peace, liaised between the Spanish government and the terrorist group. The unsuccessful efforts to put an end to violence were followed by another failed and short-lived engagement of the Carter Foundation.[20] In spite of the legitimization that ETA would extract from the acceptance of international mediators in negotiations between the terrorist group and the Spanish government, the latter agreed to the participation of the Henri Dunant Centre, based in Geneva, in the period before and after the 2006 truce declared in March of that year.[21] As part of that legitimization process derived from the internationalization of the conflict pursued by ETA, the terrorist group was also successful in its demands to the Spanish government when in October 2006 the European Parliament endorsed by a narrow margin the 'peace initiative in the Basque Country' (Pagola 2006).

ETA AND THE IRISH MIRROR

The influence that the events in Northern Ireland during the past decade have had on ETA's strategy constitutes another pattern of internationalization. Nationalist politicians in the Basque Country have regarded the Northern Ireland as a so-called 'peace process' which may serve as a model for the resolution of their own conflict. However, the search for a similar strategy towards peace in the Basque Country has been characterized by the distortion of the Irish model. Basque nationalism's interpretation of the Irish process is based on the two following wrong assumptions: that the formation of a pan-nationalist front offered the Republican movement, made up of the IRA and Sinn Fein, an alternative through which they could achieve their objectives and compensate for the weakness evidenced in their electoral and social support; and that the IRA's cessation of violence was a direct consequence of the British and Irish government's recognition of the right to self-determination.[22] Basque nationalists and ETA misrepresented the reality of the Irish context ignoring that, as prominent IRA figures have admitted, the 'peace process' had required Republicans to swallow very 'bitter pills'.[23]

Nonetheless, ETA was particularly interested in drawing parallels with the Northern Ireland context since the Basque group could use it as an example for the Spanish government to engage in negotiations with a terrorist organization. Thus, one of Batasuna's leaders stated 'Ireland was a mirror for us', adding, 'so was the republican movement', for the following reason: 'Negotiation was always regarded here in the Basque Country as something suspect. But Sinn Fein and the republican movement showed us that negotiation did not have to lead to political treachery. If it could happen in Ireland, why not in the Basque Country?' (Woodworth 1998). However, ETA's maximalist demands in subsequent contacts with Spanish democratic parties confirmed that the terrorist group was ignoring the advice al-legedly put forward by Sinn Fein politicians who had recommended Batasuna to be 'realistic' about what could be achieved in such a process (Sharrock 1998).

ETA and Batasuna were particularly seduced by the successful internationalization of the conflict achieved by Sinn Fein and materialized in the involvement of international figures in the Northern Ireland process in various forms. US Senator George Mitchell became the chair of the talks that culminated in the Belfast Agreement signed in April 1998.[24] Former Finnish Prime Minister Harri Holkeri was also part of the Mitchell Commission, which had been created with the aim of assessing how and when decommissioning should occur. Former Finnish President Martti Ahtissari and one of the leaders of the African National Congress Cyril Ramaphosa were to become independent arms inspectors. Retired Canadian General John de Chastelain was appointed Chairman of the International Commission on Decommissioning, which consisted of two other members: Brigadier Auno Nieminen from Finland, and Andrew Sens, a US diplomat who had acted as senior foreign and defense policy aide to President Bill Clinton. The former US president was himself a very active player in the process that led to the Belfast Agreement, granting Gerry Adams a visa in 1994 and welcoming the IRA leader on various occasions the White House while he was in office (Sharrock and Davenport 1997). The nationality and background of these figures allowed the IRA to present itself like a real army signing an armistice rather than as a terrorist group that had forced, through violence and intimidation, its objectives against the will of the majority of the Irish people.

Such a metamorphosis was also implemented through the advantageous comparison of the Northern Ireland terrorist phenomenon with a far away conflict like the one in South Africa. During the process that led to the signing of the Belfast Agreement in April 1998, South Africa was used as a positive model by Sinn Fein politicians, eager to compare the IRA's terrorist campaign with the African National Congress' violent struggle for the end of apartheid (Guelke 2000, O' Malley 2001). The Republican movement has frequently compared the situation in Northern Ireland with South African apartheid and the institutionalized and systematic racism existing in certain areas of the United States. Neither of these comparisons stands up to serious analysis.[25] As Purdie has noted in his analysis of how the Northern Ireland Civil Rights Association looked for inspiration in the black movement, the discrimination suffered by blacks was undoubtedly worse and more patent than that was complained of in Northern Ireland. Adopting the style and the inflammatory rhetoric of the black movement, therefore, fuelled a natural tendency towards exaggeration and increased the tension between the Northern Ireland communities (Purdie 1990).

Therefore, the IRA and Sinn Fein put in place a very effective propaganda system, as Garret FitzGerald, former Irish prime minister, summed up: 'Their propaganda system is very focused. "We are the peace party." If you murder enough people and then stop, then you become the peace party' (quoted in Hennessy 2001). Thus, it came as no surprise that ETA and Batasuna, groups that have, for a long time, developed solidarity bonds with the IRA and Sinn Fein, would endeavour to apply similar tactics through the internationalization of the Basque conflict.[26]

After suffering intense terrorist campaigns from ethno-nationalist terrorist groups like ETA and the IRA since the late 1960s, Spain and the United Kingdom have witnessed a decrease in the activities of these groups while a new terrorist threat in the form of Islamist terrorism has emerged. Terrorism has evolved adopting a more indiscriminate form, resorting to extreme manifestations such as suicide attacks without warning that have considerably increased the dangers for the states being targeted. The current Islamist threat is also characterized by the international nature of the objectives pursued by a terrorist movement that can be described as global. This unique feature should not obscure the fact that previous terrorist campaigns like the ones perpetrated by the IRA and ETA also revealed some patterns of internationalization, albeit quite different from the current ones.

ETA and the IRA can be described as transnational movement in so far as some of their activities were planned and perpetrated beyond the territory in which the terrorist groups appeared and developed. To this extent, it should be remembered how France and the Republic of Ireland, neighbouring countries of Spain and the United Kingdom, were for some time safe heavens of the IRA and ETA.[27] Other European and Latin American countries were also used as places where terrorists planned actions or went into hiding. Most of the violence perpetrated by the IRA and ETA occurred within Spain and the UK, although occasionally other countries did witness terrorist attacks by these two groups, thus confirming their transnational nature. Furthermore, both groups developed networks of contacts and alliances with other terrorist organizations, extending their activities throughout a significant number of countries and regions.

NOTES

1. See on this issue the motivations provided by some IRA and ETA activists in Alonso 2007b and Reinares 2001.
2. ETA has been responsible for the killing of 850 people since the beginning of its campaign up to May 2003. At the same time in the second half of the 1970s, after the death of General Franco, right-wing extremists related with reactionary members of the state security agencies killed 10 people in France and 23 others inside Spain, victims presumably being chosen because of their alleged relationship with ETA. The other main terrorist group active in Spain until the 1990s has been the left-wing Antifascist Grupo de Resistencia Antifascista Primero de Octubre (GRAPO, or Group of Resistance First of October) (Alonso 2005: 143–147).
3. For an analysis on how the terrorist threat has evolved in these countries, see Alonso 2008.
4. Some of the activities of this department are analyzed in Domínguez 2006: 89–129.
5. This has been the case in spite of the opinion of ETA leaders like José Luis Álvarez Emparantza. This founder member of ETA saw the IRA as 'the armed wing of the Irish nationalist right', as opposed to the Irish National Liberation Army, a splinter group from the main IRA formed in the 1970s, which was regarded by Álvarez as similar to the Basque terrorist group (Domínguez 1998b: 115). On the Irish National Liberation Army, see Holland and McDonald 1994.
6. Interviews with IRA members carried by one of the authors, Belfast and Derry, January 2000 and March 2002.
7. Gerry Adams, president of Sinn Fein and a key IRA leader since the 1970s, has paid several visits to the Basque Country. Other Sinn Fein politicians have also endorsed some of Batasuna's initiatives, as it was the case with Alex Maskey's presence in the Basque Country at the launch of an official document in January 2002.
8. Interview with Sean O'Callaghan by one of the authors, London, February 1997.
9. For a more detailed description of the contacts with some of these countries, see Domínguez 1998b: 124–127.
10. Ed Moloney provides one of the most detailed and insightful accounts of these dealings and the interception of the Eksund in Moloney 2002: 3–33. On the Libyan connection, see also O'Brien 1993: 133–153.
11. For a thorough analysis of the transatlantic influence on the Ulster conflict and the position of successive US administrations and politicians towards Northern Ireland and the IRA, see Wilson 1995; and Guelke 1988: 128–152.
12. For a more detailed account of NORAID activities, see Holland 1999: 27–62.

13. Interview by one of the authors with former IRA member who was dispatched to the Asian country by the IRA leadership.
14. Committee on International Relations, US House of Representatives, *Summary of Investigation of IRA Links to FARC Narco-Terrorists in Colombia*, 24 April 2001; Investigative findings on the activities of the Irish Republican Army (IRA) in Colombia. Prepared by the Majority Staff of the House International Relations Committee, *The Irish Times* (8 April 2002).
15. For a thorough analysis of the complex system of organizations linked to ETA, their actions and the nature of such a relationship, see Mata 1993.
16. On the rationale behind the banning of ETA's political wing, see Alonso and Reinares 2005: 270–272.
17. To this extent, notorious has been the involvement of certain figures, who have shown a deep lack of knowledge of the causes and consequences of ETA's terrorism. Consequently they have aligned themselves with ETA's agenda becoming conveyors of the terrorist group's propaganda. Father Alec Reid, who acted as an intermediary between the IRA and the British government, is probably the best example. On his damaging role in the Basque Country, see Alonso 2004: 695–713; 2007a.
18. In 1991 ETA activist Ángel María Ezquerra Andueza was arrested in possession of one of these documents. More documents on this issue were found in possession of other ETA activists arrested in March 1998.
19. It should be mentioned that ETA has often used television footage to identify their targets. Spanish police discovered TV footage of a raid in Cahors (France) in which three ETA members were arrested with 500 kg of explosives. The policemen who were coming in and out of the house raided had been identified as targets by ETA's activists.
20. The exchange of messages between ETA and the Spanish government delivered by Pérez Esquivel is summarized in Domínguez 2006: 248–252.
21. In March 2006, ETA declared a 'permanent ceasefire' that was 'officially' ended in June 2007. For the duration of the truce the terrorist group had remained active continuing with the economic extortion of individuals and the acquisition of weapons and explosives. In December 2006 a bomb detonated by ETA at Madrid's international airport killed two people.
22. For a detailed analysis of the misrepresentation of the Irish model, see Alonso 2004: 695–713.
23. Morrison D 1999. Some examples of the distorted interpretation of the Northern Ireland process carried by Basque nationalist with the aim of adopting a favourable model for the Basque context can be seen in Gallastegi 2004; Toda 2002; *Gara* 2002.
24. For a personal account of Mitchell's role in the talks' process, see Mitchell 1999.
25. See, for example, Patterson 2002: 128–131, 160–161, 192–199.
26. In that line Batasuna has resorted to the prolific use of the word 'peace' in many of its documents and statements replicating Sinn Fein's attitude since the late 1980s. See, for example, Alonso 2002.
27. In 2003, Europol warned of ETA's attempts to extend some of its actions to Portugal with the aim of setting up an infrastructure that would counter the weakening of the organization that the proactive measures of the French authorities had caused the terrorist group (Beltrán de Otálora 2007).

2

TRANSNATIONAL LINKS AND 'LOCAL CONNECTION': LATIN AMERICA AND GLOBAL TERRORISM

Khatchik DerGhougassian

INTRODUCTION

The 11th of September 2001 altered the concept of global terrorism in a distinctive way. It has blurred the distinction between the local and the international in terms of linking the violent act with a political aim. Likewise, the 'war on terrorism' that the George W. Bush administration declared immediately after the attacks on the World Trade Center and the Pentagon has broadened the battlefield of counter-terrorism beyond the traditional offense/defense strategic logic and went on to embrace 'pre-emption' along the guideline of the 2002 National Security Strategy.[1] The 'war on terrorism' has been institutionalized through domestic measures, including the creation of the Department of Homeland Security and the USA Patriot Act[2], as well as international practices ranging from unilateral decisions of military interventions to cooperative initiatives.

Among the instruments of this institutionalized 'war on terrorism' are the US State Department's lists of terrorist organizations and states that sponsor terrorism.[3] The contributor is grateful to his student,

Juliana Plencovich, for her help in the research concerning the State Department's list of terrorist organizations. The list was established as early as 1976, yet it gained a special meaning within the context of the shift of US counter-terrorism strategy from containment to pre-emption. Interestingly, from 1976 to 1983 the report was entitled *Patterns of International Terrorism*; then till 2004 it was renamed as *Patterns of Global Terrorism*; and since 2004 it has been labelled as *Country Reports on Terrorism*. The .shift is not coincidental; it shows the impact of the changing patterns of the international order—from bipolar to unipolar—on strategic thinking on terrorism. It is within this framework that the phenomenon of terrorism is perceived, defined and used for policy purposes. Nor is the focus on specific countries from 2004 onward without a rational background. It is an effort to provide a concrete road map for political and military action in the practical use of a very abstractly defined concept. Thus, specifying countries in the very title of the report is also the initial step of dividing the world into 'either with us, or with the terrorist' antagonistic camps, as formulated in President Bush's 20 September 2001 address to a Joint Session of Congress following the 9/11 attack.[4] The same logic is structured more specifically with the 'axis of evil' metaphor referring to North Korea, Iran and Iraq in President Bush's 29 January 2002 State of the Union address in Congress.[5]

According to the April 2007 *Country Report on Terrorism*, only four Latin American groups are defined as terrorist organizations: Fuerzas Armadas Revolucionarias de Colombia (FARC); Ejército de Liberación National (ELN, or National Liberation Army); Autodefensa Unida de Colombia (AUC, or United Self-Defense [forces] of Colombia); and Sendero Luminoso (Shining Path). The first three operate in Colombia, whereas Sendero Luminoso is Peruvian. Of the four organizations, only the AUC is rightist. Cuba is named by the US as a 'state sponsor of terrorism', whereas Venezuela is characterized as 'not fully cooperating' in the war on terrorism. This pattern of US perception of Foreign Terrorist Organizations (FTO), as they are officially characterized in the State Department's reports, remained practically unchanged for Latin America since 11 September 2001. The 2006 *Country Reports on Terrorism* (Chapter 2) mentioned that no Islamist groups or terrorist cells operated in Latin America. The region, therefore, has not been seen as a hotspot in the US-led 'war on terrorism'.

Yet, if a shift is made from the perspective of FTO and states sponsors of terrorism to the broader phenomenon of terrorism in Latin America in its historical evolution, current manifestations, and potential threats, this moderately optimistic assessment about a region immune from major international terrorist threat becomes questionable. To start with, in the 1970s and 1980s, Latin America was considered as one of the two regions, along with the Middle East, where anti-US terrorist attacks were the most frequent. In the 1970s and early 1980s, terrorism was sometimes employed as a tactic by rebel groups in Argentina, Uruguay, and Chile. Moreover, at least in the case of the Argentine Montoneros, there were attempts to establish links with Palestinian organizations operating in Lebanon. During the Reagan administration, the US focus shifted from South America to Central America and the Andean region—mostly Peru. Whereas the civil conflicts in Nicaragua and El Salvador were characterized mostly as guerrilla warfare, Sendero Luminoso, and the other Peruvian leftist guerrilla, Movimiento Revolucionario Tupac Amaru (or Tupac Amaru Revolutionary Movement) relied heavily on terrorist attacks both in rural areas and big cities. By the end of the 1980s, as well as during the 1990s, yet another shift occurred in the perception, definition, and manifestation of the terrorist threat in Latin America, with the growing focus on the link of drug trafficking with terrorism. This agenda shift has taken place along with a geopolitical displacement of the main US counter-terrorist strategy from Peru to Colombia, a country that since then had remained a top priority on the US agenda in Latin America. The concept of 'narcoguerrilla' appeared in late 1980s and became 'narcoterrorism' in the aftermath of 11 September 2001.

This dual agenda and geopolitical shift deepened in the 1990s in the context of the acceleration of the process of globalization after the end of Cold War, as well as the emergence of transnational Islamist terrorism. Two terrorist attacks, both in Buenos Aires, were the first cases of Islamist terrorism in the region: the bombing of the Israeli Embassy in 1992 and of the Argentine Jewish Community Centre (AMIA) in 1994. Officially, both attacks were linked to Iran and the Lebanese Hezbollah sponsored by Iran. Nevertheless, there have been serious doubts about the nature of this linkage that was criticized as partisan and politically motivated, opened a public debate and divided the Argentine political class and opinion.[6] Yet, beyond the confusion and the politicization of the issue, the terrorist attacks in Argentina highlighted—*a posteriori*—at least three aspects of the current debate about the global features of terrorism: potential 'local' connections in terms of sympathies, interests or ideological allies, including the formation of sleeper cells; financial transactions to support terrorism; and connection between transnational terrorism and the rise of anti-US sentiments.

How to conceptualize the internationalization of terrorism in Latin America in its historical evolution and how to evaluate it in the post-11 September 2001 context? This chapter tries to answer these questions. Although it relies on empirical data, including organizations, facts and significant cases of terrorism in Latin America, it goes beyond documented reporting on the so-called 'terrorist organizations' of the present and the past and their international linkages. Instead, it proposes an analytical framework to understand better the patterns of internationalization of terrorism in Latin America in a historical perspective. This framework, hopefully, should help to both evaluate the past performance of armed groups in the region in their effort to establish international links as well as the present context of terrorist connections from local to global.

One of the basic arguments made in this chapter is that terrorism as a violent tactic of political struggle is an exception rather than the rule in Latin America. Guerilla warfare and state repression is what has usually characterized the Latin American context of political violence. Moreover, compared to Middle Eastern, mainly Palestinian, organizations and even to West European groups (such as the IRA or the Basque ETA) and, for instance, to the Liberation Tigers of Tamil Eelam (LTTE), Latin American armed groups, including groups that have used terrorist means, with some rare exceptions, developed regional links at most. One of the explanations is provided by the relative 'isolation' of Latin America from the main East–West fracture line of the Cold War. Despite the prestige of the 1959 Cuban Revolution and the efforts of exporting the model as well as Havana's moral and, to some extent, material support to Latin American left-ist organizations, Cuba never played a leading role in supporting a regional insurrection, nor could it—or even wanted to do—do so. Furthermore, the Cuban insurrection model stressed more traditional tactics of guerrilla warfare and never emphasized—indeed even opposed—the use of terrorist means. The heroic figure of Ernesto Che Guevara or the moral leadership of Fidel Castro for the Latin American left has always been more a source of inspiration than a vehicle of the internationalization of the revolutionary struggle. In fact, counter-insurgency and counter-terrorism cooperation between Latin American military dictatorship under the US supervision to fight revolutionary movements and/or repress political dissidence (such as the infamous Condor Plan) may have been more organized and militarily efficient than the cooperation of the current governments that have endorsed the Doctrine of National Security.[7]

Therefore, in order to understand the 'internationalization' of Latin American organizations employing terrorist means, the conceptual comprehension of terrorism in the context of its historical evolution needs to be clarified first. The need to understand the process of securitization defined as 'the power politics of [the] concept [of security]' (Buzan et al. 1998) requires an analyst who can connect the two faces of the same coin—terrorism and counter-terrorism. Another basic premise for the same purpose is the importance of the dual consideration of changes in the political agenda and geopolitical shifts. These two conceptual bases provide a ground for a critical appraisal of the phenomenon of terrorism in Latin America, and, hopefully, should help to design rational policies aimed at preventing the threat without jeopardizing essential values including democracy, civil liberties and human rights.

The following analytical framework, first, conceptualizes the historical evolution of terrorism, and then discusses the evolution of terrorism in Latin America, with a purpose to highlight the regional and international links of the local armed groups. Finally, the chapter focuses on the present international context in the aftermath of the attacks of 11 September 2001 in an attempt to critically evaluate the potential local connections of global terrorism. Some general guidelines, critical for a rational consideration and prevention of transnational terrorist threats, are summarized in the conclusions.

INTERNATIONALIZATION OF TERRORISM: A HISTORICAL BACKDROP

Terrorism as a phenomenon is usually defined as an abstraction. The US State Department's *National Strategy for Combating Terrorism*, published in February 2003, for instance, defines terrorism as: 'premeditated, politically motivated violence perpetrated against noncombatant targets by subnational groups or clandestine agents' (The White House 2003). This abstraction notwithstanding, any analytical effort to deal with an issue related to terrorism faces a definitional dilemma of the concept, which consists in either adopting a partisan conceptualization facilitating its implementation for policy purposes, or viewing terrorism as 'a multidisciplinary challenge' that 'requires the ability to translate between the fields of criminology, comparative politics, economics, history, international relations, psychology, sociology, theology, and arguably others' (Cronin 2004). Avoidance of partisanship when defining the concept of terrorism for policy purposes is practically impossible because of the inherent political dimension of the concept. It is often said that one's terrorist is another's freedom fighter. Indeed, because of the impossibility of a broad definitional consensus, the efforts to formulate, and agree on, a universal definition of terrorism in international law has so far failed. As for the multidisciplinary approach, it might well explain why scholars of terrorism were never able to establish a discipline called 'terrorismology'. The definitional dilemma of the concept also explains the failure of communication between the policy makers and the academic community on terrorism-related matters.

A departing point for defining terrorism for the purposes of this study should be the motivations behind the phenomenon. Do the motivations behind terrorist acts in Latin America indicate real or potential links between local and foreign groups? Three concepts are used in the chapter to analyze the patterns of internationalization of terrorism in Latin America from the motivational perspective: terrorism as strategic calculation; terrorism defined in its historical context; and a 'long wave' approach that is needed to understand the evolution of terrorism. In addition, as also in line with these three concepts, a framework of analysis in the patterns of internationalization of terrorism in Latin America is suggested.

There are two broad approaches to the study of the motivations of terrorists. The first one is the psychological approach according to which psychological forces are behind the terrorist action that is rationalized later on: '*Individuals are drawn to the path of terrorism in order to commit acts of violence,* and their special logic, which is grounded in their psychology and reflected in their rhetoric, becomes the justification for their violent acts' (Post 1998). The other approach understands terrorism as an expression of political strategy. Terrorist behaviour, rather than emanating from psychological incentives, is interpreted as 'the resort to violence as a willful choice made by an organization for political and strategic reasons'(Crenshaw 1998). The second approach provides a better perspective to study patterns of internationalization of terrorism. As Crenshaw explains, this analytical approach assumes that terrorism displays a collective rationality, with a radical political organization as the central actor selecting terrorism out of the range of perceived alternative tactics to achieve a political goal on the basis of their comparative efficacy. This intentional choice is made by the way of reasonable regularized decision-making process (Crenshaw 1998).

If terrorism is the outcome of strategic calculations, the main question then is in regard to the conditions in which terrorism becomes an attractive choice. Hence, it is neither the absence of other paths, nor ideological incentives, that determines the decision to resort to terrorism, but primarily the belief of the undertaker that the outcome of the terrorist action is beneficial rather than harmful for their cause. The question about the conditions for terrorism to prevail also appears to be important for the study of patterns of its internationalization. Thus, if social learning is inherent in the rational choice perspective of a conceptual definition of terrorist motivations, the decision to internationalize terrorism is primarily based on incentives related to the search for either sources, or logistic support, or innovative forms of struggle to maximize the performance of the group at home. An internationalization pattern is to be successful only if the interest of a local terrorist organization is met with the interests of a group based outside the territory in which the former operates. Therefore, ideology is not viewed as a primary motive for internationalization or, at least, does not explain successful internationalizations. In fact, according to the rational choice logic, perhaps one of the reasons why internationalization of terrorism has historically not been successful in Latin America (for instance, in contrast to the Middle East) is because the prime motive of that pattern has been ideological without a real, material interest to support it. In other words, Latin American armed groups that resorted to terrorism had no real incentives to expand their struggle beyond their local (national) battlefield.

This interpretation of internationalization as a rational choice based on mutual interests and material incentives aiming at the maximization of the struggle at home might raise objections in at least three ways. First, the approach is too close to a framework for analysis of state behaviour, while terrorist organizations are non-state actors with motivations and incentives quite different of state entities that by definition are more powerful. Second, the ideological factor should not be downplayed, as non-state terrorist organizations that challenge state powers do tend to have a stronger inclination for engagement with identities beyond their homeland. Ideology and identity factors gain further importance if the international linkages are defined in terms of transnational—secular or religious—anti-systemic ideological schemes and organizational structures that challenge the international order. Finally, a key element of terrorist action—the violent spectacle aimed at producing a massive psychological impact—suggests a form of rationality beyond the mere materialistic incentives of internationalization. Modern terrorism operates in a virtual space where mass media from TV news to the Internet defines the battlefield, and, hence, defies at least the territoriality assumption of any action defined along the line of the logic of state behaviour.

One way of answering these challenges to the theoretical assumption of a rational motivation behind the terrorist action is to follow Ekaterina Stepanova's distinction of two types of terrorism other than the leftist, rightist or other classic 'terrorism of the peacetime': (*a*) the traditional 'terrorism of conflict' linked to the concrete agenda of a particular armed conflict, and (*b*) the more recent 'super-terrorism', or 'mega-terrorism' that has a much broader agenda and goals, such as challenging the existing world order, and does not have to be tied to any particular local or regional armed conflict (Stepanova 2003). This approach does not deny the rationality assumption of terrorist behaviour: it confirms three main criteria of terrorism—its political goals, civilians as its primary targets, and its asymmetrical nature—that are inherent to the rational behaviour of terrorists (Stepanova 2006). But it does not establish any direct link between rationality and patterns of internationalization. Yet, by distinguishing these two broad types of terrorism, Stepanova helps foresee the conditions that lie behind the phenomenon and thus to characterize the historical context in which it happens. This is important for the patterns of internationalization of terrorism in Latin America because the phenomenon in the region is primarily, if not exclusively, of the conflict-related type that initially limits the level of action to the local (national) one. To look at the mega-terrorist phenomenon in Latin America, the analysis needs to focus on the potential links of the local and the global, or rather, the local connections of the global phenomenon (for this, see the last section of this chapter).

Finally, terrorism as a 'planned show', to use Mannoni's conceptualization, is not apart from the prime consideration of the existence of a set of 'rules of a relatively regular functioning', as terrorist attacks 'are planned and respond to a strategy inhabited by a political ideology' (Mannoni 2006: 68). Hence, planning a terrorist attack as a public show reveals the strategic importance that mass media, especially television, gained for groups resorting to terrorism in a certain historical period—most evidently since 1968 when Palestinian organizations 'discovered', and made active use of, the television as a propaganda tool in their struggle. With regard to Latin America, the question to ask relates to the extent to which the spectacularization of terrorism as a turning point in its internationalization became important for terrorist organizations in the region. It is also interesting to see which mass media from the ones with a local, regional or international reach have been important for them as an information and propaganda tool in their strategy.

The perspective of terrorism as strategic calculation brings up the question of the conditions in which the decision to use terrorism is made. In other words, terrorism is understood in its political context defined as the historical, social, economic, ethnic, and even psychological factors that impact the thought, behaviour and activity of terrorists (Whittaker 2003). In other words, there is a causal relationship between terrorism and its environment: terrorism, on the one hand, is the consequence of certain conditions of that environment and, on the other hand, has an impact on its environment (Crenshaw 2001). Three theses formulated in line with this approach are useful for the purpose of this essay. First, terrorism as a political and social phenomenon may enjoy sympathies and support at least from a segment of the society in which a terrorist group operates. Second, as the process of violence is interactive, responsibility for terrorist actions is often shared, and the resort to terrorist means by non-state actors may well be provoked by state policies. Third, it is not only objective factors that explain terrorism. The symbolic or perceptual context in which terrorist actions take place could well be defined subjectively and is contingent to the comprehension of the phenomenon as a political issue—as self-representation of those who use terrorism, and as the government's or public's construction of the same phenomenon (Crenshaw 2001).

The need for contextualization of terrorism allows a discussion about the historical course of the phenomenon that Rapoport frames as a 'wave,' which is defined as 'a cycle of activity in a given time period—a cycle characterized by expansion and contraction phases' (Rapoport 2004). This approach is particularly useful for the study of patterns of internationalization because one of its features is precisely the international character of the 'wave': according to Rapoport, 'similar activities occur in several countries, driven by a common predominant energy that shapes the participant groups characteristic and mutual relationships' (Rapoport 2004). He identifies four waves of modern terrorism since its emergence in the 19th century: 'anarchist', 'anti-colonial', 'the New Left' and 'religious'. Each wave has a different energy driver. Rapoport does not overlook nationalism that is present in each wave, yet the 'wave' as a generic term indicates a phenomenon that transcended national aspirations even during the process of decolonization. A unique relationship is established between the 'wave' and terrorist organizations: 'a wave is composed of organizations, but waves and organizations have very different life rhythms. Normally, organizations disappear before the initial wave associated with them does' (Rapoport 2004). This is particularly true for 'the New Left' wave in which organizations lasted for the average of two years, yet the wave generated enough energy to create successor organizations. All Latin American terrorist organizations, for instance, came into being with the emergence of 'the New Left', but outlived this 'wave'. The question is whether the groups that are still active in Latin America have retained some of the characteristics of the past 'wave', and why.

While the 'wave' approach does not tell us much about the details of patterns of internationalization, two critical factors outlined by Rapoport as crucial for the birth of modern terrorism can be observed throughout the successful waves: the transformation of communications and transportation patterns and the doctrine, or culture, of terrorism as created, developed and spread by the 19th century Russian writers. In fact, the concept of 'energy' generated by the 'wave' would have remained abstract if it were not for these two critical factors. Yet, when focusing on patterns of internationalization, one needs to go beyond the generalities of a 'wave as energy' to look for further details about the incentives and the historical context as critical factors. Therefore, the framework of analysis for patterns of internationalization includes three conceptual elements: the 'wave' approach, the rational political motivation and the historical context.

When can the patterns of internationalization of terrorism be observed in Latin America? What are the strategic calculations that lie behind the decision of an armed group to establish international links? In what historical context have such decisions been made? These are the three questions to guide the study of the historical evolution of terrorism in Latin America and its patterns of internationalization. They are addressed in the following section.

TERRORISM IN LATIN AMERICA: THE 'THIRD WAVE'

The 'wave' approach suggests that modern terrorism is an international phenomenon. In fact, '[a] wave by definition is an international event' (Rapoport 2004). Nevertheless, it says little, if anything, about how the process of internationalization occurs, except for some general observations about the factors that could have played a role in this process. Thus, for the first 'wave', several factors could have led to the internationalization of a phenomenon born in czarist Russia. While the dominant anarchist ideology and motivation behind the choice for terrorism and the successful strategy for terrorist campaigns put forward by leading anarchist activists played their role, waves of immigration from Russia and Europe to the Ottoman Empire and the Americas also had a major impact. Latin America was not immune to this wave. However, anarchist terrorism was rather confined to specific countries that received massive immigration from Europe by the end of the 19th century. It hardly reached the regional level. Among these countries, Argentina became known as the one where anarchist activism led to a brutal repression of workers and rebels by the first government elected by universal suffrage after 1916 when the so-called 'Saenz Peña law' was passed in the parliament.[8] But even in Argentina, terrorist acts were not common in anarchist activism, with some notorious exceptions such as the bombing of the first offshore branch of Citibank in Buenos Aires (the first offshore bank in history).[9]

The principle of national self-determination is at the heart of the second wave of terrorism that Rapoport labels as 'anticolonial wave'. The principle of national self-determination was adopted after World War I at the Versailles Peace Conference. The victors applied it 'to break up the empires of the defeated states (mostly in Europe)' (Rapoport 2004). But they also undermined the legitimacy of their own empires that were now legally characterized as 'mandates' by the League of Nations. Twenty five years later, successful terror campaigns were launched in 'territories where special political problems made withdrawal [of colonial imperial powers] a less attractive option' (Rapoport 2004), such as Palestine, Algeria, Northern Ireland, and Cyprus. 'Second wave' terrorists changed both the language to describe themselves and the tactics. While the common international heritage of a revolutionary tradition was still acknowledged as a common bond, invoking national heroes became more important, ethnic diasporas became more active and efficient in supporting groups fighting in the homeland and foreign states with kindred population getting active. These features of the second wave explain why it did not reach Latin America. First, there were no colonial empires in Latin America at that time. The most important ongoing national liberation movement—the struggle led by Augusto César Sandino[10] against the military presence in Nicaragua—was a classic guerrilla war that did not involve terrorism. Second, most Latin American governments and leaders were the so-called 'populists', and their social and economic policies enjoyed mass support.

Terrorism emerged in Latin America in the late 1960s and during the 1970s in the context of the third, 'New Left', wave.[11] However, before analyzing the patterns of internationalization of Latin American terrorist organizations, it is important to follow Roman Ortiz in distinguishing three tactics of political violence: violent mass mobilization, guerrilla warfare, and terrorism. The first tactic involves actions to disturb public order and social life in order to impose certain political agenda. The second tactic—guerrilla warfare—is defined as irregular armed actions aimed at the physical destruction of military, administrative and social means that sustain a given political status quo; guerrilla warfare requires a conscious effort on behalf of the group to organize a social and territorial base where it could generate the human and material resources needed for an armed struggle. The third tactic—terrorism—is distinguished from guerrilla warfare in that the violent action aims at a psychological impact in addition to the physical destruction of the target; terrorists need fewer resources than guerrilla fighters and a social and material base is not considered a precondition to launch a terrorist strike (Ortiz 2004: 203, 224–226).

These tactics are rarely used in an isolated manner. On the contrary, political organizations tend to combine them with such legal instruments as propaganda or participation in the political process.

The selection of a tactic depends on how the group perceives its environment and the resources it has (Ortiz 2004). Therefore, it is often difficult, if at all possible, to distinguish between a guerrilla group and a terrorist organization. The Colombian FARC, for instance, is clearly a guerrilla movement, yet have used terrorism. In an attempt to overcome this difficulty, the chapter relies on the US State Department's list of FTO to analyze terrorism in Latin America, even as it does not endorse uncritically the US official definition of terrorism. This choice is justified not only by the fact that in the 1970s Latin American armed organizations appeared on the US State Department's list, but also by the striking anti-US character of the 'New Left' terrorism. While one-third of the international attacks in the 'third wave' involved US targets, especially in Latin America, Europe and the Middle East, the US itself, driven by the Cold War rivalry, supported terrorist activity in countries such as Nicaragua and Angola (Rapoport 2004).

The two main sources of the third wave, according to Rapoport, are the Vietnam War (as a model for effectively defeating a superpower), and the emergence of the Palestinian Liberation Organization (PLO) on the international scene. The centrality of the PLO for other groups, in terms of terrorist activity, 'was strengthened because it got strong support from Arab states and the Soviet Union and made training facilities in Lebanon available to the other groups' (Rapoport 2004). The importance of PLO for the international spread of the third wave also lies in the successful discovery of the importance of mass media, especially TV, and the use of these means in the political struggle. Mass media played the key role in transmitting the message a terrorist act sent. Finally, PLO was the first organization to understand the importance of financial independence and to use the globalizing financial system to diffuse and diversify the capital it gained by donations, aid or illegal means (Napoleoni 2003). Plane hijacking, kidnapping and hostage tacking, assassinations of diplomats and government officials, and attacks on foreign embassies became the favourite tactics used by the 'third wave' terrorists.

The turning point for the evolution of political violence in Latin America in modern times was the 1959 Cuban revolution that overthrew the Batista dictatorship. The successful guerrilla campaign popularized the *foco* theory, where a small revolutionary group could create a territorial basis and over time and persistence in struggle successfully overthrow a bourgeois government to replace it by a popular one (Feldman and Perälä 2004: 106). Cuba provided facilities and support to leftist Latin American organizations that later on tried to launch guerrilla campaigns in Venezuela, Bolivia, Peru, Colombia, and Guatemala, among others. Most of these campaigns launched in rural areas were unsuccessful, although some groups, such as the Colombian FARC and ELN, survived. It is with the urbanization of the guerrilla warfare by the late 1960s that terrorism emerged as a major tactic. Indeed, having critically reviewed the failure of the previous armed campaigns, leftist groups decided not to confine insurgencies to rural areas in times of rapid urban development and the growth of urban population.

As early as in 1962, young leftist activists in Venezuela formed Movimiento Revolucionario de Izquierda (MIR) or the Revo-lutionary Left Movement, an urban guerrilla group that aimed at destabilizing the Rómulo Betancourt government through assaults, robberies, bombs, and kidnappings. MIR never received popular support and was finally neutralized (Feldman and Perälä 2004). Yet, the turning point for the urbanization of the guerrilla warfare, hence the inclusion of terrorist tactics in the armed struggle, has been the death of the Cuban-Argentine guerrilla leader and *foco* theorist, Ernesto 'Che' Guevara, in Bolivia in 1967. Observing the failure of several attempts of rural *focus*, the Brazilian leftist ideologue and rebel leader Carlos Marighella promoted the use of terrorism to both provoke State repressive reaction, hence to blame the State, as well as transform the political crisis to armed conflict. Groups in-spired by the Cuban model, yet following Marighella's path of the urbanization of the guerrilla warfare, emerged in Argentina: Fuerzas Armadas de Liberación (FAL), Fuerzas Armadas Peronistas, Ejército Revolucionario del Pueblo (ERP), and Montoneros; Brazil: Accion por la Liberacion Nacional, Vanguardia Revolucionaria Armada and Var Palmares; Chile: Movimiento de Izquierda Revolucionaria, or MIR; and Uruguay: Tupamaros. Other groups that came to the scene in the 1970s and the early 1980s, such as Movimiento 19 de April (M-19) in Colombia, Frente Patriótico Manuel Rodriguez in Chile following the Pinochet coup d'état in 1973 and Frente Farabundo Marti de Liberación Nacional in El Salvador, the Frente Sandinista de Liberación Nacional in Nicaragua and Fuerzas Armadas Rebeldes in Guatemala, mixed the classical rural guerrilla warfare with terrorist attacks, often against urban targets.

Urban guerrilla warfare and terrorist attacks started in Brazil in 1968 in the geographical triangle of Rio de Janeiro–Sao Paolo–Belo Horizonte. In October 1968, Brazilian rebels killed a high-ranking US military officer and in the following year kidnapped the US Ambassador who was later released after 15 leftist rebels were freed from prison. Terrorist actions continued after the killing of Marighella in November 1969, with the kidnapping, in 1970, of the German Ambassador in exchange for 40 other political prisoners. In Argentina, the FAL, in 1970, kidnapped the Consul of Paraguay, and the following year, the ERP kidnapped in the city of Rosario the Honorary Consul of Great Britain, who was released after the government distributed free meals in the poor neighbourhoods of Argentine big cities. The ERP also used terrorism, mainly the kidnapping of wealthy businessmen, for ransom—the best-known operation in this sense has been the kidnapping of the head of the Argentina branch of Esso, for the liberation of whom the ERP received 14 million USD. However, it were not these small revolutionary groups that had the greatest effect on North American and European terrorist organizations, but the urban guerrilla group called the Uruguayan Tupamaros. It made its appearance on the political scene in October 1969, on the occasion of the second anniversary of the death of 'Che' Guevara, with the occupation of a medium urban locality, Pando, about 25 km from the capital Montevideo. One of the most spectacular operations of the Tupamaros has been the kidnapping of the US expert Dan Mitrione, a delegate of the US government who was a consultant to the Uruguayan police. Upon the failure of the negotiations with the government for the release of political prisoners, including the main leader of the movement, Raúl Sendic, Mitrione has been executed (Chaliand and Blin 2006).

All these groups operated mainly at the local level and their main external source of support and inspiration was Cuba. This does not mean that there was no cooperation between different groups. However, this cooperation was extremely limited or even reduced to inter-personal links. The Joint Revolutionary Coordination (Junta Coordinadora Revolucionaria) that ERP (Argentina), ELN (Bolivia), MIR (Chile), Frente Patriótica de Libertação Nacional (FREPALINA, National Liberation Front), Paraguay, and Tupamaros (Uruguay) tried to form in 1976–1977 has never been effective. Perhaps the most successful of all Latin American groups in establishing external links has been the Argentinian Montoneros, a Peronist organization of leftist nationalist ideology. As early as in 1972–1973, the leadership of the Montoneros made contacts with the PLO and established a working relationship. The contact was first made with a Palestinian delegate in Europe. Later on, Montoneros signed an agreement on logistics, documentation and transportation of arms with the PLO. This cooperative agreement was made public in 1977 when the chairman of the PLO, Yasser Arafat, received two Montoneros leaders, Mario Firmenich and Fernando Vaca Narvaja, in Beirut. The agreement had a secret clause concerning military cooperation. Accordingly, Arafat's organization, Al Fatah, offered training facilities, military instructors, RPG-7 missiles and other arms to the Montoneros. The Montoneros, in turn, agreed to set up a plant of plastic explosives in South Lebanon under the supervision of an Argentinian chemist. The agreement worked for a year and a half, but in September 1978 it ran the risk of being exposed when the head of the Montonero Army, Horacio Mendizábal, made it public at a press conference in Beirut. His act, intentionally or not, provoked a joint Israeli–Argentine intelligence operation against the plant and the Montoneros' base in Beirut. The Montoneros also used Spain and Mexico as recruitment bases for what was aimed to be the Contraofensiva (the counter-offensive operation) against the Argentine military dictatorship—a plan that ultimately failed (Larraquy 2006).

Terrorism in Latin America was certainly not an exclusively leftist phenomenon. In the 1970s, the Triple A (Argentine Anticommunist Alliance) murdered those who officially were labelled as 'subversive,' that is, left-wing activists, and even Peronist trade union leaders, despite the Triple A's claim of being Peronist, too. Nevertheless, this type of terrorism was even more localized although it often enjoyed the support of the military. It is in the 1980s that the right-wing terrorism emerged, under the auspices of and with support from the United States. It was practised by groups ranging from El Salvadorian Death Squads to the guerrilla-terrorist organization of the Nicaraguan Contras. Gradually, these right-wing groups, as well as the leftist guerrillas, have established connections with drug traffickers in order to provide funds for their activities.

'Third wave' terrorism in Latin America faded away even before it did so in other regions in the early 1980s. The main reason was the military defeat of these groups in their own countries and the lack of the popular support they hoped to build up for their struggle. With the return of democratic governments in the 1980s, most of Latin

American leftist armed organizations went through the transformation process experienced by all the Latin American left. In particular, they abandoned the idea of revolution and declared support for progressive change to fully embrace democracy (Castañeda 1993). As terrorism was entering its fourth, 'religious,' wave, following the 1979 Islamic Revolution in Iran and the emergence of Islamist resistance to the Soviet occupation of Afghanistan since 1979, a dual shift was underway in Latin America. Political violence first moved from South America to Central America in the 1980s and then moved to the Andean region in the 1990s and the US counter-insurgency agenda was gradually replaced by the 'war on drugs'. Both developments had their impact on the patterns of internationalization of terrorism in Latin America.

THE 'DRUG CONNECTION' AND BEYOND: TERRORISM IN LATIN AMERICA IN THE 1980s–1990s AND AFTER 11 SEPTEMBER 2001

The fourth wave of modern terrorism has Islamist extremism at its heart. 'Islamic groups have conducted the most significant, deadly, and profoundly international attacks. Equally significant, the political events providing the hope for the fourth wave originated in Islam, and the successes achieved apparently influenced religious terror groups' (Rapoport 2004). Judaic, Sikh, Hindu, Buddhist and Christian extremists have also used terrorist means and the LTTE in Sri Lanka and some other secular groups have actively employed suicide bombings. Still, most of the armed religious groups that employed terrorism in the end of the 20th century and in the early 21st century have been Islamists and generated from the larger—and growing—Islamic communities, both in Muslim countries and in Muslim diasporas elsewhere. At the same time, the number of terrorist groups in countries of mostly Christian tradition decreased from 200 active in 1980 to 40 in the next decade. While the anti-US character of the 'third wave' persisted in the 'fourth wave' in an even more evident form, it has been more specifically aimed at the evacuation of the US bases from Islam's Holy Lands and the defence of Muslim lands from the US and Western interference and, more generally, has often been viewed as a form of the larger 'clash of civilizations'.

Despite its birth in the 1980s, the fourth wave became a dominant feature of global terrorism only with the end of the Cold War. At least until the 1987 Reagan–Gorbachov summit when the two superpowers agreed to reinitiate arms control negotiations after Moscow decided to pull out of Afghanistan, international security issues and agenda were defined within the Cold War paradigm of bipolar confrontation. Thus, for the United States, Islamist terrorism was still mostly synonymous with terrorism supported by Iran (while terrorism sponsored by Syria and Libya at that time was primarily of the secular nationalist/left-wing bent). It was mainly perceived as a side effect of the US–Soviet confrontation or as an opposition to the US policies in the Middle East. In other words, Islamist 'fourth wave' terrorism was primarily identified with radical Shia organizations, such as the Lebanese Hezbollah, whereas the Sunni Mujahedeen in Afghanistan were labelled as 'freedom fighters'.

In the same way, in Latin America, the leftist regimes of Cuba[12] and Nicaragua were perceived as Soviet allies and thus labelled as sponsors of international terrorism, while the Contras who combined guerrilla warfare with terrorism were referred to as 'freedom fighters'. While, on the one hand, the process of democratization in South America led to a sharp decrease of terrorist activity in Uruguay, Argentina, Brazil, Chile, Bolivia and Colombia, where most former guerrilla organizations became political parties; in Central America, on the other hand, the pattern of internationalization of the 'third wave' terrorism did not change. Indeed, it was only by the late 1980s, and in the context of a new US–Soviet rapprochement, that the conflicts in Central America—civil wars in Nicaragua and El Salvador, unrest and armed insurgency in Guatemala, as well as the use of Honduras territory as a base for operations by the Nicaraguan Contras—came to an end with the 1987 Esquipulas II peace agreement.[13] Meanwhile, US–Latin American relations entered a new phase in which the so-called 'war on drugs' and its institutionalization as part of Washington's security agenda became an increasingly important factor and, in fact, the dominant one in the 1990s. At the same time—and for the same reason—the epicentre of terrorism/counter-terrorism struggle shifted from Central America to the Andean region (first, to Bolivia, then to Peru and, finally, to Colombia).

Guerrilla-terrorist organizations that were active in the late 1980s—Sendero Luminoso and Tupac Amaru Revolutionary Movement (MRTA, or Movimiento Revolucionario Tupac Amaru) in Peru and FARC and ELN in Colombia—were not the prime agents in the transnationalization of drug trafficking. Rather, they used their growing involvement in illicit drug business ranging from the control over the coca cultivation, drug production, and local drug trade to some limited involvement in international narcotrafficking as a source of income. Drug profits were almost the only source of income for the hard-line Maoist Sendero Luminoso whose Maoist doctrine prevented them from reaching out for financial support from the Soviet Union or Cuba. Moreover, they have always claimed that their role was limited to 'taxing' drug trafficking in the so-called 'liberated zones' under their control and that they were not involved in production of or international trade in drugs. In any case, Washington was quick to label them 'narcoguerrillas' and, since 11 September 2001, as 'narco-terrorists' outlining the symbolic context in which the nature of terrorism has been defined and counter-terrorist policies formulated. While drug trafficking and the 'war on drugs' have been the prime factors for the path of internationalization of terrorism in Latin America, it should be stressed that the main agents in the process of internationalization were not the groups officially labelled as 'terrorist organizations', but the already internationalized, or even globalized, drug cartels of Medellín and Cali in Colombia. The former, under the leadership of Pablo Escobar, made particularly intensive use of methods most commonly associated with terrorist attacks, such as the use of car-bombs and kidnappings, for instance, to prevent the extradition of Escobar to the United States.[14]

Of course, terrorism used by drug cartels can hardly meet the criteria of 'political violence' in the sense of politics as a struggle for power to either conquer the state or to impose an agenda, as the drug cartels had only one item on their political agenda—to prevent an extradition. Yet, in any other sense, including the psychological impact, violent methods used by drug cartels met the basic definition of terrorism. It is only after the dismantling of the cartels in Colombia that the FARC, the ELN, and the newly formed right-wing AUC, along with small drug traffickers—often labelled as 'cartelitos', or 'little cartels'—moved into the business of drug trafficking to fill the vacuum. Nevertheless, according to most experts on drug trafficking, the huge profits generated from the drug business made it increasingly difficult for both rebel and pro-government paramilitary organizations to withdraw from it or even to make a clear distinction between their financial activity and political agenda. This combination partly explains why any peace process has become extremely difficult to pursue and sustain in Colombia. Meanwhile, the US counter-narcotics policies embedded in the so-called Plan Colombia that was put forward by the Clinton administration in 1999, and its expansion to the Andean Initiative by the Bush administration in 2001 as well as the homogenization of counter-narcotics and counter-terrorism campaigns in the aftermath of 11 September 2001, created a destabilizing context characterized by confusion of struggles and aims.[15]

The pattern of internationalization of terrorism in Latin America in the context of the 'fourth wave' is, therefore, closely related to the globalization of organized crime, especially to drug trafficking. In other words, it is no longer ideology, logistic facilities or purely the need to finance insurgent activity that is the main driving motivation for Latin American guerrilla-terrorist organizations to build external links— rather, it is the interest in the unprecedented levels of income that drug trafficking provides. In this sense, *the pattern of internationalization of Latin American terrorism has no real connection with the 'fourth wave' Islamist terrorism*. The only characteristic that the internationalization of terrorism in Latin America shares with the 'fourth wave' terrorism is the growing independence of armed non-state actors from any state sponsorship.

Nevertheless, as mentioned in the introduction to the chapter, two terrorist attacks against Jewish and Israeli targets in Argentina in the early 1990s first raised the issue of internationalized Islamist terrorism (by a radical resistance movement based in Lebanon) in the region. Not surprisingly, following the 11 September 2001 terrorist attacks in the United States, the issue of transnational Islamist terrorism has been included into the US–Latin American agenda. In fact, despite the legal case against Iran as the main instigator of the attack against the AMIA and the official accusations against the Lebanese Hezbollah as the executor (Lanata 2006), doubts about the real motivations and actors behind the bombings of the early 1990s have not been dispelled.

Nevertheless, the attacks drew attention to the so-called 'local connections' of foreign terrorists who were behind these terrorist acts and the prosecution focused on those who had provided facilities and other logistical support to the terrorists. The investigation highlighted two interrelated aspects of interest for the study of patterns of internationalization of Latin American terrorism within the context of the 'fourth wave'. The first aspect concerns the relationship of the criminal underworld with transnational terrorism, while the second concerns terrorist financing in the more general sense. No solid legal case concerning these matters has been opened in Argentina so far. While some retired policemen who did not hide their anti-Semitic attitudes and a person connected with the criminal underworld in the Province of Buenos Aires have been charged on 29 October 2004, the Argentine Supreme Court dismissed these charges.[16] Still, the link of the attack to criminal elements has never been seriously questioned. As for the financing of terrorism, straight after the bombing the so-called Tri-Border area of Argentina, Brazil and Paraguay, and especially the Paraguayan city of Ciudad del Este, appeared on the agenda of the investigation. Allegedly, the active Arab-Muslim community of the city could provide a safe haven for the terrorists before and after the attack. However, any official, journalistic or research investigation has so far failed to find any connection with Islamist terrorism, despite the bad fame of Ciudad del Este as a capital for illicit activities ranging from drug trafficking to money-laundering and all kinds of smuggling (Mello 2007). The only evidence linking the Tri-Border area with 'fourth wave' terrorism has been some fund-raising activity for Hamas and Hezbollah which was claimed by the January 2007 Intelligence Report of the US Senate Committee on Foreign Relations. According to this report, no Islamist terrorist cells operate either in Latin America in general, or in the Tri-Border area in particular.[17] However, the Argentinian government was quick to react and demanded from the United States a 'show' of evidence establishing any connection (Alconada 2007b).

However, terrorism experts express growing concerns about the potential for expansion of Islamist terrorism in Latin America, due to the new waves of immigrants from the Middle East and Southeast Asia into the region, including the Caribbean countries and free trade zones of Iquique (Chile) and Colon (Panama). According to Zambelis, 'as a result of intermarriage and conversion, Islam is becoming one of the fastest growing religions in Latin America, and there is some evidence that Islamic missionaries based in Spain and their regional affiliates are making inroads into disenfranchised and underserved indigenous communities in Latin America that had previously been the target of evangelical Christian sects for conversion. The competition between Muslim and Christian missionaries for prospective converts has even led to confrontation and violent clashes in the Mexican state of Chiapas' (Zambelis 2005: 8). However, there is no evidence to conclude that the spread of Islam in and off itself leads to radicalism, let alone to violence, especially in the form of terrorism. Rather, 'most Muslim converts see Islam as a way to reassert their identity and see conversion as a form of social and political protest in societies where they are marginalized and experience discrimination' (Zambelis 2005).

Some other experts, however, see 'the risk of a terrorist attack against western interests in Latin America or in the Caribbean' as a real one (Huste 2007). Muslim immigration from the Middle East and the Indian sub-continent has been going on for two centuries: today, Muslims in Latin America and the Caribbean number two million, with most of them living in the five most populated countries: Argentina, Brazil, Mexico, Columbia, and Venezuela.[18] Muslims have been accepted in these societies and have managed to integrate well. However, since the 1990s, there have been increasing attempts to organize Muslim communities throughout the continent. One of the most active and developed organizations has been the Islamic Organization for Latin America created in 1992 with headquarters in Buenos Aires. Among its objectives are the establishment of special contacts between Muslim religious communities and the authorities of various countries, and of 'fluid' contacts between these communities and the diplomatic representatives of the locally accredited Islamic countries (Huste 2007). While this regional organization per se cannot be linked to violence or terrorism, a speculative line of reasoning has tried to combine it with expanding influence of Islam in the region and the two attacks of the early 1990s (mentioned in the preceding) to construct 'evidence' so as to make a case for a potential threat of Islamist terrorism. This alarmist approach also tries to build upon sympathies for the Lebanese Hezbollah on the part of some radical left-wing groups in the region and Tehran's efforts to establish and upgrade relations with the growing number of left-wing governments in Latin America, and also warns about the threat of two radicalisms joined together in their anti-American approach—the pro-Iranian Shia radicalism and the social–Bolivarian left-wing secularism (Huste 2007). The clearly biased and speculative nature of this approach not-withstanding, two considerations have to be taken into account for a potential Islamist threat in Latin America: the potential of a strategic alliance between (far) leftist movements and Islamist fundamentalism against the US 'imperialism' and the increased anti-US moods in Latin America. Both concepts are deliberately used in their most abstract form as, so far, there are no empirical proofs relating any FTO to a local, Latin American, rebel/leftist/anti-US organization or movement making a concrete case of an international linkage of terrorist organizations. As a long-time observer of Latin American politics states:

> ...apart from the two anti-Jewish actions in Buenos Aires, Latin America has managed to keep at arms length from the political and religious conflicts of the Middle East. This is reflected in a Nielsen poll that shows only 1 per cent of its population worrying abut terrorism, compared to 7 per cent for the world population. This is even more remarkable considering some countries on the region (such as Colombia and Peru) have homegrown terrorism without the need of the imported variety. (Kouyoumdjian 2006)

A final consideration would be the potential of a terrorist attack on energy resources in Latin America, if targeting energy resources, in countries such as Algeria (The Jamestown Foundation 2007), eventually becomes a persistent feature of the 'fourth wave' terrorism. One of these targets could be the Venezuelan oil fields, and, indeed, despite the tensed relations between Washington and Caracas, the Bush administration has declared itself publicly ready to cooperate with the Chávez government to neutralize al-Qaeda's threat (*El Universal* 2007).

In summation, it should be stressed that a detailed analysis of any links between the 'fourth wave' terrorism and Latin America reveals only a potential threat. It is primarily related to the growing connection between terrorism and organized crime, the rise of anti-US feelings in Latin American societies, the so-called 'left-turn' of the governments in the region, expanding Muslim communities, and the availability of soft targets, especially the energy sector. None of these factors, however, suggest more than a mere speculation about an imminent threat of the 'fourth wave' terrorism in Latin America. Moreover, the three latter factors appear only in rhetoric—seldom interested and partisan, often biased—aiming more at confusing rather than clarifying the terrorist phenomenon, most probably for political purposes. Overall patterns of internationalization of terrorism in Latin America in the context of the 'fourth wave' are related mostly, if not exclusively, to the involvement of the 'third wave' guerrilla-terrorist organizations in drug trafficking. This is the major pattern of internationalization of local groups, in addition to some evidence of the continuing patterns of a 'third wave' type logistics and training cooperation, such as the one between the FARC and the IRA (or the post-IRA groups).[19] The 'fourth wave' terrorism in Latin America is a potential threat at most, which consists of a search for 'local connections' of terrorist organizations from the main battlefield of the 'war on terrorism': the Greater Middle East expanding from North Africa to Pakistan and Afghanistan. Otherwise, it can hardly be imagined that a new generation of Latin American terrorist organizations would espouse *jihad* as their way for political change.

CONCLUSION

Terrorism in Latin America emerged mostly by the end of the 1960s as a feature of the urbanization of guerrilla warfare. However, it has rarely been an end in itself, nor even the preferred form of political struggle. Terrorist tactics, including assassinations, bombings and kidnappings, were used for propaganda purposes and punitive aims. They were employed to provoke a violent reaction from the state or for extortive purposes (much of the kidnapping or hostage taking activities were aimed at obtaining the release of political prisoners and/or getting financial means for the struggle). Though right-wing organizations, such as the Argentinean Triple A, as well as the governments and military dictatorships, also used repressive actions against civilians (campaigns of state terror) to eliminate opponents, including killings and especially the so-called 'disappearances', terrorism as such in Latin America in the 1970s was primarily the New Left, or the 'third wave', phenomenon and had an anti-US character. However, despite having the Cuban Revolution as a model and a point of reference and despite occasions of any direct or indirect help from the Castro regime, the Latin American rebel movements that resorted to terrorist tactics failed to create solid international links such as those established by terrorist organizations in the Middle East or Asia. The main reason is that, despite their internationalist rhetoric, the guerrilla movements, especially in their urban version, which implies more frequent use of terrorist means, were mostly local phenomena. Their struggle was national to the extent that except for the common general enemy—the United States characterized as an imperial power—there was no common Latin American identity as a project—such as the one, for example, where pan-Arabism motivated non-Palestinian Arabs to join the PLO. Another reason might be the harsh policies of the governments of the region, mostly military regimes, and brutal repression of the guerrilla movements and in fact of any opposition. Also, the military dictatorships in Latin America cooperated closely with the United States following the logic of the US National Security Doctrine. One of the contributing factors could also have been the absence of large and affluent Latin American immigrant communities in Europe or the United States at that time that would have been organized and motivated enough to help their fellow nationals, as did the Irish descendants in the United States and elsewhere who supported the IRA armed struggle. Thus, despite its integration into the general context of the Cold War, Latin American terrorism did not get internationalized to a great extent. Attempts to build enduring international connections such as the ones undertaken by the Montoneros and the Palestinian groups in Lebanon were rather the exception than the rule.

In all, the 'third wave' terrorism in Latin America came to a practical end with the return of democracy in the 1980s, even though the armed conflicts in Central America—classical guerrilla wars labelled by the US strategists as 'low intensity warfare'—continued up until the end of that decade. In fact, the impact of democratization and the en-gagement with democracy in terms of a farewell to arms and active demobilization has been so deep that recently democratized South American countries, mainly Argentina and Brazil, assumed an active mediating role in the process of the pacification of Central America (Hirst 1988). By the time the 'fourth wave' of terrorism was making its emergence on the international scene, political violence, particularly armed struggle, was ceasing to be a major option in the so called Southern Cone sub-region where democracy in Argentina, Brazil, Uruguay, and Paraguay has also accelerated the process of integration. In the Andean region, however, especially in Peru and Colombia, guerrilla insurgencies continued and, in fact, started to more actively employ terrorist means in both urban and rural areas. This recrudescence of terrorist violence coincided with the rise of the 'war on drugs' that became a priority issue on Washington's international security agenda. The involvement of guerrilla movements in drug business, especially after the dismantling of the big drug cartels in Colombia, paved the way for these organizations to establish transnational links. Hence, the newest pattern of internationalization of guerrilla organizations, labelled as FTO by the State Department, has been most closely related to the drug connection. This pattern of internationalization was not driven by ideological links, or search for tactical or logistical cooperation or even the need to establish strategic alliances with other insurgent movements. The main rationale for this pattern has been driven by financial needs and considerations. Whether the drug income has corrupted the political struggle and has become an end in itself is a related, but different question, which is not exactly the topic of the chapter and deserves a separate analysis. In addition to the terrorism–narcotics link that constitutes the essence of the contemporary pattern of internationalization of rebel movements in Latin America, there have also been some surviving patterns typical of the previous, 'third wave' of terrorism, such as the FARC–IRA/post-IRA training and logistics cooperation.

The 'fourth wave' of terrorism, which is identified with religious movements, and especially Islamism, and has proved to be the most internationalized, even globalized, has not yet manifested itself in Latin America. Except for the two bombings in Buenos Aires, the Israeli Embassy in 1992 and the Jewish mutuality centre, AMIA, in 1994, there have been practically no other Islamist terrorist attack registered in the post-Cold War; not even in the aftermath of 11 September 2001, despite all the alarming news about a possible use of Latin America as a base to mount attacks on US soil. The reasons for this lack of expansion of the 'fourth wave' to Latin America seem rather obvious. First, the strategic battlefield of Islamist terrorism, particularly the one associated with the radical Sunni Islamism of the al-Qaeda type, is the so-called Greater Middle East, which expands from the north of Africa to Central Asia with a special emphasis on countries like Iraq, Pakistan, and Algeria. Second, it is the United States that remain the transnational Islamists' main strategic target: so far, performing such an attack in a Latin American country has not seemed to be of much relevance to them. Third, Europe, more than any other region, seems to be the region where the 'fourth wave' of terrorism is most likely to expand, due to the existence of a large Muslim population and growing sympathies for radical Islam at least among certain segments of the Muslim communities—which is not the case of Muslims in Latin America. Fourth, despite the widespread anti-US feeling in Latin American societies and particular dissatisfaction with the Bush administration, the ideological divide between religious and leftist-secular groups is too wide to think about any probability of cooperation or connection between them. So far, there has only been some empirical evidence of fund-raising campaigns for Islamist organizations, a fact that, per se, can hardly prove any specific terrorist connection.

Overall, there is little, if any, probability of a pattern of internationalization of terrorist activities in Latin America to develop along the lines typical of that of the 'fourth wave', mainly transnational Islamist terrorism. The 'fourth wave' of terrorism could reach Latin America only in case the most active Islamist organizations plan to create local connections in forms of sleeper cells or active militants. However, neither the strategic logic of the Islamist struggle, nor the empirical evidence has so far made a strong case of such a perspective in South America.

NOTES

1. For more detail, see F. Calle and K. DerGhougassian 2003.
2. Uniting and Strengthening America by Providing Appropriate Tools Required to Intercept and Obstruct Terrorism Act of 2001.
3. The contributor is grateful to his student, Juliana Plencovich, for her help in the research concerning the US State Department's list of terrorist organizations.
4. The full text of President Bush's address can be found at <http://www.americanrhetoric.com/speeches/gwbush911jointsessionspeech.htm>, last accessed on 12 January 2008.
5. The full text of President Bush's 2002 State of the Union address can be found at <http://www.americanrhetoric.com/speeches/stateoftheunion2002.htm>
6. The most important questioning of the Hezbollah–Iran link to both attacks came from Jorge Lanata and Joe Goldman who conducted an independent investigation and reached a different conclusion about the possible source of the bombings (see Lanata and Goldman 1994). When the affair re-emerged on the political agenda in 2006, Lanata reiterated his criticism in his article, 'Tócala de nuevo, Nisman'.
7. For details, refer to Abramovici 2006–07. See also Gallego, Eggers-Brass and Gil Lozano 2006.
8. On anarchism in Argentina, see Falcón 1984: 129; Suriano 2001: 361; and Suriano 2005: 95. On the repression of the workers' movement in Patagonia, see Bayer 1986.
9. Marcelo Zlotogwiazda and Luis Balaguer (2003) have included the episode of the bombing, quoting Osvaldo Bayer in their book *Citibank vs. Argentina: Historia de un país en bancarrota*, pp. 25–30.
10. Augusto César Sandino (1895–1934), Nicaraguan rebel and guerrilla leader known as 'the General of free men' fought against the US military intervention from 1927 to 1933. The US Marines left Nicaragua in 1933 following US President F.D. Roosevelt's 'good neighbourhood policy' in Latin America. Despite the peace agreement with president Juan Bautista Sacasa that put an end to the armed conflict in Nicaragua on 2 February 1933, Sandino, who had dismantled his 6000-men strong rebel army, was murdered in a plot organized by the head of the US-organized and trained Guardia Nacional (National Guard), Anastasio Somoza García, on 21 February 1934.

11. The contributor wants to express his gratitude to his research assistant, Florencia Raskovan, for her help in the elaboration of the part concerning the historical perspective of terrorism in Latin America.

12. It is worth noting that it is only in 1982 that Cuba was first included in the US State Department's list of states sponsoring terrorism.

13. On 7 August 1987, the presidents of five Central American countries, namely Oscar Arias Sánchez (Costa Rica), José Napoleón Duarte (El Salvador), Vinicio Cerezo Arévalo (Guatemala), José Azcona Hoyo (Honduras) and Daniel Ortega Saavedra (Nicaragua), signed an agreement in the Guatemalan city of Esquipulas, known as the Esquipulas II peace agreement, which set the procedure to establish a lasting peace in Central America. The main points of the agreement, which does not mention any particular country and speaks for 'Central America', refer to national reconciliation; end of hostilities; democratization; free elections; ending help to insurrectionary movements and irregular forces; prohibition of the use of the national territory for aggression against another country; negotiations for security arrangements, verification, control and limitation of armaments; dealing with the problem of refugees and displaced people; cooperation, democracy and freedom for peace and development; international supervising; and an agenda for the execution of the agreement. The document is available at <http://www.congreso.gob.gt/Docs/PAZ/Acuerdo%20de%20Esquipulas%20II.pdf>. On conflicts in Central America, see Rouquié 1992, p. 407.

14. There is a vast literature about drug trafficking and the performance of drug cartels, as well as the involvement of insurgency and guerrilla movements in the drug business. See, for instance, Bagley and Walker III 1994: 549; Clawson and Lee III 1998: 292. Mark Bowden (2001) has investigated the rise and the brutal fall of the Medellin cartel kingpin, Pablo Escobar, in *Killing Pablo: The Hunt for the World's Greatest Outlaw*.

15. The initial idea of Plan Colombia came from Colombia's president Andrés Pastrana (1998–2002) and consisted of initiating peace negotiations with the guerrilla. According to Pastrana's view, Colombia's priority was ending the civil strife; as for drugs, it was considered a social problem the solution of which was to come along with peace and stability. The plan asked for international assistance and help to begin peace negotiations with the guerrilla. For the Clinton administration, however, the priority was fighting drug trafficking; hence, after the US Undersecretary of State Thomas Pickering's visit to Bogotá on 10 August 1999, the Clinton administration accepted the proposal but nevertheless reverted the priority, which consisted first of a counter-narcotics strategy followed by peace negotiations. The US Congress approved this new version of Plan Colombia on 13 July 2000 (Public Law 106–246) consisting of seven points. Plan Colombia was expanded to the Andean Region upon president George W. Bush's proposal on 9 April 2001. The new Andean Regional Initiative included Bolivia, Brazil, Ecuador, Panama, Peru, and Venezuela, and consisted of a total annual budget of 882.29 million USD. In the aftermath of 11 September 2001, on 2 August 2002, five days before the newly elected Alvaro Uribe took office, the US Congress expanded the authority of the State Department to use the funds available for Colombia. It also permitted the use of the money for a 'unified campaign' against drugs and guerrillas (see Cepeda 2004: 221–228).

16. The AMIA affair is known as Case 1156 'Pasteur 633 Atentado (Homicidio, Lesiones, Daños).

17. Alconada 2007a: 8. The Congressional Research Service Report for Congress, in turn, cites the 2006 terrorism report to state, '...the United States remains concerned that Hezbollah and Hamas were raising funds among the sizeable Muslim communities in the region but stated that there was no corroborated information that these or other Islamist extremist groups had an operational presence in the area.' See Sullivan 2007: 3. Fund-raising actvities in the Tri-Border are also mentioned as a major concern for the US–South American relations by the head of the US Southern Command Admiral, James Stavridis, in an interview in Buenos Aires: see Corbacho 2007: 32–36.

18. The Egyptian 'Al-Ahram' gives a figure of 8 million Muslims in Latin America, see Kouyoumdjian 2006 (unpublished analysis provided as a personal email to the contributor of the chapter, used with permission of A. Kouyoumdjian).

19. For more detail, please refer to Chapter 1 in this volume.

3

TRANSNATIONAL TIGERS: LIBERATION TIGERS OF TAMIL EELAM'S PAW ACROSS THE GLOBE

Ramani Hariharan

INTRODUCTION

The Liberation Tigers of Tamil Eelam (LTTE), also known as the Tamil Tigers, have been fighting for the creation of an independent state of *Tamil Eelam* in Sri Lanka for a little over three decades.[1] They are perhaps the most well-organized insurgent organization in the world.[2] The Federal Bureau of Investigation (FBI), in a press release on 10 January 2008, said, 'the Tamil Tigers are among the most dangerous and deadly extremists in the world.' Posing the question, 'Why should you care?', the report stated, 'because its ruthless tactics have inspired terrorist networks worldwide, including the al-Qaeda in Iraq' (The Federal Bureau of Investigation 2008).

The LTTE has many firsts to its credit. It is perhaps the only insurgent force with capability to carry out conventional and unconventional operations on land, sea, and air. As one of the earliest practitioners of suicide bombing, the LTTE, through the Sea Tigers, its naval wing, has successfully extended the suicide attack techniques to the high seas to fight the Sri Lankan Navy. Its technological improvisation has seen the conversion of its air force fleet of piston-engine light aircraft into a rudimentary light bomber force. The LTTE is well-known for the use of propaganda and psychological warfare techniques with great effect. It is also perhaps one of the few insurgent groups that have fully integrated the reach of cyber space to its operational and propaganda advantage.

Led by Velupillai Prabhakaran, the LTTE is also known for its ruthlessness, audacity and utter disregard for international human rights and humanitarian concerns. It is known for using terrorist methods in its insurgent operations. In the late 1990s, it gained notoriety for killing its victims with a burning car tyre tied around their necks. The LTTE has used terror tactics to eliminate other Tamil political leaders and members of rival Tamil insurgent groups.

The organization has also shown great resilience to bounce back from operational setbacks. Its history is scarred with wars with the armies of India, which it fought once, and Sri Lanka, which it engaged twice. Since December 2005, it has been fighting the Sri Lankan security forces for a third time. In the three decades of its existence, the LTTE is estimated to have lost over 20,000 cadres.[3]

The LTTE is essentially a guerrilla organization supported by a political wing and an intelligence wing working under it. In addition to guerrilla and terrorism capabilities, the LTTE also possesses conventional war competence. The LTTE's conventional forces took part in defensive and offensive operations against the Sri Lankan military forces in the two spells of the Eelam wars between 1996 and 2000. They have also been seen in action in operations in the eastern province during 2006–07.

Sri Lankan President Mahinda Rajapakse's 20 September 2007 estimate of the LTTE strength at 8,000 to 10,000 armed combatants, including a core of 3,000 to 6,000 trained fighters, appears to be correct (Badwar 2007). Considering its loss of around 1,000 cadres in operations since the 20 September 2007 statement, the LTTE's strength in the north is assessed as 5,000 frontline cadres, and 2,000 executive, administrative and political elements. About 1,500 recruits and child soldiers are probably available as second line reinforcements. In the east, the LTTE has 400 cadres dispersed in small groups fighting for their survival. The LTTE has its own artillery and armoured elements. The armour is made up of a small number of tanks captured from the security forces. The LTTE has a wide range of artillery guns and mortars as well as some multi-barrel rocket launchers that provide it enhanced firepower.[4] It is also known to possess a few shoulder-fired surface-to-air missiles in its arsenal.[5] However, these have not been seen in action so far in the present operations.

The LTTE's Black Tigers—as the highly motivated suicide cadres of the organization are known—have been used with terrifying effect. Until 2006, 273 Black Tigers have lost their lives in various operations. Their prominent victims include two Sri Lanka presidents—Ranasinghe Premadasa and Chandrika Kumaratunga—Kumaratunga survived the attack, although she lost an eye. Former Indian prime minister, Rajiv Gandhi, and scores of Sri Lankan ministers, parliamentarians, senior army officers and Tamil leaders of rival militant groups and intellectuals have been victims of the Black Tigers (Hariharan 2006b).

However, more Black Tigers have lost their lives in naval operations, than on land. According to one report, 194 out of the 273 suicide warriors killed in action were Black Sea Tigers. With their stealth capability, using fishing fleets as cover, Black Sea Tigers have destroyed over 301 Sri Lankan naval craft. The daring, but failed, assassination attempt by Black Tigers on the life of Sri Lankan army chief, Lt. Gen. Sarath Fonseka and the successful assassination of Maj. Gen. Parami Kulatunge, deputy chief of Sri Lankan Army, in 2006, have shown that the Black Tigers continue to remain the primary strike force of the LTTE.

The LTTE's naval arm—the Sea Tigers—has an estimated strength of 1,500 cadres. It has a variety of operational craft including a few Fast Attack Craft (FAC) captured from the Sri Lankan Navy. The Sea Tigers' boats are generally armed with machine guns, rocket launchers and cannons. In all probability, command boats are fitted with radar.

It would be of interest to note that the LTTE is perhaps the only insurgent force in the world that boasts of an 'air force'. It is a small force of about four light aircrafts, two helicopters and a few micro light aircrafts with limited operational capability. The fledgling air force carried out three daring bombing missions of the Katunayake, a Sri Lankan air force base near Colombo; the forces' Jaffna air base at Palali; and some oil storages near Colombo in the year 2007. Though these forays caused no major damage to the Sri Lankan installations, they boosted the LTTE's image and caused tremendous psychological impact and panic in Colombo.

A unique feature of the LTTE is the use of women soldiers in combat. The LTTE's all-women units include two brigades: a mortar regiment and a Women's Sea Tiger wing. A third unit—the Vasanthi regiment—took part in the Mavilaru-Thoppigala operations in the Batticaloa region of the eastern sector during the first half of 2006.

According to an intelligence estimate, 2,200 women cadres, including 1,121 cadres from the oldest unit, the Lt. Malathi Brigade, have been killed in operations up to 2006.

From the beginning, Prabhakaran had developed a vision for the LTTE in which other militant or political groups would have no space. To fulfil this vision, the LTTE ruthlessly eliminated thousands of militants belonging to other Tamil insurgent groups from 1982 onwards and it continues to do so even now. According to the estimate of a Tamil militant group, the LTTE is responsible for the death of 7,000 Tamil political activists.[6]

The LTTE's international support network played a key role in the scheme of things, particularly in the growth phase of the LTTE after 1990. From 1992 onward, the LTTE had been using its global network to acquire modern weapon systems to upgrade its arsenal strength and firepower.

With the growing global emphasis on fighting terrorism, the international community has become increasingly aware of the LTTE's incendiary mix of terror and intimidation in its operations even beyond the shores of Sri Lanka. India banned the LTTE in 1991 after a LTTE suicide bomber assassinated former Indian Prime Minister Rajiv Gandhi on 21 May 1991. The United States included the LTTE in the list of Foreign Terrorist Organizations in 1997. The United Kingdom banned it in 2001, while Canada and the 27 member-States of the European Union followed suit in 2006 after LTTE's hand was suspected in the assassination of Sri Lanka's Foreign Minister Lakshman Kadirgamar. The LTTE is also banned in Malaysia. In spite of the proscription in 32 countries, the support from sections of the Tamil diaspora continues to sustain the LTTE and its military operations.

ROOTS OF LTTE'S TRANSNATIONAL GROWTH

The LTTE is a degenerated manifestation of the failure of the democratic polity of Sri Lanka to address the grievances of the ethnic Tamil minority population that has been articulated for over the last five decades. The organization has cleverly used the historical grievances of the Tamils and their feeling of alienation from the mainstream of Sri Lanka, and has sought to create a unique status for itself as the 'saviour' of Tamils from Sinhala chauvinism. The transformation of the LTTE from a local militant group into a full-blown insurgency and terrorist movement with tentacles in almost all parts of the world is intimately connected with the exodus of Tamil population from the country as refugees to escape repressive measures of the Sri Lankan state. The continuing quest for their rights among Tamils, both at home and abroad, constitutes the basis of the LTTE's international support network.

However, the LTTE has no clear-cut ideology for Tamil Eelam, although in 1983 there was an articulation for the creation of a socialist Eelam (Balasingam 1983). But at present, socialism does not figure in the organization's pronouncements. The LTTE has ingeniously utilized Tamil nationalism, often degenerating into chauvinism, as the rallying point for Tamils worldwide to draw support for its war efforts.

SRI LANKA'S TAMIL DIASPORA

Tamil is an ancient Dravidian language, spoken by nearly 74 million people (1997 estimate), most of who live in the state of Tamil Nadu in south India and in the north-eastern parts of Sri Lanka. Tamil is a live and vibrant language with a rich literary and cultural tradition. The language serves as a focus of identity and heritage for Tamils all over the world. During the last two centuries, Tamils have migrated from India and Sri Lanka to different parts of the world. In many countries like Australia, Canada, Fiji, France (Réunion), Malaysia, Mauritius, South Africa, Singapore, and the United Kingdom, Tamils form the major population segment among migrants of South Asian origin.

The Tamils living overseas include Tamils of Indian and Sri Lankan origins. There are subtle social and cultural differences between these two communities. They have been broadly maintaining their distinct identities. However, despite such minor differences, Tamil ethnic populations across the globe have retained their strong allegiance to Tamil cultural traditions. Historically, the growth of Sri Lankan Tamil diaspora came about in three distinct waves. These coincided with the periods of ethnic upheavals and riots. The language riots of 1958, introduction of standardization rule in 1971, and the 1983 anti-Tamil riots were the major happenings that triggered the large scale movement of Sri Lanka's Tamil population as emigrants and refugees. The first two waves were smaller and made up of people aspiring to improve their opportunities in more equitable societies. However, the

1983 pogrom saw the exodus of nearly 200,000 Tamils during the course of a decade. These refugees, now spread over 50 countries, form the hardcore of Tamil diaspora directly affected by the Sinhala–Tamil confrontation. Unlike the earlier emigrants, many of them belong to the poor and less qualified segments of population. The LTTE's armed insurgency has a special appeal in this category of Tamils.

The number of Sri Lankan Tamils living abroad had been estimated between 700,000 and one million. However, the estimate of 510,000 people including 101,000 refugees appears to be a more realistic figure (Tamiltigers.net. 1997–2005). Sri Lanka's Tamil refugees are in major concentrations in 15 countries, with notable numbers in India (98,629), Canada (92,010), UK (60,000+), and Germany (60,000+). Probably India has at least an equal number of Sri Lankan Tamil refugees who have merged with the population. However, numbers alone do not translate into support for the LTTE or an independent Tamil Eelam.

In order to build its support network, the LTTE has successfully leveraged three distinct beliefs of Sri Lankan Tamil diaspora. These are: Tamil nationalism, perceived threat to the Tamil identity and their homeland, and their low standing in a demographically Sinhala dominated society.

RISE OF TAMIL NATIONALISM

Sri Lanka's ethnic Tamils form 12.7 per cent of the total population of 20.92 million people.[7] However, two other Tamil speaking segments of the population, most of them Muslims—listed officially as Moors (7 per cent), and Tamils of Indian origin (5.5 per cent) have maintained their distinct political and social identity. The Tamils had been demanding equitable treatment ever since Sri Lanka became independent in 1948.

The rise of Dravidian ethnic consciousness as a dominant political force in Tamil Nadu in the 1950s influenced the thinking of large sections of ethnic Tamils in Sri Lanka.[8] The Sri Lankan Tamils struggling for their rights against Sinhala majority domination found the Dravidian political parties' emphasis on the distinctness of Tamil identity relevant to their situation.

However, from 1956 onward, Sinhala nationalism became a major factor in politics with increased dominance of Sinhala language and culture, leading to progressive alienation of Tamils from the national mainstream. The non-violent protests of Tamils yielded no results. On the other hand, in 1972 a revised national constitution favouring the Sinhala majority was introduced. As a result, even moderate Tamil leaders started talking of creating an independent Tamil Eelam state as the only solution (Nesiah 2006).

In the1977 elections, the Tamil United Liberation Front (TULF), a political front demanding the creation of Tamil Eelam, scored a thumping victory in Tamil areas. However, the government used political trade-offs to stave them off rather than incorporate them. The failure of TULF politicians to produce results eroded their credibility among Tamils and Tamil militant groups took over the political leadership. Between 1977 and 1987 as many as 35 Tamil militant groups sprouted all over the north and east of Sri Lanka. This period also saw the rise of Velupillai Prabhakaran and the emergence of the LTTE as a powerful insurgent force. At the same time, the use of armed forces by the state to stamp out the militant activity also increased.

INDIAN INFLUENCE

India and Sri Lanka enjoy close political, cultural, and religious links. Tamils in India, with their linguistic, cultural, and family ties have always been sympathetic to the Sri Lankan Tamils' struggle. The 1983 pogrom against the Tamils in Sri Lanka came as a rude shock to the people of India. Tamil Nadu received thousands of Tamil refugees—including militants who came in the wake of the riots—with open arms. A sympathetic government of India helped the militant groups with arms and military training. A large number of LTTE cadres were also among the Tamil militants of various groups trained in India. At the same time, India also made efforts to reconcile the differences between the Sri Lankan government and the Tamils. Although the efforts failed, they culminated in the signing of the India–Sri Lanka Agreement in July 1987.

Under the agreement, Sri Lanka agreed to devolve limited autonomy to a united northeast province, considered as the traditional Tamil homeland. India agreed to help end Tamil militancy and disarm the militants. Although the agreement did not meet all the demands of Tamils, it provided a good opportunity for both sides to create a climate of confidence to resolve the issue peacefully. India dispatched an Indian Peace Keeping Force (IPKF) to Sri Lanka to enforce the agreement. All Tamil militant groups, including the LTTE, had initially agreed to conform to the agreement. However, the LTTE refused to give up its arms because it doubted the sincerity of Sri Lanka's intentions to adhere to the agreement. Moreover, the agreement did not meet LTTE's goal of creating an independent Tamil Eelam (Hariharan 2007). In a bid to disarm the LTTE, Indian troops were locked in battle with them between 1987 and 1990. The LTTE suffered heavy casualties at the hand of Indian troops and took refuge in the jungles of Vanni.

The political changes in India and Sri Lanka in 1989–90 ultimately resulted in the withdrawal of the IPKF from Sri Lanka in 1990. The Indian operations against the LTTE drew a lot of global attention to the LTTE as it had survived the Indian army. It was LTTE's strong political links in Tamil Nadu that influenced the change in Indian government policies that resulted in the pull-out of Indian troops from Sri Lanka.

The war with India was a valuable learning experience for the LTTE. With the Jaffna and Mannar coasts in northern Sri Lanka, and an hour's journey by speedboat, Tamil Nadu offered an attractive sanctuary and supply base for the LTTE even during the war. Moreover, about 100,000 Sri Lankan Tamils who had taken refuge in Tamil Nadu enabled the LTTE to operate clandestinely. The LTTE has built strong asset base in Tamil Nadu ever since it gained a foothold in 1983. In the past it had used its contacts in the Indian state to garner support from politicians and officials of Tamil Nadu. Therefore, it was comparatively easy for the LTTE to merge with the population and operate with some impunity in Tamil Nadu.

However, the support for the LTTE in Tamil Nadu declined dramatically after the LTTE assassinated Rajiv Gandhi in 1991. But, Tamils continue to passively support the Sri Lankan Tamil struggle for autonomy. It continues to be an emotive issue that influences public opinion. Therefore all political parties in Tamil Nadu carefully calibrate their actions on the Sri Lankan Tamil issue. India has a coalition government in which the Dravida Munnetra Kazhagam (DMK), the ruling party of the state of Tamil Nadu, is an important ally. So both the DMK and the Indian government have been extremely careful in handling this issue relating to Sri Lanka (Hariharan 2006a). After the

Eelam War restarted in December 2005 and the Sri Lankan refugee inflow into Tamil Nadu increased, almost all political parties in Tamil Nadu called for Indian action to protect the Tamils. Even within the ruling DMK, particularly among the middle level of leadership, there are members who were strong supporters of the LTTE in the past (Chawla 1997). Undoubtedly, they will continue to play an important role in shaping the DMK's relationship with the LTTE, which is lukewarm at present. For the LTTE, using Tamil Nadu's political influence to its advantage will always be a priority.

The LTTE had been sourcing Tamil Nadu for the manufacture of castings and parts required for the manufacture of rockets, landmines and hand grenades for sometime now. The LTTE is also reported to be engineering links with the ultra Leftist Maoist insurgents (*South Asia Tribune* 2005). Equally dangerous is its reported deals with the United Liberation Front of Asom (ULFA) to procure arms from Thailand through Bangladesh (dailyindia.com 2006). Both the insurgent groups have been waging war against the state in central and northeast India, respectively.

TRANSNATIONAL ACTIVITY

EARLY STAGES OF DEVELOPMENT

The LTTE's 1987–90 war experience brought home the importance of international support for its struggle. During this period the LTTE also probably understood the importance of international lobbying, and the use of international forums through front organizations.

Historically, the United Kingdom and Sri Lanka have enjoyed close ties, a relationship that dates back to the colonial times. The English language, familiar systems of administration, and education made the United Kingdom a favourite destination of Sri Lankan Tamil migrants. The United Kingdom has a large Sri Lankan Tamil community estimated at over 100,000. In Greater London alone eight British Sri Lankan Tamils are serving as local councillors at present. According to published estimates, Sri Lankan Tamils own more than 5,000 businesses in the country. More than 20,000 of them are in highly professional jobs. A large number of them are employed in retail jobs in petrol stations and fast food outlets.[9]

Even during the early stages, the Tamil struggle in Sri Lanka found a lot of support among Tamil expatriates in the United Kingdom. Expatriate Tamil students, many of them leftists, formed the Eelam Revolutionary Organization of Students (EROS) in London in 1975. The EROS helped Tamil militants acquire military training under the Palestine Liberation Organization (PLO). The LTTE also took advantage of this link and sent its cadres for training in 1978–79. During this period, the LTTE is also reported to have sent its cadres for training with the Hamas and other Palestinian militant groups in Libya, Lebanon, and Syria. The LTTE had also sent its cadres for training with the Mossad in Israel. The LTTE opened its London office around this period. It became part of the Tamil community's efforts in London to internationally publicize the Tamil cause.

The LTTE's overseas operations have come a long way since then. Over the years, the LTTE's international operations have become transnational in character with lateral linkages between LTTE cells working in different countries.

TRANSNATIONAL STRATEGY

The creation of independent Tamil Eelam as the only way for salvation for Tamils appears to be the core belief of Prabhakaran.[10] The LTTE cells in the midst of the Tamil diaspora are engaged in the following domains of overt and covert action to further this core belief:

1. *Political*: Take over Diaspora centres of influence to promote the LTTE cause with official bodies through lobbyists; cultivate influential persons in academic and political spectrum; organize protests and marches through local community leaders on issues appealing to the Tamils for indirect propagation of the LTTE; leverage legal options and loopholes to help LTTE and its cause through professionals and NGOs, sympathetic to the LTTE.
2. *Financial*: Collect funds to sustain LTTE and its activities at home and abroad on a regular basis; carry out investment and business operations under cover names to yield handsome returns from legal entities; use covert avenues for money making, for example trafficking people, procurement of false travel documents, gun running; use humanitarian and development issues of Tamils

   in Sri Lanka to help collect funds legitimately and transfer them
   to the LTTE.

3. *Operational*: Procure arms and military equipment and organize
   their transportation to Sri Lanka; arrange professional advisors
   among the diaspora for helping the LTTE in operations; collect
   information on technology development in warfare and arma-
   ment; disseminate operational news and visuals of operations
   through web and print media to further psychological warfare
   objectives;collect intelligence on activities of anti-LTTE organizations, particularly of Tamil diaspora and take action to curb
   them; and similarly, to carry out coercive action, and, if necessary, to eliminate leaders and persons acting against the interest
   of the LTTE (*Asian Tribune* 2007b).

4. *Social and cultural*: Create or take over social and cultural organizations (including places of worship) serving the diaspora
   to finance and influence actions in support of LTTE; use NGOs
   to act as fronts to cultivate and build links with other international NGOs and international agencies.

It is not clear how much support the LTTE enjoys among the Tamil
diaspora because the LTTE representatives often use intimidation and
coercion to gain support (*Asian Tribune* 2007a). However, at present,
with most of the Sri Lankan Tamil political parties toeing the LTTE
line, many find the LTTE as the only effective force to fight Sinhala
chauvinism.[11]

TRANSNATIONAL OPERATIONS

Although the LTTE is said to have its tentacles in as many as 52 countries,
Australia, Canada, India, Norway, the United Kingdom, and the
United States may be considered as the 'frontline states' for LTTE's
transnational activity. France and Switzerland also play important part
in this set-up. Based on the local status of LTTE, the countries may
be grouped for their sensitivity to LTTE's transnational operations
as follows:

1. As discussed earlier, India occupies a unique status, with the
   state of Tamil Nadu being the home of the Tamil community.

Although the LTTE is banned in India, it enjoys a love-hate relationship with Tamils. Despite official action to curb the LTTE activity, it continues to source India for supplies and low technology military equipment.

2. Australia, Canada, France, the United Kingdom and the United States had been traditionally tolerant of the LTTE's propaganda and public mobilization activities until 2006. In Australia, the LTTE is not banned but treated as a terrorist organization under counter-terrorism laws. The United Kingdom banned the LTTE in 2001 but was still tolerant of the LTTE's non-militant activities. As a result, London had been the headquarters of the LTTE international secretariat, where Anton Balasingham, Prabhakaran's advisor and LTTE's chief theoretician, provided the organization's external interface till his death in 2006. France was the centre of the LTTE's European activity in the late 1990s. However, since 2006, as a member of the European Union, it has been enforcing control on both overt and covert LTTE activities. Canada, like the United Kingdom, is a major bastion for the LTTE. Once again, although the organization is banned in Canada, the LTTE will continue to utilize Canadian soil for its sustenance and activities for some more time to come. The United States is an important centre for the LTTE's propaganda, fund-raising, and arms procurement activities. Although it was proscribed in 1997, curbs were placed only since the American involvement as a co-chair in the peace efforts in Sri Lanka in 2002. In all these countries the LTTE has been trying to use both its political connections and existing democratic avenues of protest to influence public policies.

3. In Norway and Switzerland, the LTTE enjoys freedom of action as long as it does not conflict with the laws of the land. While Switzerland offers limited scope, the LTTE has been fully exploiting the opportunities that Norway offers to further its interests. However, both Switzerland and Norway have a special relationship with the European Union and, as a result, of late, they have been taking action against some of the illegal activities of the LTTE that have been ignored in the past. However, some more transnational activities may be expected of the LTTE which might be centred in Norway in future, as the environment in the European Union, North America and most of Asia is increasingly becoming risky for its operations.

All the 'frontline' countries have large concentration of influential Sri Lankan Tamils. Their democratic societies respect the freedom of expression. They also have flourishing free market economies. So bulk of the LTTE's fund-raising activities, business operations, propaganda, lobbying, and public protest are concentrated in these countries. The LTTE has used the existing cleavages within the democratic polity in many of the countries to further its cause. This is done through local politicians, and elected members of public office who are dependent on the votes of Tamil diaspora, and front organizations. According to one report, the LTTE has taken systematic action to 'plant' handpicked Tamil volunteers who have language skills and computer literacy to work in the office of selected parliamentarians to exploit possible pro-LTTE leanings. The offices of Australian, Canadian, Norwegian, and the United Kingdom parliamentarians are said to be places where such volunteers operate (*Asian Tribune* 2006a). While the report has not been confirmed, it is well within the realms of LTTE's capability to carry out such an operation. A recent example is the futile attempt made by Tamil sympathizers of the LTTE in December 2008 to infiltrate the United States Presidential election campaign of the Democratic aspirant Senator Mrs Hillary Rodham Clinton (Abeysekera 2008). Sri Lanka government's poor human rights record has provided enough opportunities for local politicians to express their indirect support to the LTTE.

TRANSNATIONAL FUNDING AND ARMS PURCHASE

The Jane's Intelligence Review (JIR) report of August 2007 has analyzed in detail the present transnational set-up of the LTTE for arms procurement and funding. The LTTE has two principal directorates for funding and arms purchase (Athas 2007). According to the report, the *Aiyanna* Group probably controls the international intelligence as well as fund collection operations under the direction of the LTTE's chief of intelligence Shanmugaligam Sivashanker, better known as Pottu Amman.[12] It also manages the global front organizations of the LTTE.

The Office of Overseas Purchases, known by its nickname 'KP department', works under the direction of Kumaran Padmanabhan, better known as KP. KP is LTTE's seasoned arms procurer and trafficker. In the past, in addition to arms procurement, he had been responsible for operating the LTTE's merchant shipping fleet. The report has identified Kampuchea as an important source of arms for the LTTE. North Korea, Afghanistan, Lebanon, Cyprus, Greece, Turkey, Ukraine, and Thailand were identified as other sources of weapons supply.

According to the JIR report, the LTTE generates an estimated sum of USD 200 to USD 300 million every year. This would explain the large sums it was prepared to spend in procuring arms abroad. The transnational character of LTTE's arms procurement was revealed in a FBI sting operation in August 2006. In this operation, the FBI arrested 13 Sri Lankan ethnic Tamils domiciled in the United States and Canada for multiple crimes connected with the LTTE. The crimes included attempting to purchase illegal arms from FBI agents posing as arms dealers in Long Island in New York, attempting to obtain classified information, conspiring to bribe United States public officials in an effort to remove the LTTE from the United States State Department's list of Foreign Terrorist Organizations, and dealing in illegal financial transactions with the LTTE. The wish-list of arms included up to 100 Russian-made SA-18 shoulder-fired, surface-to-air missiles, 500 AK-47 assault rifles and other weapons (*Asian Tribune* 2006c).

The apprehended Tamils were also accused of attempting to use the LTTE front organizations, including the Tamil Rehabilitation Organization (TRO) to bribe United States' State Department officials for obtaining classified documents containing information relating to the organizations. Among those arrested was a British doctor, Murugesu Vinayagamoorthy alias Dr Moorthy, a senior LTTE intermediary from New York for aiding the LTTE by facilitating the purchase of American rockets and British submarine technology (Ministry of External Affairs, Sri Lanka 2007).

In yet another operation in Baltimore in the United States, four LTTE agents, including three foreign nationals were arrested for seeking to provide material support to the LTTE between April and September 2006. The Singapore national, Haniffa Bin Osman pleaded guilty to conspiracy charges, while Haji Subandi and Erick Wotulo, both Indonesian citizens, pleaded guilty of attempting to illegally export arms for the LTTE. Thirunavukarasu Varatharasa, a Sri Lankan citizen, has also pleaded guilty for attempting to export arms and ammunition for the LTTE. The weapons list included state-of-the-art firearms, machine guns and ammunition, surface to air missiles, and night vision goggles (*Baltimore Sun*, reproduced in the *Daily News* 2006).

In a separate operation, the FBI arrested six persons—including four Tamils and two Indonesians—in Guam in October 2006 when they deposited 700,000 USD with undercover agents in Maryland as a down payment for millions of dollars worth of missiles, sniper rifles, submachine guns and grenade launchers for the LTTE.

The LTTE's transnational 'business operations' are both legal and illegal. According to a study by Vijay Sakhuja, a naval analyst, the LTTE had in its inventory 12 to 15 ships, trawlers and smaller vessels in the 1,000 to 1,500 tons DWT (dead weight tonnage) range. These were used for commercial shipping activity mostly in the Southeast Asian waters. Flying flags of convenience, they were involved in 95 per cent legitimate cargo trade, while the balance of 5 per cent was used to carry LTTE supplies. The LTTE is also suspected to have augmented its merchant fleet by hijacking of vessels and changing their names and physical characteristics. For instance *MV Sik Yang,* a 2,818-ton Malaysian cargo ship which sailed from the South Indian port of Tuticorin on 31 May 1999 was later confirmed as having been hijacked by the LTTE. In addition to this, LTTE's hand is suspected in the hijacking of seven other ships from 1995 to 1998 (Sakhuja 2006). However, the Sri Lankan navy, in a series of operations carried out in the Indian Ocean off Sri Lanka's coast between 17 September 2006 and 11 September 2007, destroyed seven tramps said to have belonged to the LTTE merchant fleet carrying arms and military supplies. With these successes, the navy claims to have crippled the LTTE's inbuilt capacity to transport illegally procured military supplies in its own bottoms.[13]

Indian fishing boats poaching in Sri Lankan waters are often seized by the LTTE. In an incident of its kind, on 26 April 2007, the LTTE had hijacked an Indian fishing trawler 'Sri Krishna' off the South Indian coast after killing its 12-member crew. In May 2007, it was sighted off Maldives and sunk by the Maldives coast guard killing its LTTE crew. The trawler was apparently used to unload and transport arms for the LTTE (Sangameswaran 2007). The hand of LTTE cadres is suspected in a number of other illegal activities including credit card frauds in Singapore, fraudulent drawing of money using credit cards of customers at petrol stations in the United Kingdom and passport frauds in India and Norway.

LTTE IN CANADA

The LTTE activity in Canada has been well-documented since1997 (Mackenzie Institute 2000). However, in the past, Canada had shown reluctance to curb the activities of LTTE operators perhaps for the fear of offending the Tamil diaspora vote banks, particularly in Greater Toronto area.

The political influence of the LTTE in Canada became more visible after the fourth round of war between the LTTE and Sri Lanka had started in December 2005. According to Martin Collacott, former Canadian High Commissioner in Sri Lanka, the FBI had identified Canada as LTTE's major source of illegal fund-raising because the federal Liberal government 'in an effort to bolster support in the Tamil community' refused to classify the LTTE as a terrorist group despite several recommendations of the Canadian Security and Intelligence Services.[14]

The control of LTTE gangs became one of the election issues and when the Conservatives came to power, Canada banned the LTTE in April 2006. Despite the ban, LTTE continues to wield considerable influence in the Canadian polity. This was dramatically demonstrated in June 2007 at a Tamil community civic rally held at Scarborough to protest against the Sri Lanka government's continued violation of human rights of Tamils in Sri Lanka. Politicians of Canada's three largest political parties expressed solidarity at the gathering even as hundreds in the crowd waved LTTE flags and displayed large portraits of the LTTE leader, Prabhakaran (Adler 2007).

The Sri Lankan Tamils in Greater Toronto Area are concentrated especially in areas like Scarborough, East York and North York and in the Markham municipality. Outside of Toronto, the LTTE have also been very active in Montreal and parts of British Columbia. In Toronto, the Tamil radio stations and tabloids openly support the LTTE and, in turn, get advertisement support from some of the known pro-LTTE Tamil businessmen. With this vicious cycle in operation, the LTTE is able to influence the Tamil public in these areas, which gives them political clout despite the ban. According to a report of

6 November 2006, 13 Tamils who contested the municipal, local council and school trustee polls in Toronto had the blessing of the LTTE (Siva Sunderam 2006).

Activities of Tamil criminal gangs' association with the LTTE were known to the Canadian authorities even in 2001. In October 2001, 101 of them were deported to Sri Lanka for immigration violations. Immigration authorities had described some of them as a 'group of military-trained terrorists from Sri Lanka' who help raise money for the LTTE (Bell 2006). Until the LTTE was proscribed, the emblem of the LTTE was displayed at the venue of cultural shows organized by the Tamil charitable organizations like the TRO, the World Tamil Movement (WTM), the Federal Association of Canadian Tamils (FACT), and the politically active Canadian Tamil Congress (CTC), even if there was no mention of the LTTE.

The LTTE fund-raising activities through extortion has gained notoriety for sometime now. Even as early as December 2004, Ms Jo Becker, Advocacy Director for Human Rights Watch (HRW) Children's Rights Division, had estimated Tamil Canadian funding of the LTTE at USD 1 to 2 million per month (*Toronto Star* 2004).

In March 2006, HRW published 'Funding the "Final War": LTTE intimidation and extortion in the Tamil Diaspora', a report documenting the LTTE's use of extortion and intimidation against Tamils in Canada and the United Kingdom to raise funds for its operations, and to silence critics of its human rights violations (Human Rights Watch 2006). According to this study:

> In Toronto, home to the majority of Canadian Tamils, LTTE representatives typically press families for C$2,500 to C$5,000, while some businesses have been asked for up to C$100,000. In London, many families are asked for £2,000 and businesses are approached for amounts ranging from £10,000 to £100,000. Tamils in Norway and France report being approached for similar amounts.

The damaging indictment was based on research conducted over a period of five months through interviews with members of the Tamil community in Toronto, Canada; London, UK; Geneva, Switzerland; and Düsseldorf, Germany with focus on the Tamil communities in Canada and the United Kingdom.

Perhaps based on this report, Canada proscribed the LTTE as a terrorist entity on 8 April 2006. The Royal Canadian Mounted Police (RCMP) is investigating the WTM in Toronto and Montreal, reported by HRW to be involved in acts of intimidation and extortion to secure funds for the LTTE. For the last four years, the RCMP are investigating illegal transfer of funds to the LTTE through the WTM, Scarborough, and have identified 63 suspects (Bell 2007).

The LTTE is also reported to be involved in illegal smuggling of people in Canada through its network. According to a report, the rate for trafficking per person worked out to about CAD 42,000 in 2006 (Siva Sunderam 2006).

LTTE'S UK CONNECTIONS

The United Kingdom banned the LTTE on 28 February 2001, although the LTTE has continued to be active in the island nation. The Sri Lankan Tamil community's good local and international connections and the studied indifference of British authorities to take action to curb LTTE's freedom were undoubtedly the reasons for the LTTE to make London its international headquarters. Broadly, there are three ways in which the LTTE has managed to establish its tentacles of support in the United Kingdom. According to Dominic Whiteman, pro-LTTE Tamil councillors elected from North and East London (Ealing Road, Wembley, East Ham, Croydon, Walthamstow, Tooting, etc.) have formed close links with Labour Party leaders (Whiteman 2006).

Until 1990, when the LTTE had not completely cannibalized other Tamil groups, there was considerable rapport among Tamil expatriates in the United Kingdom. Over the years, a number of common assets to further the Tamil cause and assist Tamils in distress were created in the United Kingdom. Typical of these is the Tamil Rehabilitation Organization (TRO), which for a number of years had kept itself free from involvement with Tamil militancy. However, over a period of time, the LTTE covertly took over control of its operations. Progressively, the LTTE managed to infiltrate or gain control of these organizations.

The LTTE often uses muscle power to take over profitable Tamil community organizations. This was dramatically brought out in 2005 when LTTE held two visiting British citizens, Rajasingham Jayadevan and AK Vivekanathan, captive for two months in Sri Lanka. The two trustees of a Hindu temple at Wembley were held hostage till they transferred the temple to Sivayogam Trust controlled by a well-known LTTE activist, Nagenthiran Seevarathnam. The two hostages were released only after British government intervened (Brockett 2005). The Sivayogam Trust also runs another temple at Tooting, London. Seevaratnam was suspended as trustee in May 2007 by the Charity Commission over alleged links with the LTTE under the Terrorism Act, 2000 (Clover 2007). The funds of the Tooting temple have also been frozen.

After the death of Anton Balasingham, who headed the LTTE in London, Arunachalam Chrishanthakumar alias Shanthan, became the LTTE leader in the United Kingdom, and president of the British Tamil Association. The Scotland Yard had charged Shanthan and the LTTE head of finance in London, Goldan Lambert, under the Terrorism Act, 2000 with providing support to the LTTE. Shanthan has also been charged with being a member of the LTTE, encouraging support for the LTTE, and receiving funds to be used for the purpose of terrorism. On 5 July 2007, a British court froze all bank accounts of Shanthan and that of his wife (Ministry of External Affairs 2007).

THE US ACTIONS

International coordination with a number of countries—Canada, Indonesia, Sri Lanka—has been the most significant aspect of the United States' operations against the LTTE's transnational activity. This enabled the American intelligence and security agencies to bust the LTTE cells trying to procure arms and carry out money laundering activities discussed earlier. The United States is also extending intelligence cooperation to the Sri Lankans, which has probably enabled them to interdict and destroy at least seven ships carrying arms and ammunition for the LTTE as was mentioned earlier (*Daily Mirror* 2007).

On 25 April 2007, the Joint Terrorist Task Force of the federal law enforcement agency, arrested Karunakaran Kandasamay alias Karuna, the LTTE chief of the United States operations, and four others in the New York suburb of Queens on the charge of providing material support for the LTTE by fund-raising. Karuna was charged with raising money through the LTTE front organization, World Tamil Coordinating Committee (WTCC). More significantly, he had also arranged meetings in Vanni between the LTTE leaders and its supporters from the United States (Jeyaraj 2007). In 2004, the LTTE allegedly undertook a major worldwide campaign to raise money for its planned offensive against the Sri Lankan government in late 2005. In support of the offensive, Karuna held fund-raising events in November and December 2004 at a church and a public high school in Queens, New York, and a school in South Brunswick, New Jersey.

FRANCE

Although the Lankan Tamil population in France is not as high as in the United Kingdom, the LTTE has established strong roots in the country over the years. In fact, the LTTE's international spokesman, Laurence Thilagar, used to operate from Paris in the past. However, the TRO's close links with the LTTE had drawn the attention of French authorities particularly after the British Charity Commission removed the TRO's charitable status in the United Kingdom as it found that they were not able to account for the application of funds satisfactorily.

On 1 October 2006, the Swiss police arrested Vinayagamoorthy, secretary of the TRO in the Swiss-French border, while carrying EUR 18 million in cash. The French Anti-terrorism Directorate investigating the LTTE arrested him on 1 April 2007 after establishing that the amount recovered from him, ostensibly for Tamil refugees, was in fact to provide material support to the LTTE in violation of French and European Union laws. Close on the heels of this incident, on 5 April 2007, Nadaraja Matheenthiran alias Parithi alias Regan, the head of LTTE Paris branch and 13 others of Sri Lankan origin were arrested. They face multiple charges including extortion, physical violence, and illegal confinement against Tamils settled in France, and for financing terrorism and associating with a terrorist organization. Others arrested include Duraisamy Aravindhan alias Metha, LTTE chief of propaganda for Europe.

The extent of the LTTE's propaganda operations has also drawn adverse reaction from the French. They closed the Tamil Television Network (TTN), which operated out of Paris through satellite service provider Globecast. These actions have put the LTTE operations in France on the back foot.

AUSTRALIA

Ever since the FBI sting operations in August 2006, Australian authorities have been investigating Tamil Coordinating Committee and the TRO operations in Australia and had carried out searches of Tamil homes in Melbourne and Sydney. On 1 May 2007, the Australian Federal Police in Melbourne arrested Sivaraj Yathevan, the LTTE agent in charge of Eela Murasu, a Tamil community paper, and Arooran Vinayagamoorthy. Both of them were charged with terror offences after unearthing a massive fraud that siphoned off the money collected from the Australian public for Tsunami relief into the coffers of the LTTE. An accountant Arumugam Rajeevan, who is alleged to have worked for the LTTE, was arrested for dispatching AUSD 600,000 to the LTTE in Sri Lanka (Markham 2007).

SUSPECTED LINKS WITH ISLAMIST TERRORISTS

In the late 1990s, the LTTE had established links with the *Mujaheedin* operating in Afghanistan and procured some arms including surface-to-air missiles. A report by the International Institute of Strategic Studies (IISS), London, 'Military Balance 2005/2006' has referred to the emerging links between the LTTE and the al-Qaeda movement. However, these links are believed to be commercial rather than ideological. Considering the Pakistan Inter Services Intelligence's (ISI) long history of nurturing Islamist terrorists, the LTTE and the ISI would certainly consider the option of joint operations, that would be mutually beneficial, and if necessary in any third country in South Asia.

RESPONDING TO THE LTTE'S TRANSNATIONAL OPERATIONS

Over the years the LTTE has built a strong global network with the help of Sri Lankan Tamil diaspora to further its objectives in Sri Lanka. Its transnational character with extensive political, military, criminal, financial and shipping linkages has enabled it to develop a seamless and time-tested supply chain. This chain is kept operational with financial contributions of the Tamil diaspora. In the past, the LTTE managed to procure arms from many countries including Afghanistan, Bulgaria, Cambodia, Croatia, Myanmar, Mozambique, the Czech Republic, North Korea, South Africa, Thailand, and Ukraine. The LTTE sourced explosives, low technology weapon parts, fuel, medical supplies, and other essentials from India. The LTTE had been using the traditional informal money transfer channels of *Hawala* to send the funds collected abroad.

Most of the countries including the west and India had given the LTTE a lot of leeway in its arms procurement and funding operations on their soil. However, the 9/11 attacks in the United States and the global war on terrorism have brought in controls on arms trafficking, money laundering and illegal transfer of money and greater surveillance of the LTTE activities. A number of international protocols on security of shipping and maritime traffic of men and material have been introduced.

Sensitive to the changing global scene, the LTTE signed a ceasefire agreement with the Sri Lankan government in 2002. It agreed to participate in a peace process underwritten by four powers—the European Union, Japan, Norway, and the United States (referred to as co-chairs of the Tokyo donors' conference). Although the ceasefire was fairly effective for the first two years, there were gross violations and killings, initially by the LTTE and then by the government forces, escalating into full-fledged war from December 2005.

In response to the Sri Lanka government's request to the international community to dismantle the LTTE's transnational support network, the 'frontline states' started taking action to curb the LTTE' activities in their countries. Broadly, these actions were aimed at arresting those involved in illegal LTTE activities including extortion, arms procurement, trafficking, and money laundering activities. However, the LTTE's transnational human resources and propaganda machinery, by and large, remain intact. One reason for this is the interpretation of laws relating to proscribed organizations in different countries.

However, there is latent sympathy for the Tamil struggle for autonomy among sections of the diaspora. Unless this is addressed politically in Sri Lanka, the hold of the LTTE' on the diaspora cannot be permanently broken. The international community, which has been coordinating the actions to sever the LTTE transnational network, should also address this issue politically with greater vigour. Otherwise they will be involved in a long haul on this issue with their Tamil populations.

India occupies a unique position in the scheme of things and needs to do more to reduce the relevance of the LTTE for the Tamil cause by taking fresh initiatives in Sri Lanka.

NOTES

1. *Tamil Eelam* refers to the region considered by the Tamil speaking people of Sri Lanka as their traditional area of inhabitation. It comprises the present day northern and eastern provinces and Puttalam district of the northwestern province. In the context of the Tamil insurgency, it refers to the independent state of Sri Lanka's Tamil speaking people. The LTTE currently administers some of the land claimed for Tamil Eelam. This includes the entire district of Kilinochchi, most of the district of Mullaittivu, and parts of the districts of Mannar, Vavuniya and Welioya. However, a majority of the Tamil Eelam region including, the districts of Jaffna, Ampara, Trincomalee, Batticaloa and Puttlam have been taken over by the government of Sri Lanka.

2. There is some semantic confusion in popular usage of the terms militancy, insurgency and terrorism. In this article these terms mean the following:

    (a) *Militancy*: The act of taking, or readying to take strong or violent action through an aggressive posture or act.
    (b) *Insurgency*: Uprising or rebellion against the state.
    (c) *Terrorism*: Systematic or organized use of violence and intimidation to force the government or community, etc. to act in a certain way or to accept certain demands of insurgents. In the context of Sri Lanka, the LTTE has been using terrorism as a tool in the insurgency war against the state.

3. Reliable data on LTTE casualties is not available. This figure has been interpolated from the figures given by www.ltttnet.netfast.org, a LTTE web resource. According to this site the LTTE suffered the loss of 17,903 combatants between 27 November 1982 and 24 November 2005. According to the Sri Lankan government's Media Centre for National Security, the LTTE lost 3,087 cadres between 1 December 2005 and 2 August 2007. http://www.nationalsecurity.lk/statistics.php. The total LTTE casualty figure, during the period between 27 November 1982 and 2 August 2007, is 20,990.

4. For analysis of strengths and capabilities of the LTTE, see Hariharan 2006c.

5. During search operations in August 2007, Sri Lanka troops recovered 'Igla' surface to air missile from one of the LTTE caches in the Thoppigala area in the eastern province. The missile was probably unserviceable.

6. See Jayasuriya 2006. The report has quoted EPRLF leader Thurairatnam as saying that LTTE had killed 3,000 EPRLF cadres and 7,000 'democratic Tamil political activists'.

7. Total population figures as per CIA World Fact book estimate of 16 August 2007. https://www.cia.gov. For analysis of ethnic population figures, see Nesiah 2006: 88–89. Population figures after the 1981 census do not reflect the ethnic composition that prevailed before the 1983 anti-Tamil pogrom. In 1991, there was no census due to insurgency conditions. The 2001 census figures do not include the population totals of most of the Tamil areas in the north and the east that are affected by insurgency as well as those who had fled the country as refugees. In this paper, the population percentages (as given in the following) have been taken from the 1981 census and have been used as the basis (2001 census percentages are given in brackets as current reference):

(a)	Sinhalese	73.9 (81.9)
(b)	Sri Lanka Tamil	12.7 (4.3)
(c)	Indian Tamils	5.5 (5.1)
(d)	Sri Lanka Moors (Muslims)	7.0 (8.0)
(e)	Others	0.8 (0.7)

8. The TULF leader Amirthalingam had referred to this aspect in a conversation with the author in 1988.

9. See 'Sri Lankan Tamil diaspora', *Wikepedia,* available at http://en.wikipedia.org.

10. However, Prabhakaran has compromised his stand on this issue on more than one occasion, probably for political reasons. His initial acceptance of the India–Sri Lanka agreement of 1987 and the signing of the Oslo Communiqué in 2002, where the LTTE had 'agreed to explore a solution based on a federal structure within a united Sri Lanka' are two such examples. However, this did not stop Prabhakaran from saying, 'The uncompromising stance of Sinhala chauvinism has left us with no other option but an independent state for the people of Tamil Eelam,' in his Martyrs Day statement on 27 November 2006.

11. LTTE's terror tactics managed to coerce Tamil politicians and militants of all shades, barring a few, to come under the pro-LTTE umbrella political body—Tamil National Alliance (TNA)—to represent the LTTE viewpoint in the parliament of Sri Lanka.

12. The Tamil letter 'Aiyanna' is the phonetic equivalent of the alphabet I, which is normally the acronym used for intelligence in military parlance.

13. TV interview of Vice Admiral Wasantha Karannagoda, Commander of the Sri Lanka Navy, 2 February 2008. www.asiantribune.com.

14. See, *Asian Tribune* 2006b. According to Collacott, 'By 2000 the Toronto police Tamil Task Force estimated that Canada's largest city was home to as many as 8,000 members of Tamil terrorist factions, most notably the Tigers.'

4

JIHAD OR JOI BANGLA: BANGLADESH IN PERIL

Subir Bhaumik

INTRODUCTION

Bangladesh's emergence as an independent nation in 1971 was one of the most significant events in the post-colonial world. The break-up of Pakistan exposed the weaknesses, the 'artificiality' of the nation-state that was created after the partition of the Indian subcontinent in 1947 as 'the homeland for Indian Muslims'. Many post-colonial states, with diverse peoples within their boundaries imposed by the colonial rulers, have faced the kind of crisis that broke up Pakistan. But most of these states survived, Pakistan did not. The strong surge of Bengali linguistic nationalism since the 1952 language movement made Bangladesh a reality, although its people paid a huge price for liberation. Nearly 3 million Bengalis, of all religions, were killed by the Pakistani military and its collaborators, more than quarter of a million Bengali women were dishonoured and more than 10 million people were displaced during the eight months of civil war. It is this aspect that makes the Bangladesh struggle one of the bloodiest post-colonial conflicts.

The success of the Bengali nationalist movement was made possible by a favourable correlation of multiple factors like geography, linguistic and racial homogeneity, the weaknesses of the Pakistani nation-state, and the regional political environment that pitted India against Pakistan in total support for the Bengali irredentist movement. It stands out in stark contrast to the long but rather unsuccessful efforts for creating a Palestinian homeland or the failure of the Nasser-led Arab nationalist movement to create a secular, greater pan-Arab state in the Middle East. These failures indicate that neither religious nor linguistic homogeneity, nor the presence of a common enemy—in this context Israel—are sufficient factors by themselves to create and/or sustain modern nation-states. On the other hand, and at the other end of the spectrum, the failure of the Muslims of Thailand and Philippines to break away from the parent country dominated by Buddhists or Christians and create separate nation-states, despite the presence of huge Muslim countries like Indonesia or Malaysia in the immediate neighbourhood, is another interesting aspect.

Therefore, neither the strength of 'Bengali identity' nor the factor of 'Indian intervention' can be underestimated in the success of the Bangladesh liberation war. Also not to be underrated is the failure of the military-dominated Pakistani state in creating a democratic power-sharing arrangement that would have given due political representation and power to the Bengalis and economic returns to the resource-rich eastern wing. Or for the matter, the vast territorial distance between West and East Pakistan that made the military holding effort in the East by a West-dominated Pakistan army a long-term impossibility, especially after India began to support the Bengali separatist movement.

But the joy of the liberation war victory was short-lived. Within four years of Bangladesh's independence, a bloody military coup in August 1975 led to the assassination of the country's founding father, Sheikh Mujib-ur-Rehman, and many of his senior political colleagues and members of their families. The coup not only unleashed 'a legacy of blood' (coups and counter-coups, revolts and mutinies), but it also derailed the process of institutionalization of the spirit of secular Bengali nationalism. As Bangladesh slipped into Pakistan-type military rule, both the military dictators, Zia-ur-Rehman and H.M. Ershad, almost in quick succession, not only rehabilitated the pro-Pakistani fundamentalist political groups and personalities, the defeated pro-Islamist forces of 1971, but also effected long-term changes in the basic structure of the national constitution. Zia was the first to undermine the spirit of 1971 when he introduced the Fifth Amendment that replaced 'Secularism', 'Bengali Nationalism', and 'Socialism' as national principles with the 'Sovereignty of Allah'. General Ershad gave the Islamization process a huge push when, in 1988, he declared

Islam as the state religion by introducing the Eighth amendment to the constitution.

The military dictators were desperate to create a political support base for 'cantonment politics' by undermining the country's largest political party, the Awami League, and its secular allies. A definite way in which they could achieve their goal was by promoting and consolidating the space for Islamist politics that had been greatly reduced but had never quite disappeared after the dismemberment of Pakistan. Mujib-ur Rehman chose to assert the 'Muslimness' of the Bangladesh nation by deciding to join the Organization of Islamic Countries (OIC). His government also announced a general amnesty that saved the defeated Islamist forces of 1971—the Razakars, the Al-Badrs, the Al-Shams and other collaborators of Pakistan army—from total decimation. Mujib was under some pressure from his own supporters to organise mass trials of the 'war criminals' of 1971, but instead, he focussed on controlling the revenge-killings and vendetta against these elements rather than bringing them to justice.

The military dictators Zia and Ershad began active encouragement of the Islamist political groups such as the Jamaat-e-Islami (JeI), which had opposed the cause of Bangladesh's freedom. General Zia rehabilitated the JeI leader, Gholam Azam, and allowed the party to regroup. Ershad steadily purged the army, the intelligence services, and other administrative echelons of pro-1971 forces and replaced the *muktijoddhas* (freedom fighters) with 'repatriates' (who remained loyal to Pakistan in 1971 and only later returned to Bangladesh). Although Bangladesh returned to democracy in 1991, the country's subsequent governments played no role in checking the growing support base of the Islamist parties. In 2001, the Bangladesh Nationalist Party (BNP) founded by the assassinated General Zia-ur-Rehman came to power with the active support of the JeI. In the subsequent five years, Bangladesh was, for the first time since its liberation, ruled by a coalition that comprised the JeI and other Islamist groups who had opposed the break-up of Pakistan. Not surprisingly, this was the time when the country's fledgling Islamist terror groups gained unprecedented strength and Bangladesh came to be seen as 'the second front of Islamist terror' in South Asia and as a key link between the Islamist terror structures of West and Southeast Asia.[1]

The chapter will seek to trace the course of this resurgence of radical Islam in Bangladesh and examine the external linkages of the country's religious parties and the zealot terror groups who are seeking to turn the erstwhile East Pakistan into a safe haven and a regrouping zone for armed Islamist activity in Asia. This resurgence of militant Islamist groups have been made possible by *(a)* patronage to such forces from the corridors of power, first by the military dictators and subsequently by the governments of Begum Khaleda Zia, *(b)* liberal funding and other forms of support received from Islamist organizations of Middle East and the west, *(c)* failure of the Awami League and its secular allies to sustain a political and social offensive against the Islamist forces by raising the issue of 1971 crimes against humanity, and *(d)* change in the global and regional environment, the surge of Islamist militancy before and after 9/11 and the rise of Hindu fundamentalist forces in India leading to the BJP's coming to power.

JAMAAT-E-ISLAMI:
FOUNTAINHEAD OF RADICAL ISLAM

The JeI, the leading religion-based party in Bangladesh, is the fountainhead of radical Islam in the country. During 2007 and the beginning of 2008, most activists of other radical Islamist groups, after their arrest, have confessed to close links with JeI leaders. It is no coincidence that after the JeI came to power in 2001 and formed a coalition government with the BNP, the activity of the radical Islamist groups touched a new high in the country. Bangladesh is home to around 11 per cent of the world's Muslim population and more than 90 per cent of its nearly 145 million people are Muslims, the majority of them living in rural areas. They are victims of poverty and illiteracy and, thus, are susceptible to influence exerted by sustained religious propaganda, especially in a charged atmosphere like the one that has come to be after 9/11. It is significant that although the JeI's main branch is still located in Pakistan, the country of its origin, and although it has branches all over South Asia—in India, Sri Lanka and Afghanistan—it is only in Bangladesh that it has managed to share power.

> This has helped the Jamaat make some concrete moves towards creating an Islamist state based on Shariah law. They have managed to gain important positions within government while hiding their links to militancy—a key factor in destabilising government systems which the movement seeks to eventually dismantle and replace. (Blackburn n.d.)

The Jamaat-e-Islami was founded in Lahore in 1941 by Maulana al-Mawdudi, a Pakistani journalist, who wanted to prevent Muslims from succumbing to what he saw as perverse ideologies such as nationalism, women's liberation, and socialism. Mawdudi believed that the tenets of Islam could justify his vision of a perfect Muslim state that would be ruled by a powerful unelected elite and where strict Shariah law would replace secularism and progress.

Mawdudi was heavily influenced by the Ikhwan al-Muslimeen (Muslim Brotherhood), which is centred in the Middle East. He was a friend of Sayeed Qutb, a leading radical Islamist leader, who advocated creating an Islamist vanguard for a violent *jihad* against non-believers and even Muslims who opposed the creation of a fundamentalist Islamist state. Mawdudi's belief in violent *jihad* for the establishment of an Islamist state was tempered by a tactical recognition of the need to initially work through the established political system—hence the felt need for a political party to take the Islamist movement to the people which could subvert the system and create an Islamic state of his dreams.

For Mawdudi, the timing was all-important—the switch from legitimate political activity to *jihad* could only take place after the Jamaat leaders were satisfied they had enough support for their vision of an Islamic state. In Bangladesh and elsewhere in South Asia, the Jamaat has thus combined legitimate political activity with covert support for violent *jihadi* groups that it nurtures and backs. It works through the democratic system, but never believes in it. The Jamaat-e-Islami's constitution made it clear that it wants to establish the 'Islamic way of life for the greater well-being of mankind' through Dawa and Islamic finance.

After the emergence of Bangladesh in 1971, the JeI was banned in view of the adoption of secularism as state policy. In 1976, immediately after the assassination of Mujib-ur Rehman, when the Islamic Democratic League (IDL), led by Maulana Abdur Rahim, obtained permission from the government, the Jamaat activists began to operate under the banner of IDL. Some Jamaat leaders even contested the general elections of 1979 as nominees of the Democratic League, and six of them were elected. Since the late 1970s, the Jamaat has been steadily rehabilitated by Bangladesh's military dictators, Generals Zia and Ershad. In 1979, General Zia withdrew the ban on religion-based political parties and the JeI Bangladesh was formally revived. Maulana Abbas Ali Khan was elected as acting Amir of Jamaat, later being replaced by Gholam Azam.

The Jamaat gained some legitimacy when it joined the two major parties, Awami League and the BNP, in the huge street protests that finally brought down the Ershad government in 1991. Since then, the Jamaat has steadily expanded its party organization and support networks. Though its vote share has remained below 10 per cent and it has never won more than 18 seats in the 300-member Jatiyo Sangsad (National Parliament), the Jamaat was crucial for the victory of the coalition that was opposing the Awami League that had completed its five years in office. In the 1986 elections, the Jamaat secured 10 seats in the National Parliament. Five years later, after the fall of Ershad, the Jamaat contested in 35 constituencies and secured 18 seats in the 1991 parliament elections. The party supported the BNP in forming the government.

But in 1994, the Jamaat surprised many by supporting the Awami League in their movement for introducing a caretaker government system to conduct elections. To intensify the movement, the Jamaat members of the parliament resigned their seats in December 1994. But this did not augur well for the Jamaat and it could win only three seats in the 1996 parliament elections. The popular movement for 'trial of war criminals' spearheaded by the Ghatak O Dalal Nirmal Committee (Committee for the Elimination of the Killers and Collaborators of 1971) put the Jamaat on the defensive, as many of its top leaders were linked to the massacres and other crimes during the liberation war. The movement also helped the Awami League win the 1996 elections and come back to power after being out of it for 21 years. But the Jamaat recovered its lost ground and won 17 seats in the 2001 parliament elections after working out an electoral alliance with the BNP. More importantly, for the first time in independent Bangladesh, the Jamaat was in government as part of the victorious coalition and its alliance with the BNP was crucial to keep the Awami League out of power. Indeed, it was during these five years (2001–2006), when the Jamaat remained in government, that Bangladesh witnessed the most violent phase of Islamist radical activity, the peak of which was the incident of more than 450 serial explosions in the country on 17 August 2005.

Mawdudi's ideological and organizational alliance with the Ikhwan-al-Muslimeen laid the base for the Jamaat's external linkages that has been so crucial for its growth. The two groups share institutions such as the International Islamic Universities (IIUs), the Islamic Foundation UK (its trustees Ali Ghali Himmat and Ahmed Idris Nasreddin of the Ikwhan/al-Taqwa Bank have been designated terrorism financers by the United States and the United Nations) and charities such as the World Assembly of Muslim Youth (WAMY) and the International Islamic Charitable Organization (IICO). Abdullah Azzam, a founder of Hamas and Osama bin-Laden's former mentor, taught at the IIU-Islamabad in Pakistan. The alliance, meant to promote the global pan-Islamist cause, played a key role in checking the influence of Nasser-style nationalist Arab regimes that had strong Soviet backing during the Cold War. It gained legitimacy and strength when western governments like the US and the United Kingdom and their allies in the Islamic world—like Saudi Arabia and Pakistan—backed the alliance to tackle Soviet communism. These governments financed and trained the supporters of this alliance to fight and defeat the Soviet forces in Afghanistan in 1979. Osama Bin-Laden's involvement with the global Islamist movement dates back to the heady days of the Afghan war.

Mawdudi was also a founding member of the Saudi-based Muslim World League (MWL) along with Wael Hamza Jalaidan, who is later said to have cofounded the al-Qaeda along with Osama Bin-Laden. Set up in 1962 to counter Nasser-type Arab nationalism, the MWL was originally based in Geneva but it moved to Jeddah in 1969. In 2005, the MWL brought Qazi Hossain Ahmed of JeI Pakistan and Maulana Motiur Rehman Nizami, Amir of JeI Bangladesh, to discuss strategies to strengthen the pan-Islamist movement in South Asia. The late Said Ramadan, a co-founder of MWL with Maulana Mawdudi, helped JeI Pakistan organize its student branches in the 1950s. Ramadan is the son-in-law of Hasan al-Banna, the founder of the Muslim Brotherhood (Grare 2001).

Abdullah Azam of the Muslim Brotherhood is the spiritual mentor of Osama Bin-Laden and was the prime global recruiter for the Afghan *jihad*. The JeI Bangladesh is a part of this global pan-Islamist movement and it will be naïve to imagine it as a 'moderate Islamic group', as the former US ambassador to Bangladesh Mary Ann Peters used to describe it. Its legitimate political identity is further strengthened by its expanding student organization, the Islami Chatra Shibir (ICS), which provides the recruitment base for more radical Islamist groups like the Harkat-ul-Jihad-al-Islami (HUJI) or the Jamaat-ul-Mujahideen.

The Jamaat-e-Islami in Bangladesh was closely involved with the war crimes during the 1971 war of liberation and its bigotry and recourse to terror is evident in its pursuit of sectarian violence against the Ahmadiya sect in Pakistan and Bangladesh. The JeI-Bangladesh has been repeatedly linked to terrorist organizations since 2001 and the majority of leaders and terrorists belonging to the Jama'atul Mujahideen Bangladesh (JMB) and the Jagrata Muslim Janata Bangladesh (JMJB) have long records of involvement with Jamaat and its student wing, the Islami Chatra Shibir. The Islami Bank Bangladesh Limited (IBBL) is also linked to militancy and is controlled by the Jamaat. The IBBL's foreign sponsor banks have previously been accused of moving huge funds to the al-Qaeda linked militants and for supporting radical Islamism in other countries. Yassin Qadi's family has been designated by the US and the UN as financier of Islamist terrorist activities globally. Qadi is a Saudi businessman and is the son-in-law of Sheikh Ahmed Salah Jamjoom, a former finance minister in the Saudi government and a foreign sponsor of IBBL. The Kuwaiti-based Revival of Islamic Heritage Society (RIHS), suspected for financing the 17 August serial bombings in Bangladesh, also had accounts at the IBBL.

The close links between the IBBL and the International Islamic University (Chittagong) is proof of how the Jamaat-MWL-Muslim Brotherhood triangle has increased its influence in education and Islamic financial sectors in Bangladesh. The Jamaat-Shibir Bangladesh has also acted as a funding conduit for the ISI and the JeI Pakistan. In the year 2000, Indian intelligence agencies intercepted communication from Jamaat leaders indicating huge movement of funds transferred through Jamaat-Bangladesh to the Muslim United Liberation Tigers of Assam (MULTA) from Jamaat-Pakistan. Indian prime minister, Manmohan Singh and national security adviser, M.K. Narayanan have both referred to Bangladesh as a launching pad for terrorist activities against India, even naming Bangladesh nationals as being responsible for a series of major explosions in Bombay, Varanasi, Hyderabad, and Ayodhya. These attacks have multiplied exponentially since January 2004 and in the three years that followed, India has been the worst affected by terrorist incidents.

India, with 3,674 deaths in 3,032 terrorist-related incidents in the forty months since January 2004, was rated as the second worst affected country globally in terrorist attacks. Iraq, which recorded 29,070 deaths in 12,718 terrorist-related incidents in this period, was right at the top, but even Afghanistan, with 2,405 deaths in 1,682 incidents, was behind India (*The Times of India* 2007). Indeed, there was invariably a Bangladesh footprint in almost all the notable terrorist attacks in India. Either Bangladesh nationals were directly involved in the attacks or they had used Bangladesh to plan their attacks and enter India from that country. Understandably, Manmohan Singh was scathing in his attack when he described Bangladesh as 'a security concern, which offered opportunities to our enemies who seek to incite terrorism in India' (*The Hindu* 2006).

MULTA is a terrorist organization that is working towards turning Assam, a state in North East India, into an Islamic enclave to be run by Shariah law. The group has been involved in bombings and assassinations in Assam and has been recruiting activists with funds received from groups such as JeI Bangladesh. MULTA works closely with the HUJI-B and is funded by Pakistan's Inter Services Intelligence (ISI). HUJI-B has been added to the US and UN list of terrorist organizations, because it is allied to Osama Bin-Laden's International Islamic Front (IIF). The network wants to create a *Brihot Bangladesh* or 'Greater Bangladesh' by merging Muslim communities from North East India into Bangladesh. The ICS, too, is believed to have been involved with this militant network and is working in tandem with the Students' Islamic Movement of India (SIMI) to support the network. In 2002, Salim Sajid, SIMI's financial secretary, was interrogated and he confessed to the fact as to how ICS and JeI Bangladesh were closely working with the SIMI to plan and attack Indian interests. The groups have been meeting in West Bengal under the banner of the 'Islamic Action Force'.

SIMI was the student front of the Indian branch of the Jamaat-e-Islami and follows the thoughts and teachings of Mawdudi. It has a history of supporting the Taliban and the al-Qaeda. Its cadres are believed to have been responsible for several recent bomb attacks in India: in Varanasi, New Delhi, and Mumbai, resulting in high casualty rates. SIMI is also working with Lashkar-e-Toiba (LeT), Hizb-ul-Mujahideen (HM) and Jaish-e-Mohammed (JeM) which are based in Pakistan. These are also members of the International Islamic Front. In 2003, Indian Muslims working in Middle Eastern countries were contacted and recruited by known SIMI operatives to go and fight against the coalition forces in Iraq—which is another escalation of the group's international activities.

The ICS and Jamaat are working closely with SIMI and are well aware of its current strategy to attack Indian targets. Jamaat-Pakistan and Jamaat-Bangladesh also receives backing from the Islamic Circle of North America (ICNA) and Muslim Aid branches who act as fund-raisers, missionaries, and public relations managers for the Jamaat-e-Islami movement in the west. The charities have been linked to Mueen-uddin Chowdhury and Asrafuzzaman Khan, two expatriate Bangladeshis with Jamaat backgrounds, who are suspected of being directly involved in war crimes. The two charities send money collected in the UK, US, Germany, and Australia to the Al-Khidmat Foundation/Society and Muslim Aid's Bangladeshi branch. They are both de facto arms of the Jamaat. Al-Khidmat aids militancy and helps to support the Hizb-ul-Mujahideen, Jamaat's armed wing and other groups. Hizb-ul-Mujahideen is designated by the US and UK as a terrorist organization.

In 2004, agents of Russia's Federal Security Bureau (FSB) assassinated Zelimkhan Yanderbiyev, the former vice president of Chechnya, in a car-bomb attack in Doha, Qatar. They believe he was meeting with wealthy Middle Eastern figures to collect funds for *jihad*. Yanderbiyev was a recipient of Jamaat funds to wage war on Russia. Jamaat-e-Islami is listed by Russia's Supreme Court as a leading financier and supporter of terrorism. After the 9/11 attacks, the Russian FSB provided information to the US about the Jamaat's involvement in the attacks on the World Trade Center and the Pentagon. These evidences now appear credible after the arrest of Khalid Sheikh Mohammed, the mastermind of the 9/11 attacks from a residence of Jamaat leaders in Pakistan.

The Jamaat-Bangladesh has also been involved in laundering money for groups linked to ISI, the al-Qaeda, and the IIF. As detailed above, the ICS is also involved with terrorist organizations in India and Bangladesh. The Jamaat's most important supporters outside South Asia are the ICNA and Muslim Aid, UK. The organizations operate under charitable status in the US and UK. The charities receive *zakat* from benevolent Muslim communities around the world under the guise of Muslim causes. ICNA and Muslim Aid are linked to persons believed to have been involved in war crimes during the 1971 liberation war in Bangladesh and have been linked to terrorist groups from Bosnia to Indonesia (Blackburn 2006).

Even the US State Department and the US Department of Justice are concerned over the reluctance of the Bangladesh government to investigate 45 major money-laundering cases related to international terrorism. US officials from the Department of Justice have been to Dhaka to push the case with the Bangladesh government but with very little result. Bangladesh banned the Al-Haramain in July 2004 and forced it to close office in Dhaka, but of its fourteen officials who left the country after the ban, four have returned to work with the Kuwaiti RIHS. There is growing evidence of extensive funding and missionary work by non-native Islamic charities in Bangladesh. In 2005, a combined intelligence report by Bangladesh police's Special Branch, the National Security Intelligence (NSI), and the Directorate General Forces Intelligence (DGFI) identified 10 Islamic charities/NGOs as promoters/financers of Islamic terrorist groups in Bangladesh. They were: the Kuwait-based Revival of Islamic Heritage Society (RIHS), Rabita Al-Alam Al Islami (World Muslim League), Qatar Charitable Society, Society for Social Reforms, Al-Muntada Al-Islami, International Islamic Relief Agency, Al-Forkan Foundation, Kuwait Joint Relief Committee, International Relief Organization, and Muslim Aid Bangladesh (UK).

The RIHS was blamed by Bangladesh intelligence for financing the 450 serial bomb explosions of 17 August 2005, after which its chief Abdul Aziz Khalaf Malullah visited Dhaka and called on three cabinet ministers—two of Jamaat and one of BNP—to lobby for the RIHS. Its country director in Bangladesh, Ekramuzzaman Khan, was arrested in September 2005 but was immediately released on anticipatory bail. The US had blacklisted the RIHS way back in 2002 after the detailed post-9/11 investigations. After the 17 August blasts in Bangladesh, five foreign officials of the RIHS—two Sudanese, two Algerians and one Libyan—were forced to leave Bangladesh. Before joining the RIHS, these five had worked with the Al-Haramain in Bangladesh. The Al-Haramain has been blacklisted by the US as a fund-laundering front of the al-Qaeda. Sustained US pressure forced Dhaka to arrest Asadullah Al-Ghalib, chief of the militant Ahle Hadith Andolan Bangladesh (AHAB), who had helped the RIHS construct over 1,000 mosques, 10 Madrassas, four orphanages and even a kidney dialysis centre in Bangladesh.

The inclusion of Muslim Aid Bangladesh in the list of suspect charities raised the heckles as its chairman Maulana Abdus Sobhan was a legislator of the JeI in Bangladesh. The charity is part of Muslim Aid UK with five sub-branches: Muslim Aid Pakistan, Muslim Aid Bangladesh, Muslim Aid Asia (Indonesia), Muslim Aid Australia and the Germany-based Muslime Helfen. The links of the Muslim Aid's Australia branch with the Dewan Dakwah Islamiyah Indonesia (DDII), a radical organization, was exposed by the ABC News (Australia). The DDII has close links with the same Jemaah Islamiah

(JI) that was responsible for the infamous Bali bombings. The Muslim Aid network is the key link in the Islamist terror chain that connects groups like the HUJI of Bangladesh and the JI of Southeast Asia. They swap fighters and use each other's bases, training facilities and safe houses to evade western intelligence. Many of JI's activists, and those from the Islamist groups in Thailand's south, have received training in the HUJI's bases in Ukhia that is located between Chittagong and Cox's Bazar. Furthermore, there is increasing evidence that this transnational terror structure has grown on the shoulders of the vast organizational network of the Jamaat-e-Islami (Bangladesh) and the Islami Chatra Shibir, particularly in the Chittagong–Cox's Bazar region (Lintner 2004).

THE JANISSARIES OF ALLAH

The Afghan war attracted many a Muslim from all over the globe. The defeat of the powerful Soviet forces boosted their confidence and strengthened their resolve to start similar 'holy war campaigns' in their own countries and regions. Thirty four Bangladeshi *jihadis* died in the Afghan war but the survivors, who initially functioned under the Pakistan-based Harkat-ul-Jihad-al-Islami-al-Alami, got together under the leadership of Abdur Rehman Farooqi and formed the HUJI of Bangladesh. During his conversations with Osama Bin-Laden, Farooqi insisted that it should not be clubbed with the HUJI of Pakistan led by Qari Saifullah but should be treated as an independent entity (Bhaumik 2002). But the formal announcement of the formation of HUJI-Bangladesh was made in the Dhaka Press Club on 30 April 1992 after the Islamists had returned from Afghanistan. But, in a way, many of the HUJI leaders had old connections with the Jamaat–Shibir combine. When the Islamic world called for a *jihad* (Holy War) against the Soviet intervention in Afghanistan, the Jamaat-e-Islami, Islami Chatra Shibir and other Islamist groups of Bangladesh responded by sending volunteers from its Madrassas to fight the Afghan *jihad*. Those fighters who survived the Afghan war were responsible for forming the HUJI.

A top HUJI leader known to the contributor since the 1970s (but whose identity cannot be disclosed for reasons of his security) told him in 1996 that it was Osama Bin-Laden who met the Bangladeshi *jihadi* contingent near Khost on 11 February 1989 and impressed upon them the need to turn Bangladesh into a Dar-ul-Islam. 'For the Sheikh (as Osama is referred to), Bangladesh was a Dar-ul-Harb or land of infidels and he said that that should not be the case because the majority of its people were Muslims,' the HUJI leader said.[2] This leader was present at the meeting with Bin-Laden, along with Abdur Rehman Farooqi, Abdul Salam Muhammad alias Fazlur Rahman, Mufti Abdul Mannan, and Shawkat Osman alias Farid. Since after Farooqi's death, a few months after the meeting with Bin-Laden, the other three have led the HUJI in Bangladesh. From the outset, the HUJI-B's primary mission was to establish a Taliban type Islamic rule in Bangladesh. And their slogan said it all: *Amra Hobo Taliban, Bangla Hobe Afghanistan* (we will become Taliban; Bangladesh will become Afghanistan). Following the footsteps of Taliban, it began to regard music, dance, theatre, and cinema—key aspects of Bengali culture and nationalist expression—as corrupting influences on the Islamic way of life and as symbols of Hindu–Christian cultural domination.

In the initial period, HUJI-B used the favourable regime of Begum Khaleda Zia, between 1991–1996, to strengthen the organization and recruit both locals and foreigners as its members. There was one instance when 41 HUJI-B cadres were arrested with firearms on 19 February 1996, who were subsequently sentenced to life imprisonment by the court, but were released on bail by Bangladesh's high court during the second term of the Begum Khaleda Zia Government (2001–2006). Although, Madrassas—mostly financed by Arab charities—were the primary source of funds for recruitment, the HUJI also recruited a great deal from among the Rohingya Muslim refugees from the Arakan province of Myanmar, who had fled from their native land allegedly due to religious persecution and have been in refugee camps in the Chittagong-Cox's Bazar area for close to two decades. Later, the HUJI also started recruiting from Muslim-dominant areas of West Bengal and Assam and elsewhere in India. The ISI helped train the first flood of HUJI recruits, many of whom were even sent to fight alongside local separatists against the Indian security forces in Jammu and Kashmir.

After the Awami League led by Sheikh Hasina came to power in Bangladesh in June1996, the HUJI suffered some setbacks. Hundreds of its activists and collaborators were arrested. But it soon started striking at secular intellectuals and even tried to kill Sheikh Hasina by bombing a rally at Kotalipara that she was to address. The prime accused in this case, Mufti Abdul Hannan Munshi, was later arrested in Bangladesh, whereupon he confessed that he had been assured 'safe shelter' in Bangladesh by top functionaries of the BNP–Jamaat government. With a view to translating the objective of the al-Qaeda in action, Osama Bin-Laden in association with the terrorist groups from Egypt, Pakistan and Bangladesh, and elsewhere in Asia and Africa announced the formation of the IIF and issued a *fatwa* on 23 February 1998, calling for attack on all Americans including civilians. Laden seeks to replace the existing west-dominated global political structure with a Caliphate, that will bring back the glorious days of Islam. Apart from Bin-Laden, other signatories of this *fatwa* included Abdul Salam Muhammad alias Fazlur Rahman of the 'Jihad Movement of Bangladesh' (an activist of HUJI-B), Ayman-al-Zawahiri and Rifai Ahmad Taha alias Abu Nasir of Egypt and Sheikh Mir Hamzah, Secretary of the Jamiat-al-Ulema-e-Pakistan. Fazlur Rehman is part of the HUJI-Bangladesh triumvirate, indeed, perhaps its best-known ideologue (Fishel 2005).

After becoming a constituent of the IIF, HUJI-B increased its violent attacks on the Hindu minority, progressive intellectuals like poets, journalists and liberal Muslims. Bangladesh intelligence reports indicated that the HUJI-B had drawn up a list of 28 prominent intellectuals, including National Professor Kabir Choudhury, writer Taslima Nasreen, and the Director General of the Islamic Foundation, Maulana Abdul Awal. It attacked poet Shamsur Rehman, bombed a Bengali cultural programme in Jessore, set off explosions on Bengali New Year Day and drew up a plan to kill Sheikh Hasina. Bangladesh Home Minister Mohammed Naseem disclosed during his visit to India in 1999 that he had confided to the then Indian home minister, L.K. Advani and the then West Bengal chief Minister, Jyoti Basu, about the presence of HUJI-B operatives in India. He said that 'his government had definite information about HUJI militants taking shelter in India particularly in West Bengal, to flee from the crackdown unleashed by Awami League Government after the bombing attempt of Kotalipara'.[3]

With the help of the ISI and the patronage of the Islamists it became easier for the HUJI-B operatives to merge with various Muslim groups in states like Assam, West Bengal, Uttar Pradesh, and Delhi and set up their cells there. Various reports suggest that in addition to its links with Indian separatist groups like the United Liberation Front of Asom (ULFA), it also maintained links with terrorist groups outside Bangladesh, including Jaish-e-Mohammed (JeM) and Lashkar-e-Toiba (LeT) in Pakistan. The HUJI's 'India Operations Commander'

Jallaludin alias Babu Bhai, after his arrest in Lucknow during an encounter with the Uttar Pradesh police, has admitted to close links between the HUJI-B, the JeM and the LeT.[4] This includes mutual swap of operatives for operations, mutual use of bases and safe houses and logistical networking for increasing operational capability and reach. Mohammad Salim, the prime accused in the New Jalpaiguri explosion incident on a train carrying Indian troops during the 1999 Kargil War was an activist of the HUJI-B.

The HUJI was helped by the two Islamic fundamentalist parties, the Jamaat-e-Islami and the Islami Oikyo Jote, who were part of the ruling coalition during the 2001–2006 phase. The arrival of a sizeable number of Arab and Afghan Mujahideens of the al-Qaeda and Taliban, who were forced to flee Afghanistan after the fall of Kandahar in December 2001, helped the HUJI strengthen its hit-force and training programme (Perry 2002). The Islami Oikyo Jote's chairman, Azizul Huq, who was said to be a member of HUJI's advisory council openly expressed support to the Taliban and the al-Qaeda. HUJI-B sheltered these Mujahideens and then helped them melt away to various conflict zones in Asia. Intelligence reports in India and Bangladesh suggest that Osama Bin-Laden's deputy, Ayman-al-Zawahiri, paid several visits to Bangladesh during the BNP–Jamaat government's tenure in power (2001–2006) to supervise these processes. With powerful patrons in the government and financial support from Osama Bin-Laden and Saudi Arabia, Pakistan, and other Islamic countries through the Muslim non-governmental organizations in Bangladesh, HUJI-B emerged as a potential threat to global security. Its present chief Shawkat Osman alias Farid and general secretary, Imtiaz Quddus remained active both in Bangladesh and India.

Indian and Bangladeshi intelligence suggest that the HUJI-B may have up to 15,000 activists trained in the use of arms and explosives. The contributor's own source inside the organization paints a somewhat different picture. He says that the HUJI-B has trained up to 10,000 activists in the last 10 years, but only half of them are active as regular salaried cadres. Thirty per cent of these activists play a 'sleeper role' in Bangladesh, India, and elsewhere in South and South East Asia and they are only activated for special purposes during operations—as couriers of explosives and weapons, for ensuring safe passage of action groups and for gathering intelligence on assigned targets. It is a priority, the contributor's source states, that they are not exposed and do not end up with detailed profiles on computers of the Central Intelligence Agency or other national intelligence agencies. The source also states that another 20 per cent of the trained activists have left Bangladesh for other battlegrounds of the world as far as Chechnya and the Philippines. Most of the 'global jihadis' of the HUJI-B, the source says, were the Myanmarese Rohingyas, who were among the most passionate fighters for the pan-Islamist cause, while, according to him, most local Bangladeshi recruits of the HUJI-B prefer to stay in the country for action in the India–Bangladesh region. Some of them have joined up with homegrown terrorist groups to provide support for grassroot level expansion of the structure for Islamist terror.[5]

THE GRASSROOT ISLAMISTS

While the Jamaat-Bangladesh and its student body, ICS, provided a nation-wide legitimate socio-political network for promoting the cause of an Islamic state based on Shariah in Bangladesh, the HUJI-B serves as the sword of militant Islam in the country and the region beyond. It has emerged as the critical linkage between the national and the global pan-Islamist terror project. But during the last few years, a number of homegrown Islamist vigilante groups have emerged and thrived in Bangladesh with active patronage of the Jamaat and its coalition partners. These vigilante groups not only create local conditions favourable to a Shariah-based Islamist state, but are also seen as important partners in the larger project to establish Dar-ul-Islam by violence, terror and intimidation. While the Jamaat-Shibir are expected to create favourable political conditions for Islamization and the HUJI is supposed to take on established governments by systematic use of terror, these local Islamist vigilantes are expected to sweep clean areas of 'evil influences' and create ideal local conditions for the creation of an Islamic state. They are also expected to identify and provide recruits for the larger *jihad* even as they employ many of them to fight locally.

The JMJB is one such group, which shot into the headlines during the first phase of the BNP–Jamaat coalition government. Bangladeshi media reports have indicated that the JMJB is an outgrowth of the Islamist militant, JMB. Indeed there is considerable overlap between the leadership of the JMB and the JMJB. Other reports have indicated that the JMJB is a youth front of the outlawed militant group, the HUJI-B. The JMJB's senior leader Maulana Abdur Rahman, who is also the chief of JMB, says that JMJB was formed in 1998. However, when the JMJB first came to limelight on 1 April 2004, it was also known by other names like Mujaheedin Alliance Council, Islami Jalsha, and Muslim Raksha Mujahideen Oikyo Parishad. The JMJB follows the ideals of the Taliban militia and propagates a movement based on 'jihad'. Its chief, Abdur Rahman had said: 'Our model includes many leaders and scholars of Islam. But we will take as much (ideology) from the Taliban as we need.'[6]

It has explicitly stated on more than one occasion that it does not subscribe to the prevailing political system in Bangladesh and that it would 'build a society based on the Islamic model laid out in Holy Koran and the Hadith.' The JMJB function with an avowed objective of neutralizing the left-wing extremists, but its professed long-term goal is to usher in an 'Islamic revolution' in Bangladesh through 'jihad'. The JMJB had created strong bases mostly in northwest Bangladesh, in the districts of Rajshahi, Satkhira, Naogaon, Bagerhat, Jessore, Chittagong, Joypurhat, Natore, Rangpur, Bogra, Chittagong, and Khulna, operating out of a well-knit network of mosques and Madrassas (seminaries). The JMJB has also established at least 12 camps at Atrai and Raninagar in the Naogaon district, Bagmara in Rajshahi district, and Naldanga and Singra in Natore district. In these camps, the HUJI veterans trained the JMJB cadres in use of arms and explosives, and the motivation campaign was conducted through recorded speeches of Osama Bin-Laden and video footages of warfare training at the al-Qaeda's camps in Afghanistan.

The JMJB's former chief Siddiqul Islam alias Azizur Rahman alias Omar Ali Litu alias Bangla Bhai, who was later hanged in the Kashimpur jail in March 2007, had claimed that JMJB commands the strength of 300,000 members across the country. He had told Bangladesh newspapers that the group had about 10,000 full-time activists and spends up to 700,000 Taka on them every month. This appears to be an exaggeration, but intelligence agencies suggest that JMJB, during its peak, had 4,000 activists and 20 times as many ardent supporters who would be available for mobilization and action. JMJB activists, during their actions in 2004, were seen with firearms, but most used swords, other sharp weapons, hammers, and even hockey sticks. They had access to explosives but of a crude kind.

The highest decision-making body of the JMJB is the seven-member Majlish-e-Shura. Apart from Siddiqul Islam and JMB chief, Abdur Rahman, other members of the council included Ashikur Rahman,

Hafez Mahmud, Tarek Moni, and Khaled. Information regarding the Shura, after the 30 March 2007 executions, is not available. 'Commander' Bangla Bhai hailed from the Bogra district and claimed that as a college student, he had joined the ICS. Bangla Bhai had also claimed that he quit the ICS in 1995 after the Jamaat accepted female leadership, which according to him was profane. On the other hand, Maulana Abdur Rahman was reported to have worked at the Saudi embassy in Dhaka between 1985 and 1990. He studied at the Medina Islamic University in Saudi Arabia and has reportedly travelled to India, Pakistan, and Afghanistan, among other countries. His most recent visit to Pakistan was reportedly in the year 2003.

The JMJB reportedly has a three-tier organization. The first tier of the outfit consists of activists called *Ehsar* who are recruited on a full-time basis and act at the behest of the higher echelons. The second tier, known as *Gayeri Ehsar*, has over 100,000 part-time activists. The third tier involves ardent supporters who cooperate with the JMJB. According to JMJB leaders, the whole country has been divided into nine organizational divisions. Khulna, Barisal, Sylhet and Chittagong have an organizational divisional office each, while Dhaka has two divisional offices and Rajshahi three. The outfit also had committees in each village, and villagers were being forced to join the committees. If anybody refused, he was branded as a 'collaborator' of the Purbo Bangla Communist Party and taken to the JMJB 'trial centre'.

The JMJB leader Maulana Abdur Rahman stridently denied any foreign links but is known to have made several visits to Saudi Arabia, Pakistan, and Afghanistan and secured huge funds from Islamic charities to build mosques and seminaries but it is only expected that some of these funds were diverted for building the group's 'armed muscle'. It is also well known that the JMJB enjoyed support of certain members of the ruling BNP and the JeI. The former deputy minister for land revenue, Ruhul Kuddus Talukder Dulu, had close links with the JMJB, and media reports suggest that Bagmara's BNP joint secretary, Besharat Ullah, reportedly addressed the first rally of the JMJB. At the peak of JMJB's vigilante actions, the cabinet committee on law and order led by BNP minister, Abdul Mannan Bhuiyan ordered the arrest of Bangla Bhai for taking 'law into his own hands'. But three BNP ministers belonging to Rajshahi—Aminul Haq, Fazlur Rahman Patal, and Ruhul Kuddus Dulu—opposed the police action saying that the JMJB was on a 'pro-people mission' freeing the northern region from the left-wing extremists.

The JMJB also enjoyed support among certain sections of the police. For instance, Noor Mohammad, divisional inspector general of police in Rajshahi, told *The Daily Star* on 5 May 2004, that Bangla Bhai and his operatives were assisting the law enforcers in tracking down the left-wing outlaws. He said, 'We've asked police stations to support them whenever they go to catch outlaws.' Reportedly, he justified such an action by indicating that: 'You know Sarbahara [left-wing extremists] men have been quite active in the region for many years and it is not possible for the undermanned and under-equipped police to hunt them down. Aziz [Bangla Bhai] is now helping us.' When the police finally started its crackdown on the JMJB and the JMB, some of their top officials in the area were transferred or punished. The JMJB and JMB's funds came from both local level extortion and also from non-native Islamic charities like Rabeta-e-Islam and Islami Oytijjho Sangstha. Until the end of the BNP–Jamaat coalition government in October 2006, the JMJB activists had carried out more than 150 reported vigilante operations in different regions, including murders and attacks on people, particularly non-Muslim minorities, and their activists had been involved in raising protection money from traders.

Like the JMJB, the JMB led by Sayek Abdur Rehman had also emerged as a powerful Islamic vigilante group—again during the tenure of the BNP–Jamaat coalition government. It also had a seven-member Majlish-e-Shura, like the JMJB, which is the central governing body. The JMB had 16 regional commanders and a district head for each of Bangladesh's 64 districts. The overlap with JMJB becomes clear, as its one-time chief 'Bangla Bhai' was a member of the JMB Majlish-e-Shura. A high ranking JMB member had told the media that the group had also developed a 'suicide squad' and the family of every member of the squad was earmarked for a compensation of up to 100,000 Taka on his death.[7] The JMB chief, Sayek Abdur Rehman had told the media that his group had 10,000 trained full-timers and 100,000 part-timers. This again appears to be an exaggeration, but it is possible that both the JMB and the JMJB had the same set of people working for them in many districts.

After exposure of their activities in the Western press (Griswold 2005), the Bangladesh government came under huge pressure from western donor nations to act against these Islamic vigilantes. The BNP–Jamaat coalition government was forced to act. In five to six months, the top leadership of both the organization was targeted through sustained paramilitary operations. On 30 March 2007, JMJB chief, Siddiqul Islam alias Bangla Bhai was hanged in the Kashimpur jail, where he was kept since his arrest on 6 March 2006 from the remote Rampur village under the Muktagachha sub-district of Mymensingh. Hanged on the same day were five other top militants of the Jama'atul Mujahideen Bangladesh, including its 'supreme commander' Sayek Abdur Rahman. All these militants including Siddiqul Islam had been pronounced guilty by the Supreme Court of involvement in the killing of two judges in Jhalakathi in November 2005. On 4 March 2007, President Iajuddin Ahmed had rejected their mercy petitions paving the way for their execution.

Bangladesh's military-backed interim government claims that they have effectively neutralized the JMJB–JMB vigilante groups ever since they took charge in October 2007. It has explicitly committed itself to the western 'war against terror' and it would not like to do anything that would jeopardize Bangladesh's high level of involvement in UN peacekeeping operations. These operations are not only crucial for improving Bangladesh's global image but also to ensure lucrative financial returns for the army's rank and file. Therefore, the same security forces that looked the other way during the vigilante activities of the BNP–Jamaat regime, appear to be making a concerted effort during the interim regime to weed out grassroot Islamist groups who were 'taking law into their own hands'.

But while the Awami League and the BNP has come in for some severe punitive action and large number of their top leaders have been jailed for graft, corruption, involvement with violent activities and misuse of power, the JeI has emerged largely unscathed. And while the JMJB–JMB has lost its teeth, the HUJI-B has been largely untouched. That it is not striking in Bangladesh and is concentrating on actions in Indian territory or elsewhere may be part of a tactical design, but by no means indicates that the HUJI has been weakened. The interim government claims to be 'cleaning up' politics and society in Bangladesh ahead of the elections slated for the end of 2008. In this, their agenda has gone way beyond their constitutional mandate of holding free and fair polls. But when queried by the Press whether the interim government would, by the same yardstick, be interested to bring to book the 'war criminals of 1971' to clean Bangladesh of fundamentalist bigots, the former information advisor of the interim government barrister Mainul Hossain said it is not possible 'after so many years'. The west, which has been impressed by the anti-corruption drive of the military-backed interim government, needs to realize that the decimation of the two major political parties, particularly the Awami League, will only create a huge vacuum, an irreplaceable void, and that would only work to the advantage of fundamentalist parties like the JeI. And with the renewed growth of the Jamaat-e-Islami (Bangladesh), the janissaries and the grassroot *jihadis* would be back in business.

NOTES

1. A series of articles and media reports since 2002 has referred to Bangladesh as a 'cocoon of terror' and the possible venue of the 'next Islamist Revolution'. The contributor's article 'Bangladesh: The Second Front of Islamic Terror' published in 'Terrorism and Low Intensity Conflicts in South Asian Region', edited by O.P. Mishra and Sucheta Ghosh, (Delhi, Manak Publishers, Delhi, 2002) was the first to raise the alarm. Bertil Lintner's 'Bangladesh: Cocoon of Terror' in the *Far Eastern Economic Review*, 4 April 2002, was the next big piece on these lines. Alex Perry's 'Deadly Cargo' in *Time* magazine, 14 October 2002, exposed the arrival of 150 Taliban/al-Qaeda fighters to Chittagong by ship, and the shelter they received from Bangladesh military intelligence and local Islamists, pointing to Pakistan-type intelligence-Islamist collusion. Elisa Griswold's 'The Next Islamist Revolution' in *The New York Times* magazine, 23 January 2005 provided details of the Islamist vigilante and terrorist activities at the grassroots. The *National Geographic's* documentary on the al-Qaeda, aired in late 2002, had a large section on the activities and pan-Islamist linkages of the Islamist groups of Bangladesh. *Terror Sans Frontiers: Islamist Militancy in North East India* (2004) and *Bangladesh: Treading the Taliban Trail* (2006) were two of Jaideep Saikia's important works that loud-hailed the issue.
2. Interview with the HUJI leader was conducted by the contributor secretly in Ramna locality in Dhaka on 13 October 1996, quoted in Bhaumik 2002.
3. Interview conducted by the contributor with Bangladesh's former home minister, Mohammed Naseem and aired over the BBC Bengali Service on 11 December 1999.
4. Summary of Interrogation Report of Md. Jallaludin alias Babu Bhai made available to the contributor by a senior official of the Indian Intelligence Bureau.
5. The HUJI leader in question is a member of the organization's central executive committee. The contributor has known him since the mid 1970s when he was an activist of the Islami Chatra Shibir. He later completed his Islamic education and was sent to fight in Afghanistan as a volunteer. He was one of the Bangladeshi Islamist present at the meeting with Osama Bin-Laden on 11 February 1989 at Khost where Laden mooted the idea of forming a 'jihadi' brigade in Bangladesh to transform it from a Dar-ul-Harb to a Dar-ul-Islam. This leader is an old friend and a prized source but the contributor's communication with him has remained one-way after a last meeting at a house in Ramna, Dhaka, on 13 October 1996, and the contributor

is not in a position to disclose his identity for reasons of security. All that can be said is that he is disillusioned with the global salafi agenda and the Afghan–Arab domination in the movement. The source has faxed or couriered the contributor several important HUJI documents including photocopies of the minutes of their top-level meetings.

6. For details see the website of the Jagrata Muslim Janata Bangladesh (JMJB): http://www.satp.org/satporgtp/countries/bangladesh/terroristoutfits/JMJB.htm, last accessed on 26 November 2008.

7. For details, see http://www.dailystar.net/magazine/2006/09/cover.htm, last accessed on 26 November 2008.

5

EXTERNAL LINKS OF THE MAOIST INSURGENCY IN NEPAL

Bishnu Raj Upreti

INTRODUCTION

The main focus of the chapter is to analyze the external links of the Communist Party of Nepal (Maoist), CPN (M), during the period of active 'people's war' in Nepal (13 February 1996 to 21 November 2006). The main reason for choosing to examine the external links of the Maoists as the subject of the chapter is to show that even in the case of Nepal, which seems more 'domestically' oriented compared to all other insurgencies covered in this volume, some degree of internationalization of the movement's activity does take place. The case of Nepal is thus quite different from most other cases discussed in this book and only shares certain features with some of the Latin American insurgencies discussed in Chapter 2.

The chapter shows that Maoist insurgency is a localized one and confined primarily to the national context. However, the insurgency did establish some cross-border links and some aspects of its activity have been internationalized to a limited extent. The most prominent international dimension of the Maoist insurgency is, of course, its internationalist leftist ideology. Further, their link was also expanded for practical and logistic reasons such as buying arms and obtaining funding (though limited), and so on.

In the aftermath of 11 September 2001 attacks in New York and Washington, the United States and India labelled the Maoist insurgency in Nepal as 'terrorism', too.[1] Since then, the term 'terrorist' was increasingly used by some of the media, analysts and politicians, both in Nepal and abroad, to characterize the Maoists. However, comparing the homegrown, socio-political Maoist movement in Nepal with armed groups systematically employing terrorist means is a gross over-simplification. A comparison with a transnationally active terrorist network with a global agenda, such as the al-Qaeda, is completely misleading.[2] The treatment of the Maoist insurgency through the lenses of the ongoing global campaign against terrorism[3] originates from a lack of understanding of the socio-political conditions in Nepal and is driven by political biases and prejudices. As the chapter argues, the Maoist insurgency, as a locally-based, non-Islamist, leftist armed movement with its activities confined to the territory of Nepal and with a specific national agenda of socio-political transformation, is radically different from either most locally-based terrorist armed groups, let alone transnational terrorist networks. The Maoist insurgency has clear objectives and political agenda, strictly limited within the national boundary and a clearly organized structure. Its main goals have been to dismantle the feudal, centralized, top-down, autocratic structures of the monarchical state, to put an end to exclusionary governing practices, to establish the rights of the poor, marginalized, and discriminated sections of society and to build an inclusive federal republican state. Hence, the Maoist insurgency is a classic socio-political resistance movement. However, some aspects of the activities of Maoists were guided by terrorist tactics.

THE CONTEXT

CAUSES OF THE MAOIST INSURGENCY

In this section a brief discussion on different sources of armed insurgency is presented. They are grouped into structural sources, international sources, triggers and catalysts and presented in Table 5.1.

TABLE 5.1
Sources of Social Tension and Violent Conflict

Structural sources	International sources	Triggers and catalysts
Political sources, Socio-economic sources (caste, class, religion-based discriminations and inequalities; poverty and unemployment; social exclusion; and so on), Geographical isolation, Constitutional and legal issues, Ideological sources	Changes in international context; Interests of powerful nations (political, strategic and military interests), economic interests (natural resources: gas, oil, water, forestry); historical legacy; religious factor	Vested interests, Catalyst trigger events (for example, the Royal massacre in Nepal on 1 June 2001), Failure of political leadership, Psychological factors (revenge and retaliation), Irresponsibility factor and culture of denial

Source: Compiled by the author from his various publications.

While international factors have hardly been the prime causes of the outbreak of armed insurgency, they had played a role. According to the Tenth Five Year Plan prepared by the National Planning Commission of Government of Nepal International aid to Nepal had amounted to trillions of rupees (National Planning Commission 2002), but has for more than five decades failed to address root causes of conflict such as poverty, injustice, discrimination, exclusion, malgovernance, to help provide for basic needs and to protect the fundamental rights of people. According to experts who examined the impact of donor assistance on Nepal's development:

> ...despite a heavy donor presence and sustained high levels of aid to Nepal (with foreign agencies contributing some 60% of Nepal's development budget) and the existence of a wide variety of development programmes, that number of people falling below the poverty line has not decreased over the last twenty years. There can be little doubt that, even after half a century of development interventions Nepal is still in crisis. (Seddon and Hussien 2002)

The government of Nepal was determined to crack down on the Maoists through military means with the help of the USA, the UK, and India. However, every effort of the government has failed. While the detailed analysis of why the crackdown on the Maoists has not been successful and of various dimensions of the Maoist insurgency can be found elsewhere,[4] a brief overview will suffice here.

TACTICS USED BY MAOISTS

The Maoist insurgency in Nepal was launched in February 1996, following the government's rejection of a Maoists' ultimatum demanding radical social and political reform, and lasted for a decade until the late 2006. It was started as small rebellion in four hill districts of mid-western Nepal with very few hand-made weapons and small number of fighters. Their 40-point demands[5] put forward as a starting point for the insurgency included:

1. Nationalist demands (nullification of the 1950 Treaty between India and Nepal and the Mahakali Treaty, delimitation of the entire Nepal–India border, closure of the Gorkha recruiting centres, introduction of the system of work permits for foreigners, end to the monopoly of foreign capital in Nepal's industry, trade and economic sector, end to 'the cultural pollution of imperialists and expansionists...' [Upreti 2004b: 368–69, Annex 1], NGOs and INGOs).

2. Political reform (a new constitution to be drafted by the people's elected representatives; end of all the special rights and privileges of the king and his family; bringing army, police and administration under the people's control; abolishment of the Security Act and all other repressive acts; release of political prisoners and withdrawal of false charges against them; end to police operations in the different parts of the country; and so on).

3. Social and economic demands reflecting concerns of the poor, women, socially excluded and marginalized groups and bringing them into the national debate (ownership of land to be transferred to those who cultivate it, confiscation of property of brokers and commission agents, guaranteed work and minimal level of wages for all, and so forth).

The insurgency was conducted in line with Mao Ze Dong's strategy of 'three weapons for people's revolution': 'the party' (to develop and maintain ideology and to formulate policies and strategies of the people's war), 'the people's army' (that is responsible for attacking the enemies and defending the areas under 'the people's' control) and 'the united front' (to consolidate friendly forces) (Tse Tung 1968).

Maoists used different tactics in expanding their insurgency. Some of their main tactics were: propaganda, creation of fear and terror, eviction of 'exploiters', 'reactionary forces' and 'informers', killings, abductions, kidnappings, and extortions, encircling towns and urban centres by controlling peripheries and villages and the like. Most of these activities were focused on the Nepalese citizens and, at times, were particularly brutal. For example, on 5 June 2005 the Maoists planted a landmine on the busy road in Chitawan, which exploded under a bus that carried a large number of passengers. Thirty eight passengers, including children, were killed and 70 more were injured in this blast.

During the decade-long armed conflict, the Maoists used different violent tactics to advance their strategic goal of weakening the state military and widening the gap between the people and the state. This was to be achieved primarily by demoralizing and creating psychological stress and fear among the supporters of the government (or, in the Maoists' terminology, 'informers', 'reactionaries', and 'opponents of the people's war'), often through the particularly brutal use of violence. However, the Maoists also threatened to take action against any foreigners, particularly US citizens, if they were involved in spying on the Maoists to the benefit of the government.

Along guerrilla attacks against the military and security targets (such as attacks on the army camps and police stations), the Maoists also used terrorist means for advancement of their political goals. The objectives of use of terrorist means seemed to be *(a)* to exert pressure on the government to address the Maoists' political agenda, and *(b)* to exert psychological pressure on their opponents and those who support the state security forces.

The Maoists' terrorist activity involved, first and foremost, numerous high-profile assassinations, such as the killing of the Inspector General of Armed Police Force in Kathmandu in 2001 that had exerted enormous pressure on the government to hold peace talks with the rebels. Other major types of terrorist tactics used by CPN (M) included kidnapping and abduction, threats of violent action, encroachment on private property (buildings and land), eviction from home and community, hit-and-run attacks, detention, extortion, attacks on the government offices, damage of public and private property (buildings, bridges, telecommunication towers, hydro-power plants, radio stations and similar assets), burning of vehicles, looting, use of landmines, and so on. The use of terrorist means by the Maoists had created widespread fear among the local population.

It has to be noted, however, that in addition to terrorist attacks against civilians and civilian objects and infrastructure and the more classic guerrilla attacks against military targets, the Maoists also used non-violent tactics such as propaganda, blockade, demonstrations, warning letters, exerting pressure on civilians to provide food, shelter or cash donations to the rebels, public notices to the military and police personnel to leave their jobs, the formation of the local *janasarkar* (the 'parallel' local people's government: people's courts, people's army units, etc.), and actions to prevent civilians from contacting the government offices.

Also, compared to other left-wing insurgent groups in different parts of the world (such as FARC and ELN in Colombia), the Maoists in Nepal less frequently resorted to terrorist means and, if they did, their terrorist activity was mainly localized. The main explanation for the limited use of terrorist means by the Maoists in Nepal is the Maoist ideology, with its emphasis on the broad, mass-based 'people's war'. Another major factor that discouraged the Maoists from the more active use of terrorist means was the pressure from international community, especially from human rights organizations. The Maoists wanted to develop and maintain good relations with the international community and they at least tried to give the impression that they were not using terrorist means. Pressure from domestic human rights and civil society movement was another reason for the less active use of terrorist means by the Maoists, as compared to some other left-wing insurgencies.

End of the Armed Insurgency

The signing of the Comprehensive Peace Agreement (CPA) on 22 November 2006 was a result of a dynamic and complicated peace process. It started a year earlier, on 22 November 2005, when the 12-point understanding was signed in New Delhi between the Maoists and the Seven Party Alliance (SPA). The alliance was formed by seven political parties to fight against the royal takeover. On 1 February 2005, the king took over the power by removing the multi-party government, detaining and/or arresting political leaders, civil society members, journalists and human rights activists, censoring media, and imposing State of Emergency and suspending all civil rights. This 12-point understanding between SPA and the Maoists helped direct the public dissatisfaction with the royal regime and was followed by a mass revolt on 6–24 April 2006, with the protesters' main demand to the king to return power to the people. The people's movement became successful and the former rivals (the Maoists and the SPA) became allies. Then the new government was formed by SPA in late April 2006. On 16 June 2006, the SPA and the Maoists signed another 8-point under-standing to proceed further towards a negotiated settlement. The Maoists maintained ceasefire and stopped fighting. Both sides wrote formal letters to the UN calling for it to get involved in monitoring arms and military forces. The decade-long insurgency officially ended in November 2006 when the SPA government and the Maoists signed the CPA.

The main building blocs for the peace process were 12- and 8-point understandings, the 25-point Code of conduct (it was a ceasefire code of conduct agreed on 26 May 2006), the constructive mediating role of the Indian leftist political parties and their leaders (particularly the Communist Party of India (Marxist)—the CPI (M)—and its leader Sitaram Yechuri), constant international pressure and support for the peace process from many European countries, popular pressure on the Maoists for the peaceful resolution of the armed conflict and, the last but not the least, the behaviour of the king who had forced the SPA leaders to make alliance with the Maoists.

Prior to the signing of the CPA, the peace process went on relatively smoothly. However, since the finalization of the Interim Constitution on December 2006, tensions between the Maoists and the SPA have mounted, mainly due to the strong resistance on the part of some powerful SPA leaders (mainly the Prime Minister and members of his Nepali Congress Party) to further much expected political changes and reforms. These tensions continued to sharpen during the formation of the Interim Legislative Parliament and were reflected in the Interim Constitution. Many SPA leaders have not been ready to deliver on their promises made at the time of the popular uprising. Neither of the parties to the agreement fully respects its provisions. Hence, the situation is not conclusive and a possibility for re-escalation of violence persisted.

EXTERNAL DIMENSION

The Maoists made a strong effort to expand their international relations, especially since 2000 when the insurgency gained strength and the social agenda (equal rights to women, socially excluded people, marginalized people, addressing poverty and discrimination, and so on) advanced by the rebels was widely backed by the Nepalese people and international development agencies.

The Maoists had also created an international department to coordinate external activities and expand support base abroad. On 23 August 2003, the Maoists' 'foreign minister' C.P. Gajurel—a senior leader responsible for international relations—was arrested in Chennai, India, while flying to London on fake travel documents to rally for the European support to the Maoists' cause. According to Gajurel, the Maoists' supporters organized rallies in 35 countries to protest against his arrest, and to demand from the Indian government his extradition back to Nepal (Upreti 2006).

IDEOLOGICAL AND POLITICAL DIMENSIONS OF THE MAOIST INSURGENCY

The armed conflict in Nepal has had a strong ideological dimension. The rebels have been guided by the Maoist ideology and strategy (Tse Tung 1968). The Maoists considered the deep-rooted oppression as part of the feudalistic mode of socio-economic relations, unpopular and elitist power structures and monarchy as a system of governance to be the main problems and saw communism, rather than 'democratic capitalism', as a solution.

The Nepalese Communist movement was greatly influenced by both the Chinese and the Soviet models. As noted by Andrew Nickson:

> ...its leaders were strongly influenced by the international dogmas currently in vogue, which they mechanically applied to Nepali reality. In addition, Nepal's geographical locations as a buffer state between Tibet (which has been invaded by China in 1950) and India, which remained the major ally of Soviet Union in the region, means that foreign support for one or other faction was explained not simply by ideological factors, as in much of the Third World at that time, but more importantly by pragmatic consideration.

The result was the Communist movement split into a myriad of competing groups. (Nickson 2003)

The CPN (M) has ideological linkages with the following organizations.

RELATIONS WITH THE REVOLUTIONARY INTERNATIONALIST MOVEMENT

The CPN (M) has been a member of the Revolutionary Internationalist Movement (RIM) since it was founded in 1984 in London at the second international conference of the hardline Maoist parties from around the world. RIM, in turn, recognized and supported the Maoists insurgency in Nepal and, in fact, 'played important role in encouraging the Maoists to go ahead with their people's war strategy' (International Crisis Group 2007b). When the Maoists started armed insurgency in 1996, RIM issued a press statement entitled 'From the Andes to the Himalayas, people's war is the only way to liberation' and praised the armed rebellion in Nepal (Onesto 2000). In one of his interviews, the CPN (M) leader Prachanda (*nom de guerre* of Pushpa Kamal Dahal) revealed that there was a constant international involvement in finalizing the decision to launch the 'people's war' (Onesto 2000). RIM provided the Nepalese Maoists primarily with ideological and political support.

One of the most specific sources of inspiration for the Nepalese insurgency was the 'people's war' waged by the Peruvian Communist Party—Shinning Path (Sendero Luminoso). Among other radical leftist groups with which the CPN (M) established official relations has been the Revolutionary Communist Party (RCP) of the United States (Thapa 2003). Another supporter of the Maoist insurgency was the World People's Resistance Movement (WPRM). WPRM organized a series of meetings, presentations, workshops and interactions in Europe and other parts of the world to get support for the Maoists in Nepal. It had also arranged for the 'sharing of experience' between the Maoists in Nepal and the Communist parties of Bangladesh, Iran, Peru, the Philippines, Turkey, and Sri Lanka. According to the International Crisis Group (ICG), at the later stage of the armed conflict (since

November 2005 onward), WPRM also sent three groups of volunteers to work on the Maoist road building project in Rolpa District.[6]

RELATIONS WITH CCOMPOSA

The Maoists were very active in expanding their links and support base in South Asia. South Asian communist parties and other leftist organizations were inspired by the Maoists' success in Nepal and hoped to expand 'revolution' to the entire South Asian region (Sharma 2003). As a result, they formed the Co-ordination Committee of Maoist Parties and Organizations of South Asia (CCOMPOSA). The founding members of the CCOMPOSA have been the CPN (M), the Communist Party of India (Marxist-Leninist)/People's War Group, the Maoist Communist Centre, the Revolutionary Communist Centre of India, the Revolutionary Communist Centre of India (Maoist), the Communist Party of India (ML/Naxalbari), Purba Bangla Sarbahara Party (CC), Purba Bangla Sarbahara Party (Maoist Punarghathan Kendra), Bangladesh Samyabadi Party and the Communist Party of Ceylon (Maoist).

Later, however, both RIM and CCOMPOSA became dissatisfied with the strategic shift of the Nepalese Maoists from 'people's war' to negotiations for peace. The major cause for dissatisfaction were disagreements with the CPN (M) on how to translate the Maoist ideology into practice and to apply the classic strategy and tactics of the 'people's war' into the new situation. In contrast to RIM and CCOMPOSA, the Nepalese Maoists concluded that strategies and tactics of the classical Maoist 'peoples' war' need to be adapted and modified to succeed in the new context and therefore should not be followed dogmatically (International Crisis Group 2007b). RIM and CCOMPOSA opposed any such changes. Hence, the ideological tensions between Maoists and their international allies (particularly RIM and CCOMPOSA) have been on the rise once the CPN (M) changed its strategy from the revolutionary war to multi-party democracy and peace.

The Maoists in Nepal were getting moral, physical, and intellectual support from several communist parties and other groups based in India. A number of non-communist Indian scholars, such as S.D. Muni and communist politicians such as Sitaram Yechuri who supported the need for Nepal to become a republic, were also directly and or indirectly supporting Maoists' insurgency. Arms and ammunition were also sent to the Nepalese Maoists from India (Upreti and Nepali 2006). The effects of the Maoist insurgency could also be seen in Bhutan where some groups started to organize resistance to the monarchy. The Bhutanese autocratic regime blamed the Maoists in Nepal for supporting the radical groups in Bhutan. However, the link between the Nepalese Maoists and the Bhutanese Maoists is not clear. Some of the Bhutanese refugees who have stayed in the camps in Eastern Nepal might have become radicalized under the Nepalese Maoists' influence and transferred that influence across the border back to their homeland.

OPERATIONAL RELATIONS

Diaspora

The role of the Nepalese diaspora in the Maoists insurgency, especially in terms of generating financial resources, was weak compared to the role played by the Tamil diaspora in raising funds for the LTTE. However, some of the Nepalese working in India, particularly the poorest and the marginalized groups, were strongly supportive of the Maoists. The Nepalese and Indian media frequently reported examples of such support in terms of providing shelter to the Maoist leaders and cadres, supplying arms and ammunitions, organizing protest rallies and mass meetings in their support, fund-raising, and the like. In Europe, the Nepalese diaspora in Belgium, particularly in Brussels, played the most active role in raising support to the Maoists back at home. From Brussels, the émigré activists coordinated Europe-wide information and communication, political and fund-raising activities. Some pro-Maoist activity of the Nepalese diaspora could also be traced in North America, Australia and New Zealand.

The main difference between the role played by the Nepalese and the Tamil diasporas in supporting armed conflicts in Nepal and Sri Lanka, respectively, was ideological. The Nepalese diaspora was primarily formed by people from the poorest lower classes who were ready to back the Maoist insurgency at home to improve their own prospects, but were not able to raise substantial financial support due to their own poor economic condition. In contrast, the role of the Tamil diaspora in the conflict in Sri Lanka was primarily driven by ethno-nationalism (ethno-separatism). Both prosperous and poor Tamil emigrants supported the LTTE. As shown by the comparison between these two cases, ethno-nationalist ideology tends to serve as a more powerful driver for diaspora support to an insurgency than a leftist socio-political ideology.

HUMAN RIGHTS ACTIVISTS

International human rights and media activists advancing the rights of the indigenous peoples, farmers, women and the poor also helped to internationalize the Nepalese issue, to the benefit of the Maoists. Human rights violation in Nepal became one of the main international concerns regarding this country. Global and regional human rights organizations such as Amnesty International, Human Rights Watch, and the UN Office of the High Commissioner for Human Rights (OHCHR) vehemently raised concerns of human rights abuses by both parties to the conflict. As the human rights activists were meeting with the Maoists leaders to discuss the human rights issues and abuses, the Maoists tried to use these contacts to establish relations with international actors.

OTHER LINKS

Allegations about the Maoists' links with separatists in Indian State of Jammu and Kashmir or even with the Taliban in Afghanistan occasionally surfaced in both Indian and Nepalese media. However, the Maoists strongly denied any such accusations and no concrete evidences of such links were found. Indian police arrested some Nepalese in Jammu and Kashmir and filed cases against them alleging that these people are Maoist cadres engaged in arms transfers, but the Indian court later cleared the defendants of all the arms transfer charges.

MAOISTS MOVEMENT IN NEPAL AND THE NAXALITE MOVEMENT IN INDIA: A COMPARATIVE STUDY

Several parallels can be drawn between the Maoist insurgency of Nepal and the Naxalites in India in terms of ideology, logistics, characters, origin, social base, operational modes, organizational forms, and violent tactics. Both movements carry out attacks against politicians, government officials, large landowners, police and other security forces. In addition to assassination attempts, both also set up land mines to draw attention to their cause.

The origin of the Communist Party of India (Marxist)—the CPI (M)—that split from the Communist Party of India in 1964 is intertwined with the 'Naxalite movement' or Naxalites, a term that derives its name from the Indian town of Naxalbari where the peasant uprising started in May 1967 and was crushed within several months. The 1967 uprising was led by Communist rebels who became associated with the CPI (M). While the original uprising was quelled, the ideology and militant activity of this largely agrarian movement continued to spread over decades and by early 1970s has even expanded to include urban guerrilla activity in Calcutta. At the same time, the high degree of fragmentation of the movement facilitated government's actions against it. In the following decades, the main split within the movement had been the one between the communists who opted for a more peaceful, parliamentary tactics and the Maoists who emphasized armed insurgency (Banerjee n.d.). By the end of the 20th–early 21st century, the Naxalites have become one of the most active Maoist rebel movements in India. Several Maoist groups such as the Peoples' War Group (PWG), the Maoist Communist Centre (MCC), the Revolutionary Youth Forum, and the Parakala Dalam have been operating under the name of 'Naxalites' and have engaged in armed activity in nine states of India. PWG, for instance, is particularly influential in Andhra Pradesh and Bihar states.

The terms 'Naxalite' and 'Maoist' are interchangeably used in Indian literature. PWG had become the broad mass base movement with strong militant capabilities even before it merged with the Maoist MCC in 2004. Once the PWG and the MCC merged to form the Communist Party of India (Maoist) in October 2004, the CPI (Maoist) became the most powerful armed opposition force in India. The Indian union home minister, Shivraj Patil acknowledged this on 21 September 2004 in his address to India's ministers at Hyderabad. He noted the rapid expansion of the left-wing extremism in more than 149 districts of more than 12 of 28 states of India (Dasgupta 2005).

By the end of the 2000s, the Naxalites, once confined to West Bengal and Andhra Pradesh, have massively expanded to more than 16 Indian states.[7] The insurgents became major political players in Jharkhand, Orissa, and Chhattisgarh. A small insurgency movement started by Charu Mazumdar and Kanu Sanyal four decades ago (in 1967) in a Naxalbari village of West Bengal has expanded to one third of India. If the insurgency continues to spread for some more years, the control over the rural India may be seized by Naxalites who claim to represent the interests of the poorest, most marginalized, landless Indian peasants.

The rapidly expanding Maoist movement in India has posed one of the biggest internal security challenges to India. India's Prime Minister Dr Manmohan Singh acknowledged the severity of the growing threat of violent left-wing extremism by stating that the insurgency is 'the single biggest internal security challenge ever faced by our country' (Menon 2008). The security challenges posed by the insurgency cannot, however, be separated from its socio-economic background. While India is celebrating its economic growth under the slogan of 'Shining India', the accompanying—and growing—highly uneven regional and social distribution of economic growth and development leaves millions of Indians below the poverty line—a phenomenon that could be called 'Shrinking India'. The growing Maoist movement is one of the main manifestations of this 'downside' dimension of rapid economic growth.

The traumatic and painful modernization, wide social disparities, the widening gap between the rich and the poor, the concentration of control over economic resources and power in the narrow elite circles, in combination with high indoctrination and radical revolutionary ideology and strategy has provided fertile ground for the growth of the Maoist movement in India. For example, over 36 per cent of the tribal population of Chhattisgarh survive only by means of primitive economy, live in endemic poverty, and suffer from diseases such as malaria, while the government is largely unable to address these problems. Not surprisingly, the tribal population provides the main base of support to the rapid expansion of the Maoist insurgency in Chhattisgarh. The Maoist guerrillas have gained control over the area, established *Janasarkar* (people's government) and people's court (*Jana adalat*) and perform quasi-governance functions such as regulation of the prices of goods and services and even implementation of some development projects such as irrigation and cooperative farming. The Maoists want to export the Chhattisgarh model to other parts of rural India. The Nepalese Maoists had applied the same approach by forming people's administration and people's courts in the villages under their control.

Not surprisingly, the Maoist leaders in both India and Nepal tend to use similar justification for their respective movements' resort to armed violence. Explaining the main reason behind the insurgency, CPI (Maoist) Secretary General Muppala Lakshmana Rao (alias Ganapathy) noted:

> When we began the struggle it was a peaceful movement on people's issues such as land, livelihood and liberation from feudal and imperial exploitation and oppression... It was only after peaceful marches, rallies, dharnas,[8] hunger strikes, general strikes went unheard or were sought to be crushed, that people were forced to restore to violent methods. (Bhattacharjya 2008)

As in the Nepalese case, the strategic approach of CPI (Maoist) was strongly influenced by the Chinese revolutionary model, although it also built upon insurgent strategy developed by Charu Majumdar in early 1960s. Much like the Nepalese Maoists in 1996–2006, the Indian Maoists have adapted classical strategy of Chairman Mao to seize power by encircling cities and urban areas from rural areas. Among other things, this strategy implies that only after the Maoists gain sufficient control over large part(s) of the country, they can contest political power at the national level, by 'hitting on the head while standing on the body'. The Indian Maoists have also established People's Liberation Guerrilla Army in the same way that the Nepalese Maoists established People's Liberation Army. Both have recruited primarily unemployed rural youth (men and women of the age between 15 and 30) from the socially excluded, marginalized groups who were sidelined by the state for decades, provided military training to the recruits, and deployed them to fight against the state security forces. Both established village militia force to defend the areas against attacks by respective state security forces. Much like the Nepalese Maoists, the Indian Maoists have also applied tactics of psychological warfare. The massacre of 18 people in Chilkhari village of Giridih district in 2008, the attack at the Rani Bodli police post in Dantewada (Chhattisgarh), the assassination of a member of parliament from Jharkhand Mukti Morcha in March 2007, an attack on a branch of the Central Bank in Sitamarhi district are some examples.

The Indian Maoists appear to be encouraged by their own success, as reflected by the statement of the CPI (Maoist) Secretary-General Ganapathy at the 'Unity Congress'. He claimed that the Congress 'has resolved to advance the people's war throughout the country and wage a mass movement against the neo-liberal policies of globalisation, liberalisation and privatisation pursued by the reactionary ruling classes under the dictates of imperialism' (Menon 2008). In other words, as in the case of the Nepalese Maoists, the Naxalite movement is determined to increasingly shift from rural-based, classic guerrilla warfare to urban mobile warfare and to concentrate on industrial areas: as stressed by Ganapathy, 'time has come to spread in the towns and identify specific targets and with impunity' (Menon 2008).

In addition to apparent parallels between the Maoist insurgency movements in Nepal and India, there have been speculations about the alleged links between the Nepalese Maoists and other insurgent groups active in India such as the United Liberation Front of Asom (ULFA), the National Democratic Front of Bodoland, the Kamatapur Liberation Organization, the United People's Democratic Solidarity, the United National Liberation Front, People's Liberation Army, People's Revolutionary Party of Kangleipak based in Manipur, All Tripura Tiger Force, and National Liberation Front of Tripura. For instance, a senior ULFA leader Ghanakanta Bora was reported to claim, following his surrender to the Indian security forces in Tinsukia district of Assam, that the ULFA had some links with the Nepalese Maoists. According to media reports, quoting both surrendered rebel leaders and India's senior military commander in Assam:

> the ULFA have set up some bases in Nepal with the help of Maoist guerrillas and the outfit was preparing to shift a large number of cadres and leaders to the neighbouring country. We have been in touch with Maoist groups in Nepal and procuring arms, ammunitions and explosives for the ULFA... (*The Himalayan Times* 2007)

However, senior Maoist leader Dr Babu Ram Bhattarai vehemently denied any such links dismissing them as 'totally baseless'. According to him, the Nepalese Maoists 'do not know anybody from ULFA and...have never had any relationship with them at any point in the past. These allegations could have been made to try and derail Nepal's peace process and drag us into dispute'.[9] In sum, while the news generated some suspicions about such links, there was no concrete evidence provided, while the Maoist leaders in Nepal have persistently rejected these suspicions dismissing them as attempts by the reactionary forces to weaken the Nepalese homegrown resistant movement.

THE MAOISTS' STRATEGY TO DEVELOP EXTERNAL LINK

The Maoists in Nepal have long focused on developing relations with the international community. When they were able to go public during the ceasefire and negotiations in 2003, they made serious attempts to build their external links and 'international relations'. In his capacity as a leader of the Maoist negotiating team at the 2003 peace talks, Dr Babu Ram Bhattarai met several foreign diplomats.[10] The Maoists have established relatively good contacts with the United Nations and were occasionally submitting 'formal letters' to the UN. This 'international affairs' strategy has been developing in the following areas.

EXPANDING SUPPORT BASE

The international support to Maoists was primarily of the ideological nature and came from organizations of close or similar, that is, radical Communist, ideological orientation. However, the Maoists were relatively successful in expanding this support base to involve even a number of non-Communist researchers, journalists and left-wing activists who were sympathetic to their cause. In securing this support, they have also drawn on the backing from the Nepalese students and migrant labourers abroad.

GAINING PUBLICITY

Many of the non-Communist sympathizers, including the international media, have been perplexed with the reasons for the success of the Maoist insurgency in Nepal at the time of the loss of popularity and diminishing influence of Communist and other leftist movements, including armed groups, around the world—a phenomenon that guaranteed a certain level of international media coverage. The brutal repressive actions by the state against the Maoists and their support base reported by human rights organizations were another reason for growing international support and sympathy for the rebels.[11] International media played an instrumental role in expanding the

Maoists' support base by creating the image of an extraordinary, unique, and therefore, mysterious rebel movement. The Maoists' successful attacks on the government military forces and barracks have also generated interest among foreign journalists, politicians, analysts, and human rights groups. Some left-wing journalists such as Lin Onesto have spent considerable time with the CPN (M) in areas of their militant activity and have gained first-hand evidence about the movement to be published in the forms of news reports, articles, books, and so on (Onesto 2005). Many dozens of such books covering all aspects of the insurgency were published within and outside Nepal.

The issue of 'Red Notice' (that is, international arrest warrant) against the Maoists by the Interpol on 12 August 2002 generated even greater attention to and interest in the movement, especially within the foreign intelligence communities. The Nepalese government's announcement of 1–5 million rupees in bounties for the heads of the Maoist leaders on 23 April 2003 only added to the movement's growing publicity (Upreti 2004b). The arrest of the Maoist leader C.P. Gajurel in August 2003 has led to wide protests, including mass rallies, from the Maoist supporters and sympathizers across India. The media in India and Nepal, as well as the broader intentional media, widely covered this story. The Maoists also managed to use this arrest to gain publicity by organizing similar protest rallies in other parts of Asia and in Europe.

OBTAINING RESOURCES

Compared to the LTTE and some other insurgent groups, the Maoists were not able to generate much of external funding or other resources. As noted above, their external support base mainly comprised students and poor migrant labourers, some of whom were affiliated or sympathized with the movement or other left-wing groups and/or have suffered from the government repression. The few well-to-do members of the Nepalese diaspora were not known to provide any financial support to the Maoists. Some foreign-based former students affiliated with the Maoists' student organization were more active in generating resources for the movement abroad. The Maoists' finance and resource has thus been mainly domestic.

THE MAOISTS' CLASSIFICATION OF INTERNATIONAL ACTORS

While the Maoists' classification of international actors is not too explicit, it appears that they generally categorize these actors as 're-actionary', 'neutral', 'sympathetic', 'supporters' or 'cadres'. In line with this approach, the governments of the United States, India and some other countries that support the US position on the Maoists, as well as organizations such as NATO, the IMF, World Bank and the WTO, have been categorized as 'reactionary forces'. Apart from some 'neutrals' (countries like Switzerland and Norway were seen as neutral by Maoists), actors that have generally supported the Maoists' causes or at least some of these causes (that ranged from the abolition of monarchy to agrarian reform), but may not agree with the strategy and/ or tactics employed by the Maoists to achieve these causes, have been categorized as 'sympathizers' (most human rights groups, university and school teachers, and some 'sympathetic' journalists would have fallen into this category). Those who have supported the insurgency financially or morally were categorized as 'supporters', while those who took a direct and active part in expanding the insurgency (that is, in fund-raising, propaganda, communications or liaison activities) were upgraded to 'cadres'. These categories have been applied at both domestic and international levels. At the domestic level, the Maoists also used classical communist terminology to denote 'the enemy': 'imperialists', 'capitalists', 'feudals', etc. At the international level, they were more selective in applying this terminology.[12]

The Maoist strategy towards India and, to a lesser extent, other countries was based on their assessment of the respective countries' 'behaviour' (Bhattarai 2004). For example, the Maoists were even preparing to fight against the Indian forces in 2004 and were digging trenches across the country on an assumption that India would get involved in Nepal's conflict. However, these anti-Indian sentiments have made a 180 degree turnabout once India facilitated the process to reach the 12-point agreement that played an essential role in the fight against the king's coup in 2005–2006.

Following the 11 September 2001 terrorist attacks, the United States had taken a very tough stance towards the Maoist insurgency in Nepal: the Maoists, like most other groups that included terrorist means in their tactical arsenal, were compared with, if not directly linked to the al-Qaeda.[13] The US government had also provided the Nepalese authorities with military, political, intelligent and economic support to crush the rebels. US Secretary of the State, Colin Powel, visited the headquarters of the Royal Nepalese Army (that has now changed its name to the Nepalese Army), met the army generals, and discussed the role of military in suppressing insurgency. Army generals had briefed him on the armed conflict and pledged financial and other support against the Maoists. All US Ambassadors who worked in Nepal paid regular visits to the army barracks and brigades located in different parts of the country and advised the army on counter-insurgency strategies. Senior US army and intelligence officials frequently visited Nepal, to directly assist the government and to occasionally visit the Maoist influenced areas in different parts of the country to assess the situation and suggest possible strategies to the army. The Nepalese security forces have also received some counter-insurgency and counter-terrorism training from the United States (both in Nepal and in USA). The USA has also supplied arms to Nepal army. The US support to the Nepalese authorities in their fight against the Maoists further stimulated the rebels to develop closer relations with anti-American forces (Upreti 2006).

Likewise, in the aftermath of 11 September 2001, India also declared Maoists in Nepal to be a 'terrorist organization'. Indian forces regularly searched for the Maoist bases and arms caches on the Indian side of the border, strengthened border security with additional troop deployments and provided the Nepalese government with the largest external military assistance, including military equipment and helicopters, to crack down on the rebels. In response, the Nepalese Maoists have strengthened links with their counterparts in India.

EXTERNAL ACTORS WITH INTERESTS ON MAOIST INSURGENCY

As noted above, some external actors had no involvement in the conflict in Nepal and provided no direct support to either the government of the Maoists, but developed a special interest in the situation there. They were drawn to it by the very fact of a Maoist insurgency that managed to gain success within a relatively short period of time in an era when violent left-wing movements elsewhere in the world were either failing or abandoning their radical doctrines and methods. Journalists, researchers, activists, and politicians were frequently visiting Nepal to study the Maoist insurgency and the political situation in general and produced a number of reports, photographs, and documentaries. Many parallels were drawn between the Maoist insurgency and the militant campaigns by other communist/leftist movements active in different periods from the 1960s to the 1980s. The CNN, BBC, and other news services broadcasted series of documentaries about the insurgency.

The Maoists were sometimes reported to have extorted money from foreigners visiting the areas under their control. Sometimes they also issued warnings banning any visits to areas under their control to be made without their prior approval. However, unlike many other rebel groups, the Maoists have not attacked or killed a single foreigner during the 10 and half years of the armed insurgency. This approach may partly be explained by the Maoists' intent to distinguish themselves from a number of left-wing insurgent groups, such as those active in Latin America, who are known to abduct and kill foreigners. It was also meant to stress that it is the monarchy and the government, not foreigners that are their enemies.

THE MAOISTS' INTERNATIONAL RELATIONS IN THE POST-CONFLICT ERA

Nepal's foreign policy is greatly influenced by the policies of its two giant neighbours—India and China (Pandey 2005). Having signed the CPA in November 2006, the Maoists declared an 'equidistant' foreign policy towards India and China,[14] fully aware of the risk of being perceived to be associated with one or the other country. The Maoists' 'foreign affairs' person, C.P. Gajurel, argued that foreign policy should not be based on the geographical and language proximity, as well as religious and cultural similarities, alone. According to him, the decisive factor in formulating the country's foreign policy should be Nepal's 'national interest'. The Maoists have been apparently concerned about potential risks in case China perceives Nepal as moving to a closer alignment with India.

However, the fact that India played a crucial role in facilitating the 12-point understanding between the Maoists and the SPA cannot be ignored. India's support to this pact was to a large extent the result of the efforts by the Communist Party of India (Marxist) and its leader Sitaram Yechuri. The CPI (M) has been a powerful member of the coalition government of India and Prime Minister Dr Manmohan Singh decided to support the peace negotiations and democratic movement of Nepal in the interest of keeping the coalition together. As a close friend of the Nepalese Maoists' political leader Dr Babu Ram Bhattarai, the CPI (M) leader Sitaram Yechuri played an important role in drawing the Maoist leadership into the mainstream political process in Nepal. Since then, the Nepalese Maoist movement's relations with India have improved.[15]

However, the relations between the Maoists and the US Government have remained bitter even after the Maoists became part of the interim government of Nepal, as the United States has continued to view the Maoist movement as a 'terrorist organisation'. The former US Ambassador to Nepal, James F. Moriarty, actively lobbied against the Maoists and publicly declared them to be the main spoilers of the peace process and to remain engaged in terrorist activity. Among other things, he claimed that the US Government was 'optimistic that the Maoist would change their behaviour after joining the parliament', but was appalled by the behaviour of the Maoists members of parliament who 'threatened other lawmakers...entered the parliament with arms' and generally 'don't like mainstream politics'. According to Moriarty, 'cleaning a garbage from a park will not absolve one of crimes like abduction, extortion or physical abuse'. Referring to his 'desire to welcome Maoist leader to the mainstream by shaking his hand', the US Ambassador acknowledged that he would 'leave Nepal without doing so', citing the failure of the Maoists 'to renounce violence'.[16] Needless to say that the wording of this and other similar statements went far beyond the standard diplomatic discourse which explains the strong criticism that they have received from the Nepalese diplomats, international experts and the media who saw these statements as attempts to interfere in Nepal's internal affairs.[17] These attempts have, for instance, led a BBC correspondent to remark that 'the Bush administration has inadvertently achieved one thing—it has created community of distaste and fear that spreads form Wisconsin to Vladivostok, Kansas to Kathmandu'.[18] At the same time, it should be noted that, in contrast to the US Government official line, the former US president Jimmy Carter has met the Maoists' leader Prachanda on 15 June 2007 in Kathmandu during his four-day visit to Nepal as a mediator in the peace process.[19]

Many European governments (especially Switzerland, Norway, Denmark, Germany, and the Netherlands) have traditionally followed a softer approach to the Maoist insurgency in Nepal on the grounds that some of the Maoists' demands were genuine calls for the long overdue political and socio-economic reform. Some of the European ambassadors or representatives have been in contact with the Maoist leadership during the time of full-fledged civil war and tried to exert pressure on the Maoists to negotiate. The Maoists's relations with the UK have also moderately improved since 2006. For example, the UK Under-Secretary of State in the Department for International Development, Gareth Thomas, met Dr Babu Ram Bhattarai and Krishna Bahadur Mahara (the two influential Maoist leaders) on 4 April 2007 while visiting Nepal.

Following the signing of the CPA, the Maoists have also started to develop relations with China, with some success (while prior to the CPA, China's stance was a very cautious one and Beijing mainly confined itself to closely watching the activities of India and in the United States in Nepal).

CONCLUSION

On the one hand, there was some 'terrorist element' to the 10-year-long Maoist insurgency, as the rebels did sometime resort to asymmetrical terrorist attacks that were either targeting civilians and non-combatants, or were intentionally indiscriminate and were aimed at creating a broader political effect. On the other hand, the Maoists did not employ terrorist methods as their main tactic and terrorism did not play any decisive role in the armed conflict. The share of 'terrorist actions' in the Maoists' overall activity was far smaller than that of the political activity. The scale of terrorist activity in Nepal was also much lower, as compared to most other conflict areas where terrorism is employed as one of the violent tactics.

While the Maoist insurgency in Nepal is a clear example of a primarily homegrown movement that has mainly relied on domestic support and resources, the Maoists effectively supplemented their political strategy with efforts to establish, expand, and strengthen their external links with different categories of actors. These efforts were focused on (*a*) expanding support base at international level, (*b*) gaining broader international publicity, and (*c*) generating financial and other resources required to support their militant activity. The Maoists were most successful in gaining international sympathy and moral support, partly with the help of the Nepalese diaspora, but were far less successful in trying to generate external resources to support their struggle.

The Maoists' external links were the strongest in South Asia and Western Europe, as compared to other parts of the world. Ideologically, they also drew upon, refined, adapted, and effectively applied the 'people's war' strategy employed by Mao in China and later by a number of radical groups, such as Sendero Luminoso in Peru.

NOTES

1. See, for example, works by Ekaterina Stepanova who wrote: 'While the phenomena of terrorism is a multifaceted one and can mean very different things to different people, the tendency dramatically reinforced by the events of 11 September 2001, to use terrorism as synonym for almost all existing forms of violence in the world (from criminal and punitive to all forms of political violence) is a misleading and unhealthy one' (Stepanova 2006: 83).
2. For more detail, see Upreti 2004b.
3. See, for example, Raj 2004.
4. See, for instance, Upreti 2004a: 136–146; 2004b, 2006.
5. For more detail, see <http://nepalresearch.community/politics/background/maodem.htm>.
6. Once they establish their base or core areas (where state security force cannot go), they started rebuilding infrastructure to show that they are not anti-development. Hence, they started very big and ambitious road construction project in Rolpa, where the state was not able to make this road (International Crisis Group 2007b: 8).
7. In particular, the Naxalites are strongly present in the states of Madhya Pradesh (mainly in the Balaghat, Mandla, and Dhindoli districts), Bihar (mainly in the districts of Patna, Gaya, Aurangabad, Jamui, Khagaria, Banka, Jehanabad, Rohtas, Buxar, and Saharsha), Maharashtra (Chandrapur, Gadchiroli, and Bhandara districts), Jharkhand (Koderma, Hazaribag, Palamau, Garhwah, Latehar, Gumla, and Chatra), West Bengal (heavily affected districts are: Midnapore, Purulia, and Bakura), Orissa (Malkangiri, Koraput, Gajapati, Rayagada, Nowrangpur, and Mayurbhanj), Andhra Pradesh (North Telangana, South Telangana, Rayalseema, and many other coastal districts), and Chhattisgarh (Naxalites have a strong presence in Jagdalpur, Jashpur, Kawardha, Bastar, Kanker, Rajnadgaon, and Sarguja distrcits).
8. *Dharna* (Hindi) is a protest sit-in demonstration.
9. On the link between the Nepalese Maoists and the ULFA, see *The Himalayan Times* 2007.

10. However, the US Ambassador refused to meet with Dr Bhattarai. See, Upreti 2004b: 445.

11. During the insurgency (since February 1996 until April 2006), the state was responsible for the two thirds of all fatalities (over 13,200 deaths), while the Maoists were responsible for the remaining third. See, Informal Sector Service Centre (INSEC) 2007.

12. *Janadesh* (3 January 2006). Janadesh is an underground Nepali weekly which is their mouthpiece.

13. According to the U.S. Ambassador, the Maoists are terrorists, under the guise of Maoism or the so called people's war, they are fundamentally the same as terrorists elsewhere, be they members of the Shining Path, Abu Sayaf, the Khmer Rouge, or Al Qaeda.

14. The importance of equidistant foreign policy for Nepal has been repeatedly highlighted by C.P. Gajurel. See Gajurel 2007.

15. For more detail, see *The Himalayan Times* (11 June 2007).

16. This statement was delivered by Ambassador Moriarty in Pokhara on 12 June 2007 (*The Himalayan Times* 13 June 2007).

17. One of such criticisms came from a renowned Nepali diplomat, the former foreign minister, and ambassador to India and the UN, Dr Bhek Bahadur Thapa. For more detail, see Upreti 2006.

18. For more details on the U.S. policy, see Lak 2007: 10.

19. Former U.S. President Jimmy Carter visited Nepal on 13–16 June 2007 to assist the peace process. During his stay in Nepal he met with Prime Minister Koirala, the Maoist leaders Prachanda and Baburam Ram Bhattarai, CPN UML leader Madhav Nepal, the head of the United Nations Mission in Nepal Ian Martin, civil society leaders and diplomats in Kathmandu.

6

TRANSFORMATION OF KASHMIR'S INSURGENCY: *AZAADI* TO GLOBAL *SALAFI*

Jennifer Lynn Oetken

INTRODUCTION

On 3 December 2000, two Islamist militants attacked the security barracks at New Delhi's historic Red Fort, leaving three fort employees dead. The next day a Pakistan-based Islamist militant group, the Lashkar-e-Toiba (LeT), claimed responsibility for the attack.[1] The organization's objective, according to the LeT founder Hafiz Muhammad Saeed, was to initiate the expansion of the Kashmir *jihad* to the rest of India (Hussain 2007: 58). Prior to the 3 December 2000 attack, the LeT had been waging a war—since 1993—with the Indian government for Kashmir's accession to Pakistan, but had limited its operations to raids on Indian security forces and military installations. The LeT was subsequently banned by Pakistan, under United States' pressure, for its role in the 13 December 2001 terrorist attack on the Indian Parliament building.[2] However, today this terrorist group continues its armed struggle for the creation of an Islamic state in Indian and Pakistan-occupied Kashmir (PoK), India, and Pakistan.

The above incident provides a glimpse of the extent to which terrorism in Jammu and Kashmir has been internationalized since the indigenous insurgency and *azaadi* (freedom) movement began in

1989. This chapter attempts to explain the process by which terrorist organizations seeking to wrest Kashmir from Indian control have internationalized their efforts. While 'international terrorism' is commonly defined as 'terrorism involving citizens or the territory of more than one country', the chapter conceptualizes the internationalization of terrorism along several additional dimensions (Black 2004).

INTERNATIONALIZATION OF TERRORISM: THE KASHMIR EXPERIENCE

Terrorism initially takes on an international dimension not only when practitioners of terror cross state borders, but also when actors receive support from transnational sources. The internationalization of support could include financial contribution, training and weaponry provided by foreign governments or transnational organizations. Terrorist outfits that recruit foreign nationals also introduce an additional international dimension to terrorism. Second, terrorism could also become internationalized when activities are motivated or are guided by an internationalist ideology. An instance of such motivation could be the attempts of the global Islamists to create an Islamic state incorporating territory from various nation-states.

The internationalization of terrorism in Kashmir has progressed along three stages between the onset of the *azaadi* movement and the present day. The first stage is the emergence of insurgency and the *azaadi* movement, which was largely initiated by the avowedly secularist, pro-Kashmiri independence Jammu Kashmir Liberation Front (JKLF). This stage entailed a minimal degree of internalization as the JKLF militant group crossed into PoK in order to receive training and arms for its terrorist activities inside India-administered Kashmir. In the second stage, terrorism is increasingly internationalized as Hizb-ul-Mujaheedin (HuM) becomes the predominant terrorist outfit in the Valley. HuM not only based its headquarters in PoK and received support from Pakistan, but its goal for Kashmiri accession to Pakistan was motivated by a conservative Islamic ideology. In the third stage, terrorism became further internationalized as numerous non-Kashmiri terrorist organizations—under the genre of 'guest militants'—undertook a 'Kashmiri *jihad*'. While these groups were based in Pakistan, where they received tactical assistance, they also drew their recruits and funding from networks operating in Afghanistan, the Middle East, and even Africa. Furthermore, their terrorist operations were motivated by a radical Islamist ideology that promoted armed struggle against perceived western domination for the liberation of all Muslims and the creation of an Islamic state.[3]

In addition, and in order to account for the transformation of terrorism in Kashmir, the chapter seeks to identify several key contributing factors that facilitated its internationalization. In turn, the case studies that are being examined in the chapter are expected to contribute to a theoretical understanding of how terrorism is internationalized in similar contexts in other parts of the world.

FACTORS THAT ABET TERRORISM

Three factors emerge as particularly important when the internationalization of terrorism is considered. These can broadly be identified in the following manner:

First, state-sponsorship of terrorism, defined as 'a government's *intentional assistance* to a terrorist group to help it use violence, bolster its political activities or sustain the organization' (Byman 2003), has frequently been regarded as the cause of international terrorism (Richardson 2005). Pakistan has assisted terrorist organizations, both actively and tacitly, throughout the different stages of terrorist activity in Kashmir. However, it is important to distinguish between different types of relationships between terrorist groups and their sponsors (Richardson 1998). In certain instances, the state will actually commission violence; in others, it will support terrorist activities that serve its interests. States exert different levels of control over terrorist organizations and provide different types of support, such as money and equipment to groups, safe haven for members or supporters of the groups, and intelligence or other means of technical assistance (Badey 1998).

Second, the domestic politics of both the target and sponsor states may also be an important factor in the trajectories of terrorism (Crenshaw 1995). It is necessary to also consider the ways in which target states may unintentionally facilitate the internationalization of terrorism. Counter-insurgency policies that are too coercive or too moderate may provoke terrorist organizations to internationalize their activities, recruitment, funding and operations. Foreign policies, government attitudes and domestic events may contribute to international sponsorship of terrorist groups operating within or against the target state. Therefore, it is also necessary to consider how the domestic politics of Pakistan (outside of its sponsorship), and India may have influenced the internationalization of violence in Kashmir.

Finally, international events and trends may also be important contributing factors in the internationalization of terrorism. While localized events may serve to precipitate international terrorism, global trends can provide the overarching preconditions. Audrey Kurth notes that 'although individual terrorist groups have unique characteristics and arrive in local specific contexts, an examination of broad historical patterns reveals that the international system within which such groups are spawned does influence their nature and motivations' (Cronin 2002–2003: 34). In the case of Kashmir's insurgency, it is possible that the collapse of regimes abroad or the proliferation of extremist Islamist militant groups in reaction to the Iranian Revolution and the Soviet invasion of Afghanistan in 1979 played an important role in the transformation of terrorism in Kashmir.

STAGE ONE: THE JKLF AND THE *AZAADI* MOVEMENT

On 1 August 1989, the JKLF officially declared its armed struggle for the liberation of the Indian state of Jammu and Kashmir.[4] During the previous year, the group had initiated its violent revolt with the 31 March 1988 bombing of Srinagar's central telegraph office, followed by five attacks on security force personnel. In 1989, there were at least 49 attacks on police, and paramilitary forces, largely in the form of sporadic strikes on such security forces (Swami 2003: 63). Through these attacks, the indigenous underground *azaadi* movement allegedly sought to force India's secession of Kashmir, for the creation of an independent, secular and democratic Kashmiri state. While there are still no clear answers as to why the JKLF initiated hostilities between 1988 and 1989, it would seem that the timing was perfect in order to capitalize on the popular discontent that characterized the 1987 elections.[5] In combination with the years of political alienation and mistreatment, rumours that the election had been rigged by the governing regime—the Jammu and Kashmir National Conference and the Indian National Congress (I) coalition—served as a critical turning point for the Kashmiris' disappointment and disillusionment with the Indian government.[6]

In addition to casting blame on secessionist militants, Kashmir's Farooq Abdullah regime and the Central Government in New Delhi insisted that the upsurge in political violence was sponsored by Pakistan (Ganguly 1997: 103). Although the insurgency was in fact the work of indigenous Kashmiri militants, the governments' suspicions were not completely unfounded. Based on historical experiences it was not unlikely for Pakistan to play a role in Kashmir's popular uprisings. The escalation of both the 1947 and 1965 Indo-Pakistan wars followed Pakistan's attempts to instigate local rebellions within Kashmir.[7] However, the extent to which the Indian government was aware, at the time, of Pakistan's designs to sponsor another insurgency in Jammu and Kashmir is unclear.

According to former JKLF leader, Hashim Qureshi, Pakistani military representatives had approached his organization by 1984 to help the JKLF prepare for the new phase of 'Kashmir liberation' (Chadha Behera 2006: 148). After meetings were held between Pakistan's Inter-Services Intelligence (ISI) and the JKLF leaders in the summer of 1984, Amanullah Khan, the present leader, officially took over the operation (Swami 2007b: 163–66). In addition to allowing Khan to set up headquarters in Muzzaffarabad, the capital of PoK, a group of young Kashmiri men received training and arms in PoK for the liberation struggle between 1987 and 1989 (BBC News 2005). Four recruits, Muhammad Yaseen Malik, Ishfaq Majid Wani, Sheikh Abdul Hamid, and Javed Ahmed Mir—together known as the 'Haji group'—would lead JKLF's operations in Kashmir. By the end of 1989 JKLF attacks on the police, Central Reserve Police Force (CRPF), Indian intelligence, and the Congress party rendered almost all government administration and political parties dysfunctional (Chadha Behera 2006: 48).

The initial round of attacks generally failed to incite the mass sentiments of Kashmiris. Edward Desmond notes that by the end of 1989, Kashmir's 'citified middle class society was largely ambivalent, if not hostile, toward the movement because it threatened to upset' a more recent 'modest but steady increase in living standards, a booming tourist trade, and peace' (Desmond 1995). The Indian government also provided only scant attention to the growing insurgent activity as it was caught up in the Bofors scandals and the impending 1989 general elections.[8] However, the circumstances changed following the JKLF's 8 December 1989 kidnapping of Dr Rubaiya Sayeed, the daughter of India's home minister. Despite the Indian government's early capitulation to the terrorists' demands to exchange Rubaiya for five imprisoned JKLF militants, New Delhi took a decidedly more aggressive approach in early 1990. On 30 January 1990, the newly elected Indian prime minister, V.P. Singh, reappointed Jagmohan as the governor of Kashmir.[9] Jagmohan's strategy was to militarize the state and by February 1990, according to certain estimates, approximately 100,000 army, CRPF, and police personnel had been deployed (Schofield 2003: 150).

In the less than five months that Jagmohan was governor, Indian and Kashmiri security forces committed a number of atrocities. The most infamous was the Gawakadal bridge tragedy were over 100 people were killed as paramilitary troops fired on an unarmed crowd demonstrating against the previous night's house-to-house search (Schofield 2003: 148). Restrictions on individual rights and liberties, such as curfews, random searches, and unwarranted arrests characterized everyday life. By the end of spring, a mass uprising—comprising Kashmiri citizens—joined in the *azaadi* movement, echoing the demands of the JKLF through demonstrations, protests and rallies. However, to state that the JKLF was solely responsible for escalating the insurgency would be attributing too much credit to the terrorist organization. Clearly the government's ruthless counter-insurgency policy was an important reason for the mass mobilization of Kashmiri citizens demanding Kashmir's secession from India.

It was in this state of political decay that militant groups seeking to liberate Kashmir rapidly proliferated in the early 1990s. Former Governor Jagmohan lists 44 different terrorist organizations that he claims were active in the state by January 1990 (Jagmohan 1991). According to Amanullah Khan, in 1991 there were 60–70 militant groups operating in the Kashmir valley (Wirsing 1994: 132). The most significant were the HuM, the al Jihad, the al-Barq, the Ikhwan ul-Musalmeen and the al Umar Mujaheedin, most of which were conservative Islamist groups that supported and sought Kashmir's accession to Pakistan. With Pakistan's support they funnelled up to 20,000 recruits into training camps located in PoK by the mid-1990s (Swami 2007b: 177–178). These groups were largely built from the political cadres who had backed the Muslim United Front (MUF) in the 1987 elections. The MUF was a broad political alliance of Islamist parties, such as the Jamaat-e-Islami and the Ummat-i-Islami. It was also backed by less explicit Islamist parties like the Abdul Gani Lone's People's Conference and G.M. Shah's People's National Conference.

While the JKLF cadre had also supported the MUF, in several key respects its goals for the *azaadi* movement, and underlying ideology, ran counter to those of the Islamist, pro-Pakistan groups. According to their manifesto, they seek to reunite the Jammu and Kashmir state as a 'fully independent and truly democratic state' and advocate, 'equal political, economic, religious and social rights' for all citizens 'irrespective of race, religion, region, culture and sex'. Their ideology suggests that there is a distinct ethnic Kashmiri identity (*Kashmiriyat*), which is entitled to the right to self-determination (JKLF n.d.). However, the group's purported commitment to equality and secularism has frequently been called into question. The JKLF, particularly its top leader, Ishfaq Majid Wani, has been directly implicated in the assassinations of several influential members among the Hindu minority populations, the Pundits. A general terror campaign directed towards the Pundit community, in addition to the assassinations, resulted in the mass exodus of Kashmir's Hindus from the Valley (Swami 2003). Also, according to Praveen Swami, there was never 'any express JKLF condemnation of the welter of rapes and killings carried out on reportedly Islamic grounds during the phase of terrorism' that first started in 1989 (Swami 2003).

Despite the JKLF's association with communal politics and violence, many people in the valley supported its ideological commitment to Kashmiri ethno-nationalist separatism. This partially explains why the JKLF bore the brunt of India's new counter-insurgency strategy, contributing to the loss of its military ascendancy early on in the insurgency. Following the replacement of Jagmohan as Kashmir's governor, the new governor, Girish Saxena helped pass the Armed Forces (Jammu and Kashmir) Special Powers Act.[10] In accordance with this act, forces could search and arrest, and—if necessary—open fire without magisterial orders. The army, moreover, was immune from prosecution for conducting such counter-insurgency activity. Lethal force was frequently used against insurgents as well as peaceful demonstrators and torture was systematically used during interrogations.[11] Between 1990 and 1992, JKLF fighters made up the majority of the 2,213 terrorist deaths (Bose 2003: 128). According to a top JKLF leader, Sheikh Abdul Hamid, the group failed to maintain its prominence because it 'did not have a long-term military strategy because the leadership believed that they would triumph by arousing international pressure against India' (Desmond 1995: 3). Given that, during 1990, many of their top leaders had been imprisoned or killed, the JKLF ran into difficulties, and was unable to restructure their strategy.

The decline of the JKLF operations immediately paved the way to the military dominance of the explicitly Islamist secessionist groups, which would internationalize the aims and the military operations of the *azaadi* movement. In their ideological call for the creation of a 'unified Muslim community', they actively supported Kashmir's accession to Pakistan. Furthermore, by serving Pakistan's national interests, the Islamist groups—the HuM in particular—would become the benefactor of training, financing and weapons supply by the Pakistani military in PoK, Pakistan and eventually Afghanistan.

STAGE TWO: HIZB-UL-MUJAHEEDIN AND KASHMIR'S 'ACCESSION' TO PAKISTAN

At the onset of the Kashmiri insurgency, Pakistan was ready and willing to provide support to the wide array of 'liberation' groups seeking its military assistance. With the defeat of Soviet forces in Afghanistan on the horizon, the Pakistani military could afford to invest a portion of its ample resources to insurgent groups operating in Kashmir. From Pakistan's perspective they would not only help revive international attention for the Indo-Pakistan territorial dispute, but they could also be used to fight a 'proxy' war against the Indian authorities in Jammu and Kashmir. However, in an effort to maintain control over the insurgency, Pakistan would quickly alter its strategy for supporting terrorist groups operating in Kashmir.

Pakistan began by sidelining the JKLF, whose goal of Kashmiri independence clearly undercut the former's agenda to unify Kashmir with Pakistan. According to the JKLF chairman, Amanullah Khan, in the spring of 1990, the ISI started harassing its leadership, hijacking recruits and began pressuring its members to join the HuM or any of the smaller, ideologically aligned groups (Desmond 1995).

The JKLF have also stated that the HuM would kill their members and tip off the Indian security forces as to the location of their hideouts (Schofield 2003: 157). By 1991 the ISI had completely cut its aid for JKLF operations and in 1992 Pakistani authorities barred Amanullah Khan and his followers from entering PoK (Bose 2003: 126; Schofield 2003: 157–158). By the summer of 1991, Pakistan's ISI had devoted its full support to the HuM. As mentioned earlier, Pakistan had been providing resources to numerous Islamist, pro-accession groups that had rushed to its border at the onset of insurgency. However, Pakistan realized that it could not carefully control the insurgency through an abundance of splinter groups, nor did it make for an efficient militant stratagem (Swami 2007b: 178).

Of all the Islamist militant groups, the HuM was best poised to become the central militant organization in Pakistan's proxy war. Not only had its parent organization, the Jamaat-e-Islami Jammu and Kashmir (JIJK), been planning an Islamist movement in Kashmir since 1983, but it had also significant ties with Pakistan's Jamaat-e-Islami. In 1984, several Jamaat-e-Islami leaders, such as Ghulam Hassan Lone, Ashraf Dar, Ghulam Ahmed Azad, and Manzurul Islam, organized groups of young men from Jammu and Kashmir for training in PoK (Rana 2004: 437). On 1 November 1989, the HuM was created out of a combination of these various groups (Desmond 1995).

The HuM's rise to prominence in the Kashmir insurgency led to the next stage in the internationalization of terrorism both with respect to terrorist operations, ideological motivation and goals. Pakistan extensively sponsored the group's operations with arms—training and headquartering it in Muzzaffarabad. The ISI also facilitated the establishment of the HuM networks throughout Pakistan and PoK. For a period of time, the HuM also had training camps in Afghanistan, until al Badr took them over by force with the help of the Taliban Administration (Rana 2004: 446–447). While the HuM's cadre was mainly recruited from Kashmir, several hundred fighters are thought to have been trained in Pakistan, and in some cases gone on to Afghanistan to fight the *jihad* alongside the Afghan *Mujaheedin*. The group's networks have also been used to recruit non-Kashmiris in Pakistan, thereby introducing non-Kashmiris into their terrorist operations. Finally, within the Pakistani society and government, there are many Jamaat-e-Islami sympathizers who significantly contributed to the HuM fund-raising and recruitment (Rana 2004: 448–449).

The widespread support within Pakistan for the HuM, as well as additional Islamist terrorist groups that would enter the insurgency, need to be understood in the context of Pakistan's domestic political developments under General Zia ul-Haq. Following Pakistan's military coup in 1977, Zia's use of Islamic religious identity to consolidate power and legitimize military rule effectively led to the Islamization of Pakistan's political, social and military institutions.[12] The government actively promoted Jamaat-e-Islami party advocates throughout all the state's political institutions. Conservative religious education dramatically increased as the Zia government funded *madaris* with *zakat*, an Islamic tithe automatically deducted from bank accounts, and cut funding for government schools. General Zia also sought to Islamize Pakistan's army and the ISI, by making religious education a central component to military training. Promotion was no longer based on professional accomplishments but one's devotion to Islam, which introduced radical Islamists into powerful positions in the military-security establishment (Hussain 2007: 12–32).

The Islamization of Pakistan effectively created a support base for conservative Islamic organizations operating in Kashmir through all Pakistani social and political institutions. However, support for the ideological as well as secessionist agendas was unmatched by the majority of the Kashmiri population. In an effort to alter the discourse of the *azaadi* movement, the JIJK and the HuM engaged in a massive propaganda effort. They distributed publications and held public meetings and rallies in an effort to convince Kashmiris that, given their Islamic identity, the goal of the liberation struggle should be accession with Pakistan. Syed Ali Shah Geelani, JIJK's influential ideologue, published a series of writings that sought to discredit and displace the JKLF agenda. According to him, Islam forbids territorial nationalism, and therefore, the creation of an independent, secular state based on an all-Kashmiri nationalism runs counter to the religious beliefs of Kashmir's Muslims. Furthermore, Kashmir's accession to Pakistan supports the establishment of ummah based on common religious beliefs.[13] The JIJK and the HuM also promoted the creation of an Islamic state based on Shari'ah or Islamic law.

While the HuM did manage to significantly internationalize the overarching ideology and goals of the *azaadi* movement due to its military dominance, it continued to face difficulties mobilizing political support and recruiting native Kashmiris to carry out its terrorist operations. Its version of conservative Islam alienated many Kashmiri

Muslims in the Valley because it proscribed local Sufi practices, such as offering prayers at Sufi shrines and graves of Sufi saints (Chadha Behera 2006: 155; Bose 2003: 131). Additionally, many Kashmiris supported the JKLF's independence platform. According to the JKLF, in 1993 the group still retained 85 per cent of the people's support, a figure that has been corroborated even by HuM sources (Schofield 2003: 174). A significant degree of resentment developed towards the HuM not just for hijacking the *azaadi* movement for Pakistan's cause, but also because of the assassinations which they carried out, primarily of many high profile pro-independence leaders and JKLF supporters (Bose 2003: 131–134).

Nevertheless, the HuM remained the leading terrorist group operating in Kashmir throughout the mid-1990s. It directed the agenda of the *azaadi* movement by dominating smaller pro-Pakistani groups and keeping a strong hold on the All Party Hurriyat Conference (Hurriyat). The Hurriyat was established in February 1993 as a political alliance between 26 secessionist parties, as a mean to establish a degree of political legitimacy for their demands. Two political events of 1992 also increased support for the Islamist goals and ideology. Following the collapse of the Soviet-installed Najibullah regime in Afghanistan, many *Mujaheedin* from Pakistan and Afghanistan were ready to fight another *jihad* in Kashmir. Pakistan helped channel many of these Islamist militants into the HuM's various networks in India-administered Kashmir, PoK and Pakistan. The demolition of the Babri Masjid in Ayodhya, and the subsequent communal riots, in combination with an ever-growing Hindu nationalist movement inside India, mobilized Muslims throughout India and Kashmir.[14]

Following the HuM's rise to dominance in the insurgency, attacks on Indian forces dramatically increased to 3,413 in 1992; between 1993 and 1995 they hovered around 2,500 (Swami 2007b: 174). However, by 1996 a superficial quietude came over Kashmir. Armed conflict was less visible, now located mainly in the rural remote areas of the Valley and Jammu's Doda district. Two years earlier, JKLF leader, Yaseen Malik, had declared his group's cessation of armed struggle and desire to engage in political negotiations with all the concerned parties—India, Pakistan and Kashmir alike (Schofield 2003: 174). In 1996 attacks on security forces dropped to 1,432 and continued to stay in the low thousands until 2001 (Swami 2007b: 174). In light of the de-escalation in violence, the Indian government decided to reinstall a civilian government in Kashmir by holding both state-level and national-level elections. The Hurriyat boycotted the elections and demanded tripartite talks between India, Pakistan and the representatives of the *azaadi* movement. Their boycott failed and the election results brought the National Conference back to power and Farooq Abdullah as the chief minister of Jammu and Kashmir.

Amidst this attempt by the Indian government to quell the insurgency and establish some degree of political normalization, Pakistan increased its support for a new group of terrorist organizations committed to waging *jihad* in Kashmir. The emergence of the Islamist groups marked a new stage in the internationalization of terrorism in that their cadre consisted of non-Kashmiris who had been fighting Soviet occupation in Afghanistan. Furthermore, a radicalized version of Islam adopted among a transnational community of *Mujaheedin* would result in the transformation of Islamist groups' goals. Although initially these groups may have adopted a pro-Pakistan agenda, later their terrorist activities were driven by a larger global Salafi movement and would expand into India.

STAGE THREE: TRANSNATIONAL ISLAMIST TERRORISM IN KASHMIR AND INDIA

Frequently, the rise to prominence of Islamist groups in Kashmir during the late 1990s has been attributed to a deliberate strategy on Pakistan's part to marginalize the HuM—exactly in the manner it had conducted itself with the JKLF (Byman 2003; Chadha Behera 2006). However, there is little evidence to substantiate this claim. There is no indication that Pakistan's intelligence services withdrew the support it had previously provided the HuM, nor that its influence had subsided (Chalk 2001). This group's leaders have consistently chaired the United Jihad Council, which was created in 1999 by seven Pakistan-based Islamist organizations. Rather, Pakistan's strategic decision to sponsor Islamist terrorist operations in Kashmir must be understood in the context of Pakistan's role in international politics during the late 1970s and 1980s. In this light, the ways in which terrorism was increasingly internationalized is also better understood.

It was during this time that the state became the central launching point for the Afghan war against the Soviet forces that had occupied Afghanistan in 1979. Between 1979 and 1989, approximately 35,000 young Muslims from all around the world, particularly the Middle East, went to Afghanistan to fight the Soviet occupation. While this campaign was extensively funded by the Central Intelligence Agency (CIA) of the United States, and Saudi Arabia, Pakistan's ISI controlled the recruitment, training, and distribution of American weaponry to the Afghan *Mujaheedin*. Due to the Islamization process that had gripped Pakistani political, social and military institutions, Islam was integrated into the ISI's training manuals for the Afghan fighters. Many of the *Mujaheedin* had also attended Pakistani and Saudi *madaris* that taught a conservative and radicalized version of Islam (Hussain 2007: 16–18). The Afghan resistance movement had transformed itself into a global *jihad* against the communist enemy.

Following the end of the Soviet withdrawal from Afghanistan in 1989, a huge number of militarily trained and ideologically driven *Mujaheedin* lay at the disposal of the ISI. While Pakistan was motivated to use this mobilized force to carry out its regional interests in Afghanistan and Kashmir, it also sought to distance itself as a state that sponsored terror. In 1994, the ISI began 'privatizing' terrorism by establishing terrorist bases in Afghanistan, paying the Jalalabad Shura (warlords) to take charge of the bases and making various Islamist parties and organizations within Pakistan responsible for training and arming the *Mujaheedin* (Sood and Sawhney 2003: 34). They received religious training within conservative Deobandi[15] and Wahhabi Ahl-e-Hadith *madaris*, which instilled the belief that Islam required the liberation of all Muslims through violent and armed struggle. Young men from Pakistan and Kashmir desiring to fight the Kashmir *jihad* were trained and fought with Afghan, Saudi and other foreign nationals. Many of these foreign nationals would also take up the cause to unify Kashmir with the Islamic state of Pakistan.

The majority of the terrorist organizations involved in the Kashmiri *jihad* were created out of this international context and later Pakistani military's strategy to harness their potential. The most prominent groups were LeT, Harkat-ul-Mujaheedin (Harkat) (originally established as Harkat-ul-Ansar), and al-Badr.[16] In the year 2000 another extremist terrorist outfit, the Jaish-e-Mohammad (JeM), came into existence.[17] Initially their terrorist activities were not dissimilar to those of the HuM. The groups, particularly the LeT, would conduct raids on Indian police and security forces. The Harkat-ul-Ansar, on at least four occasions, abducted and held foreign tourists and security forces hostage for the release of their arrested leaders.[18] However, it was soon evident that these Islamist organizations had introduced new international dimensions to the terrorism in Kashmir.

During their training in Afghanistan many Islamist leaders established international connections with Islamist extremist organizations, such as the Taliban and the al-Qaeda. For example, Harkat leader, Farooq Kashmiri Khalil, signed the al-Qaeda's 1998 declaration of 'holy war', calling on Muslims to attack Americans and their western supporters. The LeT has endorsed the eradication of democracies on the basis that they were 'inherited from the 'alien' west' (Bedi 2001). In 1999, several Kashmiri 'freedom fighters' belonging to the Harkat hijacked the New Delhi bound Indian Airlines flight IC 814 from Kathmandu to force India to release three of its incarcerated leaders. This crisis laid bare the link between the group and the Taliban as the hijackers made their final landing in Kandahar in Afghanistan. Taliban soldiers guarded the plane with more than 155 hostages as negotiations were carried out (Hussain 2007: 61). Maulana Masood Azhar, one of the leaders released during the Indian Airline hijacking incident and the founder of the JeM, had extensive ties to Osama Bin-Laden. After his release, Azhar travelled to Afghanistan on several occasions to meet Bin-Laden, who is believed to have extended generous funding for the JeM (Bedi 2001).

The Islamists' ultimate allegiance to the greater Islamic struggle, as opposed to its Pakistani sponsor, was soon revealed during the Kargil war between India and Pakistan. In 1999, the Pakistan army's Northern Light Infantry dressed as irregulars infiltrated the Line of Control (LoC) in India's Kargil sector of Jammu and Kashmir's Ladakh area, partially in an attempt to reinvigorate the waning insurgency in Kashmir. While Islamists from LeT, the Harkat, and al-Badr also took part in the operation, the operation predominantly involved the Pakistani military. Furthermore, the Pakistan army had disguised its troops as civilians in an effort to spin the infiltration as insurgency of Kashmiri 'freedom fighters'.[19] When the Indian army discovered that well over 800 Pakistani troops had occupied key positions in the strategic heights of the LoC, it retaliated with intensive counter operations as well as limited air strikes. Once India quickly turned the tables on the Pakistani army and the United States exerted pressure on Pakistan, the Pakistan Prime Minister, Nawaz Sharif, was forced to call off the infiltration and demand that the troops withdraw (Ganguly 2001). The Islamist organizations involved in the operation were outraged by Sharif's order and viewed it as Pakistan's betrayal of the

Kashmir *jihad* (Sikand 2001). Earlier they had warned that if Pakistan asked them to withdraw under foreign pressure they would destroy the Sharif government (Schofield 2003: 211). According to the LeT chief, Hafiz Saeed, this marked the second phase of their operations when 'the *jihad* would spread all across Kashmir. It would spread to every peak, every forest and every path' (Schofield 2003).

After the Kargil war, it was apparent that the Islamist groups were no longer fighting for Pakistan's cause, but for a pan-Islamist agenda to liberate all Muslims from India. In November 1999, a few months following their withdrawal from Kargil, Saeed officially declared that the *jihad* was no longer limited to liberating Kashmir, but would be extended to the rest of India (Schofield 2003). This phase of the *jihad* was accompanied with a new terror tactic, the *fidayeen* attack. Similar to suicide terrorism, a heavily armed militant will gain entry into their target and fight until they run out of ammunition and are killed, in most cases, blowing themselves up along with ammunition that would take toll of the targets as well. The LeT initiated this deadly tactic in the summer of 1999, and perfected it in November that year when it attacked the Indian army's Corps Headquarters at Badami Bagh in Srinagar, killing several troops and officers (*Indian Express* 1999). Less than a month later, two LeT *fidayeens* launched their attack on New Delhi's Red Fort.

On 20 January 2000, Azhar's newly formed JeM joined the LeT in this new phase of *jihad*. The JeM was founded by Masood Azhar following his release from an Indian prison in exchange for the Indian Airlines flight hostages. In 2001 alone, the LeT and JeM carried out 29 *fidayeen* attacks against police, paramilitary and army camps, and government installations in Jammu and Kashmir (Bose 2003: 141). On 1 October 2001, the JeM attacked Kashmir's state assembly building in Srinagar by blowing up an army jeep filled with explosives outside the entrance, after which at least two militants seized control of the building (BBC News 2001). Despite the fact that Pakistan's president, Pervez Musharraf, denounced the attack as an act of terrorism, India warned that it would send troops into PoK and destroy the militant camps operating from the area (Hussain 2007: 104).

The Islamist groups brought India and Pakistan to the brink of war on 13 December 2001, when JeM *fidayeens*, with LeT assistance, raided the Indian Parliament building while it was in session—symbolizing an attack on the entire Indian nation. The next day India's foreign secretary demanded that Pakistan stop all activities of the

LeT and the JeM, arrest their leadership, and freeze their financial assets. Musharraf refused on the grounds that the proof of Pakistani involvement was inadequate and warned that Pakistan would retaliate if India took military action. Within a week India launched 'Operation Parakram', in which tens of thousands of Indian troops were mobilized near the LoC, in an effort to threaten Pakistan with military strikes if they did not stop sponsoring cross-border terrorism.[20] Pakistan responded in kind and the two states teetered on the edge of another international conflict. Under the threat of war and United States' pressure, on 12 January 2002, Musharraf placed a ban on the LeT and the JeM and detained up to two thousand of its members.[21] In June 2002, following additional Islamist attacks on Indian army barracks in Kashmir, Pakistan signed the Musharraf–Armitage treaty and pledged to permanently stop the infiltration of Islamist militants into Kashmir.

Initially, it was apparent that Musharraf was reluctant to completely cut off support to the Islamist militants. The initial ban on extremist groups did not apply to PoK or the semi-autonomous tribal areas bordering Afghanistan. This not only enabled militant organizations to shift infrastructure and cadres to these regions, but it provided a safe haven for hundreds of Islamist militants returning from Afghanistan after the collapse of the Taliban regime in December 2001, many of which were ready to join the *jihad* in Kashmir. Pakistan was also selective in its crack down on Islamist groups. Even after the US placed the Pakistani-based HuM on its list of proscribed terrorist organization in 2002, Pakistan was not willing to ban the group. According to Pakistan's interior minister, its illegal activities in Pakistan, or any other territory it controls, have been 'curbed'. Pakistan continues to stand by its position that the HuM is an organization of Kashmir 'freedom fighters' that functions in India's Jammu and Kashmir, therefore making a ban inapplicable (Reddy 2007). In 2003, Pakistan did 'officially' cut support for cross-border terrorism, which resulted in a significant decline in the infiltration rate across the LoC and the number of attacks on Indian security forces.[22]

However, it is difficult to determine the extent to which these groups have further internationalized their fund-raising, recruitment, weapons supply and training in order to maintain their operations. Islamist organizations continue to receive ideological and material support from Islamist hardliners within the Pakistani army and the ISI. Within Pakistan, they continue to have access to a reservoir of ideologically driven youth. Despite Pakistan's ban on terrorist organizations in 2002, these groups and their parent organizations are still able to carry out their operations underground or under the guise of a new name.

CONCLUSIONS: FOURTH AND FINAL STAGE?

Recent claims have emerged that the al-Qaeda is now operating within Kashmir. After the 11 July 2007 Mumbai mass-transit bombings, an Indian journalist received an anonymous phone call, in which the caller praised the attack, and proclaimed the arrival of a new militant group, Jammu and Kashmir al-Qaeda (Baldauf 2006). In the summer of 2007, a video recording was circulated among media organizations in Srinagar, stating that the first chapter of the al-Qaeda has opened in Kashmir (Bukhari 2007). Given past connections between Islamists and the al-Qaeda, the arrival of the al-Qaeda does not stand outside the realm of possibility, but the Indian government has yet to verify these claims. While this may indicate the beginning of a fourth stage in the internationalization of terrorism, two important questions remain: first, is Pakistan actually committed to permanently stopping its support for terrorist groups that are willing to fight its proxy war with India? Second, can terrorist organizations successfully operate in Kashmir without a degree of Pakistani support?

Based on the present analysis, Pakistan has not only provided support for terrorist activities and Islamist organizations throughout Kashmir's insurgency, but its sponsorship has also been the most critical factor contributing to the internationalization of terrorism. In the first stage, during the onset of the insurgency, Pakistan provided a minimal level of international support to the JKLF. However, its extensive sponsorship of the HuM's cross-border operations changed the ideological orientation of the liberation struggle. As the HuM came to dominate the insurgency in Kashmir, the overarching goal of terrorism was internationalized, in that it aimed for Kashmir's accession to Pakistan, and not the creation of an independent, secular and democratic state. The ideological orientation of terrorism in Kashmir was further internationalized as Pakistan began to more actively sponsor a variety of Pakistan-based Islamist organizations with international links to Afghanistan and other transnational groups. While initially these groups supported Pakistan's cause for Kashmiri accession, it soon adopted a pan-Islamist agenda—the liberation of all Muslims for the creation of a single, united Islamic state. As a result it extended the *jihad* to the rest of India.

The fact that Pakistan still regards Kashmir as essential to its identity as an Islamic state and strategically important territory, it is unlikely that Islamabad would completely cut off its support to terrorist outfits that continue to serve its national interests. This seems to be the analyses of the present, despite the fact that in a major shift from Pakistan's long-standing position, Pakistan People's Party chairman, Asif Ali Zardari, whose party (at the time of writing in end February 2008), is set to take over the reins of the country, has expressed his readiness to set aside the Kashmir issue to focus on other aspects for improving relations with India. Indeed, the aftermath of the February 2008 elections, Pakistan has witnessed violence, perpetrated by Islamists. Furthermore, the legacy of political and social Islamization, and Pakistan's involvement with the Afghan war has wedded hardliners within the army and the ISI to conservative Islamist organizations and the Islamist groups they sponsor. Islamist groups continue to infiltrate the LoC and carry out terrorist attacks irrespective of the injunction issued by the Pakistan army's Major General Khalid Mahmood to terrorist leaders to end all cross-border operations (Hussain 2007: 111–112). While the groups to a certain extent operate on their own, the ISI has always maintained tight control over such groups. The agency provides Islamists with training camps, access to weaponry and funding. While these groups have received sizeable contributions and donations from foreign sources (primarily Saudi Arabia), the ISI is responsible for funnelling such money into Pakistani bank accounts that are opened under the auspices of political, religious and charitable fronts (Chalk 2001). Therefore, it is believed that even a scaled-back terrorist operation in Kashmir require some level of coordination with the Pakistani army and intelligence services. Regardless of Pakistan's claim that it is impossible to completely seal the Indo-Pakistan border, infiltrators must still travel via routes guarded by the Pakistan army, which suggests a degree of institutional consent (Swami 2007a).

Musharraf's ability to maintain his political power in Pakistan is also affected by the support he receives from the Islamist groups. On several occasions, government leaders and Musharraf himself have been targeted by these groups. On 14 and 25 December 2003, two assassination attempts were carried out against Musharraf. Pakistani authorities believe that Islamists, particularly the JeM cadre, carried out the attacks in response to his policy that denies protection to the remaining al-Qaeda and the Taliban forces fighting against the United States led-coalition and the new policy stance on Kashmir. Furthermore, the military-security establishment is also thought to have played a role in the assassination attempts, as the attack on his heavily guarded motorcade could only have occurred with the aid of the military, paramilitary, the police, and the intelligence agency (Reddy 2004).

More recent events further demonstrate the inability of Musharraf's government to control Islamist terrorism and violence within its own borders. During the second half of 2007, Pakistan witnessed a dramatic increase in suicide terrorism—52 acts of terrorism are said to have occurred during this time period (Raman 2008). The escalation in violence appears to be a backlash against the Pakistani military raid on the Lal Masjid in July 2007 after students barricaded themselves in the Mosque (Behuria 2007). The assassination of Pakistan's former Prime Minister Benazir Bhutto on 26 December 2007 further aggravated the situation. Although a teenage boy was arrested on suspicion that he was involved with the assassination, it is not yet clear as to which organization is responsible for the act.[23] The youth has connections to the Tehrik-e-Taliban, a terrorist network from South Waziristan, headed by Pakistani Taliban leader, Baitullah Mehsud. However, as was the case in the Musharraf assassination attempts, questions of whether the ISI played a role in Bhutto's killing continue to linger (*The Times of India* 2008a). In any event, it would be interesting to watch the developments in a post-election Pakistan.

Finally, India's role in the internationalization of Kashmir's terrorism also needs to be assessed. The Indian government's history of the political mishandling of Kashmir, as well as its brutal counter-insurgency policies, did provide the pretext for Kashmiri secessionists to look towards Pakistan for military assistance. In fact, former Jammu and Kashmir governor, Jagmohan, holds that New Delhi's use of brute force to deal with the crisis is the reason that enabled separatism to gain real headway in 1990. The success of Pakistan's sponsorship of terrorism was subsequent to India's failure (Wirsing 1994: 115). In the later stages it is also possible that the rise of Hindu nationalism, particularly the demolition of the Babri Masjid, provided mobilized support for the Kashmir *jihad*, and later to liberate all Muslims from India. As Praveen Swami states: 'The failure of successive Indian governments to vigorously defend its secular culture had tragically contributed to the nightmare it now confronts' (Swami 2003: 85).

NOTES

1. In 1990, LeT was established in Afghanistan as the military wing of Markaz-ud-Dawa-wal-Irshad (MDI), an Islamist fundamentalist organization. MDI is affiliated with the Wahabi Ahl-e-Hadith sect of Pakistan.
2. On this day terrorists attacked the Indian parliament with explosives and AK-47 rifles. Nine policemen, a parliament staffer, and five terrorists were killed in the attack. For further information, see (Embassy of India 2008).
3. Praveen Swami aptly notes that there are 'considerable continuities of thought and action which cut across organizations', in Swami 2003: 56. However, it should be noted that breaking down the internationalization process into stages is not only theoretically useful, but also provides analytical clarity when describing the complex history of terrorism in Kashmir. Nevertheless, the contributor will attempt to account for these continuities at various points in the chapter.
4. It should be noted that the JKLF came into being as early as 1971, when one of its operatives, Hashim Qureshi, hijacked an Indian Airlines plane and commandeered it to Lahore.
5. Swami notes that even by 1989 the JKLF was still unprepared for an armed engagement with the Indian state (Swami 2003: 63).
6. For a detailed analysis of the structural and proximate causes for the insurgency, see Ganguly 1997.
7. For a detailed account of the 1947 and 1965 wars, see Brines 1968.
8. In the late 1980s the Indian prime minister, Rajiv Gandhi was caught up in a series of corruption scandals, including his alleged acceptance of kickbacks from the defence contract from the purchase of Swedish field artillery pieces, the Bofors 155-mm howitzers.
9. Farooq Abdullah immediately resigned as chief minister alleging that Jagmohan had dismissed him as chief minister during his first governorship and because he believed Jagmohan to be anti-Muslim.
10. Jagmohan was replaced following the assassination of Mirwaiz Maulavi Farooq and the incident were CRPF officers opened fire on his funeral procession, killing dozens of innocent civilians. The Mirwaiz is perhaps the most important hereditary and respected Muslim religious figure in Kashmir. While his assassin is unknown, blame has been apportioned to both the Indian government and the HuM.
11. For a comprehensive study on Hizban rights violations in the early part of the crisis see, Hizban Rights Watch and Physicians for Hizban Rights 1993.
12. For a thorough account of the political radicalization of Islam in Pakistan, see Abbas 2005.
13. For an insightful discussion of Geelani's writings and philosophy see Chadha Behera, 2006.
14. The Babri Masjid is a Muslim mosque that is believed by many practising Hindus to have been erected on the exact spot where the Hindu god Rama was born. In the

1980s, the Bharatiya Janata Party (BJP) and the Rashtriya Swayamsevak Sangh (RSS) used it as a political rallying point to gain support for the Hindu nationalist cause. For more details, see Hardgrave and Kochanek 2000, pp. 189–192.

15. It must, however, be noted that the Dar-ul-Uloom denounced all acts of terror as unislamic, severing its umbilical cord with the Islamist brand of Islam propagated by the Taliban and others claiming to follow the Deoband school's teachings (*The Telegraph*, 26 February 2008).

16. Harkat-ul-Ansar was banned by the United States in 1997 due to its association with Osama Bin-Laden.

17. For complete descriptions of these terrorist organizations and their activities, see Rana 2004.

18. See, South Asia Terrorist Portal, available at http://www.satp.org/satporgtp/countries/india/states/jandk/terrorist_outfits/harkatul_mujahideen.htm.

19. For a thorough account, see Malik 2006: 94–97.

20. For a detailed account of Operation Parakram, see Sood and Sawhney 2003.

21. For an excellent analysis of the limitations of India's coercive diplomacy in meeting demands of the Pakistani government, see Ganguly and Kraig 2005.

22. While the figures vary on the actual number of infiltrations and attacks on security forces, all show a significant downward trend. See for instance, *Kashmir News* 2007.

23. See *Times of India* 2008b. It should also be noted that initially after Bhutto's assassination, Adnkronos International (2007) reported that a spokesman for the al-Qaeda terrorist network called the news agency and claimed responsibility for the killing.

Part Two

INTERNATIONALIZATION OF TERRORISM: REGIONAL AND GLOBAL THEATRE

7

CIRCLE OF DESIGN: 'PROXY WARS' IN NORTH EAST INDIA

Jaideep Saikia

INTRODUCTION

The proximity or vulnerability to alienation is an important aspect that determines the geo-strategy of a region. The vulnerability to alienation, in this context, entails proximity to 'outer lands', which although not overtly hostile, possess a measure of, or potential for, sustained outward subversion. Indeed, if this theory is to count as being even minimally correct, then the fact that the northeast of India[1] explicitly qualifies as a region of strategic importance, and as a result the security considerations of the region, threatened by way of the strategic encirclement,[2] cannot be glossed over. This is despite the fact that the region is sometimes considered to be inconsequential to India's geopolitical colossus, a distant outpost of a forgotten empire.

At any rate, the peripheral nature of the region has not driven New Delhi to follow the policy that had prompted the British to occupy the region in 1826, with the Treaty of Yandaboo[3] that was concluded between the Burmese and the British, whereby *on 24 February 1826 the King of Burma 'renounced all claims' upon, and agreed to 'abstain from all future interference with the principality of Assam and its dependencies'* (Barpujari 1992). The region, despite its non-homogenous character,[4] has also been provided with an amalgamated identity, and is both recognized and governed by New Delhi as a single entity. The term

'North East', therefore, is not only a geographical identity that has been artificially created, but also one that drives New Delhi's political, economic and security policies for the region.[5] But, the differences between the various states that make up North East India are apparent: an Angami of Nagaland has as much in common with a Bodo of Assam as would a Ukrainian with a Georgian, despite the fact that—in common comprehension—both an Angami and a Bodo are tribals, just as, in the case of the comparison that is being made, the Ukrainian and the Georgian once belonged to a single political entity, namely the Union of Soviet Socialist Republics. Such indistinct notions have also provided the region with a character of a 'security zone', much of which is a result of New Delhi's policy towards the bordering nations, propelled, to a considerable extent, by a sense of circumspection, and the need, consequently, to create a buffer zone.

It must also be noted that the cautious outlook towards the region is also because of the impressionistic comprehension in New Delhi about North East India. For instance, the appearance, culinary tradition, attire and custom of much of the region, when exhibited in New Delhi or the rest of India, seem alien to the mainstream Indian. At times, the population from the northeast in the metropolitan cities of India is collectively and derogatively termed as 'chinkies'.[6] Such aspects have also led to alienation. The social mosaic that make up the region is derived from movements of people from a variety of regions: the rulers of medieval Assam, the Ahoms, for instance, came from across the Patkoi mountain range and the Irrawady river from the Shan states, and the region bears a modicum of social affinity with the peoples of South East Asia. In fact, the movement from the east took place in the medieval era, with the arrival of the Ahoms. Therefore, while it is important to comprehend the socio-cultural innards that characterize North East India, and the ways in which these differ from the rest of India, it is also important to refer to the important socio-cultural and historical connections between the region and the rest of India. After all, most of Assam, and the plains of Manipur and Tripura have been Hinduized, with the forebears of the present caste Hindus in Assam owing their origins to places such as Kanauj in the Indian mainland. But, apart from a former governor of Assam, Lt Gen. (Retd) S.K. Sinha, who attempted to highlight the ancient, medieval and modern day links between the two, New Delhi has done almost nothing to assimilate the region into the greater Indian ideal, and has certainly not made any efforts to include North East India into its nation-building enterprise. Indeed, unrest has erupted in the region largely because of the insensitivity of New Delhi towards the region. Furthermore, it would not do to thrust upon the region an ideation of nationhood without allowing a mature passage of time. New Delhi must understand that there is similarity in the religion, and even the culture that have been adopted by the indigenous people of the region. But it has all but turned a blind eye to this important aspect. Indeed, there are aspects in the socio-religious practice in the region that have distinct indigenous flavour, but that is not tantamount to stating that there are no commonalities. Indeed, it is such similarities that must be highlighted, and far-sighted personages such as Lt Gen. (Retd) S.K. Sinha sought to incorporate this aspect, and place a state like Assam on the Indian stage. But, with his exit, the exercise fell through, and at the time of writing, the divide between the northeast and the rest of India (primarily New Delhi) has grown. Insurgent organizations like the United Liberation Front of Asom (ULFA) and certain Karbi, Dimasa, and Manipuri groups have become conscious of the increasing chasm, and are beginning to target Hindi-speaking people in the region, perhaps because such actions do not necessarily raise the heckles of the indigenous people, attracting instead the attention of New Delhi that the insurgents seek. The new generation has also noticed the attitude of New Delhi and the insurgents. While the racial profiling approach of mainstream India has had an effect on the victims, the victims in turn are becoming radical and anti-Indian, not necessarily by taking recourse to the gun, but by demanding autonomy, redressal of problems such as unemployment, the institution of discriminatory and 'draconian' acts, centrist condescension, and corruption. In certain parts of North East India, earlier Hinduized populations are beginning to retrace their roots to their age-old ancestry. This is becoming evident with certain members of the younger generation adopting names that indicate their earlier identities.

The demographic invasion is another explanation for the insurgency and unrest in North East india. One of the primary reasons for the emergence of insurgency movements in Tripura and Assam is the demographic invasion from Bangladesh that has overwhelmed Tripura, and is close to transforming Assam's population pattern.[7] It has become the considered opinion of the people of the region that not only is New Delhi disinterested in containing the illegal migration that is endangering the indigenous identity, but also certain national political parties are actually encouraging the process in order to utilize the illegal migrant population as vote-banks. Among the slew of protests that are being raised is the fact that while the border between Pakistan and India-administered Kashmir and Punjab can be fenced (in order to prevent infiltration) in record time, the border between India and Bangladesh is yet to be completed despite the fact that it began much earlier. The conspiracy of vote-banks, New Delhi's insensitivity and even a reported security force-migrant mafia nexus in the border that reportedly goes up all the way to New Delhi, and one which economically benefits from the illegal migration are reasons that keep the region aflame. Of course, the attendant problems of unemployment, lack of development, and socio-political desertion add to the sense of neglect.

But, in all fairness, at least the guarded policy that typifies New Delhi's policy of perceiving the North East India as a 'defence zone' not only has a history, but also—as was stated in the opening sentences of the chapter—a reason, because the 'encircling nations' have displayed, at some point in time or the other, the potential for subversion of this strategic region. Furthermore, the partition of the subcontinent consigned the northeast to the periphery, connecting it to mainland India only by a tenuous 22 km long corridor situated near Siliguri.[8] Indeed, North East India shares only 2 per cent of its boundary with India, the rest 98 per cent of its borderlands abut alien lands that surround it in a strategic embrace. Such aspects, as also the fact that, 'as the crow flies, the region is closer to Hanoi than to New Delhi' (Hazarika 1994: xv), perhaps also aids the perception of North East India as an 'outland'.

Therefore, the realities that divide mainland India from the northeast are striking. Inimical forces that have encouraged separatism, insurgency, and terrorism in the region have utilized the opportunities that have led to the alienation, and have not lost an opening to 'fish in the troubled waters'. It must also not go unrecorded at this juncture that the fires of separatism and insurgency have certain legitimate historical basis, as in the case of Manipur which was annexed by India without due process. Economic and socio-cultural alienation—compounded after independence by the geographical distance—contributed to the estrangement. Indeed, with the possible exception of Kashmir, and to a certain extent the northern and western parts of Bengal, no other region in South Asia provides the prospect that North East India provides to hostile forces. The 'proxy war' phenomenon must be understood from this perspective as well. It is not a matter in doubt that countries such as China, Pakistan, and Bangladesh have used the aspects that separate the region from the rest of India to further the divide.

POLITICS OF PROXY

After the independence of India, and the accompanying division of the subcontinent, the countries in the region have been at war with one another. However, apart from a few 'limited' or comparatively short-scale wars,[9] the conflicts have been that of 'proxy wars', namely the sponsorship of insurgencies and terrorist groups to bleed, pester and humiliate one another. Providing insurgents or terrorists of an enemy country with safe havens, arms, training, and the like, is a phenomenon that is embedded in the post-colonial state policy and diplomacy of South Asia. The countries in the region have fought shy of engaging one another in protracted wars—of the sort Iraq and Iran were engaged in during the 1980s—but they have not concluded peace as well. Analysts have argued that 'proxy wars' in the region makes up the grey area between war and peace, and sponsorship of insurgency and terrorism has been the preferred policy alternative for the post-colonial nation-states in South Asia. According to Subir Bhaumik, 'South Asia possesses ideal conditions for sponsored insurgencies—its constituent parts are incomplete and artificially formed nation-states consisting of ethno-religious groups in uneasy cohabitation and has also witnessed a certain institutionalization of the phenomenon' (Bhaumik 1996). Indeed, scholars are of the opinion that South Asia even possesses a tradition of 'proxy wars', with reference in ancient history to Chanakya's[10] advice to his Emperor that a 'war of attrition' against a foe is more effective than a full-fledged war. As aforesaid, in the case of the Iraq–Iran wars, South Asian nations do not have the economic wherewithal to wage long drawn wars; a couple of months of full-scale war would exhaust the countries and take the economies back by years. The countries in the region are aware of this aspect, and have, therefore, adopted Chanakya's prescription of the more effective way to wage war against an enemy: a 'low-cost offensive posture', or war by proxy.

Therefore, even as Pakistan continues to support the terrorist groups in Kashmir, Bangladesh has become the most important 'bureau' of Pakistan's Inter Services Intelligence (ISI) in the region. It is from its erstwhile eastern wing that Pakistan launches their covert operations in India's mainland and North East India. Pakistan's sustenance and aid to the insurrection in Kashmir has already been documented in Chapter 6. It would suffice, therefore, to inform further that Pakistan has 'activated' a second front against Kashmir, from Bangladesh, in order to pin down Indian security forces in North East India from being deployed in Kashmir. Also, the violence that has erupted in India, particularly after 9/11 has indisputably proven the hands of Islamist groups of both Pakistan and Bangladesh, with active support from their respective intelligence agencies. This has become evident from confessional statements of apprehended and surrendered Islamist cadres in Assam.

Indeed, in the case of South Asia, countries have attempted to settle scores by taking advantage of the insurgencies in the rival countries. The distinctive aspect that characterizes this phenomenon is the response that nation-states provide. The region's geopolitics is defined to a considerable extent by reciprocal patronage of insurgencies over sustained periods of time, and at times, as was the case when India supported East Pakistan's freedom fighters, by embarking on a full-scale military intervention. Only countries such as Sri Lanka, Bhutan, Maldives, and Nepal have more or less refrained from entering into the game of 'proxy war'. But, the other countries of the region, namely Pakistan, China (a key factor in South Asia), India, and Bangladesh have almost perfected this into a near-acceptable form of offensive diplomacy. Therefore, if Pakistan aids the global *Salafi* movement in Kashmir, India had supported the 'Mukti Bahini' (freedom fighters) in Bangladesh, ensuring primarily that a hostile Pakistan is rid of an eastern flank. Also, if India backed the Amdo and the Khampa insurgents against Chinese occupation of Tibet in the past, the Chinese responded by aiding the North East Indian insurgent organizations. If Islamabad backed the Khalistan groups in Punjab, and later organizations such as the National Socialist Council of Nagalim (NSCN) and the ULFA, New Delhi reportedly backed the Mohajir outfits in Pakistan's Sind province. Indeed, even the unrest that had gripped China's Tibet Autonomous Region during the run-up to the Beijing Olympics in March 2008 might have been facilitated by a 'look-the-other-way' option of India, even as it allowed the United States to embarrass Beijing during a crucial period for China. It is also possible that New Delhi seized an opportunity and, thereby, embarked on such a course of action because it wanted to send a message to Beijing to stop making statements that pertained to its purported claim over India's Arunachal Pradesh. It is such action that illustrates the ways in which 'proxy wars' are waged in South Asia. The 'strategic encirclement' of North East India and the attendant problem of New Delhi's insensitivity has made the region into a veritable 'proxy war' playfield.

THE NORTH EAST INDIAN SCENARIO

The Naga insurgents were perhaps the first to seek and receive aid from a foreign country. Subir Bhaumik writes:

> The Naga insurrection, brewing since the unilateral declaration of independence by the Naga National Council a day before India gained independence, became more intense in the later 1950s. Pakistani support materialized immediately after the Naga National Council leader, Angami Zapu Phizo, crossed over to East Pakistan in December 1956; just after the Naga militants had taken to armed struggle. Pakistan continued to support the underground Naga movements...The Pakistani also negotiated Chinese aid, in training and equipment, for the Nagas after the 1962 Himalayan border war left Peking momentarily hostile towards New Delhi. (Bhaumik 1996: 31–32)

Nirmal Nibedon, perhaps North East India's finest chroniclers of conflict, records the Naga group's arrival in People's Republic of China. He writes:

> ...some time in January 1967, Thinsolie and Muivah with their tired men reached Yunnan. They were surrounded by 'tall' Chinese soldiers. 'We have come from Nagaland for training. Your leaders know about our coming.' The Chinese received them as credentials were checked. Someone remarked: 'How can you short men fight a mighty nation like India?' 'Major' Tangti Ao looked back defiantly. He was only five feet tall! (Nibedon 1983: 167)

Forty-one years have passed since the Chinese soldier made that sarcastic comment, but New Delhi is no closer to arriving at a solution with the Nagas, although a ceasefire was signed on 25 July1997, completing almost 11 years. Indeed, it is the Naga groups—primarily the National Socialist Council of Nagalim (Isaac–Muivah: NSCN-IM)—that are (despite the ceasefire) making the presence felt not only in Nagaland, but also in Arunachal Pradesh, Assam, and Manipur. The international linkages that had been engineered with the arrival of the Nagas in China after an arduous 97 day trek have survived—if no longer in Yunnan, then certainly in the NSCN (IM) camps in Bangladesh such as Galilee, Ruma, Barchari, Mahmuan, Salopi, and Tindu forest. It may also be noted that the NSCN (IM) has started providing a different dimension to its internationalization programme by bringing in a foreign agency called *Kreddha*, a Netherlands-based non-governmental organization, which is going to be instrumental in conceptualizing a framework of relationship between the Indian government and the Nagas on the areas of convergence, divergence or joint control. It is interesting that New Delhi should approve such a course of action, especially because it has always been against third-party negotiation. But, the Netherlands connection should not surprise watchers of the Naga peace process, which, as days pass, is becoming increasingly mired in controversy. On the other hand, in the case of the ULFA, which continues to be banned, the secretary general of the organization, Anup Chetia, had made its way to the Unrepresented Peoples' Organization in Geneva under the pseudonym of a John David Salomar, an alias and attendant credential that must certainly have been facilitated by either Bangladesh or Pakistan, just as these two countries provide thousands of false passports to Indian insurgents, including the ULFA chief of staff, Paresh Barua, who travels around the world under the alias of Kamruddin Zaman Khan. An important aspect of the internationalization endeavour is certainly the aid an insurgent or terrorist group receives from a foreign country to travel unfettered and in order to drum up international support for the 'war-efforts' back home.

The Chinese aid to the Nagas, and later to other insurgent groups, in North East India have been considerable. But, it has been confined primarily to some training, and provision of arms. Indeed, even the ULFA had ventured into China. In his admission to the contributor, Lohit Deury, an important staff officer to ULFA's chief of staff, Paresh Barua, speaks (after his surrender to the Assam Police in 2000) about Operation Chilarai and Lachit—ULFA missions to the province of Yunnan in 1986. Deury, then a Lance Corporal, also speaks of Paresh Barua accompanying the mission. Deury speaks of the Kachin liaison, the border towns of Sema and Mon from where Paresh Barua made trips to places in China where 'uniformed' Chinese officials met the ULFA Chief of Staff. Deury also spoke of a 'Black House,' an arms conduiting agency of China. While it has not been either substantiated or proven that such an agency exists, the fact remains that arms with Chinese markings have found their way into North East India. Therefore, the existence of a small arms conduiting agency in Yunnan from which arsenal for the northeastern insurgents emerge cannot be ruled out. This is especially so because reports have alluded to a Yunnan Navigational Bureau that is being run by a retired Chinese PLA officer. The organization reportedly deals in small arms and some of its major clients are the insurgent groups in North East India. However, such reports are quite anecdotal in nature, and it is the opinion of the contributor that even if such an agency exists, it does not have the official patronage of Beijing. The contributor's visit to China and the discussions he had with Chinese think tank leaders also seem to reveal that the Chinese have stopped all aid to the insurgents of North East India, concentrating instead on their 'harmonious development,' and concerns such as Taiwan and the presence of powers like the United States of America in the region that are seeking to obtain a sturdier foothold in the region, including places such as North East India.

At any rate, the aspect that cannot be disputed is the route the small arms are taking to enter North East India. According to the contributor, there are two major routes. One is from places such as Chiang Mai in Thailand, which winds its way into the Renong coast, from where trawlers ferry the arms to ports in Bangladesh. The other route originates in Yunnan from where barges in the Irrawady River carry consignments to the southern Myanmarese port of Sittwe. Once again, the arms are carried by ship to places such as Chittagong and Cox's Bazaar in Bangladesh. The route from Bangladesh to North East India and other parts of India is through land, bifurcating midway to cater to the needs of various insurgent groups in different parts of the North East India, as well as for the Maoists in Chhattisgarh and thereabouts. On 2 April 2004, a consignment of arms was seized in the Bangladesh government-controlled Chittagong Urea Fertilizer Limited jetty. A raid—reportedly triggered off as a result of an anonymous call from Indian interests—conducted on two fishing trawlers, *MV Khawja* and *FT Amanat*, on the east bank side of the river Karnaphuli in Chittagong unravelled a huge cache of arms.[11]

It is not a matter of surprise that Bangladesh has been chosen as the port of entry for illegal arms. It has emerged as an important front for terrorism, both homegrown and international. Indeed, there are over a hundred camps in Bangladesh that belong to the insurgent groups of North East India alone,[12] with senior leaders of the ULFA and the All Tripura Tiger Force (ATTF) staying in Dhaka as 'official guests' of the Bangladesh government, which has refused to extradite such leaders. It is from these camps that most anti-India operations are carried out. It is also no longer a matter of any doubt that there has been official patronage towards the insurgent groups of North East India ever since the 1950s. But the engineering of the ISI–ULFA nexus during the early 1990s heralded an important chapter in the 'proxy war' phenomenon.

Since the ULFA stands as the most important and belligerent insurgent outfit in North East India at the time of writing, the contributor deems it fit to record some of the important ways in which the links between the two has grown.

A record of some of the early events and meetings that had taken place between the two provides the progression of the linkage.

1. In the month of November 1990, the ULFA decides to send Munin Nobis and Partha Pratim Bora alias Javed to Bangladesh to contact the ISI in Dhaka for arranging supply of arms and ammunition. They were instructed to set up a base camp in Bangladesh.

2. Munin Nobis sets up a base camp in Dhaka in 1990 with the help of a Col. (Retd) Faruque of the Bangladesh Freedom Party and Gani Shapan of the Jatiyo Party. Nobis rents a house at Moghbazar in Dhaka.

3. Munin Nobis assumes the name 'Iqbal' and contacts Shamsul Siddique, the second secretary in the Pakistan Embassy in Dhaka. Contacts with the ISI are established through Siddique.

4. Munin Nobis visits Pakistan to negotiate with an Islamist group headed by a Mustafa Ali Jubardo for the impartment of training to ULFA cadres on payment.

5. The vice chairman of the ULFA, Pradip Gogoi visits Dhaka in January 1991, and contacts an ISI officer called Haque and signs an agreement for the impartment of training to ULFA cadres. He also meets another ISI officer, one Jalal.

6. After the agreement with the ISI, Munin Nobis summons a group of ULFA members for training in Pakistan in April 1991. Pradip Gogoi accompanies a six-member group to Islamabad for training with the ISI.

7. Hari Mohan Roy alias Rustabh Choudhury of the ULFA along with 10 other ULFA cadres undergo training in camps organized by the ISI in Pakistan in 1993. Hari Mohan Roy obtains a passport under the name of Jamul Akhtar of Bangladesh.

8. According to a statement of the former ULFA leader, Lohit Deury, the ULFA's foreign secretary, Sasadhar Choudhury has provided information about the Indian army's location in Assam to the ISI in Kathmandu in exchange for payment in US Dollars.

9. At least a dozen ULFA cadres visited Pakistan to train in the use of the Pakistan military produced Programmable Time Delay Device (PTDD). It may be noted in this context that PTDD is the explosive that the ULFA has been primarily using in Assam, including during the infamous 15 August 2004 explosion in Dhemaji that has taken the life of many innocent civilians including women and children.

10. According to a reliable source, a meeting was held on 25 June 2007 in the Bangladesh's Directorate General of Forces Intelligence (DGFI) Head Quarters in Dhaka. The meeting (that was attended by representatives of the DGFI and the ULFA) took a decision, among others, that the ULFA must work not only with Bangladeshi terrorist groups like the Harkat-ul-Jihad-al-Islami (HUJI), but also mainstream Islamist organizations such as the Lashkar-e-Toiba and the Jaish-e-Mohammad. If the above information is correct, then the future would witness an entirely different sort of violence. However, it must be mentioned here that there are agencies that have sought to spread such information in order to defame a particular insurgent group in the eyes of the populace. For instance, certain agencies had spread the word that the ULFA had joined the United Jihad Council. The allegation had no basis.

However, the ISI is (at present) training cadres belonging to the ULFA, ATTF and Islamist groups in various insurgency tactics, including mortar firing and in the use of explosives, later on the lines of car, motorcycle and cycle bombs. These are reportedly undertaken in 'official' training ranges in Bangladesh. The confession of an ULFA cadre is telling in this regard. Responsible for a number of mortar attacks that took place all over Assam in 2002, including the Indian Air Force's Airmen Mess in the outskirts of Guwahati, Dipamoni Kalita alias Seema Biswas states (according to a reliable source) after her surrender to the Assam Police:

> On 30 September 2001, at about 5:30 in the morning, two vehicles came to our place. The two NDFB, the two NSCN (K) cadres, Dilip Roy and I boarded one of the vehicles while five other persons boarded the other vehicle. The five persons looked like army personnel... They imparted training with respect to handling and operation of RPG-7 and 60 mm mortar...we underwent training for 14 days in all. On the last day of the

training we had range practice and I fired 12 shells from 60 mm mortar while Dilip fired three shells from the 60 mm mortar...from the language spoken by the instructors one could guess that they were non-Bangladeshi and could be Urdu speaking people. They were smart like army personnel.

Myanmar cradled most of the insurgent groups in North East India, with training, safe haven and arms. It is also reported that Beijing continues to have some influence over Yangon, and although Myanmar does not display the same sort of overt hostility as Bangladesh, its relationship with India is marked with sporadic and detached concern. Indeed, despite assurances that Myanmar would act against the insurgents in the Myanmar Naga Hills,[13] such assurances and consequent actions have only been cosmetic in nature. It is reported that the action against the ULFA and the NSCN (Khaplang) in early 2007 was preceded with 'early warnings' to the northeastern insurgent groups by Myanmarese villagers who had been warned by the Myanmarese army. Consequently, the 'jungle-bashing' by the Myanmarese army largely amounted to 'raids' only on empty insurgent camps in Takyemkok and Longloung, even as the insurgents shifted their camps southwards to places such as Sake Hi, Maimong, and Wayok.

New Delhi has, however, adopted a strategy of positive engagement with Yangon, which according to the contributor is prudent. It is also true that Myanmar does not actively support the insurgent groups—apart from non-institutional subterfuges that take place in the lower echelons of the Myanmarese army, primarily for money. To that end the Tatmadaw is not hostile to New Delhi, and North East India does not fall in its ambit of 'proxy war'. Indeed, it is the semi-governed area of Kachin State that provides the Indian insurgent the haven, and since these areas are not entirely under the control of Yangon, a Bhutan-like operation against the ULFA is deemed difficult. It must also be understood that even Bhutan, a country that has a unique relationship with India, was able to act against the ULFA after a great deal of pressure, and time. A repeat of Operation All Clear in Myanmar and Bangladesh is next to impossible. If at all, New Delhi would have to adopt stern measures on its own to neutralize the Indian insurgent groups billeted in foreign soil—actions that it is perfectly capable of. But, it has not done so, perhaps because of the weak-kneed policies of certain policy managers in New Delhi, or because the powers that are of the opinion that diplomacy would still help. In the past, there has been cooperation between the Myanmarese army and the Indian army: Operation Golden Bird in the mid-1990s was an important cooperative venture in which a large number of important insurgents were apprehended along with arms. But that was about the last— New Delhi has since been content with high-level visits, assurances and handing over of list of camps and insurgents in Myanmar and Bangladesh. It is important to realize that Indian insurgent camps exist in Myanmarese and Bangladeshi soil, and of crucial importance are the operations that are being carried out in North East India from these countries. Upper Assam, the Tirap, and Changlang districts of Arunachal Pradesh and the Mon district of Nagaland are directly affected by the presence of the insurgents in the Myanmar Naga Hills. Bangladesh's direct aid and sustenance have been documented. The 'proxy war' phenomenon would continue and innocent Indian citizens would continue to be killed until New Delhi realizes that there are ways and means to guard the interests of its citizens, however peripherally placed they may be.

But despite the fact that North East India is an active theatre of 'proxy wars,' and international links have taken deep roots in the region, with almost all insurgencies, separatist and autonomy movement looking outwards toward the encircling nations for anti-India sustenance, the phenomenon constitutes a special case. While the insurgency movements in the region have sought and received support from the 'encircling countries,' almost all such movements have remained loyal to their founding principles, and accusation that occasionally appear in the media are to a considerable extent the creation of opposing forces in order to discredit such movements in the eyes of its parish. The insurgencies that have erupted in Manipur and Tripura continue to be separatist in nature, as indeed was the case with the one that had gripped Mizoram.[14] Indeed, with the probable exclusion of the ULFA, who has reneged on the ideology that gave birth to it,[15] as aforesaid, almost all insurgent groups in North East India continue to remain faithful to their original agenda. Therefore, if there has been internationalization of the movements in North East India, it has only been by way of insurgent groups looking for aid in their war against India. It is not tantamount to adopting the ideologies of the 'allies' in revolution. For instance, the Naga groups that sought and received aid from the Chinese during the late 1960s were reluctant to be drawn into the People's Republic's communist philosophy, perhaps because of the fact that the influence of Christianity; and 'Christ for Nagaland'[16] became and continues to be the dominating principle for the NSCN. Similarly, the internationalization efforts of the United National Liberation Front, the People's Liberation Army of Manipur, the National Liberation Front of Tripura and the All Tripura Tiger Force were that of groups seeking sustenance, safe havens and, in certain cases, aid from their alien chaperons. Neither the Mizo National Front, during the period of rebellion, nor insurgent groups from Manipur and Tripura at present, have linked their cause with the climatic revolutionary or terrorist agenda that characterizes the world today. The al-Qaeda, for instance, has little or no mandate in North East India, and much of what has been made out to be an Islamist agenda in the region has been confined to groups such as the People's United Liberation Front of Manipur (with only anecdotal corroboration about its links with the al-Qaeda) and certain Islamist groups in Assam like the Muslim Liberation Tigers of Assam and the imported Islamist organization such as the Harkat-ul-Mujahideen. Indeed, even in Assam, the agenda that goads the Islamist organizations had not been influenced by the al-Qaeda in the manner that the terrorist organization was able to sway organizations in Bangladesh such as Jama'atul Mujahideen Bangladesh (JMB), Jagrata Muslim Janata Bangladesh (JMJB) and the HUJI. This aspect was, to a considerable extent, the result of the secular character that pervades the Muslim population of North East India who entered the region way back in 1198 AD and had become an inalienable part of the region. Indeed, certain instances of the Islamist subterfuge have actually been detected as a result of the direct aid that indigenous Assamese Muslims have provided to the authorities.[17] Furthermore, the Islamist agenda in the region, too, have a different bearing, and most of the demands that initially goaded the Muslim youth to take to the path of arms have little or nothing to do with the ideologies or objectives of groups such as the al-Qaeda, but for, what the contributor considers as being, perfectly valid demands.[18]

But, an alien programme imported from Bangladesh is beginning to appear in North East India. The agenda has a pan-Islamist bearing. It has the illegal migrant population as its parish, and has begun to take roots primarily as a result of the illegal ingress of Bangladeshis into Assam and the other states of North East India, and the pan-Islamist motivations that are goading them to take part in the global *Salafi* movement. At the time of writing in March 2008, few indigenous Assamese Muslims have found cause or motivation in such an agenda. Indeed, a section of Assamese Muslims that had gone to Pakistan-occupied Kashmir, Pakistan, and Afghanistan have returned in disillusionment, as they realized that the motivation for which they had gone for such training would not be fulfilled by linking their cause with the global Islamist movement. The demands of these people were, as aforesaid, quite valid and targeted at the socio-political and economic upliftment of their fellowmen in the North East India, and were quite localized and narrow in its approach. But, during the course of their training in Pakistan-occupied Kashmir and/or Afghanistan, they were imparted lessons about *shahadat* (martyrdom) for the cause of Islam, the extermination of the non-believer and the creation of *Nizam-e-Mustafa* in Assam. All these aspects were quite alien to the Assamese Muslims that had lived in harmony with the rest of their brethren for centuries. The disenchantment was also as a result of the ill-treatment that was meted out to the Assamese Muslims in the Islamist camps by their Pakistani and Afghanistan instructors and counterparts, some of which was because of the docile nature of the former as also because of their small built and inability to perform certain physically challenging tasks such as mine-clearing.

But, the above disillusionment notwithstanding, the security situation in North East India is beginning to witness a distinctive trend. An unusual order of extremism that has traditionally been known to exist is beginning to appear in the region. Islamist terrorism—with motivation and objectives—has begun to take urgent roots in the region. This movement has entered the secular space of the region from the fanatically resurgent Bangladesh that abuts the region, and if reports are anything to go by, is all set to take up the trenches that the ethnically based insurgent movements would have left behind. A robust internationalization movement—as is the case in Kashmir—would then herald the arrival of religious fanaticism and divide. At this time, and as aforesaid, it is analyzed that the growing illegal migration population in Assam and the other states of North East India would provide the pioneers for the growth of the predicted agenda. This conspiracy seems to be gaining ground particularly after Operation Enduring Freedom and the 'detalibanization' of Afghanistan, when active remnants of the al-Qaeda and the Taliban entered Bangladesh, which borders North East India. The region is also heir to myriad subterfuges by the ISI of Pakistan and the DGFI of Bangladesh, intelligence agencies that are beginning to expand their aid to the insurgent organizations of North East India by including Islamist groups in the region. Indeed, this has been compounded by the fact that the 'military-led' interim government in Bangladesh has—despite assurances to New Delhi—not acted (at the time of writing) either against the Indian insurgent groups operating from its soil, nor against the groups such as the Jamaat-e-Islami and the HUJI. Cosmetic action that has been taken against homegrown Islamist organization like JMB and JMJB have amounted to little, and the prognosis that the contributor wishes to make at this time is that the Islamist situation in the region is merely experiencing a lull—perhaps because of the heightened sense of surveillance and action against them in certain parts of the world, especially Pakistan, as also the fact that the military in Dhaka realizes that it does not have the legitimate mandate of the people of Bangladesh. Sections of the military that are responsible for guiding both the Indian insurgent groups and the Islamists have, therefore, counselled a tactical quietude for sometime. Furthermore, the atmosphere in Bangladesh is not conducive either. Certain important Bengali officers of the then Pakistan army who had joined the freedom fighters in 1971 against the Pakistan army have got together to form what has been named as the 'Sector Commanders Forum.' The Forum's agenda includes the banning of the Jamaat-e-Islami from politics and the trial of the war criminals. Indeed, cases have been filed against some of the Jamaat-e-Islami leaders who sought to term the liberation war as a civil war. But the security establishment has not taken any action against the anti-liberationists. This aspect also speaks volumes about the hidden agenda of certain 'Pakistani sympathisers' in the Bangladesh army. One of the biggest terrorist strikes in North East India was the one that was perpetrated on 30 October 2008 when nine explosions were set off in Assam's capital city, Guwahati, and other places in lower Assam. Although the initial needle of suspicion had pointed to Islamist groups, investigation has revealed that the blasts were the handiwork of the ULFA and the NDFB, the latter group involved despite it having entered into a ceasefire with New Delhi. Subir Bhaumik has argued that the pro-Pakistani lobby in the Bangladesh army influenced the ULFA and the NDFB to set off the explosions (the first of the explosions was in Tripura's capital city, Agartala by the ATTF). Bhaumik states that the Bangladesh army wanted to thwart the fresh efforts by Bangladesh's interim government to normalize relations with India, and those by the Bangladesh army chief, General Moen U. Ahmed who wants to establish stronger military-to-military ties with India. The 'rogue elements' in the Bangladesh army expected that large-scale explosions would trigger off an Indian outcry against Bangladesh, leading to a surge of anti-Indian sentiment within Bangladesh. Such emotion would lessen the chance of the secular and pro-India political party, the Awami League. It seems to be clear to observers like Bhaumik that the pro-Pakistan lobby in the Bangladesh army and Pakistan itself is resorting to a variety of subterfuge to ascertain that the Awami League does not come to power, which by all reckoning is a certainty.

The events in Bangladesh (the chapter began by showcasing the proximate nature of the 'encircling nations') have an important effect on North East India. Not only are the Indian insurgent groups sitting pretty in the country, but also, it seems that, the Islamists in the country are entering Assam and the rest of North East India. As was elucidated earlier, such Islamists are utilizing the illegal Bangladeshi migrant population in Assam to promote their agenda, which at this time, is primarily to use North East India as a gateway to the rest of India, where large-scale perpetration of violence has been, and is, on the Islamist fare. Matters have not helped the situation with Assam having not only a sizeable illegal migrant population, but also a long and porous border with Bangladesh, which has a predominantly Muslim population. Moreover, the population of the four geostrategically positioned districts of Assam has become Muslim majority (and five others have more than 35 per cent Muslim population)—a direct consequence of the illegal migration from erstwhile East Bengal, East Pakistan, and now Bangladesh. The Islamist militant movements in the region have found an organized parish in the illegal migrant population whose ideology and socio-religious commitments continue to be informed by experiences from across the border.

But, the insurgencies in North East India have been waged largely on ethnic lines, with nearly every insurgent organization owing its origins to an ethnic distinctiveness. Rebellion was egged on by identities that dissented against the imposition of other identities. Although, the chapter is not about the clash of ethnic identities, the fact of the matter is that North East India is an ethnic mess. Nirmal Nibedon had written about this aspect in his seminal book *North East India: The Ethnic Explosion*. The late Nibedon had stated:

> It is the ethnic explosion. Make no mistake about it. Have no doubts about it. World governments, more so in India and the South East Asian countries, will have to closely study the case of the ethnic minorities, whether they are Kachins and Karens of Burma, the Mizos or the Ahoms of India. The ethnic minorities of India, particularly those of the Mongoloid stock, will deserve more attention. For, gone are the days when small bands of proud tribesmen fought and defended themselves with poison-tipped arrows. Today, in the 1980s, the ethnic minorities are wielding sophisticated

weapons and engaging national armies in combat, unceasingly. In brief, they are all zealously guarding their ethnic identity. (Nibedon 1983: xiii)

But, as has been examined in the chapter, the ethnically-based insurgencies would be overshadowed by an alien agenda. Indeed, the 'proxy war' phenomenon would only receive a fillip with the entry of urban terrorism into North East India, the one that is beginning to experience a distinct international dimension, dovetailing it with agendas like that of the HUJI, Lashkar-e-Toiba, and the al-Qaeda.

NOTES

1. The northeast of India comprises of the states of Arunachal Pradesh, Assam, Manipur, Meghalaya, Mizoram, Nagaland, and Tripura. Collectively these states are also referred to as the 'Seven Sisters'.
2. The northeast of India borders Bangladesh, Bhutan, China, and Myanmar. Nepal is placed slightly afield near the Siliguri corridor, which connects the region to the rest of India. The northeast of India is perhaps the only region in South Asia to be situated amid five countries.
3. The British occupied the region primarily for commercial reasons, namely the abundance of tea and oil in the area. Indeed, while it brought the plains of Assam under its direct administrative ambit, it kept the hills only under partial control, perhaps because the colonial rulers saw no profit in completely dominating the hills.
4. While it is true that the present states of Meghalaya, Mizoram, and Nagaland were districts of Assam, the fact of the matter is that they were all unique in their identities. This is precisely why they had to be accorded Union Territoryhood and eventually statehood. It is also important to note that insurgencies in Mizoram and Nagaland broke out even when they were part of Assam. Manipur and Tripura were, of course, independent principalities that were annexed by India with the coming of independence in 1947. Arunachal Pradesh was formed out of the erstwhile North East Frontier Agency, a region that was not only loosely governed by the British, but much of whose territory was under Tibetan sway. Indeed, the present claims of the People's Republic of China to Arunachal Pradesh hark back to that era.
5. For instance, there is a ministry of Development of North Eastern Region in the Indian union ministry, a North East Council, and major ministries of the Indian government have a North East department/desk.
6. Perhaps in a bid to describe their mongoloid features.
7. The Tripura insurgent groups, the All Tripura Tiger Force and National Liberation Front of Tripura came into existence primarily because of the assertion of the tribal population of Tripura, which had been reduced to a minority in the state as a result of the massive influx from Bangladesh, and before it, East Pakistan. On the other hand, the United Liberation Front of Asom (ULFA) was formed as a militant manifestation of the agitation against illegal migrants from Bangladesh that was being spearheaded by the Student's of Assam.

8. While the North East India had easy access to the Bay of Bengal and other parts of India before the partition of the subcontinent in 1947, the partition and the creation of East Pakistan (present Bangladesh) severed the links, committing the northeast to a distant, almost inaccessible corner of India.

9. The Indo-Pak wars of 1947, 1965, 1971, and 1999 can safely be characterized as 'limited' wars (although the one fought in 1971 was fought in two fronts, defining it, therefore, as a 'short-scale' war). The Indo-China war of 1962 and the skirmishes that have occurred thereafter, too, fit the definition of 'limited' or 'short-scale' conflict.

10. Author of Arthashastra, and one time prime minister/adviser of Emperor Chandragupta Maurya.

11. The seizure list of the Chittagong Metropolitan Police states that the arms and ammunition recovered include 690 7.62 mm T-56-I Sub-Machine Guns (SMGs); 600 7.62 mm T-56-2 SMGs; 150 40 mm T-69 Rocket launchers; 840 40 mm rockets; 400 9mm semi-automatic spot rifles; 100 'Tommy Guns'; 150 rocket launchers; 2000 launching grenades; 25,020 hand grenades; 6,392 magazines of SMG and other arms; 700,000 rounds of SMG bullets; 739,680 rounds of 7.62 mm calibre; and 400,000 bullets of other weapons. Most of the arms and ammunition were reportedly of Korean, Italian, Chinese, and American make. The shipment has reportedly armed an entire armed division of the Bangladesh army. Speculation has been rife about which group the arms were meant for. Security analysts and officials are of the opinion that it was probably meant for a number of separatist groups in North East India as well as the Indian Maoists.

12. Dhaka, however, continues to deny the existence of such camps. Almost all meetings between the Bangladesh Rifles (BDR) and the Indian Border Security Force (BSF) ends up with denial by Bangladesh, and instead the latest trend is that BDR hands over a list of Bangladeshi insurgents that are wanted in that country, but are reportedly hiding in India.

13. Important camps of the Indian insurgent organizations are located in the Myanmar Naga Hills. The General HQ of the National Socialist Council of Nagalim (Khaplang) and the 28th Battalion HQ of the ULFA are situated in the area, as are certain Manipuri groups in the Sagaing division of Myanmar.

14. With the signing of the Mizo Accord, the Mizo National Front, the organization that had spearheaded the movement, gave up their separatist ideals and returned to the mainstream, and indeed, its leaders joined the Indian polity and governed the state after swearing allegiance to the Indian constitution.

15. The ULFA has reneged on an important aspect of its ideology when it became more or less silent on the issue of illegal migration from Bangladesh. The contributor is of the opinion that this was initially occasioned by the geostrategic compulsions of the ULFA, namely the need for safe havens, launching detachments and training facilities in Bangladesh. The ULFA, moreover, took training from both the ISI and the Bangladesh intelligence service, becoming subservient to it on many occasion. However, the unilateral ceasefire by two companies of the ULFA's 28 Battalion (which is also considered to be its strongest) on 24 June 2008 because of difference with its central leadership and disillusionment with the latter about the 'real issues of Assam' such as the illegal migration from Bangladesh into Assam also showcases the commitment of the militant groups in North East India to their founding principles.

16. The manifesto of the NSCN clearly states, 'to us, the sovereign existence of our country, the salvation of our people in socialism with their spiritual salvation in Christ, is eternal and unquestionable.' NSCN Manifesto, (Preface), GPRN, Oking, 31 January 1980. See NSCN manifesto 1980.

17. In 2001, cadres of the Harkat-ul-Mujahideen surrendered to the Assam police, and as the then Director General of Police of Assam, Hare Krishna Deka informs the 'surrender was facilitated through the active help of nationalist Indian Muslim villagers alone.'

18. The aims and objectives as displayed in the various documents produced by the Islamist groups in Assam, for instance, are interesting. Unlike the ethnic militant groups such as the ULFA, the NDFB, or the NSCN, the charter of demands of the Islamist organizations does not normally carry a clause of secession from India, though a few have stated goals about the establishment of separate Islamic homelands. Indeed, most of the MFO demands are perfectly valid. The MULTA demands in Assam, for instance, include:

- Thirty per cent reservation in education and employment for Muslims.
- Establishment of a Muslim court in Assam.
- Reservation of seats in the Legislative Assembly for the Muslims of the Barak Valley.

8

INTERNATIONALIZATION OF TERRORISM AND ITS LIMITS IN THE MIDDLE EAST

Amos N. Guiora

INTRODUCTION

A discussion of terrorism must be preceded by a definition of the term. Only then is it possible to clearly specify the subject matter to be analyzed. When approaching such a broad subject, it is necessary for reader and writer alike to narrow down the focus. Otherwise, it will be impossible to distinguish the trees from the forest. Furthermore, critical issues will not be satisfactorily addressed. The unlimited boundary encompassed in discussions regarding the Middle East necessitates a narrowing of the scope of the examination. To that end, the chapter limits the discussion to the analysis of two issues within the Palestinian terrorism paradigm: the difference between global and local terrorism, and the role of religion as a motivating factor.

The chapter differentiates between different paradigms of Palestinian terrorism. Hamas[1] should be distinguished from the Palestine Liberation Organization (PLO). The PLO—before it came to be the Palestinian Authority (PA)—was a secular terrorist organization focused on achieving local goals, while openly seeking assistance and support within a global context from the Soviet Union and other international secular terrorist organizations. Hamas, on the other hand, while locally focused, is a radical Islamist fundamentalist terrorist organization that does not perceive itself as part of a global *Salafi* movement.

Before proceeding forth with the discussion it is important to address why the contributor is discussing Palestinian terrorism. His 19-year long career in the Israel Defence Forces (IDF) has provided him with extensive experience in the legal and policy aspects of operational counter-terrorism—aspects that facilitates this discussion. His postings have included those of: prosecutor in the West Bank Military Court where Palestinians suspected of committing acts of terrorism were brought to trial; assistant to the West Bank Legal Advisor where he wrote legal opinions regarding the imposition of sanctions on Palestinians, including administrative detentions, house demolitions and deportations; Judge in the Gaza Strip Military Court, where the contributor presided over hearings of Palestinians accused of terrorism-related crimes; Legal Advisor to the Gaza Strip where he provided senior IDF commanders legal and policy advice regarding operational international law as it pertains to counter-terrorism.

As a result, the contributor has spent thousands of hours with thousands of Palestinians accused of terrorism-related crimes ranging from stone-throwing to killing Israelis or fellow Palestinians suspected of collaborating with Israel. The Palestinian terrorists he prosecuted, judged, and against whom he recommended sanctions, represented a cross-section of Palestinian terrorist organizations. These individuals were affiliated with the PLO, Hamas, the Islamic *Jihad*, the Democratic Front for the Liberation of Palestine, the Popular Front for the Liberation of Palestine, various splinter and localized groups of the larger organizations, and 'lone' terrorists neither beholden to, nor acting at the behest of, a particular terrorist movement.

The contributor has not, to the best of his knowledge, professionally encountered a member of the al-Qaeda although he has met individuals espousing views similar to, and in support of, Bin-Laden and the al-Qaeda.

Each of these terrorist suspects impressed upon the contributor his/her absolute determination and dedication to the establishment of a Palestinian state. To that end, the Palestinians, male and female, young and old, single and married, parents and children, have engaged in acts of terrorism against a wide variety of Israeli targets. The essence of Palestinian terrorism as articulated by these individuals was to serve a 'local' purpose: Palestinian statehood. It was not related to what many have referred to as 'international Islamist terrorism'.

PALESTINE LIBERATION ORGANIZATION

A proper understanding of the interplay between Palestinian and international terrorism necessitates recourse to history. In the aftermath of the 1967 Six Day War (Ajami 1992: 31), Israel occupied the West Bank, the Gaza Strip, the Sinai Peninsula, the Golan Heights and East Jerusalem. It is important to note that the PLO, which became the primary Palestinian terrorist organization under Yasser Arafat's leadership,[2] was not 'born' in response to the occupation. Rather, on 1 January 1965, Arafat declared the organization's twin purposes: to eliminate the state of Israel and to establish the state of Palestine.[3]

In the aftermath of the Six-Day War, Arafat established the PLO headquarters in Amman, Jordan. King Hussein concluded in September 1970 that the PLO posed a threat to the Hashemite Kingdom (consisted of Bedouins and Palestinians) and brutally expelled them[4]. From Jordan, the PLO moved to Lebanon where its strongest presence was in Beirut and southern Lebanon. The PLO was headquartered in Lebanon until 1982 when Israel, in response to a PLO attack on the Israel Ambassador to Britain, entered Lebanon. As a result of the Lebanon War and the deployment of American marines to Lebanon, the PLO was forced to withdraw from Lebanon and subsequently moved to Tunis. Upon the establishment of the PA in the aftermath of the Oslo Accords in July 1994, Arafat left Tunis and came to the Gaza Strip (Avalon Project at Yale Law School).

Experts are generally of the opinion that from 1967 to 1985, in the West Bank and the Gaza Strip (the 'Areas'), the Palestinians did not react violently to the Israeli occupation (Lesch 1990). This lack of armed resistance was clearly distinct from PLO terrorism outside the Areas committed by PLO members not residing in the West Bank or the Gaza Strip. A partial list includes the following attacks: Savoy Hotel in Tel Aviv (*Time* 1975), Ma'alot schoolhouse (*Time* 1974), Lod Airport attack (Canadian Broadcast Corporation) carried out by the Japanese Red Brigade, which operated loosely under the PLO (*PBS* 2006),

Munich Olympics (*Time* 2002), and the Tel Aviv Coastal road attack (*Time* 1978).

While the PLO was supported by the former Soviet Union[5] and was consequently aligned with left-wing terror organizations including Germany's Baader-Meinhof (BBC News 2007b), Italy's Red Brigade, (Federation of American Scientists 1998) and Japan's Red Army (Federation of American Scientists 2003) the organization was not perceived to be a 'full member' of the international socialist or communist movements. To that end, while the PLO trained at Soviet-funded training camps and benefited from professional association with like-minded terrorist organizations, the organization's focus was 'local', not international.

In that spirit, the PLO was a secular, nationalist terror organization devoid of religious trappings or undertones. Although Arafat was a devout Muslim, the organization reflected his secular tendencies. A Palestinian state under his control would not have been dominated by the *Sha'ria*[6] and education would have been secular, not driven by fundamentalist Islam.

The PLO is not considered to be a part of international terrorism, as the phrase is understood and defined by scholars (Laqueur 2004). Bruce Hoffman describes international terrorism as being geographically unbounded, where terrorists attack foreign targets not necessarily related to, or connected with, the terrorist organization (Hoffman and Hoffman 1995). Hoffman writes:

> International terrorism disdains any concept of delimited areas of combat or demarcated battlefields, much less respect of neutral territory. Accordingly, terrorists have repeatedly taken their often parochial struggles to other, sometimes geographically distant, third party countries and there deliberately enmeshed persons completely unconnected with the terrorists' cause or grievances in violent incidents designed to generate attention and publicity. (Hoffman 2006)

Akin to other terrorist organizations whose goal was local—rather than global—the PLO accepted Soviet largesse for specific purposes divorced from 'globalism'. The PLO's focus was two-fold: the establishment of the state of Palestine and the destruction of the occupying state, which is Israel. To that end, assistance was welcomed from international sources. However, the PLO did not reciprocate by furthering the ambitions of other European terrorist movements (Rickman 2000). In short, the PLO was not a part of international terrorism.

THE INTIFADA, 1987-1994

In December 1987, the Palestinians, in response to a tragic car accident in which a number of Palestinians were killed, took to the streets in protest. The remonstration was initially in the Gaza Strip, and spread shortly thereafter to the West Bank. Within a few days, what came to be known as the 'Intifada',[7] was in full force—thousands of Palestinians were participating in massive demonstrations against Israeli occupation. While the IDF was clearly caught off-guard,[8] so was the PLO leadership in Tunis. The Intifada became increasingly violent as demonstrations quickly progressed from burning tyres to throwing stones, and then to throwing Molotov cocktails.

The Intifada's initiative and leadership were local. The burden of punishments (incarceration, administrative detention, house demolition, and deportation), and the loss of life (of active participants and innocent bystanders) were borne by Palestinians living in the West Bank and the Gaza Strip. Not only did the Tunis-based PLO not provide assistance or leadership, but also other, established terrorist organizations (Democratic Front for the Liberation of Palestine, Popular Front for the Liberation of Palestine) were similarly uninvolved. The Intifada was, in its essence, a true grass roots uprising against the Israeli occupation. It is unclear whether local Palestinians felt emboldened and encouraged by major terror attacks previously committed by the PLO (in Israel and Europe). What is apparent is that the acts from within (the Areas) clearly influenced the Israeli government.

THE PALESTINIAN AUTHORITY

In the aftermath of the Oslo Accords and the establishment of the Palestinian Authority, Arafat assumed the position of Ra'is ('President' or 'Chairman') of the PA. Soon, corruption became rampant. Foreign investors and donor nations alike, particularly those from Europe, poured enormous amounts of money into the PA. A significant portion of those funds made their way into Arafat's private bank accounts and vast international holdings. The long-term victims are the Palestinian people who never received sufficient funding enabling the building of a politically viable and economically stable entity.[9] The short-term loser was the PLO's leadership of the PA, voted out of office in 2006.

HAMAS

The winner of the 2006 Palestinian election was Hamas (BBC News 2006), an Islamist terrorist organization whose covenant calls for Israel's destruction.[10] Unlike the secular PLO, Hamas is a religion-based Islamist terrorist organization. Created in the Gaza Strip in the mid-late 1980's as the Palestinian chapter of the Islamic Brotherhood, Hamas 'exploded' onto the scene in 1989 with the kidnapping and killing of two Israeli soldiers, Avi Sasportas and Ilan Sa'adon. Hamas argues that the organization has two separate and distinct branches: one branch provides social services to its membership (akin to 'cradle to grave' care taking); the other, Iz al-Din al-Kassam,[11] responsible for terrorist attacks. Israel, however, argues that these branches are indistinguishable and that any distinction is artificial.

Hamas' most significant contribution to operational terrorism has been the further development and improvement of the sophisticated infrastructure required to achieve a successful suicide bombing attack. Hamas' suicide bombing attacks have exacted a heavy toll on the Israeli population: over 3,000 killed (*The Observer* 2006), thousands more wounded, (Israel Ministry of Foreign Affairs 2004) and also resulting in economic hardships including a reduction in tourism and foreign investment (Frisch, citing Haim Barkai 2006). Additionally, a series of particularly 'successful' suicide bombings in the spring of 1996 led to a change of Israel's government.[12]

In the spring of 2007, Hamas and the PLO engaged in what many experts termed a Palestinian civil war in the Gaza Strip. The long-festering feud for control of the PA has resulted in the deaths of PLO and Hamas members and, in some cases, their families. The raging gun battles in the streets of Gaza were not only over money and power but also, and perhaps more importantly, the shape of the future Palestinian state. Most commentators assume that a Palestinian state is inevitable. Therefore, the question is not if there will be a Palestinian state, but will the Palestinian state be secular (PLO) or Islamic (Hamas).

PALESTINIAN AND INTERNATIONAL TERRORISM: ONE AND THE SAME?

The question naturally leads to the fundamental issue that this chapter seeks to address: the relationship between Palestinian terrorism and international terrorism.

The aftermath of 9/11 included a heightened sense of awareness about the threat of global terrorism. The attack drew the world's attention to a global threat called 'Islamist terrorism'. Whether the operative term should be Huntington's 'clash of civilizations' or 'Islamofascism',[13] the implication is the same: Islamist extremists are prepared to go to great lengths to kill as many westerners as possible and cause significant damage to western assets. Also targeted are Arab regimes (Egypt, Jordan, and Saudi Arabia) accused of allowing the west, particularly the United States, to penetrate—actually, to defile—Arab society. To that end, from the perspective of Islamist terrorists, western and certain Arab regimes are legitimate targets.

However, this does not inherently suggest that Hamas' efforts to destroy Israel and establish a religious[14] Palestinian state are directly linked to international, Islamist terrorism. In order to address this question it is critical to inquire whether international, Islamist terrorism actually exists, or is it a product of media spin, anxious governments threatened by attack, or a combination of both.

The contributor has suggested that contemporary Islamist terrorism is the 'new Hundred Year war'.[15] This does not suggest—explicitly or implicitly—that the phenomenon is a clash of civilizations. It does propose, however, that western society is confronted by a determined foe whose actions are predicated on a particular interpretation of the religious text of the Muslims, the Koran.[16] Obviously, not all Muslims are terrorists, and not all Arabs wanted to blow up the World Trade Center. Therefore, there is a need for extreme caution when one engages in such discussion.

It is critical to understand what is at stake. What is at risk is not a threat by *all* Muslims, but clearly by *some*. Such an interpretation may seem overly simplistic, legal, or unnecessarily mired in argument, but the requirement to engage and understand subtle distinctions is critical.

APPLYING THEORY TO PRACTICE

Applying the nuanced approach articulated above to the West Bank and the Gaza Strip requires a careful analysis of some the following issues:

1. On whose behalf is Hamas acting? Who is supporting Hamas? What are the larger issues at play?

2. What are the motivations of the 'foot soldier' willing to blow himself up tomorrow afternoon in a Tel Aviv restaurant? What can be done to prevent such actions?
3. What is the role of religion in terrorism? Has Islam been manipulated, if not perverted, by various organizations and regimes?
4. What are the limits of free speech?
5. What social and economic conditions are at play?
6. What is the most effective means of reaching out to millions of school-age children taught to hate western values? How much—if at all—is the west expected to 'understand' Islamist terrorism?
7. What is the responsibility of leaders such as Egyptian President Hosni Mubarak in the face of Islamist terrorism? What is the role of European nations facing significant demographic upheavals resulting from an open border policy?

The above list is not exhaustive. Nevertheless, in order to productively engage the issue of Palestinian terrorism, it is necessary to be highly selective in determining which questions to address.

Accordingly, the questions the contributor proposes to address are the following:

1. On whose behalf is Hamas acting?
2. Who supports Hamas and why?
3. What are the motivations of the suicide bomber acting on behalf of Hamas?
4. What is the relationship between religion and terrorism?

ON WHOSE BEHALF DOES HAMAS ACT?

If Hamas acts under the umbrella of international terrorism to advance a global cause, then the answer is that Hamas members act on behalf of a global concept. Conversely, if Hamas acts on behalf of a local, specific goal, rather than 'globalization', then it is not part of the international terrorist fabric. So, which is it? From varied and extensive conversations with Hamas 'senders' (those who send the suicide bombers) and 'doers' (the suicide bombers), the contributor's overwhelming impression is that the suicide bombers were driven by an absolute sense of local mission, related exclusively to the Palestinian people and unrelated to a larger objective.

To that end, the answer to this critical question is that the organization was established for the specific purpose of establishing a religious Palestinian state. The internationalization of terrorism is, at most, a by-product from which the organization may benefit. Certainly, funds supporting Hamas travel a circuitous international route (significant funds originate in the US and the UK). However, that fact alone does not inherently make Hamas a part of international terrorism.

Any terrorist organization—local or international—is obligated to ensure that its coffers are full: 'If nothing else is clear, it is understood that terrorists generally have a wealth of funding sources to draw from in order to finance their terror' (Baldwin Jr. citing Osher and Eichenwald 2004). While the financing of terrorism is international, the terrorism it supports is not necessarily international: 'Hamas believes that Islam is completely different to the ideology of Mr Al-Zawahiri. Our battle is against the Israeli occupation and our only concern is to restore our rights and serve our people. We have no links with any group or element outside Palestine' (FOX News 2006).

Therefore, although Hamas actively seeks funding from any available source—local or international—the essence of the organization remains unaffected. Accordingly, the conclusion is that Hamas is acting solely on behalf of the Palestinian people.

WHO SUPPORTS HAMAS AND WHY?

Hamas is supported by Palestinians living in the West Bank and the Gaza Strip who voted for the organization either because of religious devoutness or disenchantment with the PA's corruption. However, the available literature (Levitt 2005) suggests that the organization's core supporters are religious Muslims desirous of a Palestinian state as articulated by the Hamas. This means Hamas supporters desire a Palestinian state that is a religious, non-secular entity. What remains unclear is the extent to which Sha'ria would be imposed under such a government and whether the future Palestinian state would resemble Iran or a more moderate version of political Islam.

The fact that Hamas is, at its core, an Islamist terrorist organization does not inherently imply that it is a member of international Islamic terrorism. Reports (CBS News 2002; *Jerusalem Post* 2006) suggest that the al-Qaeda and the Hezbollah have both sought to gain a foothold in the Gaza Strip by sending terrorists to participate in the Hamas terrorist attacks. However, the Hamas did not send members either to fight in Lebanon (during the summer of 2006) alongside Hezbollah or to Iraq to assist the al-Qaeda. Neither did Hamas support the Taliban in Afghanistan. The significance of this cannot be overemphasized; it unequivocally demonstrates that Hamas is *not* an active participant in external Islamist terrorism (external defined as beyond its immediate geographic region). What remains to be analyzed is whether Hamas' internal efforts are an integral component of international Islamist terrorism.

MOTIVATION OF THE SUICIDE BOMBER

As discussed by Professor Robert Pape,[17] the primary motivations of suicide bombers are not—contrary to popular wisdom—inherently religious. In making his case, Pape analyzes the LTTE in Sri Lanka who, according to Pape, were the initial practitioners of suicide bombing in the contemporary age. According to Pape, LTTE did so for purely nationalist reasons, divorced from religious considerations. While the Tamil Tigers may be acting out of secular and nationalist motivations, it is suggested that the Hamas suicide bombers are motivated by a number of considerations, primarily religion.

According to documented cases, a number of Palestinians decided to become suicide bombers after witnessing the humiliation of family members by the Israel Defence Forces, particularly at check-points. To that end, these individuals are determined to avenge the humiliation. Similarly, a Palestinian whose loved one was killed by the IDF has strong motivation to exact a similar price on Israelis. For this category of bombers who witnessed humiliation of their kin, it is suggested that the primary motivation is neither religious nor nationalist; rather, a basic human emotion not unique to Islamist or Palestinian terrorism.

An additional category of bombers are Palestinians who are convinced that their economic and social condition is such that eternal reward (paradise) is preferable to a life devoid of opportunity and upward mobility. As a group, they are vulnerable to religion or other 'higher' offerings and promises of a higher calling. In the case of Islam, the higher calling proffered is martyrdom (*shahadat*) and the promise of purity, eternal heaven, and 72 virgins awaiting the martyr (*shahid*) in heaven. Bruce Hoffman (Lecture, University of Utah, 1 March 2007) suggests that the controversy regarding whether the Koran promises martyrs 72 virgins is largely irrelevant since potential suicide bombers believe this to be true. Hoffman's fundamental thesis is that mere belief in the promise of 72 virgins is sufficient motivation, regardless of whether the Koran actually articulates their existence.

A third category, particularly prevalent in the heyday of Saddam Hussein, was predicated on financial considerations. The former Iraqi leader paid the families of successful suicide bombers 20,000 USD, for those only injured 10,000 USD (CBS News 2003, FOX News 2002). Similar to the individuals motivated by familial humiliation, financial considerations are also 'practical' ones that transcend religious and nationalistic motivations.

The contributor proposes that the fourth category is the most prevalent: individuals convinced that the most effective and important contribution they can make to the establishment of a religious Palestinian state is by committing a suicide bombing. The contributor has presided over innumerable remand hearings for individuals who failed in their attempts to perpetrate such attacks owing either to technical failure or because the General Security Services (the Israeli security service, similar to the American Federal Bureau of Investigation) had prior information regarding their intentions. Such individuals clearly acted out of a sense of advancing Islamist terrorism solely relevant to the Gaza Strip and the West Bank. The entire focus was local.

While suicide bombers in Iraq read religious texts that motivate Palestinian bombers, their applications and motivations are distinguishable. While the Koran and its interpretations are often identical to both, the practical application is specific to the context in which the suicide bomber operated. Walter Laqueur cautions:

> Many terrorisms exist, and their character has changed over time and from country to country. The endeavour to find a 'general theory' of terrorism, one overall explanation of its roots, is a futile and misguided enterprise... Terrorism has changed over time and so have the terrorists, their motives, and the causes of terrorism. (Borum, citing Laqueur 2003)

While the 9/11 actors saw themselves acting on a global stage, the Hamas suicide bomber has a much smaller and more focused stage.

While perhaps sympathetic to global Islamist terrorism, Hamas is not an explicit member of, nor contributor to, the furtherance of goals such as those espoused by the al-Qaeda.

RELIGION AND TERRORISM

This is perhaps the most crucial aspect in the present examination as it goes to the heart of the most important issue. In discussing the issue of religious underpinnings for terrorism, it is critical to emphasize what the chapter does *not* discuss: it does not inherently blame organized religion for the religion-based actions of its followers. It does, however, assume that religious training and indoctrination impacts the world-view of millions of people. In the context of the present discussion, the question is whether the religious indoctrination of the Hamas is akin to the religious foundation of suicide bombers elsewhere. Furthermore, if the answer is in the affirmative, what is its significance?

Articulated in a different manner, the chapter questions the stereo-typical notion that suicide attacks committed by Hamas and Islamist terrorists elsewhere in the world (while similar in method and justified by identical Koranic texts) are in actuality one and the same. Is it fair to say that they belong to the same cult of international terrorism simply because individuals in both groups use suicide bombing and the Koran? The answer is no. While both seek guidance and justification from the same religious text, they are not motivated by the same political and individual considerations.

While religion is what Hamas and internationally oriented Islamic fundamentalists have in common (religion as a common, primary motivator), terrorists acting on behalf of the latter do not share the same goal(s) as terrorists acting on behalf of the former. The same religious text is used for different purposes; Hamas for a narrow (local) purpose; international oriented terrorism (of which Hamas is not a part) for broader goals and purposes.

The commonality of religion does not inherently mean a commonality of purpose and motivation. That is not intended to gainsay the absolute centrality of religion as a motivator for the contemporary terrorist. It is to unequivocally advocate that similarity of religious beliefs does not inherently imply globalism. Bluntly put, the contributor's fundamental assumption is that the final thoughts of a Hamas suicide bomber are more likely to be about a religious Palestinian state rather than the World Trade Center.

CONCLUSION

In the over-heated geopolitical environment that characterizes contemporary analysis of terrorism, the easy assumption is that all Islamist terrorists belong to international Islamist terrorism. It is the contributor's fundamental thesis that the Hamas—as the religious counterpart to the secular PLO—has its proverbial eye on the same endgame: a Palestinian state.

While a Hamas-led state will likely be more religious (although the extent is unknown), the fundamental goal of Hamas leadership is geographically locale-specific. Perhaps the late Tip O'Neal's famous phrase—'all politics is local'—most appropriately describes both the Hamas and the PLO with the one significant difference previously alluded to. While the Hamas and other Islamic-based terrorist organizations read the same texts, they do not share the same specific goals and aspirations. Religion can be a mutually shared motivator, but the means and goals it justifies need not be inherently similar.

NOTES

1. 'Hamas' is an acronym; the group's actual name is the Islamic Resistance Movement.
2. Yasser Arafat, winner of The Nobel Peace Prize 1994. For details, see Abrams 1999. See also *Time* 2004.
3. Refer to the *Palestinian Charter*, in The Avalon Project 1968; see also Tq Shang 2001.
4. This treatment inspired the name of the terrorist organization 'Black September,' which was responsible for the Munich Olympic Games massacre. See *Time* 2002.
5. Until the end of the Cold War, with the collapse of the former Soviet Union in 1989.
6. Islamic law.
7. 'Intifada' literally means ridding, throwing off, or shrugging off.
8. In 1987 (prior to the Intifada) the Ministry of Defence released a glossy publication in which the Head of the Coordinator of Government Affairs for the Territories (Shlomo Goren) wrote that the Palestinian residents of the West Bank and Gaza Strip benefited from the Israeli occupation. Needless to say, Goren came to rue the publication and his words.

9. The Palestine Authority is not a state; whether it is a 'quasi-state', 'semi-state'; 'state-minus' is a matter of legal interpretation and political opinion but it clearly does not meet the international law definition of a State.

10. For reference, see Avalon Project 1988; see also BBC News 2007a.

11. Iz al-Din al-Kassam is named after a Palestinian cleric who in the 1920s and mid-1930s led an Islamist organization fighting the British mandate authorities and Jewish communities in Palestine; see also Levitt 2004.

12. Prime Minister Peres (who assumed office after Prime Minister Rabin's assassination) was defeated by the head of the opposition party (Likud), Benjamin Netanyahu. The suicide bombings were 'blow-back' for the targeted killing of Yiheah Ay'ash ('the Engineer') a senior Hamas operative responsible for the deaths of hundreds of Israelis.

13. Refer to NPR 2006. ('The first time it was used in the mainstream press was back in 1979, in a *Washington Post* article describing Iran's Ayatollah Khomeni as an Islamic Fascist. Since then, the phrase has morphed into 'Islam-o-fascist'. That word appeared in a 1990 article in the British newspaper *The Independent*, which argued that authoritarian governments are the norm in the Islamic world.')

14. The degree of Islamic observance in the Palestinian state is unclear.

15. For details, see, cleveland jewishnews.com/articles/2006/08/11/news/local/bcover0811.txt.

16. With respect to acting in the name of interpretation of religious texts, it is important to note that Christian extremists have killed in the name of both the New and Old Testaments, and Jewish extremists have killed in the name of the Bible. One significant difference that has been the source of media and scholarly attention is that Jewish and Christian extremists—unlike Islamist extremists—do not conduct suicide bombings.

17. *NY Times* 2005; see also *Washington Post* 2005a and *Washington Post* 2005b.

9

REGIONALIZATION OF TERRORISM: JEMAAH ISLAMIYAH IN SOUTH EAST ASIA

Mohamed Nawab Bin Mohamed Osman

INTRODUCTION

In the aftermath of 11 September 2001, a new Islamist movement, the Jemaah Islamiyah (JI), appeared in South East Asia. The advent of the JI in the region has been both a source of debate as well as the cause of untold problems. This chapter aims at highlighting some of the transnational linkages of this organization, and argues that the Afghan war played a significant role in the transformation of the JI from a group with local aspirations to one that aligned itself with a larger Islamist discourse of forming a supranational Islamic state or Caliphate.

The chapter begins with a brief history of the group and its linkages to the Dar-ul-Islam rebellion in the 1950s and 1960s in Indonesia. It will then examine the impact of the Afghan war in developing JI as an active movement. Finally, it will examine the linkages of the JI to other Islamist movements in various parts of the world.

TRACING JEMAAH ISLAMIYAH

The origins of the JI can be traced to the Dar-ul-Islam movement. This movement was formed in 1942 by Sekarmadji Maridjan Kartosoewirjo to fight against Dutch colonialism.[1] Later, following independence and some disagreements with the key Islamic political party, the Masyumi, Kartosoewirjo led a rebellion in 1948 in West Java. On 7 August 1949, he announced the establishment of the Islamic Army of Indonesia, the Tentera Islam Indonesia (TII) and fought the Indonesian government. This rebellion was commonly known as the Dar-ul-Islam movement. The rebellion took place in various parts of Indonesia such as Central Java, South Sulawesi, South Kalimantan and Aceh, the leaders of each of these groups often having their own local agendas. As Greg Fealy (2005b) notes, Dar-ul-Islam was not a single or unified movement or rebellion; rather it comprised a number of regional rebellions, and communications between the various rebellions were sporadic at best.[2] For the next 13 years, Kartosoewirjo continued his struggle to establish an Islamic state. Trailed by the Indonesian army for three months, Kartosoewirjo and his men were hiding in the jungles of Java. The army finally caught up with them and apprehended Kartosoewirjo on 4 June 1962. He was later executed in September 1962.

During the New Order regime of General Suharto, a senior military officer of the Indonesian army, General Ali Moertopo revived the Dar-ul-Islam movement in order to use the group against communist insurgents in Indonesia (Cahyono 1998). It was argued that with the fall of southern Vietnam to the communists, Borneo in Indonesia was in danger of falling to the communists as well (International Crisis Group 2002b). Suharto was fully supportive of Moertopo as he felt the Islamists could be used against his main nemesis, the Indonesian communists. Later, Moertopo skillfully manipulated the remnants of the Dar-ul-Islam movement to create a bastion of threat from Muslim radicals (Al-Chaidar 1999). In 1977, the government arrested several members of Komando Jihad, a group linked to the Dar-ul-Islam movement. However, it is widely held that this group was created to discredit the Dar-ul-Islam movement and put on trial many of its key leaders (Al-Chaidar 1999). By this time, the movement began to fragment and smaller groups emerged out of the movement.[3] Abdullah Sungkar and Abu Bakar Ba'asyir led one such faction.[4] It is believed that they had joined Dar-ul-Islam in the late 1970s and became active in mobilizing radicals to the Dar-ul-Islam cause. They were arrested on 10 November 1978 in connection with meetings that they had organized with Haji Ismail Pranoto, a former Dar-ul-Islam commander, and were accused by the government of recruiting members for Dar-ul-Islam to wage a violent movement (International Crisis Group 2002a). Both

Sungkar and Ba'asyir were tried in 1982 and sentenced to nine years in prison for trying to subvert the state. In late 1982, when their sentences were reduced after an appeal, and they were released temporarily, the two fled to Malaysia.

In Malaysia, Sungkar and Ba'asyir began canvassing for support among local Malaysian businessmen for their cause. Subsequently, they encouraged members of Dar-ul-Islam to come to Malaysia to work in Malaysian companies, owned by these businessmen. For 14 years, Sungkar and Ba'asyir remained in Malaysia, living in a village in the State of Johor where they had earlier established the Lukmanul Hakim *madrasah*. JI was formally established on 1 January 1993 by Sungkar, several months after Abu Bakar Ba'asyir and he left Dar-ul-Islam.[5] Sungkar became the first *amir* (leader) of the JI. The JI is a more closely structured organization compared to Dar-ul-Islam, but its key objective was the establishment of an Islamic state in Indonesia through *jihad*.

After Suharto's fall, both Sungkar and Ba'asyir returned to Indonesia to continue their struggle. Upon the death of Sungkar in 1999, Ba'asyir succeeded him as the leader of the JI. When Abu Bakar Ba'asyir, founded the Majlis Mujaheedin Indonesia (MMI) in August 2000, the move was seen as a betrayal of Sungkar's political ideals that the JI should remain underground in their struggle to set up an Islamic state. The radicals were of the opinion that accommodation within a non-Islamic political system could contaminate the faithful and as such it was forbidden. Abu Bakar Ba'asyir on the other hand saw it as an opportunity that should not be wasted (International Crisis Group 2002a). It was believed that these internal agreements about methodology led to Ba'asyir's resignation as JI's *amir* in the year 2000. He was replaced by Abu Rusdan and, subsequently, by Abu Dujana (Abuza 2006a). The leadership of the JI under these two leaders marked a complete shift in the organization towards more violence whereby even Muslim civilian casualties were overlooked.

OPERATIONAL HISTORY OF JI

While the primary objective of this paper is not the examination of the operational history of the JI, several major attacks carried out by the JI must be mentioned briefly. It was not until 2000 that JI conducted its first terrorist attacks. As Abuza notes, the leaders spent the first six or seven years patiently building up their network, recruiting, training and attaining proficiency in terror tactics (Abuja 2005). Its earliest significant attacks were on several churches in the city of Medan in May 2000 (Conboy 2004). Following this, the group detonated a bomb close to the home of the Filipino ambassador in retaliation against the Filipino government for its attack on the Moro Islamic Liberation Front (MILF) and the JI camps in Mindanao. On Christmas Eve of the year 2000, the JI launched its most intense attack yet on some 38 churches across five provinces, which left 19 dead (*Jakarta Gatra* 2001). The JI's most deadly phase began in late 2001, when it began preparations for attacks on several diplomatic missions and public buildings in Singapore, such as the ministry of defence, ministry of education and subway stations (Singapore Ministry of Home Affairs 2003). The planned attack showed a shift in the strategy of the JI where they began targeting western interests in South East Asia. Yet, despite the seemingly organized planning of the attacks, the event could perhaps be identified as the first point of fissure within the JI. The JI leaders as Riduan Isamuddin Hambali, Dr Azahari Husin and Noordin Mohd Top believed that the time had come for the JI to wage an armed *jihad* and to take on the international system.[6] Yet, it seems that there were disagreements between Hambali and the head of the Singapore chapter of the JI, Ibrahim Maidin, about the preparedness of the JI to conduct such attacks.[7] The threat posed by the JI was further underscored by the 12 October 2002 Bali bombings. Bombs were detonated in two nightclubs frequented by western tourists. The bombs left 202 dead and scores of others injured. The bombings, the most deadly since the 9/11 attacks in the United States, marked a shift in the JI's strategy; the United States' Federal Bureau of Investigation has reported that in early 2002, senior JI leaders—meeting in Thailand—decided to attack 'softer targets' in Asia such as tourist sites frequented by westerners (Solomon and Hookway 2002). Following this, several attacks were perpetrated by the JI in 2003 and 2004 when they bombed the JW Marriot Hotel and the Australian Embassy respectively. These bombings were blamed on Dr Azahari Husin, nicknamed 'Demolition Man' and Noordin Mohd Top, both Malaysian JI operatives who are believed to be estranged from the JI leadership (International Crisis Group 2005). The Marriot attack was particularly of interest as it marked the fissure that was occurring within the ranks of the JI. In 2005, the JI terror network once again hit Bali in what has popularly come to be known as the Bali 2 attack. In this attack, three suicide bombers detonated bombs resulting in 20 deaths and more than 100 injured. Once again, the blame fell on Azahari and Top for the attacks. The split within the organization, killings of its leaders and numerous arrests of its leaders, including Hambali, have resulted in the weakening of the Jemaah Islamiyah[8] and the reduction in its capability to mount another serious attack in South East Asia. Yet, the threat of the JI cannot be taken for granted. The escape of Mas Selamat Kastari, one of the Singaporean JI operative from the prison cells of Singapore (at the time of writing) is a manifestation of this danger (*The Straits Times* 2008). Mas Selamat was one of the most dangerous JI operatives in Singapore and his escape has now enhanced the threat of JI in the region. This would especially be the case if he is able to successfully link up with JI operatives in Indonesia and plan attacks against Singapore.

THE JI IDEOLOGY

An attempt to understand the ideology of the JI must begin with the Pedoman Umum Perjuangan Al-Jamaah Al-Islamiyah (PUPJI) translated as 'General Guide for the Struggle of Jemaah Islamiyah', which is a guidebook for the JI leadership, members and followers.

The PUPJI explains that the JI is a well-structured organization with a top-down leadership formation. It also emphasizes that the Islamic state would precede a global Islamic Caliphate, which marked the shift of the JI struggle to be open enough to attach itself to an international global Islamist movement. PUPJI is also important, as Chapter XIV of PUPJI says that the JI can work with any other *jamaah islamiyah*— Islamic community—as long as it shares the same principles and goals. Any leader of a *mantiqi* or *wakalah*[9] can establish relations with others, as well as providing training to like-minded organizations in other parts of Indonesia or a South East Asian country. [10] While the leaders of JI were known to have established links with other groups even before the group's formation, PUPJI structured these relationships within its constitution. This allows it leaders to form tactical alliances with groups such as the al-Qaeda, Moro Islamic Liberation Front (MILF) and other Islamist groups in the region.

THE AFGHAN CONNECTION

The experience of the Afghan war is perhaps a watershed for the JI in building its international connections. In an effort to seek additional funds for their cause and provide proper arms training to the members of their branch of the Dar-ul-Islam, it is reported that Sungkar and Ba'asyir started establishing contacts with the *Mujaheedin*, who were waging a war in Afghanistan against communist Russia.[11] Several hundred JI operatives were sent between 1985 and 1992 to train in Afghanistan.[12] These included recruits from Indonesia, Malaysia, and Singapore.

In Afghanistan, members of the group were linked up to the *Mujaheedin* and Tehreek-e-Islami led by Abdurrab Rasool Sayyaf. It is likely that upon establishing initial contacts with the Saudis, they might have linked Sungkar to Sayyaf. Sayyaf was known for his radical interpretation of Islam. His fluency in Arabic and his studentship experience in Saudi Arabia gave him robust access to Saudi funds (Bergen 2002). Sayyaf's military academy for the *Mujaheedin* was used as a training facility for many foreign fighters, including those from Indonesia. Nasir Abbas' encounter is a useful gauge of the kind of training the recruits undergo and the kind of interaction that occurs between the future JI members and the international network of Islamists. He explained that recruits underwent three years of training known as Sinfi Awwal (first year), Sinfi Duwom (second year) and Sinfi Suwom (third year) (Abas 2005). Upon graduation from each year, recruits also doubled up as trainers. For instance a recruit in the second year would train recruits who were in their first year. The recruits from South East Asia were also rarely in the frontline of fighting with the Soviets as Sayyaf held the belief that they should remain alive to fight the 'war' in Indonesia (Abas 2005). Notwithstanding this, some of the Indonesian recruits did acquire some war experience in Afghanistan. For instance, one of the JI operatives, Mukhlas claims to have taken part in a turning point of the Afghan war, the Battle of the Lion's Den in April 1987 alongside Osama Bin-Laden (International Crisis Group 2003).

The Afghan war was significant in several ways. First, the war provided the future JI members with ample training. The division of levels, compartmentalization of cells involved in attacks, and the careful preparation of the operatives, are the hallmark of the methodology adopted by the Afghan *Mujaheedin*. They were also exposed to weapons training and guerilla tactics, which proved useful in the subsequent terrorist attacks they perpetrated in South East Asia.

Second, the war was important in shaping the thinking and concretizing the ideology of the JI. Prior to the Afghan war, the focus of the South East Asian Islamists was the establishment of Islamic states in their respective countries. After the war, they began to link themselves to the larger struggle of the Muslim world and sought instead to re-establish the Islamic Caliphate. However, both the al-Qaeda and the JI remain discrete organizations with differing, though overlapping, agenda (Abuza 2003). At a more ideological level, the PUPJI resembled many of the handbooks often used by groups such as the al-Qaeda, Hamas, and the Egyptian Muslim Brotherhood. This was the result of the cross-fertilization of ideas and practices that occurred during the Afghan war.

Third, and most importantly, the war was important in strengthening their belief in the Islamic brotherhood. This led to the building of ties between the JI and the ideologues of the al-Qaeda such as Abdullah Azzam and Osama Bin-Laden as well as with the global al-Qaeda network. It was also the point of contact between the JI and other militant groups in South and South East Asia such as the Lashkar-e-Toiba (LeT), Moro Islamic Liberation Front (MILF) and the Harkat-ul-Jihad-al-Islam (HUJI) of Bangladesh.

AL-QAEDA–JI NEXUS

OPERATIONAL COOPERATION

As highlighted in the preceding, the JI and the al-Qaeda remain two separate organizations although the two networks have developed a high degree of symbiotic relationship (Vaughn et al. 2005). At the same time, there is some overlap in membership between the two organizations. One such member is Hambali (Gunaratna 2003). Hambali had first met Osama when he was in Afghanistan and reportedly told those who were attending his religious sermons in Malaysia the exact place and date of these meetings (Simon Elegant 2002). Hambali eventually became the most important linkman between al-Qaeda and the JI, and was reportedly the al-Qaeda's operations chief in South

East Asia. Of particular importance, is his personal relationship with Khalid Sheikh Mohamed, a member of the al-Qaeda and a principal architect of the 9/11 attacks. The relationship between the two dates back to the Afghan war where both had trained together in Sayyaf's camp.[13] As far back as 1995, Khalid Sheikh and Hambali had put together a terror blueprint that has come to be known as Operation Bojinka. It was a coordinated plan to assassinate Pope John Paul II during his visit to Manila, blow up 11 US planes and fly a plane loaded with explosives into the Central Intelligence Agency headquarters in Langley, Virginia.[14] It is also widely believed that the Christmas Eve attacks and several attacks on churches throughout Indonesia were the result of cooperation between the JI and the al-Qaeda. The JI and the al-Qaeda also cooperated in areas of conflict where Muslims are seen to be persecuted. It was estimated that there were at least 200 Afghan, Pakistani and Arab al-Qaeda fighters in Maluku at the height of the conflict between Muslims and Christians there in 2000 (Yunanto 2003). A similar number of al-Qaeda fighters were also believed to be in Poso, another conflict zone in Indonesia. Many of these operatives remain active in these areas till today.[15] The confessions of Omar al-Faruq, a Kuwaiti born al-Qaeda operative in South East Asia, also conclusively prove that Ba'asyir had given him free access to JI operatives in the region for al-Qaeda's planned bombings against American facilities in South East Asia. For instance, Ba'asyir despatched weapons and men to assist al-Faruq (Barton 2004).

SHARING FACILITIES

The JI is also known to have played a supporting role to the al-Qaeda. This support often translated into coordinating meetings for the al-Qaeda in South East Asia. For instance, on 5 January 2000, an important meeting was held in Malaysia of key Bin-Laden lieutenants. Among them were top suspects in the bombing of the USS Cole in Yemen, on 12 October 2000 and two of the 9/11 hijackers, Khalid al-Mindhar and Nawaq al-Hazmi; and Ramzi bin al-Shibh, a close associate of Mohammed Atta (Abuza 2002). The JI also played host to an al-Qaeda operative seeking to form ties with the Lashkar Jihad, a terrorist group operating in the areas of Maluku and Poso where a Muslim–Christian conflict was occurring, when this operative visited Indonesia. This meeting was facilitated by JI operatives in Malaysia, including Hambali. Another supporting role played by the JI for the al-Qaeda is in the sharing of personnel, such as when Hambali sent Yazid Sufaat to Afghanistan to assist in the development of al-Qaeda's chemical and biological project (The 9/11 Commission Report 2004: 151). Sufaat was with Hambali in Kandahar, Afghanistan, in the fall of 2001, where he was working with al-Qaeda weapons experts, discussing anthrax production in South East Asia (Simpson 2003). The JI also allowed al-Qaeda operatives to train in camps run by the group throughout South East Asia. An instance of this was when a Spanish al-Qaeda operative, Louis Jose Galan Gonzales, was reportedly trained in Indonesia by a JI member who was running a terrorist camp in Central Sulawesi. Gonzales was subsequently arrested for alleged terror plans.

FINANCIAL COOPERATION

Al-Qaeda and JI cooperation was also evident in the realm of terror financing (International Crisis Group 2003). In the planning of Operations Bojinka, the JI played an important role for moving money and purchasing equipment for the production of explosives. The *modus operandi* of the al-Qaeda was to obtain some seed money and then to become self-sustaining over time (Abuza 2003). In 1994, Hambali had started a trading company, Konsojaya that ostensibly exported Malaysian palm oil to Afghanistan and imported honey from Sudan and Yemen (Abuza 2003). The firm had a financial capital of 100,000 ringgit, and 5,998 of its 6,000 shares were controlled by Wali Khan Amin Shah and Medhat Abdul Salam Shabana (Abuza 2003). It was believed that the money was initially provided for by the al-Qaeda. The company played an important role in Operation Bojinka as a front for money laundering and purchasing chemicals and equipment for the production of explosives.

The financial support that the al-Qaeda gave to the JI was utilized in several attacks. Of these the most important is the Bali bombings of 2002. The Bali bombings were the most important and successful result of cooperation between the JI and the al-Qaeda. The decision to target tourist areas frequented by westerners was inspired by Hambali. This followed the failed attempt to bomb targets in Singapore. But the fact remains that it was inspired by the al-Qaeda's own agenda of pursuing such targets. It was believed that the bulk of the funding for the bombings came from Khalid Sheikh Mohamed to Hambali.[16] Following the attacks which killed 202 people, many of whom were Australians, the al-Qaeda transferred USD 100,000 to Hambali in two installments to support the families of more than 30 people arrested in the aftermath of the blasts. It was reported that Khalid Sheikh Mohamed was jubilant over the success of the operation and had transferred the money to reward the JI (Powell 2003).

BROAD BASE ALLIANCE IN SOUTH EAST ASIA

In line with its strategy, underlined in PUPJI, of working with like-minded Islamist groups, the JI started forming alliances with various militant groups in the region. The first group that the JI allied with was the MILF. Contacts between the two groups first occurred in 1985, when members of MILF were sent to train in Afghanistan during the war. This relationship was strengthened when several members of Dar-ul-Islam went to southern Philippines to escape persecution from the Indonesian government (Abas 2005). Due to the civil war that followed the Soviet withdrawal and the fall of the communist regime in Afghanistan, the JI decided to shift their training to southern Philippines. In 1994, Nassir Abas, who subsequently rose to the rank of Mantiqi 3, was instructed by Sungkar, to go to southern Philippines at the Abu Bakar Camp run by the MILF (Abas 2005). Abas was responsible for the establishment of the Hudaibiyah Camp—a camp used by JI operatives to train. By 1997, the camp was fully functional and had between 40–60 men training within its facilities. These men included both MILF and JI members as well as some Arab fighters believed to be members of the al-Qaeda (Abas 2005). However, the relationship between the MILF and the JI was not limited to the sharing of facilities and coordinated training alone. It is believed that the attempt on the life of the Filipino ambassador in the year 2000 was a response to the atrocities allegedly perpetrated on Muslims in the Philippines. The MILF also assisted the JI in procuring materials and weapons from sources that provide the group with its own supplies (Abuza 2005). While the current status of the JI in the Philippines is uncertain, the MILF may still be providing refuge to some JI operatives (International Crisis Group 2007a).

The JI also attempted to form a broad base alliance of militant groups in the region. In order for them to achieve this, they hosted a meeting of militant groups held at the International Islamic University in Malaysia. Ba'asyir had invited leaders from groups such as the Free Aceh Movement (GAM), the MILF, the Malaysian Mujaheedin Group (KMM), the Pattani United Liberation Organization (PULO), the Islamic Mujaheedin Movement of Pattani (GMIP), the Rohingya Solidarity Organization (RSO) and the Arakanese Rohingya Nationalist Organization (ARNO) to set up the Rabitatul Mujaheedin (RU) or the International Mujaheedin Association (International Crisis Group 2002a). The key objective of the RU is to coordinate militant activities aimed against western and southeast Asian government interests. It should be noted that groups such as PULO and ARO were opposed to the use of violence, especially against civilian targets. Several follow-up meetings were held in 2000 and 2001.

Through the auspices of the RU, the JI began to cooperate more closely with members of militant groups in Malaysia and southern Thailand. The KMM formed in 1995 by Zainon Ismail, an alumnus of the Afghan war and other Afghan alumni aimed to overthrow the Malaysian government through a violent coup and establish an Islamic state. Links between JI members and KMM were established in Afghanistan. The JI 'White Paper' noted that one of the Singapore JI members bought a boat for Islamist activities in Indonesia. In turn, the 'White Paper' informs us, KMM assisted the JI to obtain ammonium nitrate to produce bombs. Another group known for its links with the JI is the GMIP.[17] The GMIP is a secessionist group aiming to form an Islamic state in the region of Pattani in southern Thailand. While there has been little evidence of joint operations or JI involvement in the southern Thailand insurgency, the GMIP may have assisted the JI operatives to evade authorities, as in the case of Hambali.[18] Another group that the JI had sought to establish is the aforesaid RSO of southern Myanmar. This organization represents Rohingya refugees in Bangladesh. The Rohingya is a Muslim minority group in Myanmar who are persecuted by the military regime in the country. Some Rohingya was known to have fought alongside JI members in Afghanistan (Lintner 2007). There are also reports, based on information derived from the interrogation of Jemaah Islamiyah leader Hambali, who was arrested in Thailand in August 2003, that indicate that he had made a decision to shift JI elements to Bangladesh, in response to counter-terrorist activities in South East Asia (Vaughn 2007).

Beyond South East Asia, the JI is believed to have ties with militant groups both in Pakistan and Bangladesh. These linkages were built during the Afghan War. JI operative Nasir Abas reported that he had helped to train several Bangladeshi militants believed to have been from the Harkat-ul-Jihad-al-Islami (HUJI) (Abas 2005). These links became more apparent when several members of the JI were arrested in Pakistan. It is believed that the JI was training its next-generation leadership in the facilities of Lashkar-e-Toiba in Pakistan with a network of students from Thailand, Indonesia, Malaysia, and Singapore (*Agence France-Presse* 2003a, 2003b). This became apparent after the interrogation following the arrests in 2003 of Rusman Gunawan, the brother of Hambali, along with a network of students from Thailand, Indonesia, Malaysia, and Singapore. These links remain relevant until today as evidenced by the substantial number of Bangladeshis and Pakistanis, known to be fighting alongside JI operatives, in Poso, Indonesia.[19]

LINKS WITH OTHER GROUPS

Beyond linkages with terrorist organizations in South East Asia, the JI also attempted to draw support for its mission and vision by engaging other Islamist groups. One such group is the Hizb-ut-Tahrir (HT). The HT was formed in 1953 by an Islamic scholar, Sheikh Taqiuddin an-Nabhani with the explicit aim of reviving the Islamic Caliphate.[20] It is today operating in more than 43 countries. The interactions between the HT and the JI can be first traced to the HT's earlier interaction with the founders of the al-Qaeda such as Abdullah Azzam. Abdullah Azzam had met members of the HT when he was in Jordan. While he rejected their more gradual and non-violent approach, he agreed with their vision of reviving the Caliphate. More interactions occurred as many former members of the HT, who grew disillusioned with the group's softer approach decided to join the al-Qaeda or groups aligning themselves with the al-Qaeda.[21] The HT was also known to have met the Taliban regime shortly after the latter took over power in Afghanistan in order to offer them assistance to revive the Islamic Caliphate, but was rejected by the Taliban.[22] The al-Qaeda operative was also critical of HT's non-violent approach and had condemned HT as a weak and moderate Muslim Group (Seraj 2003). Despite these uneasy relations, the HT in South East Asia has maintained good links with the JI.

The links between the JI and the HT is of particular interest due to the transnational nature of the HT itself. Some members of the HT go a step further to indicate that it was the HT that influenced the JI to broaden its vision of establishing an Islamic state for establishing a supranational Islamic Caliphate. In Singapore, while no clear cooperation can be established between the two groups, the HT members had met members of the JI in the country in an attempt to persuade the JI members to adopt the HT's methodology of reviving the Islamic Caliphate. The meeting was initiated in November 2001. Their attempt failed and later when members of the JI in Singapore were arrested, the Singapore's Internal Security Department arrested several members of the HT. It is believed that some of the JI detainees reported the existence of the HT network in Singapore. Interestingly, these members included a Muslim army officer who was the first Muslim to be awarded the prestigious Singapore Armed Forces scholarship.[23]

In Indonesia, clear linkages can be seen between the Hizbut Tahrir Indonesia (HTI) and the JI. Ismail Yusanto noted that he did not believe that the JI existed and the creation of the JI is part of the American and Western conspiracy against Islam.[24] The HTI members were in the forefront of defending Ba'asyir when the later was arrested for his ties with the JI and terrorism. Ba'asyir was also invited to speak at the largest ever congregation organized by the HT worldwide.[25] Ba'asyir did not attend as he was threatened with arrest by Indonesian authorities.[26] Following the congregation, a separate forum was organized by the HTI, featuring Ba'asyir as a speaker. Ba'asyir stated his support for the HTI's vision of reviving the Islamic Caliphate, stating that it is an obligation for all Muslims in Indonesia (HTI 2007). The MMI, one of the splinter groups of the JI also worked closely with the HTI in holding mass demonstrations against the Indonesian government and calling for the implementation of the Shariah in the country. In 2005, the HTI and the MMI mooted the formation of the Muslim Ummah Forum (FUI) following a series of discussions among several Muslim organizations in Indonesia. The forum aimed to revive the Islamic Shariah in Indonesia and has been in the forefront of organizing talks, forums and demonstrations towards this end. It must be mentioned at this point that despite such interactions between the two groups, the HT's influence was at an ideological level and not in the operational arena. The HT and its chapters in South East Asia remain committed to a non-violent revival of the Islamic Caliphate. Yet the interactions and close relationships between the JI (and its affiliates) and the HT in South East Asia may result in the shift of methodology of the JI itself when one observes the result of such interactions in other parts of the world. In Pakistan, the HT had been successful in recruiting members of the LeT into its fold (Perlez 2007). Similarly, in India, former members of the Student Islamic Movement of India (SIMI) are flocking to HT gatherings in India.[27] Both the LeT and the SIMI are alleged to have links with the al-Qaeda and subscribe to the al-Qaeda's ideology and methodology. At this stage it seems that many of these activists have disavowed violence and are working for a peaceful revival of the Islamic Caliphate. Thus, the close link between the HT and the JI in Indonesia may eventually result in the latter's disavowal of violence.

Today, the JI has become less of a threat to South East Asia. This is partly due to the intensive operations by various security agencies in the region to curb its activities and arrests its leaders. Most of its international links to other groups with the exception of the HT and the MILF have been significantly affected, especially after the arrest of Hambali. Its network in Malaysia, Singapore, and Australia is completely wiped out. The recent release of five more JI members in Singapore is a reflection of the success of the Singaporean authorities in rehabilitating JI members (Hussain 2008). However, the escape of Mas Selamat may lead to the strengthening of JI in Singapore. The JI in Indonesia itself has become weak and has splintered into smaller groups.[28] The most visible of these groups is the MMI. Nevertheless, its key spiritual leader, Ba'asyir is still at large and has become an important force in Indonesian politics. Observers in Indonesia believe that he may contest the next elections in 2009 or support certain Islamic parties in Indonesia. Others believe that he may even work closer with groups like the HT and utilize the HT as a vehicle for power.

CONCLUSION

The paper began by describing the history and ideology of the JI. It then traced how the international linkages with other militant groups in the region emerged as a result of the JI's involvement in the Afghan war. Its linkage with the al-Qaeda is of significance because of the extensive cooperation in operations and finances that took place between the two groups. Similarly, the JI's cooperation with the MILF gave it access to training camps and facilities that its operational imperatives necessitated. Nevertheless, the most interesting aspect that characterized JI's international links is its links to the HT. Despite the poor relations between the HT and the pan al-Qaeda network, the HT seems to have developed good relations with the JI. This relationship can bring about a positive development if the HT is able to convince members of the JI to adopt a more peaceful method of reviving the Islamic Caliphate rather than adopting a violent one. The current status of the JI states that almost all its international linkages are becoming defunct. However, it will be interesting to see how the new JI positions itself in dealing with the HT and how this will impact Indonesian and southeast Asian politics.

NOTES

1. The most comprehensive work on the life, politics and thinking of Kartosoewirjo is Al-Chaidar (1999), and for a comprehensive history of the Darul Islam rebellion, see Van Djik 1981.
2. Greg Fealy 2005b, p. 16. Also refer to pp. 18–19 of the same for details of the regional rebellions.
3. In 1974, a meeting of Darul Islam leaders appointed the Acehnese Islamic scholar Daud Beureueh as leader of the movement, a position he held until his death in 1984. Following his death, some of Kartosoewirjo's former commanders, former assistants and sons laid claim to the Darul Islam leadership. The most prominent of these were Adah Djaelani, Ajengan Masduki and Kartosoewirjo's sons, Tahmid Rachmat Basuki and Dodo Ahmad Sudarda. See Fealy 2005c: 22 and Abduh 2002: 28–40.
4. There are differing opinions among scholars about whether Sungkar and Ba'asyir were members of the Dar-ul-Islam. Martin van Bruinessen, Greg Fealy and Sidney Jones support the view that they are members while others such as ICG maintains that the two were never members of the Dar-ul-Islam. See Bruinessen 2004; Jones 2005; Fealy 2005b and ICG 2002b. For the purpose of the chapter, the contributor will take the view that they were members of Dar-ul-Islam.
5. Fealy 2005c: 25. Sometime in 1992, the two senior leaders of the Dar-ul-Islam movement, Abdullah Sungkar and an Indonesia-based man, Ajengan Masduki, fell out. Sungkar accused Masduki of having Shi'ite and Sufi tendencies and, therefore, of having strayed from *salafi* teaching. See ICG 2003: 6.
6. Their decision followed in the footsteps of Bin-Laden's 1996 Declaration of War against the Zionist-Crusader Enemy and his 1998 *fatwa* calling for the killing of American and Western civilians. See Conboy 2004: 136–138.
7. Culled from confidential sources.

8. Hambali was arrested in August 2003 in Ayutthaya, Thailand after some local Muslims in the area reported to the police about a strange man living in their midst. He was apparently planning an attack on the participants of the Asia-Pacific Economic Cooperation summit in Bangkok scheduled for October 2003. He was subsequently handed over to the United States and is now detained in Guantanamo Bay. Following Hambali's arrest, Dr Azahari Husin was believed to have assumed leadership of JI. However, in 2005, he was killed in a showdown with the Indonesian police when the later attempted to arrest him in Semarang, Indonesia.

9. Mantiqi refers to a province. The First Mantiqi covers West Malaysia and Singapore, the second Mantiqi covers Sumatra, Java until Nusa Tenggara, the third Mantiqi includes Sabah Malaysia, East Kalimantan, Central Sulawesi, North Sulawesi and Mindanao, South Philippine, while the fourth Mantiqi includes Australia. There are some Wakalah in a Mantiqi, and the Wakalah is divided into parts, small study groups as per *Pedoman Umum Perjuangan Al-Jamaah Al-Islamiyah*, Chapter 2, Article 4, Clause 2. For a more detailed explanation of these terms as well as the JI manual, PUPJI, see Pavlova 2006.

10. *Pedoman Umum Perjuangan Al-Jamaah Al-Islamiyah,* Chapter 10. For a better sense of the operational structure of JI, see Singh 2003: 45.

11. Abas 2005: 45. Nasir Abas was a former member of JI who also fought in Afghanistan.

12. See ICG, 2003: 7–10 for the list of prominent alumni of the Afghan war. This list includes Hambali who went there in 1987 and Muchlas alias Ali Ghufron, one of the perpetrators of the Bali bombings who went there in 1986.

13. Khalid Sheikh Mohamed's relationship with Sayyaf was captured in the 9/11 Report.

14. A detailed description of the plan can be found in Reeve 1999.

15. Culled from confidential sources.

16. See Abuza 2003: 54–56 for details of funding for the operation.

17. For more on the GMIP, refer to Abuza 2006a.

18. Hambali was captured in Thailand in 2003.

19. Culled from a confidential source.

20. The most important and in depth study of HT is Suha Taji-Farouki, *A Fundamental Quest, Hizb al-Tahrir and the Search for the Islamic Caliphate.*

21. Omar Shariff who attempted a suicide bombing operation in Tel Aviv, Israel was purportedly a former HT member (Malik 2003).

22. Interview with a member of Hizbut Tahrir in UK, June 2007.

23. Conversation with a former member of Hizbut Tahrir in Singapore, June 2006.

24. Interview with Ismail Yusanto, Spokesman, Hizbut Tahrir Indonesia, August 2007.

25. In all advertisements used by HTI to promote the event, Ba'asyir was featured as one of the speakers.

26. Interview with HT Indonesia leader, Muhammad al-Khaththath, August 2007.

27. Interview with member of HT India in UK, June 2007.

28. For details of its current status, see ICG 2007a.

10

AL-QAEDA
INSPIRED TRANSNATIONAL
TERRORISM: IDEOLOGY AND
ORGANIZATIONAL FORMS

Ekaterina Stepanova

INTRODUCTION

Throughout history, terrorist means have been used by militant groups of different religious orientation, often blended with nationalist and socio-political ideological elements. However, the main terrorist threat to international security in the late 20th–early 21st centuries has been posed by transnational Islamist terrorism.

The challenges posed by Islamist terrorism at the transnational level can only partly be reflected by quantitative indicators. In the period from 1968 until 2006 that is covered by available data, all religious terrorist groups, including Islamist actors, were responsible for a minority of international terrorist attacks. Even with the rise of Islamist terrorism in the late 1990s–early 2000s, the *number* of international attacks committed by Islamist terrorists has not surpassed the number of such attacks carried out by radical nationalist groups. In 1998–2006, religious—mostly Islamist—terrorists carried out 352 attacks internationally, as compared to 353 attacks by violent nationalists.[1]

This trend comes in contrast with the greater *lethality* of religious terrorism in general and the lethality of Islamist terrorism in particular, especially at the transnational level. Since the early 1990s, religious, mostly Islamist, terrorism has been far more deadly at the international level than any other type of terrorism, including nationalist terrorism. In international attacks committed over the last decade (1998–2006), 4–3 times more people (5,136) were killed by religious, almost exclusively Islamist, terrorists than by ethno-separatist and other nationalist groups (1208).[2] This correlation is hardly surprising. In contrast to violent Islamist networks that may be truly transnational, nationalist terrorism is tied to a specific national context, is generated by and operates within a national political system and primarily, although not exclusively, results in attacks that may qualify as 'domestic' or 'internal'. Also, in contrast to many secular militant organizations or groups whose ideology is not dominated by religious imperative, religious terrorists perceive their attacks as 'acts of faith'. Accordingly, self-sacrifice attacks are carried out as acts of religious martyrdom. This upgradation of a terrorist event to a 'sacred act' effectively removes some of the basic constraints on incurring mass civilian casualties and facilitates the perpetration of deadlier, larger-scale attacks addressed to a much broader audience.

The high lethality of transnational Islamist terrorism is often seen as the main threat posed by this type of terrorism. However, it is not just the high level of terrorism-related casualties that make Islamist terrorism a major—in fact the greatest—terrorist challenge for the international community in the early 20th century. First of all, sheer numbers and quantitative indicators in principle cannot suffice for an accurate analysis of terrorism. This is due to the specifics of terrorism as the use of—or threat to use politically-motivated violence in such a way that its broader consequences and impact go far beyond its immediate human costs and material damage. Terrorists' main message is directed at someone beyond their immediate civilian targets—usually at the state. Second, high lethality should rather be seen as a side-effect and a reflection of the more fundamental characteristics of the transnational Islamist terrorism. These more fundamental characteristics are its ideological goals, political agenda, overall outreach and organizational forms.

Some of these characteristics also help distinguish transnational, globally-oriented violent Islamist networks such as the al-Qaeda and the cells of a broader transnational violent movement inspired by the al-Qaeda from the more localized militant groups of Islamist orientation who combine Islamism with a strong nationalist bent and for whom Islam is only part of their identity, ideology and socio-political goals and programmes.

SUPRANATIONAL IDEOLOGY OF THE MOVEMENT

Terrorism is the use or threat to use violence against civilians and non-combatants by non-state actors, in order to achieve political, ideological or/and religious goals in an asymmetrical confrontation.[3] To 'justify' violence against civilians as a tool to exert pressure on a more powerful opponent—the state, or a group of state, or an international community of states—a militant group needs a higher degree of ideological commitment and indoctrination than it does to engage in many other forms of violence. This high degree of indoctrination and 'justification' of terrorist tactics used indiscriminately or specifically directed against civilians can only be provided and facilitated by an extremist ideology. The ideological basis for terrorism may be provided by extremist ideologies of all types and origins. This, however, does not at all mean that any such ideology (anarchism, Maoism, racism, nationalist extremism or Islamism) is inherently linked to terrorism or automatically produces it.

The main comparative advantages of the state and the international community in asymmetric confrontation with militant groups that employ terrorist means are the states' incomparably greater conventional military, economic and political power and the formal status that they enjoy in the international system as its mainstays. However, armed non-state actors that choose to use terrorist tactics have certain comparative advantages in asymmetric confrontation with the state too, both at the local and the broader transnational level. One of the two main advantages of militant-terrorist actors is precisely the very high power of mobilization and indoctrination that their radical, *extremist ideologies* have in certain segments of society. These may be parts of an ethnic or religious community or social group(s) in whose name these militant actors claim to speak and whose interests they claim to defend. Actors ready to take up arms to oppose the dominant system (national or international political order) and to go the extreme length in using or threatening indiscriminate or direct and intentional violence against civilians are by definition far more ideologically zealous, more strongly motivated and display a much higher level of resolve and commitment to their ideological goals than their mainstream opponents. In sum, extremist ideologies are one of the main strengths and strategic resources of terrorist actors in asymmetrical confrontation.

In the past, the most widespread extremist ideologies employed by groups that used terrorist means were various radical socio-revolutionary, anarchist and other left-wing currents. By the late 20th century, they have been replaced by radical nationalism and religious extremism as the most influential ideologies of terrorist groups. While at the *local* level terrorists often combine religious extremism with some form of radical nationalism, modern transnational terrorism is dominated by violent Islamist extremism of the type promoted and inspired by the al-Qaeda. This form of Islamist radicalism has taken the role of a globalized anti-system protest ideology. In playing this role, transnational violent Islamism has largely replaced the secular internationalist left-wing revolutionary ideologies of the past.

What makes the ideology of violent Islamism such a powerful driver of a transnational violent protest movement with global outreach and goals? How is the ideology of multiple cells of this transnational post-Qaeda network different from the mix of radical Islamism and nationalism that guides many more localized, territorially based Islamist groups and grassroot movements? How is it different from other radical ideologies that had global appeal and aspired to play a global role in the past, such as internationalist left-wing ideologies?

TRANSNATIONAL ISLAMISM AND LOCALIZED ISLAMIST-NATIONALIST GROUPS

Theoretically, the shared ideology of violent Islamism should appear to be one of the few things that can link the al-Qaeda or the cells of the broader transnational movement inspired by the al-Qaeda with the more localized and consolidated armed Islamist groups active in different national and regional contexts.

If a standard, albeit increasingly outdated, dichotomy of 'international—internal' terrorism is applied, terrorist activities of the al-Qaeda and post-al-Qaeda networks would automatically qualify as 'international' terrorism. As for several insurgent groups that combine Islamism with territorially based nationalism—both ethno-separatist and broader nationalist and national liberation resistance movements (such as the ones in the Palestinian territories and in Iraq)—terrorism employed by these groups is generated within the respective national context. Even as these groups' terrorist activities usually have some external logistical, financial or other dimension or cross-border implications, their main goals and agenda are confined to a particular conflict area or national context. Thus, their terrorist activities are still more accurately described as 'domestic' terrorism. Also, there is hardly any ideological unity or consolidated discourse between violent Islamist networks at a global level and many local groups of Islamist bent.

How is the transnational ideological discourse of the al-Qaeda and the post-al-Qaeda movement different from that of the more localized and nationalist-oriented groups of Islamist bent (such as the Palestinian Hamas or the Lebanese Hezbollah) whose activities have a clear territorial dimension and are mainly tied to a specific national context? What does allow us to distinguish between the former and the latter? The answer is: *global goals and outreach* of the dispersed and multiple cells of the al-Qaeda inspired movement. The ultimate goals and the end-state of both violent and non-violent Islamism at the transnational level is a worldwide Islamic Caliphate. The Caliphate is neither a classic nation state, not a purely theocratic state. Rather, it is a global political and social order, a form of government that is based on the 'direct rule of God' and is expected to unite all Muslims. Both violent and non-violent followers of this utopian 'global vision' aspire, ultimately, to create or, rather, 'restore' the supranational, quasi-religious, rather than purely religious, order and spread its power to the rest of the world.

A global goal such as the Caliphate can only be a relatively abstract one. The same is true for most other categories and notions put forward by transnational Islamist movements, including violent networks. If the end-state is a universalist, quasi-religious global order, politics is also likely to be interpreted that way—in sharp contrast to radical nationalists. Transnational Islamists' understanding and interpretation of most other basic social, political and military categories such as 'security', 'victory', 'defeat' are also very broad and abstract and by definition not confined to any specific local or national context. For instance, unlike secular groups or ethno-confessional nationalist movements for whom religion is only part of their identity and who operate main within their national political systems, the notion of the ultimate 'enemy' is usually formulated by violent al-Qaeda inspired cells in much broader, almost universal terms. While the enemy could be personalized to some extent and categorized as a 'close' enemy (impious Muslim regimes corrupted by Westernization) and a 'more distant' one (such as the USA and its allies), ultimately, it cannot be reduced to a few individuals, social class, ethnic group, state or even a community of states. Rather, their main protagonist represents some generalized and impersonalized 'evil' that in principle can only be defined in very broad and blurred categories, as a generalized notion or trend (ranging from 'the West' or 'Western-style modernization' to the entire world of unbelief, ignorance and materialism (*jahiliyyah*) or simply 'all injustice on earth').[4]

Fighting against such a broadly defined, vague, multi-faceted enemy that amounts to nothing less than 'global evil', or Satan, by definition requires a universal *jihad* with unlimited goals. These goals are centred on establishing 'the Sovereignty and Authority of God on earth' by 'an international party' rising 'with a universal faith and ideology' and 'launching an assault on the principles of the opponent' (Maududi 2004: 400). Unlike some other form of armed *jihad* such as internal *jihad* that targets 'impious' Muslim regimes or liberation *jihad* (armed struggle to drive 'occupiers' and 'non-believers' from the 'native' Muslim lands, that is, in Iraq and the Palestinian territories), the global *jihad* is a transnational and or, more precisely, supranational movement founded by Bin-Laden and the al-Qaeda. While, according to its ideologues, global *jihad* may have a series of sub-goals to be achieved along the way, including the support for the more localized internal and liberation jihads, its ultimate goal is centred on establishing Islamic rule worldwide. In this sense, of all the types of jihad as an armed struggle mentioned above, global *jihad* is the most radical one and poses the greatest challenge to international security.

In summation, the ideology of the transnational violent Islamist movement of multiple self-generating post-al-Qaeda cells active in different countries and parts of the world is truly global and universalist. The final ideological goals of this movement are not limited to confrontation with the West. They go far beyond any concrete national or even any broader anti-neo-imperialist or anti-neocolonialist agenda re-interpreted in quasi-religious categories.

This comes in contrast to most more-localized, territorially based movements of Islamist bent that usually combine Islamism with some form of radical nationalism. Many genuine Islamist grassroot social and resistance movements may gradually develop a very strong nationalist identity and ideology, with the Palestinian Hamas and the Lebanese Hezbollah as the two best-known cases in point. While theoretically, the idea of a global order centred on a restored Caliphate may remain in their list of distant goals, their real goals, agenda and activities are completely dominated by a specific national context and effectively confined to a local or, maximum, regional level.

Alternatively, some originally nationalist/separatist insurgent movements in Muslim-populated areas, such as the one in the North Caucasus (Russia), may gradually become more Islamized and acquire a professedly Islamist profile. For armed separatist movements, one of the main advantages of Islamization is often precisely its ability to internationalize a group's agenda and broaden its constituency beyond members of a certain ethnic group. The more Islamized they become, the more they can hope to appeal to a broader religious community where their message can received broader support, even if their terrorist tactics is rejected by the majority of that community.

In dealing with these localized Islamist-nationalist groups, especially if they are broad grassroot movements in a conflict or a post-conflict environment, their *ability to 'nationalize' their ideology and practical activities and to integrate them into national, state-centred political context is of critical importance.* In sharp contrast to the al-Qaeda inspired cells of transnational Islamist networks that reject the very idea of a state, the strong nationalist bent of these locally based movements still keeps them very much focused on the state. While their state-building agendas may be radically different from those formulated within the liberal Western discourse, they at least remain within the same state-based order that guides the rest of the world. This, in turn, at least leaves armed actors, including those that may have used terrorist means, with an opportunity of turning—or coming back—to the mainstream non-violent forms of political Islam (the so-called legalist Islamism, as opposed to violent Islamism). This also means that the rejection of terrorist means by some of these actors, especially by broad grassroot movements such as Hamas or Hezbollah, remains at least a plausible option.

In contrast, the violent quasi-religious movement's ideology may be markedly transnational, even supranational, to the point that it explicitly rejects any form of nationalism. The main case in point is the ideology of the original al-Qaeda and the broader transnational violent Islamist movement that it had inspired. Such an ideology cannot be integrated with nationalism in principle unless it changes beyond recognition. In that case, the option of such a transnational movement ever abandoning its terrorist tactics—at least as long as it exists—is almost completely unrealistic.

TRANSNATIONAL ISLAMISM AND GLOBAL PROTEST IDEOLOGIES OF THE PAST

The ideological vision of transnational violent Islamist cells and networks inspired by the al-Qaeda is not only universalist, but also, as noted above, goes beyond theology and purely religious outlook. It does not make a clear distinction between religion and politics on a global scale.

This phenomenon can partly explain what distinguishes the ideology shared by cells of post-al-Qaeda inspired transnational movement from, for instance, sets of beliefs of some relatively small totalitarian religious sects with a global, apocalyptical vision. The main distinction is precisely that violent Islamism—as well as Islamism in general—is a quasi-religious, rather than purely religious, ideology that views religion and politics, society and state as inseparable. This is in large part due to the holistic, all-embracing nature of fundamentalist forms of Islam where legal and normative aspects are developed in far greater detail than in other religions and confessions. In that sense, Islamism is more a comprehensive concept of social order and organization, at both the national and supranational levels, than it is a purely religious current.

In the 20th century, some other globally-oriented groups and movements that used terrorist means were guided by secular internationalist left-wing ideologies, such as radical Marxism, Maoism or Trotskyism. The major distinction between transnational violent Islamist of the present and these radical secular ideologies with global appeal that inspired international terrorists of the past is not only the religious dimension of the former. A no less important distinction is the rejection of the very notion of the 'state' as such by transnational violent Islamism. This radical transnational ideology of violent Islamism of al-Qaeda type is truly supranational and 'supra-state'. Not only does it ignore the modern concept of state—it also goes beyond the notion of the state as such. Unlike most internationalist radical ideologies that had dominated international terrorist activity in the past (with a possible exception of anarchism), transnational Islamism does not see the state as a reference point of the coming world order—it suggests a form of global social, political, religious and legal organization that is not based on states as its core units.

In the view of the ideologues of this movement, all modern states and societies are impious, inadequate and 'steeped in *Jahiliyyah*' that has encompassed the entire world (Qutb 1989: 14). Any state and society is seen as being part of *jahiliyyah* as long as it does not dedicate itself to submission to God alone, in its beliefs and ideas in its observances of worship, and in its legal regulations (Qutb 1989: 103). As noted above, the end-state of this vision—the global Caliphate—is hardly an analogue of a state in its classic sense, but rather a global socio-political-religious order. This order is seen as the one striving for an ideal 'to annihilate all systems and governments that establish the hegemony of human beings and relegate them to their servitude' (Qutb 2000: 231), and an 'all-embracing and total revolution against the sovereignty of man in all its types, shapes, systems, and states' (Qutb 2000: 228).

In sum, in terms of its international spread and appeal, the version of violent Islamism preached and practised by the al-Qaeda inspired transnational Islamists is not exactly an *internationalist* ideology (such as internationalist left-wing revolutionary ideologies of the past), but rather a *transnational* and even a *supranational* ideology. In the context of conflicting trends of globalization and fragmentation, modernization and 'reactive' archaization, it is hardly surprising that the main new ideology of modern transnational terrorism is *(a)* a *quasireligious* ideology, in contrast to the secular radical socio-revolutionary ideas of the past, and *(b)* a *supranational* ideology that, despite its religious radicalism, may unexpectedly well resonate with some of the main features of today's world, such as the erosion of state power and sovereignty.

Despite its utopian nature, the global, universalist dimension of transnational violent Islamism is one of its powerful ideological tools. It is interesting to note in this context that well before the contemporary discourse and debates on globalization emerged and became widespread, the first ideologues of modern violent Islamism (such as Sayeed Qutb in the 1950s—early 1960s) had already presented a vision that could be seen as an alternative version of globalization. This type of supranational globalism is based on, and ruled by, fundamentalist Islam but provides for the pluralism of cultural-ethno-confessional modes and patterns (on condition that their adherents recognize the primacy of the 'One God'). All this has made transnational violent Islamism not just an extremist theory, but also a powerful ideology with a surprisingly modern dimension that gives a radical quasi-religious response to the challenges of the modern, globalizing world.

TRANSNATIONAL MULTI-LEVEL NETWORKS AS AN ORGANIZATIONAL FORM

While the organizational patterns of terrorist groups may vary, the basic assumption is that the more different these structures are from those most typical of their main protagonist (the state or the international community), the harder it is to counter these non-state actors in an asymmetrical confrontation.

The structures of the al-Qaeda and of the broader and even more fragmented and dispersed follow-on transnational Islamist movement are usually described as a transitional form from a more formalized to a more amorphous, decentralized, creeping network of cells that spread in a way that, in some way, resembles franchise business schemes. These cells share the al-Qaeda's ideology, follow its general strategic guidelines and use its name as a 'brand', but are not, or not necessarily, formally linked to it in structural terms. Such a creeping network displays some of the main characteristics of what has become known as *segmented polycentric ideologically integrated network* (the so-called SPIN-structure).[5] SPIN is very flexible in structural terms and effectively adapts to the fast changing environment. This model allows many modern social protest movements to effectively resist suppressive measures by governments and to penetrate all strata of the society. The main integrating force for SPIN is its shared *ideology* that helps connect its often fragmented, dispersed, isolated or informally inter-linked elements.

The problem is that some of the main organizational strengths and specifics of the cell structure of the modern transnational violent Islamist movement cannot be explained by or reduced to its network characteristics alone. If these cells were simply organized into just another social protest network such as the anti-globalist movement, it would have been half the trouble. While networks have some structural advantages—such as greater mobility, flexibility, and adaptability—over more hierarchical organizations, they also have some serious weaknesses (most of which are downsides of their comparative advantages). The mere fact that multiple cells form a network tied by their ideological proximity and shared beliefs does not yet impose any mutual *obligations* to act upon these network elements. Networks have difficulties in decision-making and ensuring strategic coordination or implementation of any decisions. They also lack consolidated central leadership able to exercise control over the network's multiple elements and cells.

The transnational al-Qaeda inspired movement may appear as a loose network of dispersed and not necessarily connected cells scattered around the world. However, in contrast to most standard social protest networks, it demonstrates an unusually high level of effective strategic coordination and doctrinal coherence. In other words, despite the dispersed structure of this network, its cells manage to neutralize some of the main weaknesses typical of networks as an organizational form. These largely self-generating cells that emerge in different countries and parts of the world not only think, but also act as parts of the same global movement.

This structural puzzle needs an organizational explanation. Given that organizational forms of Islamist movements are to a very significant extent shaped by their ideology, any such organizational explanation should be intertwined with and supplemented by an ideological one.

HYBRID MULTI-LEVEL NETWORK

In organizational terms, the al-Qaeda and the multiple cells of the broader follow-up transnational post-al-Qaeda movement are usually seen as representing a 'new' organizational form (network) that is qualitatively different from 'old', more hierarchically structured, terrorist groups. However, years after the attacks of 11 September 2001, it no longer suffices to downgrade this dynamic, adaptive and rapidly changing organizational system to a standard network, described in the most general terms.

The spread of network forms in the late 20th–early 21st centuries marked a certain structural shift in organizational forms. This shift was most evident among the non-state actors, both those that engage in social and political activism and those who resort to violent means. In practice, however, neither the collision between networks and hierarchies, nor the distinctions between informal decentralized networks and more formal organizations are strict dichotomies. Basic distinctions between networks and hierarchies do not mean that there is no space for various intermediate structures. Most real-life structures, including terrorist groups, are structures of mixed type: they fit somewhere in between 'ideal' network and 'pure' hierarchy. In other words, they are *hybrids* that combine both network and hierarchical elements. This combination is subject to dynamic change: for instance, a decentralized organization such as the al-Qaeda in its early years can later evolve into a broader and looser full-fledged network.

In spite of the prevalence of network forms and characteristics, transnational violent Islamist movement, like most real-life structures, also displays some elements of hierarchy. This movement cannot be reduced to purely 'leaderless resistance' (a concept that was developed in the 1980s–1990s by the US right-wing white-power supremacist and network theorist and practitioner Louis Beam) (Beam 1992). In contrast, the al-Qaeda inspired transnational movement does have multiple leaders (even if these are not necessarily leaders in the classic sense of the word). It is also a multi-level rather than flat network system that displays some vertical links connecting its macro-level with sub-levels. These links are different from those typical for vertical hierarchies in that they may also be as virtual as the informal horizontal links between the movement's autonomous cells at the micro-level.

More generally, network elements are hardly entirely 'new' to organizational patterns of terrorist groups. With all the present focus on network characteristics of the al-Qaeda as the first modern super-terrorist network, certain network elements have been present—and continue to proliferate—in organizational patterns of terrorist groups of the more traditional types, including militant separatists. The fact that the first attempt to conceptualize segmented network 'urban guerrilla' employing terrorist means dates back to the late 1960s is often overlooked. Many of the tactics typical to modern 'network warfare' such as *swarming* (a convergent, breakthrough attack by many relatively small, dispersed, autonomous units striking from all direction on a same target)[6] are no less popular among the localized militant groups than among the multiple cells of the al-Qaeda inspired transnational movement. Today, network elements and forms are not only characteristics of the 'new' transnational terrorism of the al-Qaeda and the follow-up transnational movement, but are increasingly employed in organizational frameworks of more localized hybrid-structured armed groups (for example, in the Palestinian context, these groups may range from Hamas to Al-Aqsa Martyrs/Arafat Brigades).

The main defining criterion of the 'new' transnational terrorism, or super-terrorism, is not so much its network structures as opposed to hierarchical forms of organization of 'terrorism of the past'. What distinguishes modern super-terrorism from, for instance, terrorism employed for decades by the Palestinian, Kashmiri or other militant non-state actors as a tactics in asymmetrical confrontation at the local/regional level is *the level and scope of a terrorist group's goals and agenda*—global (unlimited) or limited to a certain territory and/or local, national or regional political context.[7]

The spread of network elements can be traced in organizational patterns of terrorist groups of different types and at all levels from global to local. If there are any major structural distinctions between the more localized terrorism of more traditional types and the relatively 'new' transnational super-terrorist networks, these distinctions are mostly a matter of varying correlation of network and hierarchical forms. Not surprisingly, for a transnational violent Islamist movement with a global outreach and unlimited goals the role and significance of network characteristics, elements and models would be by definition much higher than for a more localized group with goals confined to a particular national political context.

INTRA-CELL LINKS AT MICRO-LEVEL: FROM 'BROTHERHOODS' TO BLOGS

Terrorism-centred activities of the multiple, dispersed and mostly self-generating cells of the al-Qaeda inspired movement require a much higher level of intra-organizational coherence, mutual trust and personalized social obligations that the one that can be provided by standard, impersonalized network linked by shared ideology. This coherence at micro-level of individual cells is something that neither a pure network, nor a hybrid multi-level structure can be expected to provide by default. What are the main characteristics that allow the individual cells at the micro-level to hold together and engage in terrorist activity so effectively, then?

Some networks analysts wrestling with this question suggested a clan-based, 'network tribalism' concept as an answer. They argued that what helps individual al-Qaeda inspired cells to achieve a high degree of internal coherence and integration may be a cell formation pattern built upon family, kinship and clan ties and resembling a traditional, archaic extended family, or tribe.[8] However, more systematic attempts to provide psycho-sociological account of post-al-Qaeda transnational violent Islamist networks have confirmed that the members of the same (semi)autonomous cell are usually linked by close personal and intra-group relations. These relations are often established before a cell 'joins' the movement—either through getting in contact with some of other cells and leaders or simply by means of 'direct action', that is, by organizing and carrying out a terrorist attack. However, these links are not so much of the clan or family type as of they are ties based on friendship, shared regional or national background, common professional, educational and other experience.[9] This common experience may have been acquired not only, or not even primarily, in places of religious worship, such as mosques, or religious schools, but also in secular universities, engineering and technical schools and so on. In other words, the case in point is not so much an archaic 'clan-type' relationship, as it is a group of close friends with similar or common interests, an association or 'brotherhood' of like-minded people.

There is no need to reproduce in detail the specific mechanisms of radicalization and cell formation of the transnational Islamist movement, as they are context-specific and do not conform to a single pattern. Regardless of context, a relatively small group of friends gets more and more tightly integrated—usually on the basis of a combination of a general feeling of alienation from the 'imperfect', 'immoral', 'corrupt' society of non-believers surrounding them (jahiliyyah) and under the strong impression and impact of certain political and military developments, both at the national and at the international levels. In the post-11 September period, the developments that had the most powerful symbolic meaning and the strongest mobilization effect were the military intervention in Afghanistan and Iraq.[10] A group gets politicized and radicalized and finds natural guidance and ready answers to many of its concerns in Islamism and Islamic extremism. At some stage, often under the impact of a certain 'critical event', the group realizes the need to go beyond 'mere talk' and to turn to active 'propaganda by deed'. Following this, the members of the new cell which is already ripe for joining the 'movement' starts to actively search for the possibilities and means to organize an 'action'—usually, a terrorist act or a series of terrorist attacks. Such a cell may try to establish a contact with one of the veteran Islamists (of the Afghan resistance or any subsequent 'jihads'), but it may also proceed with its terrorist plans and actions on a purely self-generated basis.

It is interesting to note that people that remain closely integrated into relatively archaic, non-modernized clan structures rarely become active members of the al-Qaeda inspired transnational Islamist movement. Quite on the contrary, it is the areas of the most intensive and close contact with 'aliens', especially in Muslim diasporas and communities in Western states, especially in Europe, or areas of the extended Western economic, military, political and cultural presence and influence in the Muslim world, that provide the most favourable environment for breeding potential members of the post-al-Qaeda terrorist cells. There are also indications that the radicalization process that eventually leads to formation of violent Islamist cells with transnational agenda has become increasingly rapid, especially in Muslim diasporas in the West and has been increasingly facilitated though online information and communication activities (Europol 2007: 18–19).

TRANSNATIONAL QUASI-RELIGIOUS IDEOLOGY AS STRATEGY AND ORGANIZING PRINCIPLE

The main organizational specificity of Islamist movements—both reformist and extremist, non-violent and violent, localized and transnational—is that their structures do not simply evolve in an organic way, but are to a large extent dictated by and formed in accordance with the Islamist ideology. Among other things, this ideology does not favour strictly hierarchical organizational forms in principle, and gives a general preference to networks while retaining a strong egalitarian element.

While structures of various Islamist groups at levels from local to global are characterized by organizational pluralism, the transnational violent Islamist movement inspired by the al-Qaeda is a loose multi-level network of small, semi- or fully autonomous cells. Unlike some broad mass-based grassroot territorially-based Islamist movements (such as

Hamas or Hezbollah), the cells of this transnational movement are small, closed, tightly integrated and elitist. They are relatively isolated, that is, try to isolate themselves from the impure, corrupt, ignorant of true Islam and unjust environment (*jahiliyyah*). The way these cells see themselves as the revolutionary vanguard of the few chosen is fully in line with the concept of Islamist 'elitist vanguard' groups developed by one of the major theorists of modern radical Islamism, Dr Sayeed Qutb, as early as in the 1950s–1960s (Qutb 1989: 16–17).

The links between individual cells as well as between cells at micro-level and some of the leaders and ideologues of the movement are informal, at best. The underground nature of the individual cells, the informal character of links that tie them into a broader decentralized network, the absence of any strict vertical chain of command and, indeed, of any single, identifiable 'central staff'—all these characteristics appear to come in sharp contrast with the very active, effective and seemingly well-coordinated manner in which the movement carries out its militant and especially terrorist activities. Despite the unclear, virtual links between individual units and between the different levels of this system, it appears that they can effectively operationalize if necessary—for instance, for the purpose of carrying out a terrorist attack that involves more than one cell.

The chapter argues that this striking phenomenon can be explained by the very nature of the universalist quasi-religious ideology of the transnational violent Islamist movement.[11] The surprisingly high and effective coordination within the movement is achieved neither by means of centralized control (as in hierarchies) nor through mutual agreements, compromises and consultations (as in networks).[12] Rather, it appears that *strategic discourse and guidelines formulated by the movement's leaders and ideologues in a very general way only in and of themselves serve as a sufficient basis for effective coordination of its multiple cells' violent activity.* Since the mid-2000s, the process of consolidation of ideological discourse and strategic doctrine of the movement as a whole has been gaining strength, especially through discussions at the radical electronic websites, blogs and forums, under the guidance of and inspiration from the younger, post-al-Qaeda 'on-line generation' of radical clerics.[13] In fact, the greatest variety of organizational forms and their combinations the movement displays, the greater is the demand for such a consolidated ideological-strategic discourse, which is even seen by some observers as the equivalent of the 'true' leader of the movement.[14]

Such an effective coordination of informally linked network elements based in different parts of the world by the way of general strategic guidelines is only possible if the shared ideology that ties the system together meets certain requirements. This ideology should be formulated in such a way that it already contains 'instructions' specific enough to serve as a basis for violent actions in pursuance of its goals. In line with such an ideology, strategic goals are formulated in such a way that they may be implemented through a wide variety of means, in very different contexts and circumstances, or whenever an opportunity presents itself, but will still 'qualify' and be perceived as actions directed towards the same final goal.

The ideology of both the original al-Qaeda, and especially of the broader follow-up transnational violent movement, fully meets these requirements. This extremist ideological interpretation provides encouragement, advance approval of, and blessing for, any context-specific violent actions, including terrorist attacks against civilians. The best-known example is provided by Bin-Laden's 1998 fatwa that called for a course of action that, regardless of its context or immediate target, would always qualify as being directed towards the same 'general goal'.[15] It automatically interprets all forms of armed struggle, including terrorism against civilians, directed against multiple targets ranging from 'impious' muslim regimes to Western hard and soft targets as actions in advance of the same ultimate goal—the global order based on the direct 'rule of God'.

NOTES

1. There were only four years when the number of such incidents carried out by religious groups worldwide exceeded the annual total of attacks committed by nationalist/separatist groups. What is most worrying is that three of these four years are the most recent ones, 2004–2006, with 1994 as the fourth year. Calculations are based on the electronic data from the Terrorism Knowledge Base of the US Memorial Institute for the Prevention of Terrorism (MIPT Terrorism Knowledge Base), <http://www.tbk.org>. For a detailed graph compiled by the author on the basis of electronically generated MIPT data, see Figure 3.1, 'International terrorism incidents by nationalist/separatist and religious groups, 1968–2006', in Stepanova 2008: 56, <http://books.sipri.org/files/RR/SIPRIRR23.pdf>. Since May 2008, the MIPT Terrorism Knowledge Base was merged with and became part of the Global Terrorism Database managed by the National Consortium for the Study of Terrorism and Responses to Terrorism (START) at the University of Maryland: <http://www.start.umd.edu/data/gtd>.

2. Since 1993, religious terrorism at the international level resulted in higher numbers of deaths than nationalist terrorism in all years, except 1996 and 1999. Domestically, over the last decade religious terrorism has been just somewhat more lethal than nationalist terrorism. In 1998–2006—a period for which comparative data on both domestic and international terrorism is provided in the MIPT database—terrorist acts by religious groups resulted in 6,600 fatalities, while nationalist actors were responsible 5,643 (or 14.5 per cent lower) fatalities. For more detail, see the graph compiled by the author on the basis of the MIPT data: Figure 3.2. 'International terrorism fatalities caused by nationalist/separatist and religious groups, 1968–2006', in Stepanova 2008: 57.

3. For a discussion of definitional matters regarding terrorism, see Hoffman 2006: 1–41 and Stepanova 2008: 5–15.

4. *Jahiliyyah* is a traditional Islamic notion referring to the state of lawlessness and ignorance in the pre-Islamic period; it means 'ignorance' in Arabic and is used to denote 'ignorance of divine guidance'. It is also employed by radical Islamists to denote the current state of unbelief, ignorance and materialism in the world that is not governed by norms of fundamentalist Islam. See, for example, Qutb 1989: 14–17, 34–36.

5. According to the concept of a SPIN-structure formulated by US scholars Luther Gerlach and Virginia Hine in the early 1970s, the *segmented* nature of a SPIN-structure means that it is made of many cells, its *polycentric* character implies that it lacks single 'central' leadership, but has several leaders and centres, its *network* structure indicates that its segments, leaders and central nodes are integrated into a network through structural, ideological and personal links. Gerlach and Hine 1970. See also Gerlach 1987.

6. For more detail on swarming tactics, see Arquilla and Ronfeldt 2000.

7. The level of a group's goals may of course affect the level and type of the means that it employs to achieve those goals. For more on this, see Chapter 11 of this book.

8. This view can be referred to as 'network tribalism' concept introduced by David Ronfeldt. See Ronfeldt 2005. For a detailed critique of the concept, see Stepanova 2008: 135–142.

9. According to the data collected by the US psychologist Marc Sageman, friendship-type relations played important role for 68 per cent of active Islamists those who joined the movement while kinship and family links played the same role for about 14 per cent. As some cell members were inter-linked by both friendly and kin ties, overall, the social ties of both types played an important role in cell formation for 75 per cent of all members. Sageman 2004: 111–113.

10. As stated by a member of the Leeds cell that carried out the July 2005 suicide bombings in London, attacks 'will intensify and continue, until you [the USA and allies] pull all your troops out of Afghanistan and Iraq'. See Middle East Media Research Institute (MEMRI) 2006.

11. This movement is often referred to in the literature as 'transnational jihadi movement' or the 'Global Salafi jihad', but the editors of the volume decided not to use the term 'jihad' in this context, as the notion of 'jihad' has many meanings, and may denote non-violent as well as violent activity. It should, therefore, not be used as a synonym of 'terrorism' even when applied to 'armed struggle.'

12. For more detail, see, for instance, Mayntz 2004.

13. One of the attempts to summarize this emerging consolidated strategic discourse was undertaken by a young 'on-line generation' cleric Hamed bin Abdallah al-Ali: Al-Ali H. bin A. 2007. The key information providers and discussion moderators for this process include Al-Fajr Media Center, the Al-Sahab Foundation for Islamic Media Publication, the Global Islamic Media Front and personal websites of radical Islamist clerics and ideologues, as well as affiliated Internet blogs and forums.

14. See, for instance, Committee on Homeland Security and Governmental Affairs, U.S. Senate, *Radicalization of Global Islamist Terrorists*, Testimony by M. Sageman, 27 June 2007.

15. In this fatwa, Bin-Laden calls 'to kill Americans and their allies' as 'an individual duty for every Muslim who can do it in any country in which it is possible to do it', that is, for violent actions that can be carried out in many contexts, whenever there is a possibility to undertake them. Bin-Laden 1998.

11

TRANSNATIONAL TERRORISM: UNLIMITED MEANS?

Adam Dolnik

INTRODUCTION

Since the mid-1990s, the possibility of the use of chemical, biological, radiological, and nuclear (CBRN) weapons by non-state actors has become a topic of an extensive academic and public debate. Originally, the discussion concentrated primarily on capabilities, where the alleged ease of acquisition of CBRN materials following the break-up of the Soviet Union as well as the arguably more widespread availability of expertise needed for the production and weaponization of such agents were the main sources of concern. Later, the debate was brought to a more realistic level through the acknowledgement of technical hurdles associated with the successful delivery of CBRN agents, as well as the possible motivational constraints involved in the decision of terrorist groups to use such weapons. Another shift in the debate was represented by the claim that the rise of a phenomenon known as the 'new terrorism' had eroded these constraints. In other words, the 'new terrorists'—typically defined primarily by the religious nature of their ideology—were believed to be unconstrained by the political considerations that had traditionally led secular terrorist organizations to place limits on their violent activities (Hoffman 1998). Based on this argument, which seemed to have been confirmed by the events of

9/11, a general consensus had emerged that it is no longer a question of 'if' a mass casualty terrorist attack using CBRN weapons will occur, but rather the question of 'when' this will happen. Nevertheless, the phenomenon still remains poorly understood.

Part of the problem is the fact that the overall rise in lethality of terrorist violence is not a two dimensional proposition along the religious vs secular divide, but is also influenced by many additional dynamics and factors, most importantly, the growing level of internationalization of terrorist networks and the process of 'democratization of destructive power'. Due mainly to the rapid proliferation of advanced technologies, the presence of a large, well-funded, and highly organized group is no longer a precondition to the occurrence of significantly destructive terrorist plots, as even small groups of individuals are increasingly gaining the capacity to inflict considerable damage. Especially influential in this regard has been the boom of the Internet, which has become instrumental in significantly aiding the efficiency of terrorist operations. This has included the facilitation of easy access to astonishing quantities of instructional material that theoretically enables the terrorists to acquire useful skills, such as knowledge on how to manufacture explosives and poisons from dual-use materials, or the technical specifications of buildings, power plants, and other potential targets. Information technologies have also aided the 'new terrorists' in studying their enemies' investigative capabilities and operational procedures, thus providing the aptitude to further identify and exploit potential weaknesses and vulnerabilities. As a result, even small groups of terrorists with limited resources are now arguably gaining the capacity to organize increasingly sophisticated operations.

Given the above trends, what is the current threat level with regard to the prospects of mass-casualty CBRN terrorism? The chapter will explore this question at the technological, motivational and organizational levels. Understanding the nature of this threat is critical, as it is impossible to prepare adequately for such an event in isolation from the likelihood of its occurrence. Admittedly, any analysis that seeks to address the threat of 'CBRN terrorism' collectively as a monolithic phenomenon is inevitably too vague to be useful, given the fact that C vs B vs R vs N are very disparate threats with regards to issues such as difficulty of acquisition, potential to cause significant damage, technological hurdles involved in mass production and weaponization, and challenges posed for states on the side of detection, prevention, and response.[1] And while this analysis tries to make the necessary distinctions whenever possible, space limitations do not allow a truly comprehensive treatment of this extensive subject.

The first part of the chapter will provide a brief overview of significant past cases of CBRN terrorism, with the purpose of outlining the critical lessons for the future. The second part will focus on the exploration of the motivational side of threat assessment, and will also provide some likely behavioural characteristics of potential CBRN terrorists. The specific issue of interest will be the impact of the level of transnationalization of the respective perpetrators on their interest in CBRN. The third part will then explore the technological aspects of CBRN terrorism, focusing on the level of difficulty of acquiring and successfully weaponizing the necessary agents. In this section, various types of 'super terrorist' attack scenarios will be examined, with special attention devoted to an assessment of their technological feasibility. The lessons learned, as well as an outlook for the future will be provided in the conclusion.

LESSONS FROM THE PAST AND THEIR IMPLICATIONS FOR THE FUTURE

Despite the heightened level of attention in recent years, the threat of CBRN terrorism is far from new. One of the first incidents of *chemical* terrorism in the post-World War II environment was the 1946 poisoning of bread designated for a US prisoners-of-war camp near Nuremburg by a group of Jewish terrorists known as Avenging Israel's Blood (DIN). The attacks, in which arsenic mixed with glue was smeared onto the bottom of 2500–3000 loafs of bread succeeded in hospitalizing 207 former SS officers, but failed to kill a single person. Another noteworthy attempt was the unsuccessful 1986 plot by the apocalyptic white Christian supremacist group calling itself the Covenant, Sword, and Arm of the Lord (CSA) to poison the water supply of several large US cities with only 30 gallons of cyanide. June 1990 then marked the first time when chemical agents were used on the battlefield in a guerilla campaign, after the LTTE attacked a Sri Lankan Army encampment in eastern Kiran with canisters filled with chlorine (*Xinhua* 1990). Then on 27 June 1994, the first modern act of chemical terrorism took place in Japan, where six members of the apocalyptic cult Aum Shinrikyo released Sarin out of a van parked in a residential neighbourhood of Matsumoto, killing seven people and seriously injuring 144 others (Kaplan 2000). Finally, on 20 March 1995 the cult again used the nerve agent to attack five trains on three different subway lines in Tokyo, killing 12 and injuring 1039 in what remains the largest and most notorious unconventional terrorist attack to date.[2]

With regards to *biological* agents, the first notable incident was the unsuccessful 1972 plot by a tiny environmentalist cult calling itself R.I.S.E., to culture large quantities of *Salmonella typhi* with the plan to contaminate the water supply of several large cities.[3] The first actual bioterrorist attack then occurred in 1984, when the Rajneeshee cult used the causative agent for salmonella food poisoning to contaminate salad bars in a small Oregon town in an effort to influence a local election. The cult, which chose an incapacitating rather than lethal agent, succeeded in making 751 people ill, but no one died. Then in 1994 and 1995, four Minnesota men, all members of an extremist antigovernment group called the Minnesota Patriots Council (MPC), were the first people ever convicted of possession of a biological agent for use as a weapon under the 1989 US Biological Weapons Antiterrorism Act. The men acquired the protein toxin ricin, which is derived from castor beans, possibly to use against local law enforcement and federal officials. Although the MPC's plan was never carried out, the group was heavily influenced by right-wing extremist Christian Identity ideology, similar to the ideology that motivated the Oklahoma City bomber, Timothy McVeigh. During the early 1990s, over a dozen large scale attacks with biological agents were also carried out in Japan by the Aum Shinrikyo. Between 1990 and 1995 the group had spread botulinum toxin, the world's most toxic substance, and *Bacillus anthracis*, the causative agent for anthrax, out of street cleaning trucks, automatic suitcases and from the roof of its own compound near Mt. Fuji. However, the attacks went completely unnoticed, failing to produce a single casualty due to the fact that the cult used a nonvirulent strain of botulinum toxin, and only a harmless veterinary vaccine strain of *Bacillus anthracis*. The 1990s also witnessed two cases of loners with ties to American militia and Christian identity movements. Larry Wayne Harris, a man who in 1995 ordered plague bacteria from a Maryland culture collection was arrested three years later in possession of *Bacillus anthracis*, while Thomas Lewis Lavy was detained in December 1995 for possession of 130 grams of ricin. And finally, the 2001 attacks that utilized letters filled with *Bacillus anthracis* spores which resulted in 5 deaths were also probably carried out by an individual that fit a similar profile.

With regard to *nuclear* and *radiological* terrorism the record is even less extensive, as we have yet to see a single incident of nuclear terrorism, and the only example in which a radiological dispersal devices (RD) has actually been deployed—albeit purely for show—has been the November 1995 discovery of a 32 kg parcel containing 10–50 mCi of Cesium-137 at the Izmailovsky Park in Moscow (Lee Rensselaer III 1998). The package was found by a NTV television crew following instructions provided by Chechen terrorist Shamil Basayev, who simultaneously threatened that many such containers were placed around Moscow and could be detonated at any time to cause several 'mini-Chernobyls.' The package did not actually contain an explosive device.[4]

All of these past plots carry several important lessons. First, it is interesting to note that historical chemical and biological terrorism cases have so far been all geographically confined to developed parts of the world—more specifically the USA and Japan—possibly suggesting that the perpetrators' more frequent exposure to modern technologies could be associated with a greater likelihood of their incorporation into terrorist operations. This, of course, has significant implications for the future, given the increasing transnationalization of terrorist organizations and the rise of Islamist networks in Western countries. Due to their greater exposure to advanced technologies and the increasingly prevalent involvement of well-educated individuals, the homegrown cells may be in an increasingly suitable position to exploit CBRN for attack purposes. In addition, the rapid evolution of fields such as microbiology and their proliferation to developing countries may gradually spread this effect on a global scale.

The second lesson lies in the fact that the vast majority of the historical incidents falls into the category of crudely delivered low-level attacks that have utilized primitive agents such as potassium cyanide, arsenic, salmonella, Cesium-137, various pesticides, rat poisons and other dual-use items. Such attacks have been comparatively ineffective when it comes to creating a large number of casualties, although they have succeeded in achieving a disproportional psychological impact. Nevertheless, more potent unconventional agents have been used by terrorists only scarcely, and only two groups—Aum Shinrikyo and the unknown anthrax letter mailer(s)—have ever killed anyone by using an actual warfare agent. Given the fact that the perpetrators in both of these instances had at their disposal a large and comparatively expensive weapons programme—which in today's security environment would arguably be much more difficult to access—it seems reasonable to expect that future CBRN plots are likely to uphold the general trend of rudimentary delivery of low-end agents.

The third important lesson lies in the fact that despite our common tendency to use the term CBRN as synonymous with 'weapons of mass destruction', in most cases it was *not* the desire to produce mass casualties that had led the respective perpetrators to adopting CBR agents as their weapon of choice. In most cases, the respective groups were attracted to unconventional agents either because of their covert and difficult-to-detect nature (that is, MPC, Rajneeshees), due to their capacity to trigger disproportionate fear (that is, Chechens, anthrax letter mailer, Lavy) or simply as an inferior substitute for a temporarily degraded conventional capability (that is, LTTE).[5] In some cases, of course, the perpetrators did seek to maximize their killing potential (that is, Aum, R.I.S.E., CSA, DIN), but the lesson to emphasize here is that the commonly assumed link between CBRN and mass casualties remains an exception, as opposed to a rule.

And finally, the historical record suggests that past perpetrators of CBRN terrorism seemed to have certain distinct characteristics that set them aside from other, more 'conventional' terrorist organizations. This suggests that while any discussion about the uncertainty of terrorist organizations' interest (or lack thereof) in CBRN in the post-9/11 world is likely to be dismissed as obsolete, there is still some value in going through this exercise in order to narrow down the 'profile' of most likely perpetrators for the future. This will be the focus of the upcoming section.

MOTIVATIONAL CHARACTERISTICS OF FUTURE 'SUPER TERRORISTS'

One of the main reasons for why the historical record does not offer many past cases of CBRN terrorism, lies in the fact that most terrorist organizations have traditionally practiced a considerable level of restraint on their violent activities. Traditional terrorists have not necessarily been interested in killing a lot of people, but rather in attracting attention to their cause by killing only relatively few (Jenkins 1975). The 'old terrorists' typically showed little interest in indiscriminate killing of innocents on a large scale, as such action was seen as potentially counterproductive with regard to attracting popular support—an essential component of the fulfilment of traditional terrorist goals, such as the creation of an independent homeland or the implementation of social justice norms within the targeted state.

But while this traditional interpretation of terrorism has been the consensus for decades, many authors have observed that over the past 20 years, the phenomenon has experienced disturbing new trends. First, there seems to be a steady trend toward an increasing lethality of terrorist acts. While the deadliest incidents prior to the 1980s involved 'only' dozens of fatalities, in the 1980s and 1990s, the most lethal attacks were counted in the hundreds, and in the new millennium the plateau has reached into the thousands for the first time in history. The process of increasing lethality of terrorist operations has been accelerated even more by the events of 9/11, in part due to the empirical confirmation that even some acts of mass-casualty terrorism can receive enthusiastic endorsement from the perpetrating group's constituency. So while in the 50 years prior to 9/11 only 14 terrorist operations had resulted in more than 100 fatalities, in just six years since this date this number has more than doubled (Hoffman 2007). Quite simply, terrorism has become a significantly more lethal phenomenon than in the past.

While there are many reasons behind this accruing trend—including the terrorists' common tendency to 'out-do' their previous attacks, the desensitization of target audiences to a steady level of terrorist violence over time, and the processes of organizational splintering and the formation of new groups[6]—possibly the most important reason behind the increasing lethality of the 'new terrorism' has been the rise of violent activities motivated by a religious imperative. Bruce Hoffman, one of the most influential scholars on the subject, has identified the rise of religious motivation among terrorist groups as the primary cause of the higher number of casualties per attack in the modern era, by pinpointing several core characteristics of religious terrorists that allegedly set them aside from their secular counterparts (Hoffman 1998). These have included mainly the radically different value systems of religious terrorists, the different mechanisms of legitimization and justification, concepts of morality, mechanisms of victim dehumanization and an overall world-view. According to Hoffman, the aims of 'religious political' terrorists are defined as the attainment of the greatest possible benefits for themselves and for their co-religionists only, as opposed to the indiscriminately utilitarian goals of secular terrorists (Hoffman 1993). This allegedly further widens the gap between ends and means; 'where the secular terrorist sees violence primarily as a means to an end, the religious terrorist tends to view violence as an end in itself' (Hoffman 1993). Based on this logic, the assertion that religious terrorist groups are more likely to use CBRN weapons than their secular counterparts has become one of the few paradigms of the field of terrorism studies. However, while this interpretation of the new trends in terrorism makes intuitive sense, a grave danger lies in its mechanical application to threat assessment without further inquiry into the nature of a given organization's belief system.

Many of today's threat assessments of CBRN terrorism tend to focus simply on the general nature of the respective group's ideology (specifically along the 'religious' vs 'secular' divide), in combination with specific statements of interest in mass-casualties or 'weapons of mass destruction'. For instance, most analyses of the al-Qaeda's potential to use CBRN quickly establish intent by simply citing the following statements made by important al-Qaeda figures:

Acquiring weapons for the defense of Muslims is a religious duty. If I have indeed acquired these weapons [of mass destruction], then I thank God for enabling me to do so.
Osama Bin-Laden interviewed in *Time Magazine*
(December 1998, quoted in Innes 1999)

We have the right to kill 4 million Americans, two million of them children.
Abu Ghaith in 'Why We Fight America'
(June 2002, quoted in Middle East Media Research Institute 2002)

If a bomb was dropped on them that would annihilate 10 million and burn their lands…this is permissible.
Sheikh Nasir bin Hamid al-Fahd in 'A Treatise on the Legal Status of Using Weapons of Mass Destruction Against Infidels'
(May 2003, quoted in Boccara and Greenberg 2004)

But while these statements are a serious cause for concern and should certainly not be taken lightly, it is important to emphasize that a comprehensive threat assessment of 'intent' in the CBRN terrorism context needs to go further than the common focus on a group's declaration of 'interest.' A meaningful analysis needs to focus on the question of *how far is the given group willing to go in order to actually achieve a significant capability?* While it may be reasonable to assume that groups like the al-Qaeda would use a chemical weapon if they stumbled across one, the question we must ask is: 'how far is the respective group really willing to go to obtain it?' What level of material and human resources is the leadership willing to sacrifice, and how much is it willing to risk in terms of operational security in order to achieve a CBRN capability? If the organization is attracted to this option simply because of its desire to kill as many people as possible, why not just attack more often, at more locations, and on a greater scale with weapons that are already available and have already proven to be effective? Why invest a massive amount of precious resources into a new technology that only few, if any, know how to use and that could potentially end up killing the perpetrators themselves—all without any guarantee of success? Why risk a negative public reaction and a possibly devastating retaliation likely to be associated with the use of CBRN weapons?

As we can see from the complexity of these questions, there is clearly an additional element besides the desire to kill on a large scale that plays a decisive role in a terrorist group's decision to launch a biological or nuclear weapons programme, one so strong that it is able to offsets the currently unfavourable cost-benefit calculation[7] in favour of chemical or biological weapons over other conventional options. Empirically speaking, organizations that have in the past gone beyond merely expressing interest in chemical and biological agents have been groups for whom these weapons have had a strong expressive or emotional value, such as the desire to kill without shedding blood or the interpretation of poisons and plagues as God's tools. An example of this is the frequent reference to biblical plagues commonly used by various radical Christian groups, or the strange fascination of Aum Shinrikyo's leader Shoko Asahara who wrote poems about sarin. Alternatively, environmentalist cults—such as the Church of Euthanasia, the Voluntary Human Extinction Movement, and the Gaia Liberation Front—have interpreted diseases as 'natural' tools used by Mother Nature to eliminate the human race that has through technological advances and an inconsiderate use of natural resources caused a natural imbalance, which according to the group could only be restored by an elimination of the world's most destructive species (Dolnik 2007). Alternatively, more ideologically 'conventional' groups that place great emphasis on the principle of unconditional reciprocity may under some conditions resort to CBRN violence, especially in the case of repeated claims of having been subjected to the same treatment by the enemy—in this case the use of poisons against the population the group claims to represent. An example of this is the attraction to poisons by the aforementioned Avengers (DIN), who argued that since 6 million Jews were poisoned in concentration camps, 6 million German civilians also had to be killed in the same manner for justice to be served (Sprinzak and Zertal 2000). On a similar note, an attraction to chemical weapons can be expected from Chechen and Kurdish groups based on their claims that their constituencies have also been targeted with such weapons, and we can also expect an attraction to radiological terrorism on behalf of groups in countries such as Iraq, Bosnia or Kosovo, where much resentment has been raised by the American use of depleted uranium (DU) munitions.

It is this specific expressive component that will play a key role in the matrix of useful intelligence indicators that can be used to identify potential perpetrators beforehand. Other such indicators include high level of paranoia, an apocalyptic vision, presence of an undisputed charismatic leader displaying signs of psychological idiosyncrasies and an attraction to truly extreme violence, high level of operational and physical risk taking, membership base including members with scientific backgrounds, the group's expressive emphasis to innovation and extremely high ambitions in the operational realm (Dolnik 2007). At the same time, while these predictive indicators can provide us with a useful tool, we must be aware of the fact that the vast majority of previous CBW plots have not involved prominent terrorist organizations, but rather previously *unknown* individuals and groups that emerged seemingly out of nowhere. This means that a meaningful threat assessment needs to expand past existing terrorist organizations to include unknown actors, and that new assessment tools need to be designed to provide timely and accurate intelligence on the activities of such actors.

This is especially the case, given the increasing transformation of terrorist organizational structures from the hierarchical, political party-like formations into more loosely knit networks of cells operating without any real central command (Tan and Ramakrishna 2002). The characteristics of the worldwide network we know as the al-Qaeda, or the concept of 'leaderless resistance' embraced by the North American Christian Identity and animal rights movements, provide good examples of this phenomenon, which in many ways represents one of the downsides of globalization. Today's terrorists can easily communicate via e-mail, using commercial encryption programmes and coded messages posted on various websites and chat rooms, a fact that has resulted in an unprecedented international reach of terrorist networks and the proliferation of operational know-how among groups through knowledge sharing. Even more importantly, the proliferation of the Internet has also contributed to the rise of the so-called 'home-grown terrorism,' or the emergence of active Islamist terrorist networks in the West. Members of these small networks identify themselves with the al-Qaeda's global ideology, but essentially operate autonomously, without any direct link to the central command. This dynamic, of course, significantly influences our capability to accurately assess the threat, given the fact that the potential intent of these homegrown cells to acquire and use CBRN will rarely be identifiable beforehand. Today, one can theoretically become a 'member' of a terrorist group simply by embracing its ideology, gaining operational knowledge through manuals accessed from the Internet, and carrying out attacks in the group's name via its signature *modus operandi* and general targeting guidelines.

The unpredictability of such independent actors is especially worrying given the fact that the opening up of ranks of terrorist organizations to volunteers that have never gone through structured training or formal organizational acceptance, has contributed to the erosion of motivational constraints to engage in acts of catastrophic terrorism. Since members of such *ad hoc* groups operate without any moderating influences from the more politically and strategically conscious central leadership, this decentralization of decision making has also contributed to the deterioration of restraint that traditionally played a role in the initiation and planning of spectacular attacks.

This might especially be the case with respect to CBRN. For instance, the al-Qaeda's pre-9/11 doctrine called for the acquisition of CBRN mainly as a deterrent and counterbalance against Israeli and American non-conventional arsenals (as opposed to a first strike option) creating a setting in which any use of such technology would be carefully weighted by the leadership (Salama and Hansell 2005). In this light the continuing fragmentation of the group and the emergence of a global movement of independent and self-radicalized cells subscribing to the al-Qaeda's global ideology has arguably created a situation, in which the decision to use CBRN would theoretically be in the hands of only several individuals acting in a one-time capacity, with no real concern for the consequences. In such a setting, the motiv-ational, strategic, and political obstacles to using CBRN have become even less relevant today. This is especially true given the increased aggressiveness of the new 'al-Qaeda' doctrine with regards to CBRN, which now incorporates not only religious sanction, but even strategic preference for using such means (Salama and Hansell 2005). For an independent cell seeking guidance on Islamist websites and forums about the permissibility of employing CBRN technology to attack the enemy, the answer would be an overwhelming 'yes'. That being said, in order for a CBRN attack to actually take place, this intent would also need to be matched by the capability to acquire and effectively weaponize a CBRN agent. This question will be explored in the next section.

ACQUISITION AND WEAPONIZATION OF CBRN AGENTS

For most C,[8] B,[9] R[10] (but not N[11]) agents the acquisition step is certainly not difficult, given the fact that many weapons-usable substances have legitimate uses and are therefore relatively widely available. Further, the boom of information technologies and the Internet makes the necessary know-how for successful procurement of cultures more widely available than ever before. On the other hand, the production of large quantities of a biological agent as well as its successful weaponization (the process of producing a mass-casualty-capable delivery system for the acquired agent) is a more complex and difficult endeavour than is generally believed.[12] The difficulty of weaponizing chemical and biological substances varies greatly based on the agent of choice. Inflicting mass casualties with chemical and non-contagious biological agents such as anthrax or tularemia requires a high-tech delivery, as every victim has to come into direct contact with the agent in order to be affected.

One popular scenario for a bioterrorist attack has been the mass contamination of a city's water supply. A major difficulty of successfully perpetrating such an attack is represented by the fact that most water-borne organisms die in the presence of sunlight, ozone, or chlorine, and are therefore unlikely to survive routine water treatment processes.

One possibility would be the contamination of water post-treatment, but such operation would involve pumping enormous quantities of agent into the water distribution system while avoiding detection—not an easy feat considering the huge quantities of agent needed and the fact that the water in the pipelines is under pressure. But, even if the terrorists were to overcome all of the hurdles associated with contamination of a city's water supply, the chances of inflicting mass casualties are minimal, unless the agent used is colourless, tasteless, and odourless, in order to facilitate mass consumption. Despite the fact that this seems common sense, past plots and a review of dozens of terrorist chemical and biological weapons manuals demonstrate the lack of realization of this simple fact on behalf of most terrorist groups. Consider, for instance, the February 2002 plot to poison the water supply of the US Embassy in Rome, which has been widely cited as evidence of the al-Qaeda's 'chemical weapons' capability (Henneberger 2002). In this case, the four Moroccan perpetrators arrested in Italy were in possession of 8.8 pounds of potassium ferrocyanide—enough to theoretically kill two people, but certainly not suitable for a water-borne attack—given the fact that the agent when mixed with water tends to significantly change its colour, providing ample warning to the possible target (Croddy et al. 2002). Many similarly ridiculous historical instances could by cited.

The next commonly discussed scenario is the open-air dissemination of a non-contagious agent such as anthrax. Anthrax is the prototypical biological weapons agent—it is relatively easy to produce, it is extremely virulent, and the infection is not contagious, so the outbreak will not spread beyond those affected directly. Most importantly, anthrax forms rugged spores when exposed to environmental stresses, and these spores facilitate processing and weaponization. However, significant hurdles to effective open-air dissemination of anthrax exist as well. Anthrax can be delivered in liquid or powder form. While the liquid form is relatively easy to produce, it is much more difficult to deliver effectively because it is susceptible to clumping into heavy droplets that fall to the ground instantly, providing insufficient time for the victims to inhale the agent. Conversely, the powder form is significantly less challenging to disseminate but is much more difficult to produce; its effective dissemination requires an aerosol composed of particles between one and five microns in diameter. Production of such fine aerosol requires a sprayer system that is equipped with specialized nozzles that are not widely available. Finally, an open-air dissemination of aerosol is also highly susceptible to meteorological conditions that make targeting much less controllable.

Contagious agents on the other hand, allow for a much less efficient delivery, as it is only necessary to infect a small group of people, who can then spread the disease by secondary transmission. In this regard, the popular scenario of a suicide 'bomber' infected with smallpox and cruising along crowded city areas comes to mind. This scenario is, of course not nearly as technologically sophisticated as the scenarios mentioned above. However, obtaining the virus today is almost impossible, and even then there are very few organizations in the world that would be inclined to use such an unpredictable method; contrary to a classical suicide bombing, one of the key advantages of which is a high level of control of the circumstances under which the detonation occurs, in the 'biosuicide' attack the organizers lose any control whatsoever following the first secondary transmission of the disease. Few of today's known groups seem willing to launch a terror campaign that would have the capacity to indiscriminately eliminate not only the intended victims, but also the group's constituencies, membership and leadership, as well as their friends and families.[13] It is thus not surprising that none of the many existing biological weapons manuals inspected by the contributor has ever covered the category of contagious agents.

While the technological difficulty of obtaining a mass-casualty-capable chemical, biological or nuclear weapon is clearly the dominant reason for why the use of such weapons by terrorist organizations has been extremely rare, the comparative ease with which a radiological dispersal device (RDD) could be assembled raises the question of why there has not yet been a single incident involving the 'dirty bomb' scenario.

RDDs can be very crude and can take the form of simple placement of radioactive material in a location with the intent of causing damage, destruction or injury by the means of radiation produced by the decay of the material used, or by the dispersal of radioactive material over a larger area by the means of attaching it to a conventional explosive (Ford 1998). The damage and injury inflicted by such a device would depend greatly on the amount and type of the radioactive material used. The effects of a 'dirty bomb' would be threefold: the blast and fragmentation effects of the explosive device, radiation effects, and psychological effects (Ford 1998). Of these, the psychological implications would be the most devastating, mainly because of the automatic association of the word 'radioactive' with 'nuclear' in the minds of the majority of world population. In reality, however, more people would probably die in stampedes and car accidents resulting from the panicking population's desire to leave the affected area immediately, than from direct effects of radiation. Second in the hierarchy of destructive impact would be the damage inflicted by the blast and the fragmentation effects of the explosive device to which the radioactive material was attached. The physical damage caused by the actual radiation effects would in most instances be minimal, comprising mainly of area denial rather than mass casualties resulting from radiation poisoning. And while the possibility of a significantly lethal RDD design cannot be ruled out completely, even states with access to virtually unlimited amounts of highly radioactive materials have found this difficult. The main obstacle in this case was the handling of gamma-emitting radioactive substances, which requires the use of extremely heavy and bulky protective lead shielding. Other obstacles included the problems associated with grinding the material into the five-micron size and mixing it with an inactive solid substance to enhance dispersion and increase inhalation hazard, the variability of weather conditions, and the ability of buildings to absorb large amounts of radiation (Ford 1998). Nevertheless, the relative ease with which an RDD can be assembled combined with the immense psychological effects such a weapon has to offer, make the 'dirty bomb' scenario a threat that is very real.

ASSESSMENT OF CONTEMPORARY TERRORIST CAPABILITIES

Due to significant obstacles faced by terrorist organizations in the process of weaponizing chemical, biological and nuclear agents, most of the doomsday scenarios often cited by security agencies and sensationalist media outlets are unlikely to be fulfilled any time soon. In fact, judging by past incidents and dozens of CBRN terrorism manuals, contemporary terrorist organizations still demonstrate a relatively naïve approach to this issue. Even the al-Qaeda and its associate groups such as Jemaah Islamiyah, have demonstrated a very limited ability to acquire a significant chemical or biological capability.[14]

For instance, the al-Qaeda had initiated its secret plan to develop chemical and biological weapons—the so-called 'Project Yogurt'—as far back as 1999 (Cullison 2004). In the initial stages, the plan was to conduct a survey of literature while the organization looked to recruit a scientist to run the programme. In 2001, the al-Qaeda's third in command, Mohammed Atef, approached JI's top operational leader Hambali with a request to find a scientist who would take over the programme. Hambali introduced Yazid Sufaat, a US trained biochemist and former Malaysia military officer, who subsequently spent several months attempting to cultivate anthrax in a laboratory near the Kandahar airport (National Commission on Terrorist Attacks Upon the United States 2004). Plans were also established to set up another laboratory in Malaysia and a third lab in Bandung, Indonesia, through Sufaat's company, called Green Laboratories Medicine (ABC 2006). But while this intent may sound scary on paper, it is interesting to compare the logistics and expertise of the al-Qaeda's biological weapons programme with that of the Aum Shinrikyo, the undisputed leader in this field. Prior to deciding on the production of chemical agents, Aum Shinrikyo had conducted no less than 10 attacks with biological agents (particularly *Bacillus anthracis* and botulinum toxin), under the direction of Dr Seichi Endo, a molecular biologist who had obtained graduate degrees in genetic engineering, genetics, and medicine from the prestigious Kyoto University (J. Miller 2002). Even though the group had at its disposal an unrivalled amount of resources equalling nearly 1 billion USD, a team of no less than 20 graduate level scientists, and state-of-the-art laboratories and equipment, it failed to kill a *single* person with a *biological* weapon. Compare that with the al-Qaeda's 'Project Yogurt,' which had the startup budget of only 2000–4000 USD was based on an initial survey of literature from the 1920s to 1960s (Cullison 2004), and its chief 'scientist' only had a bachelor's degree in biological sciences and a minor in chemistry from Cal State University in Sacramento. In this perspective, the al-Qaeda's ability to kill thousands of people with biological agents seems rather questionable.

Could this reality suddenly change? The rapid scientific advances in the fields of microbiology and genetic engineering seem to suggest so, but in order to get a fuller picture one must also consider the issue of willingness and ability of terrorist organizations to adopt new technologies. History informs that terrorist organizations rarely alter their established *modus operandi*, and when they do, these changes are driven by very specific reasons (Dolnik 2007).

The first such reason comes in the event of an introduction of government countermeasures, such as target hardening efforts that serve as a direct obstruction to the tactics used by terrorists in the past. While most groups can be expected to respond by selecting substitute targets, an innovative organization will refuse to go down this path of least resistance in order to increase its probability of success. Instead, such a group will work to overcome these countermeasures by means that have not been accounted for by the enemy, often placing an emphasis on projecting an image of invincibility as well as mocking the state for failing to stop the attack despite all of its resources. In this light, certain chemical and biological agents pose a direct threat for the future, as they could be used to overcome security measures already in place at key targets such as airports. And while CBW employment in this scenario is unlikely to involve a mass-casualty-capable delivery system, even crudely delivered agents deployed onboard a commercial airliner in midcourse flight could result in very significant damage and casualties.

Another scenario in which a group can be expected to alter its operational methods in a novel direction comes in the presence of an inherent ideological pre-determination toward using certain technologies or the need to innovate in order to obtain the capability to match the level of violence associated with the respective ideological and strategic preferences (Dolnik 2007). An example of this in the CBRN realm is the incorporation of certain chemical or radiological agents into explosive devices, along the lines of the Hamas inclusion of pesticides in suicide belts for anticoagulant effect (Dolnik and Bhattacharjee 2002), or the detonation of chorine canisters recently introduced by the insurgents in Iraq. What is important to emphasize here, is that mass casualties remain an unlikely outcome even in this scenario, as most of the added agent tends to be consumed by the initial explosion. Nevertheless, the psychological effect of such operations cannot be underestimated.

The third relevant scenario of a trigger to terrorist adoption of new operational methods is an incidental or unintended acquisition of a particular human or material resource. In the CBR context this is a real threat, especially in light of the growing decentralization of the global Islamist movement and the associated phenomenon of 'self-starter groups' emerging in Western countries. If, for instance, a highly skilled microbiologist decided to launch an attack in the name of the al-Qaeda, it is likely that such a person would use the skills and technologies that he or she is most familiar with, as opposed to resorting to traditional terrorist weaponry. Given the growing prevalence of highly educated individuals actively participating in terrorist violence, the scenario of a homegrown terrorist cell attacking with a CBR capability in a Western city is becoming increasingly more imaginable. That being said, even in this scenario, where would be the significant technological obstacles standing in the way of success.

CONCLUSION

Today's terrorist organizations demonstrate only a limited potential to use CBRN agents for the purposes of launching an attack capable of causing mass casualties or significant physical damage. Nevertheless, the threat of small-scale operations involving certain chemical, biological and radiological agents is certainly real, and is most likely on the rise. Of great concern in this light is the gradually growing understanding of the difficulty of causing mass destruction with CBRN among the terrorists themselves. Whereas a decade ago the known terrorist plots and CBRN manuals demonstrated a very high level of technological naivety and ridiculous ambitions, today's organizations seem to have a greater appreciation of the technological hurdles they are facing—and seem to be reflecting on this reality by shelving unrealistic projects in favour of focusing their energy on the more feasible scenarios. Even more importantly, today's terrorists seem to have a much greater appreciation of the psychological impact that even small-scale CBRN operations will have on the population and society,[15] leading to an increasing likelihood of the occurrence of such attacks in the future. Given the importance of the primarily psychological dimension of this threat, it will be even more vital for us in the future to take these plots for what they are, and to avoid misleading interpretations of such events as 'weapons of mass destruction terrorism'.

With a longer-term outlook into the future, the issue of specific concern is the continual process of transnationalization of terrorism, and the associated rise of global decentralized networks of small cells operating independently of any central command. Given their lack of a longer-term strategic outlook and the overwhelmingly supportive views of the online Isalmist community on the issue of using CBRN, these cells are arguably going to be even less constrained in their motivation to deploy such technologies for attack purposes. While this increasing motivation in combination with our limited ability to accurately assess it beforehand is certainly a cause of concern, it must be emphasized that this growing intent is by no means matched by capability—in fact, there seems to be an inverse relationship between the two. Small groups of individuals operating in a hostile environment under pressure of the security services are likely to be in very difficult positions to breach the technological hurdles associated with a mass-casualty CBRN weapons programme. In fact, the homegrown cells typically experience very limited success in launching even small to medium-scale conventional attacks without obviation and disruption, which has led some members of the online Islamist community to call for *less sophisticated* and operationally *less challenging* attacks and plots, as a substitute to the current preference for synchronized suicide bombings. The further busting of cells in Germany, the USA, Norway, Canada, Denmark, Belgium, the UK, Australia, and the Netherlands, as well as the failure of even rudimentary attacks launched in June 2007 by a comparatively well-educated group of Islamists in London and the Glasgow airport, seem to confirm that the upcoming trend of terrorist operations will be one of *decreasing*, rather than increasing, technological sophistication. That being said the continuing process of 'democratization of destructive power' will make it easier for even small groups of individuals to wreak havoc and destruction, so the potential for the situation to eventually change in the long term cannot be ignored completely.

NOTES

1. For instance, only N and B but not R and C have the capacity to achieve 'mass destruction'. Similarly, while potential perpetrators of CBR terrorism will not be limited so much by access to materials (which is relatively easy) but more by the difficulty of effectively weaponizing them, in the case of N it is the acquisition of sufficient quantity of fissile material which represents the greatest technological hurdle.
2. For more information on Aum Shinrikyo's chemical and biological weapons activities, see the website of the Center for Nonproliferation Studies, *Chronology of Aum Shinrikyo's CBW Activities*, (March 2001).
3. This incident is sometimes incorrectly attributed to a neo-Nazi group 'Order of the Rising Sun.

4. The container, which weighed approximately 15 kg and measured 400 by 300 by 250 centimeters, was wrapped in yellow paper and plastic, and contained an ordinary piece of equipment found in the oil industry.

5. This refers to LTTE's employment of chlorine gas during the siege of a Sri Lankan Army camp in Kiran in 1990, which also came as a direct result of the group's decreasing access to ammunition following the seizure of several of the group's arms shipments (Hoffman 2000: 220).

6. Upon emergence, new violent organizations usually do not undergo the full step-by-step process of radicalization, but rather pick up at the level of violence where other organizations active in the same struggle have left off. Alternatively, many existing organizations can give birth to new formations through the process of splintering, which usually results in the new entity being more radical and more violent than the core group.

7. Consider the experience of Aum Shinrikyo, who after investing 30 million USD into *sarin* alone, succeeded in killing only 12 people in its most lethal attack—a number that pales in comparison to the 192 persons who died in the 2003 suicide attempt on the Seoul subway, which was executed by a mentally disturbed individual who used technology requiring only about a $3 investment: a paper milk container filled with gasoline and a cigarette lighter. The lesson is that even for a group that tries to maximize casualties, the cost-benefit analysis is not necessarily in favour of 'weapons of mass destruction'.

8. The acquisition of low-level chemical agents such as cyanide, chlorine or various pesticides is also relatively easy, considering the dual-use nature of these substances. A much more challenging task is the acquisition of ready-made nerve agents or key precursor chemicals needed for the production of such compounds. Other significant challenges include the safety issues involved in handling chemical agents and the difficulties of stabilizing such agents for storage purposes.

9. Many biological agents have legitimate uses and are therefore widely available through commercial repositories that isolate, preserve and distribute cultures. Even though the security of many repositories has recently been tightened, there are still many unsecured culture collections around the world from which pathogens can be purchased with few questions asked. Another factor that makes the acquisition of biological agents possible is the relative ease with which even small amounts of biological materials can be converted into large quantities. Moreover, the boom of information technologies and the Internet makes the necessary know-how for successful procurement of cultures more widely available.

10. Radiological terrorism can take the form of a radiological dispersal device (RDD) also known as a 'dirty bomb', or a sabotage of a nuclear facility. Since millions of tons of radioactive materials exist around the world, much of it unaccounted for, acquisition of RDD-usable materials is hardly inconceivable. Theft or purchase of spent nuclear fuel rods or dual-use materials such as cobalt-60, cesium-137, and irridium-192 present a wide array of opportunities. The availability of nuclear facilities that could be sabotaged is also great, considering the fact that there are 438 nuclear power reactors, 277 operational research reactors, and hundreds of fuel cycle facilities throughout the world, including uranium mills and conversion plants, enrichment plants, fuel fabrication plants, interim storage sites, and reprocessing facilities. (Nilsson A., 'The Threat of Nuclear terrorism: Assessment and Preventive Action', Presentation for the Symposium on Terrorism and Disarmament, United Nations, 25 October 2001.)

11. The biggest obstacle to nuclear terrorism remains the acquisition of sufficient quantities of fissile material. A nuclear warhead would require either 4–8 kilograms of plutonium or 15 or more kilograms of HEU, depending on the quality of enrichment and the blueprint of the device. A uranium device would require a simpler design than a plutonium one, but larger quantities of fissile material would at the same time be needed. The easiest design to construct would be gun-type device which, according to Gavin Cameron, could be 'assembled by a small group using knowledge available in open source literature, without the use of sophisticated technology at a cost of a fraction of a million dollars'. Such device, however, would require 50–60 kilograms of HEU, an amount difficult to acquire for most states, let alone non-state actors. See Cameron 1998.

12. The term 'weaponization' refers to the process of producing an effective delivery system for the acquired agent. Generally, two basic scenarios for a chemical or biological terrorist attack exist. One is a relatively crude, small-scale delivery along the lines of the 2001 anthrax letters, which can succeed in causing massive panic and disruption, but lacks the potential of inflicting significant damage in terms of loss of human life. The other scenario is a mass-casualty attack, which is much less likely, but which could potentially be catastrophic. It is the latter type of attack that is the primary focus in the chapter.

13. It is interesting to note that the Islamist manuals surveyed by the contributor, the category of contagious agents tends to be avoided completely. The al-Qaeda manual 'Military Studies in the Jihad against the Tyrants' when discussing assassination with biological agents even specifically limits the discussion 'only to poisons that the *mujaheed* can prepare without endangering his health'.

14. For excellent analyses of al-Qaeda's potential to acquire and use CBRN see Salama and Hansell 2005; Pita 2007: 480–511. For an analysis of Jemaah Islamiya, see Dolnik and Gunaratna 2007.

15. For more detail about this argument highlighted by the Kemal Bourgass (January 2003) and Dhiren Barot (November 2006) plots, see: Hoffman B., 'CBRN Terrorism Post-9/11', in Howard and Forest 2007, pp. 273–274.

APPENDIX: THE ATTACK ON MUMBAI

Subir Bhaumik and Jaideep Saikia

Ten well-trained Islamist terrorists struck India's financial capital, Mumbai, from the Arabian Sea. The terrorists got off their 'Boat Assault Pneumatic Type' dinghies and rushed into the city, indiscriminately killing everyone who came within the range of their *Kalashnikovs*. Continuing to rain fire, two groups among the 10 commandeered two luxury hotels and a Jewish hostel, while the third group carried out assault in a railway station. It was the night of 26 November 2008.

Caught unawares, Mumbai's security establishment reacted, but the planned Islamist operation not only took the lives of several police officers who had sought to launch a quick counter offensive, but the ferocity with which the attackers went about their task occasioned the induction of India's elite anti-terrorism force, the '51 Special Action Group'. In the 62-hour gun battle that ensued, the terrorists were killed, even as one of them was captured alive. Mohammad Ajmal Amin Iman alias Kasab, the apprehended terrorist, revealed that the daring operation, which took the lives of 188 persons, was planned and launched from Pakistan. India reacted in anger and in the melee of accusations and denials, the attack on Mumbai brought India and Pakistan on the brink of war for the second time since 2001. In 2001, the two countries mobilized troops for nearly a year after an Islamist outfit—once again launched from Pakistan—attacked the Indian Parliament.

A leading Pakistani author, Ahmed Rashid, has blamed the al-Qaeda for the Mumbai attack. In a BBC column posted on its website on 4 December 2008 (http://news.bbc.co.uk/2/hi/south_asia/7764475.stm), Rashid argues:

> When the Pakistan army finally stopped allowing Pakistan-based militant groups from infiltrating into Indian-administered Kashmir in 2004, groups like the LeT, Jaish-e-Mohammed and Harkat-ul-Mujahideen splintered and

fragmented. Some militants went home, others got jobs or stayed in camps in the mountains. However, the youngest and the most radicalised fighters joined up with the al-Qaeda and the Pakistani and the Afghan Taliban in the mountains of Pakistan's tribal areas on the border with Afghanistan. They embraced the global jihad to fight the US troops in Afghanistan and Iraq and later attacked the Pakistan government and the army as the Pakistan Taliban developed their own political agenda to seize power. The group that attacked Mumbai may well include some Pakistanis, or most of them may also be Pakistanis, but it is more likely that it is an international terrorist force put together by the al-Qaeda and the Pakistan Taliban, who are besieged by the Pakistan army on one side and a rain of missile being launched by US forces in Afghanistan against their hideouts on the other. The al-Qaeda is looking for some relief and a diversion. What better way to do so than by provoking two old enemies—India and Pakistan—with a terrorist attack that diverts attention away from the tribal areas? Such a move would force Pakistani troops back to the Indian border while simultaneously pre-occupying the US and the NATO countries in hectic diplomacy to prevent the region exploding into war.

There is more than a grain of truth in Rashid's analysis that an al-Qaeda diversion would preserve the extremist group's sanctuaries along the Pakistan–Afghanistan border and would provide the terrorists with some respite, especially as the US President-elect Barack Obama is planning to send an additional 20,000 US troops to Afghanistan. But it is analyzed that there is more to the Mumbai attack than what Ahmed Rashid has stated. It is about the Pakistan army and the manner it is seeking to use the militant card to play spoiler in the India–Pakistan peace moves. Indications are there that one of the masterminds of the Mumbai attack is Zaki-ur-Rehman, a 'forward desk' officer of Pakistan's Inter Services Intelligence (ISI). The terrorist apprehended in Mumbai, Kasab also revealed that the module that attacked Mumbai was trained in urban warfare in Durbari Mitho in Pakistan and in amphibious assault in Pakistan army facilities like the Mangla Dam reservoir. According to the contributors, the scale in which the Mumbai operation was mounted is not possible without military support.

Every time a democratically elected government in Pakistan has extended the olive branch to India, the army in the country has played spoiler. Pervez Musharraf—as the Pakistani army chief—initiated the Kargil intrusion in 1999 to disrupt the Lahore peace process. The Pakistan army is currently desperate to pull out from the Afghanistan border and leave the fighting to the US–NATO forces: one of the ways that this could be achieved is by sponsoring Mumbai style attacks through one of ISI's 'forward desk' that works in close concert with outfits such as the Lashkar-e-Toiba, the group to which the 26 November 2008 attack has been attributed to. The attack on Mumbai would derail the India–Pakistan peace process. It would also provide the Pakistan army an excuse to move troops from the west and deploy them in the border with India, creating thereby an atmosphere that would allow dominance of the Pakistan army in the country's politics by projecting India as a major threat.

The Pakistan army chief, General Ashfaque Qayani is concerned about low troop morale and rising desertions due to its involvement in fighting the militants it once created. He is willing to even countenance a truce with Behtullah Mehsud, the man responsible for the assassination of Benazir Bhutto. It is small wonder, therefore, that the Taliban is offering Qayani (not President Asif Ali Zardari) full support against India. When Zardari—after his election as Pakistan's President—said that India was never a threat for Pakistan, he nearly took away the very reason for existence of the Pakistan army. The statement has led to disappointment in an influential section of the Pakistan army and the ISI. The renewed military–militant nexus could be a devise to counter such a move.

CONSOLIDATED BIBLIOGRAPHY

Abas, Nasir. 2005. *Membongkar Jemaah Islamiyah: Pengakuan Mantan Anggota JI*. Jakarta: Grafindo Khazanah Ilmu.

Abbas, Hassan. 2005. *Pakistan's Drift into Extremism: Allah, the Army, and American's War on Terror*. Armonk, NY: M.E. Sharpe.

Abduh, Umar. 2002. *Al Zaytun Gate: Investigasi Mengungkap Misteri*. Jakarta: LPDI-SIKAT and Al Bayyinah.

Abed-Qotob, Sana. 1995. 'The Accommodationists Speak: Goals and Strategies of the Muslim Brotherhood of Egypt'. *International Journal of Middle East Studies* 27: 321–339.

Abeysekera, Mendaka. 2008. 'Clinton campaign drops pro-LTTE contributors', *New York*, 10 February 2008. Available online at http://www.nation.lk/2008/02/10/news20.htm

Abramovici, P. 2006–07. 'Opération "Condor", cauchemar de l'Amérique latine', *Le Monde diplomatique Manière de voir 90 'Amérique latine rebelled'*, December 2006–January 2007: 30–35.

Abrams, Irwin (ed.). 1999. *Nobel Lectures, Peace 1991–1995*. Singapore: World Scientific Publishing Co. Available at http://nobelprize.org/nobel_prizes/peace/laureates/1994/arafat-bio.html; *see also, Time Magazine*. 2004. 'A Life in Retrospect: Yasser Arafat' *Time Magazine*, 12 November 2004. Available at http://www.time.com/time/world/article/0,8599,781566-1,00.html

Abu-Amr, Ziad. 1994. *Islamic Fundamentalism in the West Bank and Gaza Strip*. Bloomington: Indiana University Press.

Abuza, Zachary. 2002. 'Tentacles of Terror: Al-Qaeda's Southeast Asian Network', *Contemporary Southeast Asia*, 24(3): 4.

———. 2003. 'Funding Terrorism in Southeast Asia: The Financial Network of Al-Qaeda and Jemaah Islamiyah', NBR Analysis, December 2003.

———. 2005. 'Al-Qaeda Comes to Southeast Asia', in Paul J. Smaith (ed.), *Terrorism and Violence in Southeast Asia*, p. 43. New York: East Gate Books.

———. 2006a. 'Abu Dujana: Jemaah Islamiyah's New Al-Qaeda Linked Leader'. *Terrorism Focus*, 3(13). Jamestown Foundation.

———. 2006b. 'A Breakdown of Southern Thailand's Insurgent Groups', *Terrorism Monitor*, 4(17).

Adler, Mike. 2007. 'Tamil community rallies at civic centre', *Toronto Community News*, 12 June 2007. Available online at http://www.insidetoronto.ca

Adnkronos International. 2007. 'Pakistan: Al-Qaeda Claims Bhutto's Death', Adnkronos International, 27 December 2007. Available online at http://www.cnn.com/2007/WORLD/meast/12/27/bhutto.dhs.alqaeda/ (accessed on 28 January 2007).

Agence France-Presse. 2003a. '2 Young Singaporean JI Members Arrested', *Agence France-Presse*, 18 December 2003.

Agence France-Presse. 2003b. 'Pakistan Probes Suspected JI Sleeper Cell', *Agence France-Presse*, 24 September 2003.

Ahmad, Hisham. 1994. *Hamas*. Jerusalem: The Palestinian Academic Society for the Study of International Affairs (PASSIA).

Ajami, Fouad. 1992. *The Arab Predicament: Arab Political Thought and Practice Since 1967.* Available at http://www.books.google.com/books?hl=en&lr=&id=Qj-UEPalcwC&oi=fnd&pg=PR9&dq=1967+Six+Day+War&ots=KMp75ExNyN&sig=p QuFm_8br9wYTpBWaF5PeF51Kz4#PPR7,M1

al Jarbawi, Ali. 1994. 'The Position of Palestinian Islamists on the Palestine-Israel Accord'. *The Muslim World*, 83(1–2): 127–154.

Al-Ali, H. bin A. 2007. *[Covenant of the Supreme Council of Jihad Groups]*, 13 January 2007, in Arabic, http://www.h-alali.net/m_open.php? id=991da3ae-f492-1029-a701-0010dc91cf69

Al-Azmeh, Aziz. 1993. *Islams and Modernities*, 2nd Edition 1996. London: Verso Books.

Al-Chaidar. 1999. *Pemikiran Politik Proklamator Negara Islam Indonesia S.M. Kartosoewirjo: Fakta dan Data Sejarah Darul Islam*. Jakarta: Darul Falah.

Alconada, Mon H. 2007a. 'La Triple Frontera preocupa en EE.UU.' *La Nación*, 21 January 2007: 8.

———. 2007b. 'Rechazo del gobierno', *La Nación*, 21 January 2007: 8.

Alonso, R. 2002. 'La manipulación del modelo irlandés', *El País Domingo*, 3 February 2002.

———. 2004. 'Pathways out of Terrorism in Northern Ireland and the Basque Country: The Misrepresentation of the Irish Model', *Terrorism and Political Violence*, 16(4): 695–713.

———. 2005. 'El nuevo terrorismo: factores de cambio y permanencia', in Amalio Blanco, Rafael del Águila and José Manuel Sabucedo (eds), *Madrid 11-M. Un análisis del mal y sus consecuencias*. Madrid: Editorial Trotta.

———. 2007a. 'Políticas antiterroristas y procesos de paz: Qué papel y qué consecuencias para las víctimas del terrorismo?', in Rogelio Alonso and Cristina Cuesta (coord.), *Las víctimas del terrorismo en el discurso político*. Madrid: Editorial Dilex.

———. 2007b. *The IRA and Armed Struggle*. London: Routledge.

———. 2008. 'The evolution of the terrorist threat in Spain and the United Kingdom: from ethno-nationalist terrorism to jihadist terrorism', in Brett Bowden and Michael T. Davis (eds), *Terror: From Tyrannicide to Terrorism in Europe, 1605–2005*, pp. 263–281. Queensland: University of Queensland Press.

Alonso, R. and F. Reinares. 2005. 'Terrorism, Human Rights and Law Enforcement in Spain', *Terrorism and Political Violence*, 17(1–2).

Andoni, Lamis. 1996. 'The Palestinian Elections: Moving Toward Democracy or One-Party Rule?', *Journal of Palestine Studies* 25(3): 5–16.

Armstrong, Karen. 2002. *Islam*. New York: The Modern Library.

Arquilla, J. and D. Ronfeldt. 2000. *Swarming and The Future of Conflict*. RAND Documented Briefing, Santa Monica, California: RAND. Available online at http://www.rand.org/pubs/documented_briefings/2005/RAND_DB311.pdf

Asian Tribune. 2006a. 'Banned Tamil Tigers infiltrate Western bases of political power', *Asian Tribune*, 5 November 2006. Available online at www.asiantribune.com

———. 2006b. 'Canadian diplomat blasts former Liberal government for funding Tiger terror in Sri Lanka', quoted from *Ottawa Citizen, Asian Tribune*, 19 September 2006. Available online at www.asiantribune.com

Asian Tribune. 2006c. 'FBI Court Document Reveals in Detail: Sri Lanka's Tamil Tiger Arms Procurement Plot', *Asian Tribune*, 16 September 2006. Available online at www.asiantribune.com

———. 2007a. 'Dirty "Sethu" and "Rowdy" Rajan found guilty of attacking Tamil Broadcasting Corporation in London', *Asian Tribune*, 31 March 2007. Available online at http://www.asiantribune.com

———. 2007b. 'Tiger gangs attack rival PLOTE members in Zurich: two Tamil in a serious condition', *Asian Tribune*, 2 May 2007. Available online at http://www.asiantribune.com

———. 2008. TV interview of Vice Admiral Wasantha Karannagoda, Commander of the Sri Lanka Navy, 2 February 2008. Available online at www.asiantribune.com

Athas, Iqbal. 2007. 'East: the aftermath', *Sunday Times*, Colombo, 22 July 2007. Available online at http://www.sundaytimes.lk

Aubrey, S. 2004. *The New Dimension of International Terrorism*. Zurich: Auflage.

Australian Broadcasting Corporation (ABC). 2006. 'Al Qaeda analyst on cricket terrorist plot claims', 10 October 2006. Full transcript of the interview with Zachary Abuza is available online at: <http://www.abc.net.au/lateline/content/2006/s1759229.htm> (accessed on 12 October 2006).

Avalon Project. 1968. 'The Palestinian National Charter: Resolutions of the Palestine National Council 1–17 July 1968', The Avalon Project at the Yale Law School. Available online at http://www.yale.edu/lawweb/avalon/mideast/plocov.htm

———. 1988. 'The Hamas Covenant 1988: The Covenant of the Islamic Resistance Movement', The Avalon Project at the Yale Law School, 18 August 1988. Available at http://www.yale.edu/lawweb/avalon/mideast/hamas.htm

———. 1993. 'Israel-Palestine Liberation Organization Agreement: 1993', The Avalon Project at the Yale Law School. Available at http://www.yale.edu/lawweb/avalon/mideast/isrplo.htm

Azem, A.J. 1977. 'The Islamic Action Front', in J. Schwedler (ed.), *Islamic Movements in Jordan*, pp. 95–144. Amman: al-Urdun al-Jadid Research Center.

Badey, T.J. 1998. 'Defining international terrorism: a pragmatic approach', *Terrorism and Political Violence*, 10(1): 90–107.

Badwar, Inderjit. 2007. 'Inderjit Badwar's interview of President Mahinda Rajapakse', *Asian Tribune*, 20 September 2007. Available online at http://www.asiantribune.com

Bagley, B.M. and W.O. Walker III (eds). 1994. *Drug Trafficking in the Americas*. Miami, FL: University of Miami North-South Center.

Bailey, F.G. 1969. *Strategems and Spoils: A Social Anthropology of Politics*. New York: Schocken Books.

Balasingam, Anton S. 1983. 'Liberation Tigers of Tamil Eelam: Our Theoretical Guide to the National Question', available online at http://www.tamilnation.org/ltte/83guide.htm

Baldauf, Scott. 2006. 'Is Al Qaeda Setting Up Shop in Kashmir?' *Christian Science Monitor*, 18 July 2006. Also available at http://www.csmonitor.com/2006/0718/p06s02-wosc.html (accessed on 1 June 2007).

Baldwin, Fletcher N. (Jr). 2004. *The Rule of Law, Terrorism, and Countermeasures Including the USA PATRIOT Act of 2001*, Florida Journal of International Law, March 2004, 16(43): 60.

Ballard, Tim., Jason Pate, Gary Ackerman, Diana McCauley and Sean Lawson. 2001. 'Chronology of Aum Shinrikyo's CBW Activities', Center for Nonproliferation

Studies, March 2001. Available online at <http://cns.miis.edu/pubs/reports/aum_chrn.htm> (accessed on 12 December 2002).

Baltimore Sun. 2006. 'Further indictments in federal arms sting', reproduced in *The Daily News*, 7 October 2006. Available online at www.dailynews.lk

Banerjee, S. (n.d.). 'Naxalbari (1967): The Naxalite Movement in India', *AsiaMedia*, n.d. Available online at http://venus.unive.it/asiamed/eventi/schede/naxalbari.html

Bar, Shmuel. 1998. *The Muslim Brotherhood in Jordan.* Tel Aviv: Moshe Dayan Center, Tel Aviv University.

Barkai, Haim. 2005. 'Hapeilut ha-Kalkalit Ha-Realit shel Milhemet Ha-Hatzmaut', in Alon Kadish (ed.), *Milchemet Ha-Hatzmaut Tashah-Tashat: Diyun Mehudash.* Tel-Aviv: Misrad Habitachon.

Barpujari, H.K. (ed.). 1992. *The Comprehensive History of Assam (Vol II).* Guwahati: Publication Board Assam.

Barton, Greg. 2004. *Jemaah Islamiyah; Radical Islamism in Indonesia.* Singapore: Ridge Books.

Bayer, O. 1986. *La Patagonia rebelde.* Buenos Aires: Hyspamérica.

BBC News. 2001. 'Militants Attack Kashmir Assembly', BBC News, Monday, 1 October 2001. Also available at http://news.bbc.co.uk/1/hi/world/south_asia/1574225.stm (accessed on 29 June 2007).

———. 2005. 'Ex-rebel Recalls "Pakistan Trips"', BBC News online, Saturday, 4 June 2005.

———. 2006. 'Hamas Sweeps Election Victory', BBC News, 26 January 2006. Available at http://news.bbc.co.uk/1/hi/world/middle_east/4650788.stm

———. 2007a. 'Palestinian Rivals: Fatah & Hamas', BBC News, 17 June 2007. Available at http://news.bbc.co.uk/2/hi/middle_east/5016012.stm

———. 2007b. 'Who were the Baader-Meinhof gang?', BBC News, 12 February 2007. Available online at http://news.bbc.co.uk/2/hi/europe/6314559.stm

Beam, L. 1992. 'Leaderless resistance', *The Seditionist*, 12 (Feb. 1992): 1–7. Available online at http://www.louisbeam.com/leaderless.htm

Bedi, Rahul. 2001. 'Kashmir Insurgency is Being 'Talibanised'', *Jane's.com*, 5 October 2001. Also Available online at http://www.janes.com/security/international_security/news/misc/janes011005_n_shtml (accessed on 1 July 2007).

Bedoya, J. 2007. 'Al menos 23 extranjeros ingresaron a las Farc mediante la modalidad de intercambios estudiantiles', *El Tiempo*, 8 September 2007.

Behuria, Ashok K. 2007. 'The Rise of the Pakistani Taliban and the Response of the State', *Strategic Analysis*, 31(5): 712–713.

Bell, Stewart. 2006. 'Canada deports LTTE extortion gang leader', *National Post*, Toronto, 31 January 2006.

Bell, Stewart. 2007. '63 suspects named in Tamil Tigers case: Judge extends probe', *National Post*, Toronto, 1 June 2007.

Beltrán de Otálora, O. 2007. 'Europol advirtió en 2003 que la banda terrorista intentaba instalarse en Portugal', *El Correo*, 22 July 2007.

Benningsen, A. 1958. 'The National Front in Communist Strategy in the Middle East', in Walter Laqueur (ed.), *The Middle East in Transition*, pp. 351–360. London: Routledge & Kegan Paul.

Bergen, Peter L. 2002. *Holy War, INC.: Inside the Secret World of Osama Bin Laden* London: Phoenix.

Bhabha, Homi K. 1994. 'DissemiNation: Time, Narrative and the Margins of the Modern Nation', in Homi K. Bhabha (ed.), *Nation and Narration*, pp. 290–322. London: Routledge.

Bhattacharjya, S. 2008. 'Red Terror', *India Today*, 11 February 2008: 33.

Bhattarai, R. 2004. *Geopolitical Specialties of Nepal and a Regional Approach to Conflict Transformation*. Kathmandu: Friends for Peace.

Bhaumik, Subir. 1996. *Insurgent Crossfire: North East India*. New Delhi: Lancer.

———. 2002. 'Bangladesh: The Second Front of Islamic Terror', paper presented at the International Seminar on 'Terrorism and Low Intensity Conflict', Jadavpur University, India, 6–8 March 2002.

Bin-Laden, O. 1998. 'World Islamic Front for Jihad against Jews and crusaders: initial 'fatwa' statement', *Al-Quds Al-Arabi*, 23 February 1998. For a translation into English, see <http://www.pbs.org/newshour/terrorism/international/fatwa_1998.html>

Bjorgo, T. (ed.). 2005. *Root Causes of Terrorism*. New York, London: Routledge.

Bjorgo, Tore. 2007. *Root Causes of Terrorism: Myths, Reality and Ways Forward*. New York, Tauris.

Black, Cofer (Ambassador). 2004. 'Introduction', in *Patterns of Global Terrorism 2003*, United States Department of State (USDS), April 2004. Available online at http://www.terrorisminfo.mipt.org/pdf/2003PoGT.pdf (accessed on 25 June 2007).

Blackburn, Chris. 2006. 'Terrorism in Bangladesh: The Region and Beyond', paper presented at the Policy Exchange Conference on 'The Rise of Political Islam in Bangladesh', London, 14 November 2006; also published in, *New Age*, 22 September 2006.

———. n.d. 'Jamaat-e-Islami: A Threat to Bangladesh?' Special Articles section, *Secular Voice of Bangladesh*. Available online at www.secularvoiceofbangladesh.org (last accessed on 26 November 2008).

Boccara, M.H. and A. Greenberg. 2004. *Islamist Websites and their Hosts Part II: Clerics*. Middle East Media Research Institute Special Report, No. 35, 11 November 2004. Avilable online at <http://www.memri.org/bin/articles.cgi?Page=archives&Area a=sr&ID=SR3504>.

Borum, Randy. 2003. *Psychology of Terrorism*. Available online at http://www.ncjrs.gov/pdffiles1/nij/grants/208552.pdf., *citing* W. Laqueur. 2003. *No End to War: Terrorism in the Twenty-First Century*. New York: Continuum.

Bose, Sumantra. 2003. *Kashmir: Roots of Conflict, Paths to Peace*. Cambridge, Massachusetts: Harvard University Press.

Bowden, Brett and Michael T. Davis (eds). 2008. *Terror: From Tyrannicide to Terrorism in Europe, 1605–2005*. Queensland: University of Queensland Press.

Bowden, Mark. 2001. *Killing Pablo: The Hunt for the World's Greatest Outlaw*. New York: Atlantic Monthly Press.

Brines, Russell. 1968. *The Indo-Pakistani Conflict*. London, UK: Pall Mall Press, Ltd.

Brockelmann, Carl. 1960. *History of the Islamic People*. New York: Capricorn.

Brockett, James. 2005. 'Temple leader tells of capture by Tamil Tigers', *Harrow Times*, London, 30 April 2005. Quoted in www.dailynews.lk

Bruinessen, Martin van. 2004. 'Traditionalist and Islamist pesantren in contemporary Indonesia', Paper presented at the ISIM workshop on 'The Madrasa in Asia', 23–24 May 2004. ISM, Netherlands.

Bukhari, Shujaat. 2007. 'Al-Qaeda Chapter in Kashmir?' *The Hindu*, Saturday, 9 June 2007. Available online at http://www.hindu.com/2007/06/09/stories/2007060906761200.htm (accessed on 10 June 2007).

Burgat, François and William Dowell. 1993. *The Islamic Movement in North Africa*. University of Texas: Austin Center for Middle Eastern Studies.

Burns, T. and G. Stalker. 1961. *The Management of Innovations*. London: Tavistock.

Buzan, B., O. Weaver, J. de Wilde. 1998. *Security: A New Framework for Análisis*. Boulder, Colorado: Lynne Reinner Publishers.

Byman, Daniel. 2003. *Deadly Connections: States that Sponsor Terrorism*. Cambridge, UK: Cambridge University Press.

———. 2005. Deadly Connections: States that Sponsor Terrorism. Cambridge: Cambridge University Press.

Cahyono, Heru. 1998. *Pangkokamib Jenderal Soemitro dan Peristiwa 15 January 1974*. Jakarta: Pustaka Sinar Harapan.

Calle, F. and K. DerGhougassian. 2003. 'El guardián del mundo unipolar y sus críticas: La Estrategia de Seguridad Nacional de Estados Unidos y la construcción del espacio alternativo', *Revista Colección*, Universidad Católica Argentina, Instituto de Ciencias Políticas y Relaciones Internacionales, año IX, no. 14 (diciembre 2003), pp. 65–97.

Cameron, G. 1998. 'The Likelihood of Nuclear Terrorism', *The Journal of Conflict Studies*, 18(2): 5–28.

Canadian Broadcast Corporation. n.d. 'Fasten your Seatbelt', Canadian Broadcast Corporation. Available at http://www.cbc.ca/fifth/fastenseatbelts/best.html; *see also* http://www.palestinefacts.org/pf_1967to1991_lod_1972.php.

Casinello, A. 1984. 'ETA y el problema vasco', paper presented at the Seminar on International Terrorism, *Instituto de Cuestiones Internacionales* (ICI), Madrid, 1984.

Castañeda, J.G. 1993. *La utopia desarmada: intrigas, dilemas y promesa de la izquierda en América Latina*. Buenos Aires, Argentina: Ariel.

Caton, Steven C. 1987. 'Power, Persuasion, and Language: A Critique of the Segmentary Model in the Middle East', *International Journal of Middle East Studies*, 1 (February 1987): 77–102.

CBS News. 2002. 'Terrorism Alliance?', CBS News (26 July 2002). Available online at http://www.cbsnews.com/stories/2002/07/26/attack/main516585.shtml

———. 2003. 'Palestinians Get Saddam Charity Checks', CBS News (13 March 2003). Available online at http://www.cbsnews.com/stories/2003/03/14/world/main543981.shtml

Cepeda, F. 2004. 'El caso colombiano', in Claudio Fuentes S. (ed.), *Bajo la mirada del Halcón. Estados Unidos-América Latina post 11/09/2001*, pp. 221–228. Santiago de Chile: FLACSO-Chile.

Chadha Behera, Navnita. 2006. *Demystifying Kashmir*. Washington, DC: Brookings Institute Press.

Chaliand, G. and A. Blin. 2006. *Histoire du terrorisme de l'antiquité a Al Quaida*. Paris: Bayard.

Chalk, Peter. 2001. 'Pakistan's Role in the Kashmir Insurgency', *Jane's Intelligence Review*, 1 September 2001. Also available online at http://www.rand.org/commentary/090101JIR.html.

Chawla, Prabhu. 1997. 'Jain commission revelations-damning the DMK', *India Today*, 17 November 1997. Available online at www.india-today.com

Clawson, P.L. and R.W. Lee III. 1998. *The Andean Cocaine Industry*. New York: St. Martin's Griffin.

Clover, Ben. 2007. 'Charity trustee suspended over "terrorism links"', *South London Times*, 21 May 2007. Available online at www.icsouthlondon.co.uk

Cohen, Amnon. 1980. *Political Parties in the West Bank Under Jordanian Rule 1948–1967*. Ithaca, N.Y.: Cornell University Press.

Commission on Human Rights, United Nations Economic and Social Council. 2004. 'Civil and political rights, including the question of torture and detention', Report of the Special Rapporteur on the question of torture, Theo van Boven. Addendum, Visit to Spain, Sixtieth session, E/CN.4/2004/56/Add.2, 6 February 2004.

Committee on Homeland Security and Governmental Affairs, U.S. Senate. 2007. *Radicalization of Global Islamist Terrorists*, Testimony by M. Sageman, 27 June 2007. Available online at <http://hsgac.senate.gov/files/062707Sageman.pdf>.

Committee on International Relations, US House of Representatives. 2001. Summary of Investigation of IRA Links to FARC Narco-Terrorists in Colombia, 24 April 2001.

Compilation of Media Reports. 2007. *LTTE The International Dimensions of Terrorism*. Colombo: Ministry of External Affairs, Government of Sri Lanka.

Conboy, Ken. 2004. *The Second Front: Inside Asia's Most Dangerous Terrorist Network*. Jakarta: Equinox.

Corbacho, A. 2007. 'El problema número uno en el hemisferio es la pobreza', *DEF Desarrollo/Defensa/Energía/Medio Ambiente*, 3(21): 32–36.

Cragin, K., P. Chalk, S.A. Daly and B.A. Jackson. 2007. *Sharing the Dragon's Teeth: Terrorist Groups and the Exchange of New Technologies*. Report prepared for the Department of Homeland Security, Santa Monica, California: RAND.

Crenshaw, Martha. 1995. 'Thoughts on Relating Terrorism to Historical Contexts', in M. Crenshaw (ed.), *Terrorism in Context*, pp. 13–14, 22–23. University Park, PA: The Pennsylvania State University Press.

———. 1998. 'The logic of terrorism: Terrorist behavior as a product of strategic choice', in Walter Reich (ed.), *Origins of Terrorism: Psychologies, Ideologies, Theologies, States of Mind*. Washington DC: Woodrow Wilson Center Press.

———. 2004. *Terrorism in Context*. University Park, PA: The Pennsylvania State Mashal.

——— (ed.). 2001. *Terrorism in Context*. University Park (Pennsylvania): Pennsylvania University Press.

Croddy, E., M. Osborne and K. McCloud. 2002. *Chemical Terrorist Plot in Rome?* Center for Nonproliferation Studies Research Story of the Week, 11 March 2002. Available online at <http://cns.miis.edu/pubs/week/020311.htm>

Cronin, A.K. 2002–03. 'Behind the Curve: Globalization and International Terrorism', *International Security*, 27(3): 34.

———. 2004. 'Sources of Contemporary Terrorism', in Audrey Kurth Cronin and James M. Ludes (eds.), *Attacking Terrorism: Elements of a Grand Strategy*. Washington DC: Georgetown University Press.

Cullison, A. 2004. 'Inside al Qaeda's Hard Drive', *The Atlantic Monthly*, 294(2): 55–70.

Daily Mirror. 2007. 'Tigers waiting for Missiles to go for full-scale war', *Daily Mirror*, Colombo, 23 March 2007. Available online at http://www.dailymirror.lk

Dailyindia.com. 2006. 'ULFA forging ties with LTTE, say police', dailyindia.com, Agartala, 2 December 2006. Available online at http://www.dailyindia.com.

Dasgupta, T. 2005. 'Whither the Naxal Comrades?', *Himal South Asia*, 18(2): 16–19.

Desmond, Edward W. 1995. 'The Insurgency in Kashmir 1989–1991', *Contemporary South Asia*, 4(1).

Dios Colmenero, J. de. 2004. 'ETA se financia en Iberoamérica', *La Clave*, 2–8 July 2004: 14–17.

Dixit, J.N. 1998. *Assignment Colombo*. Colombo: Vijitha Yapa Bookshop.

Documentos Y. 1971a. 'Zutik 63', *Documentos Y*, vol. 12, p. 351.

———. 1971b. Vol. 12, p. 396.

———. 1973. Vol. 16, pp. 447–448.

Dolnik, A. 2007. *Understanding Terrorist Innovation: Technology, Tactics and Global Trends.* London: Routledge.

Dolnik, A. and Anjali Bhattacharjee. 2002. 'HAMAS: Suicide Bombing, Rocket, or WMD?', *Terrorism and Political Violence*, 14(3): 119.

Dolnik, A. and R. Gunaratna. 2007. 'Jemaah Islamiyah and the Threat of Chemical and Biological Weapons Terrorism', in Russell D. Howard and James J.F. Forest (eds), *Terrorism and Weapons of Mass Destruction*. New York: McGraw-Hill.

Domínguez, F. 1998a. *De la negociación a la tregua.¿El final de ETA?* Madrid: Taurus.

———. 1998b. *ETA: Estrategia Organizativa y Actuaciones 1978–1992*. Bilbao: Universidad del País Vasco.

———. 2006. *Josu Ternera. Una vida en ETA*. Madrid: La Esfera de los Libros.

Druckman, Daniel and Christopher Mitchell. 1995. 'Flexibility in Negotiation and Mediation', *Annals*, No. 542.

Eichenwald, Kurt. 2001. 'A Nation Challenged: The Money; Terror Money Hard to Block', *N.Y. Times*, December 10, p. B4.

Eickelman, Dale F. and James Piscatori. 1996. *Muslim Politics*. Princeton, N.J.: Princeton University Press.

Eisenberg, Ethan. 1996. 'Democracy in Gaza: An Election Diary', *Congress Monthly*, 63(2): 9–13.

El Correo. 2002. 'El director de los servicios secretos españoles dice que ETA compra armas a las mafias de los Balcanes', *El Correo*, 8 June 2002.

El Fadl, Khaled Abou. 2006. *The Great Theft: Wrestling Islam from the Extremist*. New Delhi: Harper Collins.

El Universal. 2007. 'EUU dispuesto a colaborar con Venezuela tras amenaza de Al Qaeda', *El Universal*, 16 February 2007. Available online at <http://www.eluniversal.com> (last accessed on 9 April 2007).

Embassy of India. 2008. *Terrorist Attack on the Parliament of India*, http://www.indianembassy.org/new/parliament_dec_13_01.htm (accessed on 28 January 2008).

Engene, J.O. 2007. 'Five decades of terrorism in Europe: the TWEED dataset', *Journal of Peace Research*, 44(1): 109–110.

Esposito, John L. and James P. Piscatori. 'Democratization and Islam', *Middle East Journal*, 45(3): 427–440.

Europol. 2007. *EU Terrorism Situation and Trend Report 2007*. Europol: The Hague.

Falcón, R. 1984. *Los orígenes del movimiento obrero (1857–1899)*. Buenos Aires: Centro Editor de América Latina.

Fealy, Greg. 2004. 'Islamic Radicalism in Indonesia: A Faltering Revival?', in *Southeast Asian Affairs*, pp. 104–21. Singapore: Institute of Southeast Asian Studies.

———. 2005a. 'A Conservative Trajectory in Indonesian Islam?', *Bulletin of Indonesian Economic Studies*, 41(3).

———. 2005b. 'Half a Century of Violent Jihad in Indonesia: A Historical and Ideological Comparison of Darul Islam and Jemaah Islamiyah', in Marika Vicziany and David Wright Neville (eds), *Islamic Terrorism in Indonesia: Myth and Realities*. Victoria: Monach University Press.

Fealy, Greg. 2005c. 'Radical Islam in Indonesia: History, Ideology and Prospects', in Greg Fealy and Aldo Borgu (eds), *Local Jihad: Radical Islam and terrorism in Indonesia*. Canberra: Australian Strategic Policy Institute Strategic Reports.

————. 2007. 'Hizbut Tahrir in Indonesia: Seeking a 'Total' Muslim Identity', in Shahram Akbarzadeh and Fethi Mansouri (eds), *Islam and Political Violence: Muslim Diaspora and Radicalism in the West*, pp. 151–64. London and New York: I.B. Tauris.

Federation of American Scientists. 1998. 'Brigate Rosse Red Brigades', FAS, 8 August 1998. Available online at http://www.fas.org/irp/world/para/br.htm, updated Saturday, 08 August 1998; *see also Red Brigades Leader Tells of Ties to P.L.O., NY Times* (17 March 1982), available at http://query.nytimes.com/gst/fullpage.html?res=990CE0D8133BF934A25750C0A964948260.

————. 2003. 'Japanese Red Army (JRA): Anti-Imperialist International Brigade (AIIB)', FAS, 1 May 2003. Available online at http://www.fas.org/irp/world/para/jra.htm (last modified on 1 May 2003).

Feldman, A. and M. Perälä. 2004. 'Reassessing the causes of nongovernmental terrorism in Latin America', *Latin American Politics and Society*, 46(2).

Fishel, Kimbra L. 2005. 'Challenging the Hegemon: Al Qaeda's Elevation of Asymmetric Insurgent Warfare onto the Global Arena', in Robert Bunker (ed.), *Networks, Terrorism and Global Insurgency*. UK: Routledge.

Fitzgerald, M. 2002. 'ETA admit ties with Provos: terror groups help each other, says Basque ex-leader', *Belfast Telegraph*, 20 May 2002.

Ford, J.L. 1998. 'Radiological Dispersal Devices: Assessing the Transnational Threat', *Strategic Forum*, 136 (March 1998). <http://www.ndu.edu/inss/strforum/forum136.html>.

FOX News. 2002. 'Saddam Pays 25k for Palestinian Bombers', FOX News, 26 March 2002. Available at http://www.foxnews.com/story/0,2933,48822,00.html

————. 2006. 'Hamas Rejects Zawahiri's Support', Fox News, 6 March 2006. Available online at http://www.foxnews.com/story/0,2933,186900,00.html

Fricsh, Hillel. 1994. 'The Evolution of Palestinian Nationalist Islamic Doctrine: Territorializing a Universal Religion', *Canadian Review in Nationalism*, 21(1–2): 45–55.

————. 2006. 'Motivation or Capabilities? Israeli Counterterrorism against Palestinian Suicide Bombings and Violence'. Available online at http://www.biu.ac.il/SOC/besa/MSPS70.pdf

Gajurel, C.P. 2007. 'Foreign Policy: National Interest is the Deciding Factor', *The Kathmandu Post*, 26 April 2007.

Gallastegi, I. 2004. 'Sinn Féin y Herri Batasuna', *Gara*, 22 February 2004.

Gallego, M., T. Eggers-Brass and F. Gil Lozano. 2006. *Historia Latinoamericana 1700–2005: Sociedades, culturas, procesos polítios y económicos*. Buenos Aires: Editorial Maipue.

Ganguly, Sumit. 1997. *The Crisis in Kashmir: Portents of War, Hopes of Peace*. Washington, DC: Woodrow Wilson Press; Cambridge, UK: Cambridge University Press.

————. 2001. *Conflict Unending: India-Pakistan Tensions since 1947*. New York: Columbia University Press and Washington, DC: Woodrow Wilson Center Press, 2001.

Ganguly, Sumit and Michael R. Kraig. 2005. 'The 2001–2002 Indo-Pakistani Crisis: Exposing the Limits of Coercive Diplomacy', *Security Studies*, 14(2): 290–324.

Gara. 2002. 'ETA censura la falta de una declaración de Downing Street', *Gara*, 30 January 2002.

Gelner, Ernest. 1983. *Nations and Nationalism*. Ithaca, NY: Cornell University Press.

Gerlach, L. 1987. 'Protest movements and the construction of risk', in B. Johnson and V.T. Covello (eds), *The Social and Cultural Construction of Risk*, pp. 103–145. Boston: D. Reidel Pub. Co.

Gerlach, L. and V. Hine. 1970. *People, Power, Change: Movements of Social Transformation*. New York: The Bobbs–Merril Co.

Ghanem, As'ad. 1996. 'Founding Elections in Transitional Period: The First Palestinian General Elections', *Middle East Journal*, 50(4): 513–528.

Goplaji, Malviya (ed.). 2005. *Security Dimensions of Peninsular India*. Chennai: Centre for Security Analysis.

Grare, Frederic. 2001. *Political Islam in the Indian Sub-continent: Jamaat-e-Islami*. Delhi: Manohar Publishers.

Griswold, Eliza. 2005. 'The Next Islamist Revolution', *The New York Times Magazine*, Main Edition, 23 January 2005.

Guelke, A. 1988. *Northern Ireland: The International Perspective*. Dublin: Gill and McMillan.

———. 2000. '"Comparatively peaceful": South Africa, the Middle East and Northern Ireland', in Michael Cox, Adrian Guelke and Fiona Stephen (eds), *A Farewell to Arms? From 'Long War' to Long Peace in Northern Ireland*, pp. 223–233. Manchester: Manchester University Press.

Gunaratna, Rohan (ed.). 2003. *Terrorism in the Asia-Pacific: Threat and Response*. Singapore: Eastern Universities Press.

Harbom, L. and P. Wallensteen. 2008. 'Appendix 2A. Patterns of major armed conflicts, 1998–2007', *SIPRI Yearbook 2008*. Oxford: Oxford University Press.

Hardgrave, Robert L. (Jr) and Stanley A. Kochanek. 2000. *India: Government and Politics in a Developing Nation*. Fort Worth, TX: Harcourt Brace & Company.

Hariharan, R. 2006a. 'Engaging Sri Lanka: India's potpourri–Update no 97', *South Asia Analysis Group*, Note No. 297, 30 July 2006. Available online at http://www.southasiaanalysis.org

———. 2006b. 'LTTE and the cult of the suicide warriors', *South Asia Analysis Group*, Paper No. 1873, 12 February 2006. Available online at http://www.southasiaanalysis.org

———. 2006c. 'Sri Lanka: How strong are the Tigers?–Update No 84', *South Asia Analysis Group*, Note No. 297, 28 February 2006. Available online at http://www.southasiaanalysis.org

———. 2007. 'The discarded accord and the unwanted war', *The Hindu* (7 August 2007). Available online at http://www.thehindu.com

Harnden, T. 2002. 'Adams ally's trade in terror', *The Daily Telegraph*, 15 May 2002.

Hautsi. 1973. *Hautsi*, No. 2, September–October 1973.

Hazarika, Sanjoy. 1994. *Strangers of the Mist: Tales of War and peace from India's Northeast*. New Delhi: Penguin Books.

Henneberger, M. 2002. '4 Arrested in Plot Against U.S. Embassy in Rome', *New York Times*, 21 February 2002: A15.

Hennessy, M. 2001. 'Republicans woo young voters with softer image', *The Irish Times*, 31 July 2001.

Heru Cahyono. 1998. *Pangkokamib Jenderal Soemitro dan Peristiwa 15 Januari 1974* Jakarta: Pustaka Sinar Harapan.

Hirst, M. 1988. 'Las políticas exteriors latinoamericanas frente a la crisis subregional: putos de comparación', in Cristina Eguizábal (ed.), *América Latina y la crisis centroamericana: en búsqueda de una solución regional*, pp. 263–278. Buenos Aires: Grupo Editor Latinoamericano.

Hizban Rights Watch and Physicians for Hizban Rights. 1993. *The Hizban Rights Crisis in Kashmir: A Pattern of Impunity*, Hizban Rights Watch and Physicians for Hizban Rights, June 1993. Available online at http://physiciansforHizbanrights.org/library/documents/reports/report-1993-impunity.pdf (accessed on 26 June 2007).

Hobsbawm, Eric. 1990. *Nations and Nationalism Since 1780: Programme, Reality*. Cambridge: Cambridge University Press.

Hoffman, B. 1993. *'Holy Terror': The Implications of Terrorism Motivated by a Religious Imperative*, RAND Paper P-7834. Santa Monica (California): RAND. Available online at <http://www.rand.org/pubs/papers/P7834>

———. 1998. *Inside Terrorism*. New York: Orion Publishing Co.

———. 2000. 'The Debate Over Future Terrorist Use of Chemical, Biological, Nuclear and Radiological Weapons', in Brad Roberts (ed.), *Hype or Reality: The 'New Terrorism' and Mass Casualty Attacks*. Alexandria, Virginia: Chemical and Biological Arms Control Institute (CBACI).

———. 2006. *Inside Terrorism*. New York: Columbia University Press.

———. 2007. 'CBRN Terrorism Post-9/11', in Russell D. Howard, James J.F. Forest and Natasha E. Bajema (eds), *Terrorism and Weapons of Mass Destruction*. New York: McGraw-Hill.

Hoffman, Bruce and Donna K. Hoffman. 1995. 'The RAND-St. Andrews chronology of international terrorist incidents', RAND. Available online at http://www.rand.org/pubs/reprints/RP666/

Holland, J. 1999. *The American Connection: U.S. Guns, Money and Influence in Northern Ireland*. Dublin: Roberts Rinehart Publishers.

———. 2001. 'FARC defectors implicate IRA in training program', *Irish Echo*, 9 January 2001.

Holland, J. and H. McDonald. 1994. *INLA: Deadly Divisions*. Dublin: Poolbeg.

Hopkins, N. 2001.'Real IRA suspects extradited from Slovakia guns deal', *The Guardian*, 31 August 2001.

HTI. 2007. 'Ustad Abu: Syariah Tak Perlu Musyawarah', *HTI*, 30 August 2007. Available online at http://www.hizbut-tahrir.or.id/index.php/2007/08/30/ustad-abu-syariah-tak-perlu-musyawarah/ (accessed on 1 September 2007).

Huisken, Ron and Meredith Thatcher (eds). 2007. *History as Policy: Framing the Debate on the Future of Australia's Defence Policy*, SDSC Canberra Paper No. 167, Australian National University.

Human Rights Watch, New York. 2006. 'Funding the "Final War": LTTE intimidation and extortion in the Tamil Diaspora', Human Rights Watch, New York, 15 March 2006. Available online at http://www.hrw.org/reports/2006/ltte0306/

Huntington, Samuel P. 1991. *The Third Wave*. Norman: University of Oklahoma Press.

Hussain, Zahid. 2007. *Frontline Pakistan: The Struggle With Militant Islam*. London: I.B. Tauris.

Hussain, Zakir. 2008. 'DIY extremists a "worrying trend"', *The Straits Times* (25 January 2008). Available online at http://www.straitstimes.com/print/Singapore/Story/STIStory_199798.html

Huste, J.P. 2007. 'Latin America, the Caribbean, Islamism and terrorism', in *ESISC Analysis Notes*, 7 March 2007.

Indian Express. 1999. 'The Fidayeen—faithful to the death', *Indian Express*, Friday, 12 November 1999. Available online at http://www.indianexpress.com/res/web/pIe/ie/daily/19991112/ige12049.html (accessed on 29 June 2007).

Informal Sector Service Centre (INSEC). 2007. *Human Rights Yearbook 2007*. Kathmandu: INSEC.

Innes, J. 1999. 'Bin Laden Admits He 'Instigated' US Embassy Attacks', *Scotsman*, 4 January 1999.

International Crisis Group. 2002a. *al-Qaeda in Southeast Asia: The Case of the Ngruki Pondok*, ICG Indonesia Briefing, 8 August 2002.

———. 2002b. Indonesia Backgrounder, *How The Jemaah Islamiyah Terrorist Network Operates*, ICG Asia Report No. 43. Jakarta/Brussels, 11 December 2002.

———. 2003. *Jemaah Islamiyah in Southeast Asia: Damaged but Still Dangerous*, ICG Asia Report No 63. Jakarta/Brussels, 26 August 2003.

———. 2005. *Recycling Militants in Indonesia: Darul Islam and the Australian Embassy Bombings*, ICG Asia Report No 92. Singapore/Brussels, 22 February 2005.

———. 2007a. *Indonesia: Jemaah Islamiyah's Current Status*, ICG Asia Briefing No 63. Jakarta/Brussels, 3 May 2007.

———. 2007b. *Nepal's Maoists: Purists or Pragmatists*. Asia Report No. 132. Brussels: International Crisis Group, 2007.

Israel Ministry of Foreign Affairs. 2004. 'Hamas Terrorist Attack', Israel Ministry of Foreign Affairs, 22 March 2004. Available online at http://www.mfa.gov.il/MFA/Terrorism-+Obstacle+to+Peace/Terror+Groups/Hamas+terror+attacks+22-Mar-2004.htm

Israeli, Raphael. 1990. 'The Charter of Allah: The Platform of the Islamic Resistance Movement (Hamas)', in Y. Alexander and A.H. Foxman (eds), E. Mastragelo (contributing ed.), *The 1988–1989 Annual on Terrorism*, pp. 109–132. The Hague: Martinus Nijhoff Publishers.

Iturribarría, F. 2007. "La justicia francesa prueba la conexión entre el terrorista 'Carlos' y ETA pm", *El Correo*, 8 April 2007.

Jagmohan. 1991. *My Frozen Turbulence in Kashmir*. New Delhi: Allied Publishers.

Jakarta Gatra. 2001. 'Bandung Xmas Eve 2000 Bombers Also Used Mobile Phones', *Jakarta Gatra*, 6 January 2001.

Jayasuriya, Ranga. 2006. 'LTTE has killed 7,000 Tamils–Thurairatnam', *Sunday Observer*, 11 June 2006.

Jenkins, B.M. 1975. *Will Terrorists Go Nuclear?*, RAND Paper P-5541. Santa Monica, California: RAND.

Jerusalem Post. 2006. *Saudi religious leader blasts Hezbollah*, *Jerusalem Post*, 6 August 2006. Available online at http://www.jpost.com/servlet/Satellite?pagename=JPost/JPArticle/ShowFull&cid=1154525810323

Jeyaraj, D.B.S. 2007. 'Trouble overseas', *Frontline*, Chennai, 24(14).

JKLF. n.d. *JKLF: Our Ideology, Aims and Objectives*. Available online at http://www. shell.comsats.net.pk/~jklf/i2.htm (accessed on 23 June 2007).

Jones, Sidney. 2005. 'Terrorism and "Radical Islam" in Indonesia', in Marika Vicziany and David Wright Neville (eds), *Islamic Terrorism in Indonesia: Myth and Realities*, pp. 3–15. Victoria: Monach University Press.

Juergensmeyer, M. 2000. *Terror in the Mind of God: The Global Rise of Religious Violence*. Berkeley; Los Angeles; London: University of California Press.

Kaldor, M. 1999. *New and Old Wars: Organized Violence in a Global Era*. Cambridge: Polity Press.

Kaplan, D.E. 2000. 'Aum Shinrikyo', in Jonathan B. Tucker (ed.), *Toxic Terror: Assessing Terrorist Use of Chemical and Biological Weapons*. London: Cambridge (Massachusetts): MIT Press.

Kashmir News. 2007. 'Kashmir Insurgency Turns Deadlier,' *Kashmir Newz*, 15 March 2007. Available online at http://www.kashmirnewz.com/n000137.html (accessed on 2 July 2007).

Kassim, Anis F. 1980. 'The Palestine Liberation Organization's Claim to Status: A Juridical Analysis Under International Law', *Denver Journal of International Law and Policy*, 9(1): 19–30.

Kepel, Gilles. 1985. Muslim Extremism in Egypt: The Prophet and the Pharaoh. Berkeley and Los Angeles: University of California Press.

Khaled Abou El Fadl. 2006. *The Great Theft: Wrestling Islam from the Extremist*. New Delhi: Harper Collins.

Kjorlien, M.L. 1993. 'Hamas in Theory and Practice', *Arab Studies Journal*, 1(2): 4–7.

Knoke, David. 1990. Political Networks: The Structural Perspective. Cambridge: Cambridge University Press.

Kouyoumdjian, A. 2006. 'Islam, Chile and related matters', unpublished analysis provided as a personal email.

Kramer, G. 1994. 'The Integration of the Integrist: A Comparative Study of Egypt, Jordan and Tunisia', in Ghassan Salame (ed.), *Democracy Without Democrats? The Renewal of Politics in the Muslim World*, pp. 200–226. London: Tauris.

Kramer, Martin. 1996. 'Fundamentalist Islam at Large: The Drive for Power', *Middle East Quarterly*, 3(2): 37–49.

Krishnamurti, Lakshmi, R. Swaminathan and George W. Kueck (eds). 2003. *Responding to Terrorism: Dilemmas of democratic and developing societies*. Chennai: India: Book Venture.

Lahman, Shay. 1982. 'Sheikh `Izz al-Din al-Qassam', in Elie Kedourie and Silvia Haim (eds), *Zionism and Arabism in Palestine and Israel*, pp. 54–99. London: Frank Cass.

Lahoud, Nelly and Anthony Johns (eds). 2005. *Islam in World Politics*. London: Routledge.

Lak, D. 2007. 'Global Janandolon: It's time Americans and the rest of the world came together to stop the madness', *Nepali Times*, 15–21 June 2007: 10.

Lanata, J. 2006. 'Tócala de nuevo, Nisman', *Perfil*, 19 November 2006: 16–17.

Lanata, J. and J. Goldman. 1994. *Cortinas de humo: Una investigación independiente sobre los atentados conta la embajada de Israel y la AMIA*. Buenos Aires: Planeta.

Lapidus, Ira M. 1988. 'Islam Political Movements: Patterns of Historical Change', in Edmund Burke and Ira M. Lapidus (eds), *Islam, Politics, and Social Movements*, pp. 3–35. Berkeley and Los Angeles: University of California Press.

Laqueur, Walter. 2004. 'The Terrorism to Come', *Hoover Institue Policy Review*, August & September 2004. Available online at http://www.hoover.org/publications/policyreview/3437231.html

Larraquy, M. 2006. *Fuimos Soldados: Historia Secreta de la Contraofensiva Montonera.* Buenos Aires: Aguilar.

Lawrence, T.E. 1938. *Seven Pillars of Wisdom: A Triumph.* Garden City. NewYork: Doubleday.

Lee Rensselaer III, W. 1998. *Smuggling Armageddon: The Nuclear Black Market in the Former Soviet Union and Europe.* New York: St. Martin's Press.

Legrain, J.F. 1997. 'Hamas: Legitimate Heir of Palestinian Nationalism?', in John L. Esposito (ed.). *Political Islam: Revolution, Radicalism or Reform,* pp. 159–178. Boulder, Colo.: Lynne Rienner.

Lesch, Ann M. 1990. 'Prelude to the Uprising in the Gaza Strip', *Journal of Palestinian Studies*, 20(1): 2–5, Autumn, 1990. Available online at http://www.jstor.org/cgi-bin/jstor/printpage/0377919x/di009636/00p00042o/0.pdf?backconte xt=page&dowhat=Acrobat&config=jstor&userID=81167e82@cwru.edu/01cce440610050d15c0&0.pdf

Lesser, I., Bruce Hoffman, John Arquilla, David F. Ronfeldt, Michele Zanini. 1999. *Countering the New Terrorism.* Santa Monica (California): RAND.

Levitt, Matthew. 2004. 'Hamas from Cradle to Grave', *Middle East Quarterly*, Winter 2004. Available online at http://www.washingtoninstitute.org/templateC05.php?CID=2378

———. 2005. 'A Hamas Headquarters in Saudi Arabia?', Washington Institute for Near East Policy, 8 September 2005. Available online at http://www.washingtoninstitute. org/templateC05.php?CID=2378

Lewis, Bernard. 1992. 'Rethinking the Middle East', *Foreign Affairs* 71(4): 99–119.

Lijphart, Arend. 1994. *Election Systems and Party Systems.* Oxford: Oxford University Press.

Lintner, Bertil. 2004. 'Religious Extremism and Nationalism in Bangladesh', in Robert G Wirsing, Satu Limaye and Mohan Malik (eds), *Religious Radicalism and Security in South Asia.* Honolulu, Hawaii, US: Asia-Pacific Center for Security Studies.

———. 2007. 'Championing Islamic Extremism.' Available online at http://www. asiapacificms.com/articles/rohingya_al_qaeda/, (Accessed on 5 July 2007).

Litani, Y. 1989. 'The Militant Islam in the West Bank and Gaza Strip', *New Outlook*, 32(11–12): 40–42.

Mackenzie Institute, Toronto. 2000. 'Funding terror: The Liberation Tigers of Tamil Eelam and their Criminal Activities in Canada and the Western World', Mackenzie Institute, Toronto, Commentary no. 77, 17 March 2000.

Malik, General, V.P. 2006. *Kargil: From Surprise to Victory.* New Delhi: Harper Collins Publishers.

Malik, Shiv. 2003. 'NS Profile Omar Shariff', *New Statesman*, 24 April 2003.

Mannoni, P. 2006. 'Le terrorisme, un spectacle palnifié', in Régis Meyran (ed.), *Les mécanismes de la violence: états, institutions, individu.* Paris: Auxerre Sciences Humaines.

Maqdsi, Muhammad. 1985. *Radical Islam.* New Haven, Conn.: Yale University Press.

Maqdsi, Muhammad. 1990. 'Mobilisation islamiste et soulevement palestinien 1987–1988', in G. Kepel and Y. Richard (eds), *Intellectuels et militants de l'Islam contemporain*, pp. 131–166. Paris: Seuil.

———. 1990. 'Social Theory in the Study of Muslim Societies', in Dale F. Eickelman and James Piscatori (eds), *Muslim Travelers: Pilgrimage, Migration, and the Religious Imagination*, pp. 1–25. London: Routledge.

———. 1993. 'The Charter of the Islamic Resistance Movement (Hamas)', *Journal of Palestine Studies*, XXII(4): 122–134.

———. 1997. 'Can Islamists Be Democrats? The Case of Jordan', *Middle East Journal*, 51(3): 373–388.

Markham, Shelley. 2007. 'Tamil Tigers' roots run deep in Australia', 24 September 2007. Available online at http://www.theaustralian.news.com.au

Mata, J.M. 1993. *El nacionalismo vasco radical: discurso, organizaciones y expresiones*. Bilbao: Universidad del País Vasco.

Maududi, S.A.A. 2004. 'Jihad in Islam', Lecture given in Lahore, 13 April 1939, reproduced in Walter Laqueur (ed.), *Voices of Terror: Manifestos, Writing and Manuals of Al Qaeda, Hamas, and Other Terrorists from Around the World and throughout the Ages*. New York: Reed Press.

Mawdudi, Abu-l-'Ala'. 1982. 'Political Theory of Islam', in John J. Donohue and John J. Esposito (eds), *Islam in Transition*, pp. 252–271. New York: Oxford University Press.

Mayer, Tomas. 1990. 'Pro-Iranian Fundamentalism in Gaza', in E. Sivan and M. Friedman (eds), *Religious Radicalism and Politics in the Middle East*, pp. 142–155. Albany: State University of New York Press.

Mayntz, R. 2004. 'Organizational Forms of Terrorism: Hierarchy, Network or a Type Sui Generis?', Max Planck Institute for the Study of Societies (MpfiG) Discussion Paper 04/4, Cologne: MpfiG. Available online at <http://www.mpifg.de/pu/mpifg_dp/dp04-4.pdf>

McGuire, M. 1973. *To Take Arms*. New York: The Viking Press.

Meijer, R. 1997. *From al-Da'wa to al-Hizbiyya: Mainstream Islamic Movements in Egypt, Jordan and Palestine in the 1990s*. Amsterdam: Research Center for International Political Economy.

Mello, A. 2007. 'No man's land is everybody's business', *The Arab Washingtonian*, 23 April 2007. Available online at < http://www.arabwashingtonian.com/english/article.php?issue=14&articleID=348>

Menon, A.K. 2008. 'The Siege Within', *India Today*, 11 February 2008: 39.

Middle East Media Research Institute. 2002. Special Dispatch Series-*No. 388*, 12 June 2002. Available online at <http://www.memri.org/bin/articles.cgi?ID=SP38802>, (accessed on 31 August 2007).

———. 2006. 'Al-Qaeda film on the first anniversary of the London bombings', Transcript No. 1186, 8 July 2006. Available online at http://www.memritv.org/clip_transcript/en/1186.htm

Miller, Aaron David. 1983. *The PLO and the Politics of Survival*. Washington, DC: Georgetown University Center for Strategic and International Studies.

Miller, J. 2002. *Germs: Biological Weapons and America's Secret Wari*. New York: Touchstone.

Ministry of External Affairs, Sri Lanka. 2007. 'IC has never been so supportive to SL to fight terrorism—FM', Ministry of External Affairs, Sri Lanka, 10 August 2007. Available online at http://www.defence.lk

Ministry of Foreign Affairs, State of Israel. 1995. Israeli-Palestinian Agreement on the West Bank and the Gaza Strip. Jerusalem: Ministry of Foreign Affairs.

Mir, Mustansir. 1991. 'Jihad in Islam', in Hadia Dajani-Shakeel and Ronald A. Messier (eds), *The Jihad and Its Times*, pp. 113–126. Ann Arbor: University of Michigan Press.

Mishal, Shaul and Reuven Aharoni. 1994. *Speaking Stones, Communiqués from the Intifada Underground*. Syracuse. New York: Syracuse University Press.

Mitchell, G. 1999. *Making Peace: The Inside Story of the Making of the Good Friday Agreement*. London: William Heinemann.

Mitchell, Richard P. 1969. *The Society of the Muslim Brothers*. Oxford: Oxford University Press.

Moloney, E. 2002. *A Secret History of the IRA*. London: Penguin Books.

Morris, S. 2001. 'IRA's links with Farc and Eta revealed', *The Guardian*, 25 August 2001.

Morrison, D. 1999. 'Stretching republicans too far', *The Guardian*, 13 July 1999.

Murphy, J.F. 1989. *State Support of International Terrorism: Legal, Political, and Economic Dimensions*. Westview: Boulder, Colo.

Napoleoni, L. 2003. *Modern Jihad: Tracing the Dollars behind the Terror Networks*. Sterling, VA: Pluto Press.

Narayanswamy, M.R. 1994. *Tigers of Lanka: From Boys to Guerrillas*. New Delhi: Konark Publications.

———. 2003. *Inside an Elusive Mind–Prabhakaran*. New Delhi: Konark Publications.

National Commission on Terrorist Attacks Upon the United States. 2004. *9–11 Commission Report*. Norwalk, CT: Easton Press.

National Strategy for Combating Terrorism (Washington D.C.: The White House, December 2006). 2003. Available online at <http://www.whitehouse.gov/nsc/nsct/2006/nsct2006.pdf>

Nesiah, Devanesan. 2006. 'Sri Lankan Nationalism, Ethnic Identity and Community', in B. Raman, N. Sathiya Moorthy and Kalpana Chittaranjan (eds), *Sri Lanka: Peace Without Process*, pp 53–89. New Delhi, Samskriti.

Nibedon, Nirmal. 1983. *Nagaland: The Night of the Guerillas*. New Delhi: Lancers Publisher.

Niblock, Tim. 1991. 'Islamic Movements and Sudan's Political Coherence', in H. Bleuchot, C. Delmet and D. Hopewood (eds), *Sudan: History, Identity, Ideology*, pp. 253–268. Reading, Pa.: Ithaca Press.

Nickson, R.A. 2003. 'Democratisation and Growth of Communism in Nepal', in D. Thapa (ed.), *Understanding the Maoist Movement in Nepal*. Kathmandu: MartinChautari.

Nilsson, A. 2001. 'The Threat of Nuclear Terrorism: Assessment and Preventive Action', paper for the Symposium on Terrorism and Disarmament, United Nations, 25 October 2001.

Noorani, A.G. 2002. *Islam and Jihad*. New Delhi: Left Word Books.

NPR. 2006. *Verbal Front in the War on Terror*, 15 August 2006. Available online at http://www.npr.org/templates/story/story.php?story Id=5651001

NSCN Manifesto, (Preface), GPRN, Oking, 31 January 1980. See NSCN manifesto at www.nscnonline (accessed on 12 February 2008).

NY Times. 2005. 'Blowing Up an Assumption', *NY Times*, 18 May 2005. Available online at http://www.nytimes.com/2005/05/18/opinion/18pape.html?ex=1186545600&en=8d75c3b2eb8bd3ff&ei=5070

O'Brien, B. 1993. *The Long War: The IRA and Sinn Féin*. Dublin: The O'Brien Press.

O'Malley, P. 2001. 'Northern Ireland and South Africa: Hope and History at a Crossroads', in John McGarry (ed.), *Northern Ireland and the Divided World: Post-Agreement Northern Ireland in Comparative Perspective*, pp. 276–308. Oxford: Oxford University Press.

Office of the Commissioner for Human Rights. 2001. Report by Mr Alvaro Gil Robles, Commissioner for Human Rights, on his visit to Spain and the Basque Country, 5–8 February 2001, for the Committee of Ministers and the Parliamentary Assembly, Council of Europe, CommDH (2001) 2, Strasbourg, 9 March 2001.

Olivier, Roy. 1995. *The Failure of Political Islam*. Cambridge, Mass.: Harvard University Press.

Onesto, L. 2000. 'Red Flag Flying on the Roof of the World (Interview with Prachanda)', *Revolutionary Worker*, 20 February 2000.

———. 2005. *Dispatches from the People's War in Nepal*. London: Pluto Press; Chicago: Insight Press.

ORF series on Contemporary Asia, *Towards Peace in Sri Lanka*. New Delhi: Rupa & Co.

Ortiz, R. 2004. 'Radicalización política y violencia insurgente en América Latina: un análisis en perspectiva histórica', in Javier Roldán (ed.), *Los orígenes del terror. Indagando las causas del terrorismo*. Madrid: Biblioteca Nueva.

Osher, S. 2002. 'Privacy, Computers and the Patriot Act. The Fourth Amendment Isn't Dead, but No One Will Insure It', University of Florida law Review, 54(533): 533–34.

Pagola, J. 2006. 'Sectores de Batasuna alardean de la "victoria de ETA" tras el apoyo de la UE al "proceso"', *Abc*, 1 November 2006.

Pandey, N.N. 2005. *Nepal's Maoist Movement and Implications for India and China*. Regional Centre for Strategic Studies (RCSS) Policy Studies Report no. 27. New Delhi: Manohar Publishers and Distributors.

Patterson, H. 2002. *Ireland Since 1939*. Oxford: Oxford University Press.

Pavlova, Elena. 2006. 'From Counter-Society to Counter-State: Jemaah Islamiyah According to PUPJI', S. Rajaratnam School of International Studies (RSIS) Working Papers No. 117.

PBS. 2006. 'The Popular Front for the Liberation of Palestine', *Public Broadcasting Service* (PBS), page created on 14 February 2006. Available online at http://www.pbs.org/wgbh/amex/hijacked/peopleevents/p_pflp.html

Perlez, Jane. 2007. 'From Finding Radical Islam to Losing an Ideology', *The New York Times*, 12 September 2007.

Perry, Alex. 2002. 'Deadly Cargo', *Time*, Asia Edition 14 October 2002. Available online at http://www.time.com/time/magazine/article/0,9171,501021021-364423,00.html, last accessed on 26 November 2008.

Piscatori, James. 1983. *Islam in a World of Nation–States*. London: Royal Institute of International Affairs.

Pita, R. 2007. 'Assessing al-Qaeda's Chemical Threat', *International Journal of Intelligence and CounterIntelligence*, 20(3): 480–511.

Porath, Yehoshua. 1974. *From Riots to Revolt: The Arab-Palestinian National Movement 1929–1939*. London: Frank Cass.

Post, J.M. 1998. 'Terrorist psycho-logic: terrorist behavior as a product of psychological forces', in Walter Reich (ed.), *Origins of Terrorism: Psychologies, Ideologies, Theologies, States of Mind*. Washington, DC: Woodrow Wilson Center Press.

Powell, Sian. 2003. 'Hambali links JI to al-Qaeda cash', *The Australian*, 29 September 2003.

Purdie, B. 1990. *Politics in the Streets: The Origins of the Civil Rights Movement in Northern Ireland*. Belfast: The Blackstaff Press.

Qutb, S. 1989. *Milestones*, translated by M.M. Siddiqui. Kuwait: Al Faisal Press.

———. 2000. 'War, peace, and Islamic Jihad', in M. Moaddel and K. Talattof (eds), *Contemporary Debates in Islam: An Antology of Modernist and Fundamentalist Thought*. London: Macmillan; Basingstoke.

Raghavan, V.R. (ed.). 2007. *Peace Process in Sri Lanka: Challenges and Opportunities*. Chennai: East West Books (Madras) Ltd.

Raghavan, V.R. and Karl Fischer (eds). 2005. *Conflict Resolution and Peace Building in Sri Lanka*. New Delhi: Tata McGraw-Hill Publishing Co., Ltd.

Raghavan, V.R. and Volker Bauer (eds). 2006. *Federalism and Conflict Resolution in Sri Lanka*. New Delhi: Lancer Publishers & Distributors.

Raj, A.P. 2004. *Maoists in the Land of Buddha: An Analytical Study of the Maoist Insurgency in Nepal*. Delhi: Nirala Publications.

Raman, B. 2008. 'Suicide Terrorism in Pakistan', *Outlookindia.com*, 14 January 2008. Available online at http://www.outlookindia.com/full.asp?sid=1&fodname=200 80114&fname=raman (accessed 28 January 2008).

Raman, B., N. Sathiya Moorthy and Kalpana Chittaranjan (eds). 2006. *Sri Lanka Peace without Process*. New Delhi: Samskriti.

Rana, Muhammad Amir. 2004. *A to Z of Jehadi Organizations in Pakistan*. Lahore: Marshal Books.

Rapoport, D. 2004. 'The Four Waves of Modern Terrorism', in A.K. Cronin and J.M. Ludes (eds), *Attacking Terrorism: Elements of a Grand Strategy*. Washington, DC: Georgetown University Press.

Reddy, Muralidhar B. 2003. 'No ban, only curbs on Hizb activities: Pak', *The Hindu*, 21 May 2003. Available online at http://www.hinduonnet.com/thehindu/thscrip/ print.pl?file=2003052105390100.htm&date=2003/05/21/&prd=th& (accessed on 2 July 2007).

———. 2004. 'The Jihadist Backlash,' *Frontline*, 21(1), 3–16 January 2004. Available online at http://www.hinduonnet.com/fline/fl2101/stories/20040116004512400. htm (accessed on 1 July 2007).

Reeve, Simon. 1999. *The New Jackals*. London: Andre Deutsch Ltd.

Reinares F. 2001. *Patriotas de la muerte. Quienes han militado en ETA y por qué*. Madrid: Taurus.

Richardson, L. 1998. 'Global rebels: terrorist organizations as transnational actors', *Harvard International Review*, 20(4): 52–56.

———. 2005. 'State sponsorship—a root cause of terrorism', in Tore Bjorgo (ed.), *Root Causes of Terrorism: Myths, Reality and Ways Forward*. New York: Routledge.

Rickman, Gregg. 2000. *The PLO and Iraq in the Twilight of Soviet Foreign Policy, MERIA*, 4(3). Available online at http://meria.idc.ac.il/journal/2000/issue3/jv4n3a8. html

Robinson, Glenn E. 1997. *Building a Palestinian State, the Unfinished Revolution*. Bloomington: Indiana University Press.

Rodinelli, Dennis A. 1993. *Development Projects as Policy Experiments*, 2nd edition. London: Routledge.

Rokeach, Milton. 1966–67. 'Attitude Change and Behavioral Change', *Public Opinion Quarterly* 30: 529–550.

Ronfeldt, D. 2005. 'Al Qaeda and its affiliates: a global tribe waging segmental warfare?', *First Monday*, 10 (3), March 2005. Available online at http://firstmonday.org/issues/issue10_3/ronfield/index.html

Rouquié, A. 1992. *Guerres et paix en Amérique Centrale*. Paris: Seuil.

Sachi, Sri Kantha. 2005. *Pirabahakaran Phenomenon*. Gifu City, Japan: Lively COMET Imprint.

Sageman, M. 2004. *Understanding Terror Networks*. Philadelphia, Pa.: University of Pennsylvania Press.

———. 2007. *Leaderless Jihad: Terror Networks in the Twenty-First Century*. Philadelphia, Pa.: University of Pennsylvania Press.

Saikia, Jaideep. 2004. *Terror Sans Frontiers: Islamist Militancy in North East India*. New Delhi: Vision Books.

———. 2005. 'Template for anti-terror doctrine', *Aakrosh*, New Delhi, October 2005.

——— (ed.). 2006a. *Bangladesh: Treading the Taliban Trail*. New Delhi: Vision Books.

———. 2006b. 'Islamist Terror: Deconstructing the Paradigm', *Aakrosh*, New Delhi, October 2006.

——— (ed.). 2007. *Frontier in Flames: North East India in Turmoil*. New Delhi: Penguin Books.

Sakhuja, Vijay. 2006. 'The dynamics of LTTE's commercial maritime infrastructure', Occasional papers, Observer Research Foundation, New Delhi, April 2006. Available online at www.orfonline.org.

Salama, S. and L. Hansell. 2005. 'Does Intent Equal Capability? Al-Qaeda and Weapons of Mass Destruction', *Nonproliferation Review*, 12(3), November 2005. Available online at http://cns.miis.edu/pubs/npr/vol12/123/123salama.pdf.

Sale, George. n.d. *The Koran*, translated into English from the original Arabic. London: Warne.

Sangameswaran, K.T. 2007. 'LTTE wanted boats for smuggling arms: police', *The Hindu*, Chennai, 27 May 2007. Available online at http://www.hindu.com

Satloff, Robert. 1989. 'Islam in the Palestinian Uprising', *Orbis*, 33(3): 389–401.

Schiff, Z. and E. Ya'ari. 1989. *Intifada, the Palestinian Uprising, Israel's Third Front*. New York: Simon & Schuster.

Schofield, Victoria. 2003. *Kashmir in Conflict: India, Pakistan and the Unending War*. New York: I.B. Tauris & Co. Ltd.

Seddon, D. and K. Hussien. 2002. *The Consequences of Conflict: Livelihoods and Development in Nepal*. London: Overseas Development Institute.

Sela, Avraham and Moshe Ma'oz (eds). 1997. *The PLO and Israel: From Armed Conflict to Political Solution, 1964–1994*. New York: St. Martin's Press.

Serraj, Par Abdelhak Najib et Karim. 2003. 'Saïd Chedadi et Cheikh Najib, le chaînon manquant du 16 mai?', *La Gazette de Maroc*, 29 October 2003.

Shang, Tq. 2001. 'The Palestinian Intifada as Bargaining Signal', *Stanford Journal of International Relations*, Spring 2001. Available online at http://www.stanford.edu/group/sjir/3.1.03_shang.html

Sharkanski, Ira. 1997. 'The Potential of Ambiguity: The Case of Jerusalem', in Efraim Karsh (ed.), *From Rabin to Netanyahu*, pp. 187–200. London: Frank Cass.

Sharma, S. 2003. 'The Maoist movement: an evolutionary perspective', in D. Thapa (ed.), *Understanding the Maoist Movement in Nepal*, pp. 362–380. Kathmandu: Martin Chautari.

Sharrock, D. 1998. 'ETA sets foot on road that led to Ulster deal', *The Guardian*, 22 August 1998.

Sharrock, D. and M. Davenport. 1997. *Man of War, Man of Peace? The Unauthorised Biography of Gerry Adams*. London: Macmillan.

Shikaki, Khalil. 1996. 'The Palestinian Elections: An Assessment', *Journal of Palestine Studies*, 25(3): 17–22.

Sian. 2003. 'Hambali links JI to al-Qaeda cash,' *The Australian*, 29 September 2003.

Sikand, Yoginder. 2001. 'The Changing Course of the Kashmiri Struggle: From National Liberation to Islamist Jihad', *The Muslim World*, 91(1–2): 229–256.

Simom Elegant. 2002. 'Asia's Own Osama', Timeasia.com, 1 April 2002. Available online at http://www.time.com/time/asia/features/malay_terror/hambali4.html

Simpson, Cam. 2003. 'U.S. Seeks Access to Malaysian Al Qaeda Suspect', *Chicago Tribune*, 7 December 2003.

Singapore Ministry of Home Affairs. 2003. *The Jemaah Islamiyah Arrests and the Threat of Terrorism*. Singapore: MHA.

Singh, Bilveer. 2003. *ASEAN, Australia and the Management of the Jemaah Islamiyah Threat.* Canberra Papers on Strategy and Defence, No. 152. Canberra: ANU.

Singh, Depinder. 1992. *IPKF in Sri Lanka*. New Delhi: Trishul publications.

Singh, Harkirat. 2007. *Intervention in Sri Lanka: The IPKF Experience Retold*. New Delhi: Manohar.

Siva Sunderam. 2006. 'Three murders Sunday early hours rock the Toronto Tamil community', *Toronto*, 6 November 2006. Available online at www.independentlk.com

Sivan, Emmanuel. 1995. 'Eavesdropping on Radical Islam', *Middle East Quarterly*, 2(1): 13–24.

Smaith, Paul J. (ed.). 2005. *Terrorism and Violence in Southeast Asia*. New York: East Gate Books.

Smyth, P. 2002. 'Colombian army chief says FARC trained by IRA', *The Irish Times*, 25 April 2002.

Solomon, Jay and James Hookway. 2002. 'Bali Bomb Suspect Used Thailand as Staging Area', *The Wall Street Journal*, 7 November 2002.

Sood, Lt Gen. (Retd.) V.K. and Praveen Sawhney. 2003. *Operation Parakram: The War Unfinished*. New Delhi, India: Sage Publications.

South Asia Tribune. 2005. 'LTTE and Maoist links: Indian intelligence sounds the red alert', Report of *South Asia Tribune*, 11 July 2005, reproduced in www.colombopage.com

Sprinzak, E. and Zertal, I. 2000. 'Avenging Israel's Blood', in Jonathan B. Tucker (ed.), *Toxic Terror: Assessing Terrorist Use of Chemical and Biological Weapons*. London, Cambridge (Massachusetts): MIT Press.

Steinberg, Matti. 1989. 'The PLO and Palestinian Islamic Fundamentalism', *Jerusalem Quarterly*, 52: 37–54.

Stepanova, E. 2003. *Anti-Terrorism and Peace-Building During and After Conflict*. Stockholm: SIPRI. Available online at <http://books.sipri.org/files/PP/SIPRIPP02.pdf>

———. 2006. 'Terrorism as a tactic of spoilers in peace processes', in Edward Newman and Oliver Richmond (eds), *Challenges to Peacebuilding: Managing Spoilers during Conflict Resolution*, pp. 78–104. Tokyo: United Nations University Press.

Stepanova, E. 2008. *Terrorism in Asymmetrical Conflict: Ideological and Structural Aspects.* Oxford: Oxford University Press.

Sullivan, M. 2007. *Latin America: Terrorism Issues*, CRS Report to Congress RS21049, Washington, DC: US GPO, 22 January 2007. Available online at <http://fpc.state. gov/documents/organization/81364.pdf>

Suriano, J. 2001. *Anarquistas: cultura y política libertaria en Buenos Aires (1890–1910).* Buenos Aires: Manatial.

———. 2005. *Auge y caída del anarquismo: Argentina 1880–1930.* Buenos Aires: Capital Intelectual.

Swami, Praveen. 2003. 'Terrorism in Jammu and Kashmir in Theory and Practice', *India Review*, 2 July 2003: 56.

———. 2007a. 'Grim infiltration figures undermine troop-cut calls', *The Hindu*, 24 June 2007. Available online at http://www.hindu.com/2007/06/24/stories/ 2007062451120900.htm (accessed on 25 June 2007).

———. 2007b. *India, Pakistan and the Secret Jihad: The Covert War in Kashmir, 1947–2004.* New York: Routledge.

Taji-Farouki, Suha. 1996. *A Fundamental Quest, Hizb al-Tahrir and the Search for the Islamic Caliphate.* London: Grey Seal.

Tamiltigers.net. 1997–2005. 'Sri Lankan Tamil Migration', available online at http:// www.ttnet.netfast.org/features/migration/te_migration.html

Tan, A. and K. Ramakrishna. 2002. *The New Terrorism.* Singapore: Eastern University Press.

Taylor, P. 1997. *Provos: The IRA and Sinn Fein.* London: Bloomsbury.

Thapa, D. (ed.). 2003. *Understanding the Maoist Movement in Nepal.* Kathmandu: MartinChautari.

The 9/11 Commission Report. 2004. *Final Report of the National Commission on Terrorist Attacks Upon the United States.* New York: W.W. Norton & Co.

The Federal Bureau of Investigation. 2008. 'Taming the Tigers–From here in the U.S.', FBI, 10 January 2008. Available online at http://www.fbi.gov/

The Himalayan Times. 2007. 'ULFA Guerillas Shifting Base to Nepal', *The Himalayan Times*, 7 June 2007.

The Hindu. 2006. 'Pakistan's intentions will be on test: Manmohan', *The Hindu*, 19 October 2006. Available online at http://www.hindu.com/2006/10/19 stories/2006101919150100.htm., last accessed on 26 November 2008.

The Jamestown Foundation. 2007. *The Algiers Bombings: Al-Qaeda's Resurgence in North Africa*, Event Summary, The Jamestown Foundation, 7 April 2007. Event video is available on-line at <http://www.jamestown.org/events_details.php?event_id=30> (last accessed on 20 April 2007).

The Observer. 2006. 'Hamas in call to end suicide bombings', *The Observer* (9 April 2006). Available online at http://observer.guardian.co.uk/world/story/0,1750028,00.html

The Straits Times. 2008. 'Escape of JI leader: How can this happen in S'pore?', *The Straight Times*, 28 February 2008. Available online at http://www.straitestimes. com/Latest%2BNews/Singapore/STIStory_211368.html

The Telegraph. 2008. 'Deoband denounces terror', *The Telegraph*, Kolkata, 26 February 2008.

The Times of India. 2007. 'India tops terror toll, after Iraq', *The Times of India*, Delhi, 27 August 2007.

The Times of India. 2008a. 'ISI Blamed for Bhutto Assassination', *The Times of India*, 10 January 2008. Available online at http://timesofindia.indiatimes.com/World/Pakistan/ISI_blamed_for_Bhutto_assassination/articleshow/2688579.cms (accessed 28 January 2008).

———. 2008b. 'Teen Suspect in Benazir Murder Plot Held', *Times of India*, 19 January 2008. Available online at http://timesofindia.indiatimes.com/articleshow/2714208.cms (accessed 28 January 2008).

The White House. 2003. *National Strategy for Combating Terrorism*. Washington DC: The White House, February 2003. Available online at http://www.whitehouse.gov/news/releases/2003/02/counter_terrorism/counter_terrorism_strategy.pdf and <http://www.state.gov/documents/organization/60172.pdf>

Thornton, C. 2002. 'IRA tactics could kill Americans', *Belfast Telegraph*, 27 March 2002.

Time. 1974. (published as a news story), *Time*, 27 May 1974. Available online at http://www.time.com/time/magazine/article/0,9171,911263,00.html?promoid=googlep

———. 1975. 'Terrorism Complicates a Mission of Peace', *Time*, 17 March 1975. Available online at http://www.time.com/time/magazine/article/0,9171,912976,00.html?promoid=googlep

———. 1978. 'A Sabbath of Terror', *Time*, 20 March 1978. Available at http://www.time.com/time/magazine/article/0,9171,919454,00.html?promoid=googlep.

———. 2002. 'When the Terror Began', *Time*, 2 September 2002. Available at http://www.time.com/time/europe/magazine/2002/0902/munich/index.html

———. 2002. 'When the Terror Began', *Time*, 2 September 2002. Available at http://www.time.com/time/europe/magazine/2002/0902/munich/index.html

———. 2004. 'A Life in Retrospect: Yasser Arafat', *Time*, 12 November 2004. Available online at http://www.time.com/time/world/article/0,8599,781566-1,00.html

Toda, T. 2002. 'Si por Garzón fuera, en Irlanda no habría paz', *Gara*, 19 February 2002.

Toronto Star. 2004. 'Canada's Tamils must rethink LTTE support', *Toronto Star*, Toronto, Canada, 19 December 2004.

Tse Tung, Mao. 1968. *Selected Military Writings*. Peking: Foreign Languages Press.

Turabi, Hasan. 1995. 'Islam as a Pan-National Movement', *RSE Journal* (August), University Press.

Upreti, B.R. 2004a. 'Nepal on Fire: A Tragedy of Triple Betrayal', *South Asian Journal*, 7 December.

———. 2004b. *The Price of Neglect: From Resource Conflict to Maoist Insurgency in the Himalayan Kingdom*. Kathmandu: Bhrikuti Academic Publications.

———. 2006. *Armed Conflict and Peace Process in Nepal: The Maoist Insurgency, Past Negotiation and Opportunities for Conflict Transformation*. New Delhi: Adroit Publishers.

Upreti, B.R. and R. Nepali (eds). 2006. *Nepal at Barrel of Gun: Proliferation of Small Arms and Light Weapons and their Impacts*. Kathmandu: South Asia Small Arms Network-Nepal.

Usher, Graham. 1995. 'Arafat's Opening', *New Statement and Society*, 8(381): 25.

Van Djik. 1981. *Rebellion Under the Banner of Islam*. The Hague: Martinus Nijhoff.

Vaughn, Bruce, Emma Chanlett-Avery, Richard Cronin, Mark Manyin and Larry Niksch. 2005. *Terrorism in Southeast Asia*, CRS Report for Congress, 7 February 2005.

Vaughn, Bruce. 2007. *Islamist Extremism in Bangladesh*, CRS Report for Congress, 31 January 2007.

Vicziany, Marika and David Wright-Neville (eds). 2005. *Islamic Terrorism in Indonesia: Myth and Realities*. Victoria: Monach University Press.

Voll, O. John. 1991. 'Fundamentalism in the Sunni Arab World: Egypt and Sudan', in Martin E. Marti and Scott R. Appleby (eds), *Fundamentalism Observed*, pp. 345–395. Chicago: University of Chicago Press.

Waldner, David. 1994. 'Civic Exclusion and Its Discontents', paper presented at the annual meeting of the American Political Science Association, New York City, September 1994.

Walker, B. 2002. 'Web of terror: The blame in Spain', *Belfast Telegraph*, 22 May 2002.

Washington Post. 2005a. 'Scholarly Look at Terror Sees Bootprints in the Sand', *Washington Post*, 10 July 2005. Available online at http://www.washingtonpost. com/wp-dyn/content/article/2005/07/09/AR2005070901425_pf.html

———. 2005b. 'Suicide Bombs Potent Tool of Terrorists', *Washington Post*, 17 July 2005. Available online at http://www.washingtonpost.com/wp-dyn/content/ article/2005/07/16/AR2005071601363_pf.html

Watts, Michael. 1996. 'Islamic Modernities? Citizenship, Civil Society and Islamism in a Nigerian City', *Public Culture*, 8: 251–289.

Weizman, S. 2001. 'HAMAS Pleased with Addition of Poison to Bombs', *Associated Press*, 12 December 2001.

Whiteman, Dominic. 2006. 'LTTE Tamil Tigers and its UK-wide network', Pipelinenews.org, 17 October 2006. Available online at www.pipelinenews.org.

Whittaker, D.J. 2003. *The Terrorism Reader*, 2nd ed., New York: Routledge.

Wikipedia. 'Sri Lankan Tamil diaspora', *Wikepedia*. Available online at http:// en.wikipedia.org/

Williams, Clive and Brendan Taylor (eds). 2003. 'Countering Terror: New Directions Post 9-11', Canberra Papers on Strategy and Defence, No. 147, Strategic and Defence Studies Centre, The Australian National University, June 2003.

Wilson, A.J. 1995. *Irish America and the Ulster Conflict 1968–1995*. Belfast: The Blackstaff Press.

Wirsing, Robert G. 1994. *India, Pakistan, and the Kashmir Dispute: On Regional Conflict and its Resolution*. New York, NY: St. Martin's Press.

Woodworth, P. 1998. 'Basque leader sees peace process as way forward', *The Irish Times*, 31 October 1998.

World and Islam Studies Enterprise and the University of South Florida, Committee for Middle East Studies. 1992. 'Islam, Democracy, the State and the West', A Round Table with Dr. Hasan Turabi, 19 May 1992.

Xinhua. 1990. 'Sri Lankan Tamil Tigers Use Poison Gas Against Government Troops, Says Senior Officer', *Xinhua General Overseas News Service*, 18 June 1990, radio transcript accessed through Lexis–Nexis.

Ya'ari, Ehud. 1970. *Strike Terror: The Story of Fatah*. New York: Sabra Books.

Yunanto, S. 2003. *Gerakan Militan Islam Di Indonesia dan di Asia Tenggara*. Jakarta: RIDEP Institute.

Zambelis, C. 2005. 'Radical Islam in Latin America', *Terrorism Monitor*, 3(23).

Zlotogwiazda, M. and L. Balaguer. 2003. *Citibank vs. Argentina: Historia de un país en bancarrota*. Buenos Aires: Editorial Sudamericana.

ABOUT THE EDITORS AND CONTRIBUTORS

EDITORS

Jaideep Saikia (India) is a security and terrorism analyst based in Assam. He has authored and/or edited seven books, including, *Terror Sans Frontiers: Islamist Militancy in North East India* (2004) and *Bangladesh: Treading the Taliban Trail* (ed., 2006), *Frontier in Flames: North East India in Turmoil* (ed. 2007). He had his education at the Royal Indian Military College, Dehra Dun, St. Stephen's College, University of Delhi, and as a Ford Fellow at University of Illinois at Urbana–Champaign, USA. He has travelled widely in the USA, Europe, China, and in South and South East Asia on academic assignments, and is the recipient of many fellowships including the National Foundation for India, when he studied the security situation in Kashmir, Regional Centre for Strategic Studies fellowship for research in Sri Lanka. He also visited the US as an International Visitor on the invitation of the Department of State in its programme on 'International Crime Issues and Global Cooperation'. Later he also worked on the United Nations University project on challenges for peace building. Saikia has served the governments of India and Assam in security advisory capacities, including the National Security Council Secretariat of India as an expert on North East India. Saikia was a member of the Indian delegation for 'Track II' dialogue with Bangladesh in 2007 and is a referee for the journal, *Strategic Analysis*.

Ekaterina Stepanova (Russia) leads an Armed Conflicts and Conflict Management Project at Stockholm International Peace Research Institute (SIPRI). She has been a Senior Research Associate on non-traditional security threats at Center for International Security, Moscow Institute of World Economy and International Relations (IMEMO) since 2001. She serves on the editorial board of the journals *Terrorism and Political Violence* (St Andrews University), and *Security*

Index (CREP, Geneva). Previously, she has worked as a researcher on armed conflict and terrorism at SIPRI (2003), and a researcher at the Moscow Center of the Carnegie Endowment for International Peace (1994–2000). She has held several Russian research fellowships, was twice adjudged McArthur Research Fellow (2000 and 2003), and a McArthur NGO Fellow at King's College, University of London (1998). She is the author of several monographs, including *Terrorism in Asymmetrical Conflict: Ideological and Structural Aspects* (2008), *Anti-Terrorism and Peace-Building During and After Conflict* (2003), and *Civil–Military Relations In Operations Other Than War* (2001). Her book, *The Role of Illicit Drug Business in the Political Economy of Conflicts and Terrorism* (2005), won the gold medal from the Russian Academy of Sciences.

CONTRIBUTORS

Rogelio Alonso (Spain) is a Lecturer in Politics and Terrorism at Rey Juan Carlos University, Madrid, and he coordinates the 'Unit for Documentation and Analysis on Terrorism' in the university, as well as its PhD programme on 'Analysis and Prevention of Terrorism'. From 1994 to 2004, he was a Lecturer at the School of Economics and Politics in The University of Ulster in Belfast. He was also a Research Fellow at the Institute of Governance, Public Policy and Social Research, and at the Institute of Irish Studies, both at the Queen's University of Belfast. He holds a PhD in International Relations and a Master in Irish Studies. In 1995 Queen's University and the Irish Association awarded him with the Montgomery Medal for his research on British policy towards Northern Ireland. In 2005, his article 'Pathways out of terrorism in Northern Ireland and the Basque Country' in *Terrorism and Political Violence* (winter 2004) won the award of the Spanish Association of Political Science for the best article published in an academic journal. Dr Alonso's most recent book, *The IRA and Armed Struggle* (2007) is based on the widest sample of personal interviews with former IRA members ever carried out. He is the author of three other books on terrorism and has written numerous chapters in collective books as well as articles in academic journals such as *Terrorism and Political Violence* as well as *Studies in Conflict and Terrorism*. He acts as book review editor for the journal *Democracy and Security*, and is a member of the editorial board of *Studies in Conflict and Terrorism*.

Subir Bhaumik (India) is BBC's correspondent for eastern India and author of the book, *Insurgent Crossfire: North-East India*, which he completed as the Queen Elizabeth House fellow in the University of Oxford in 1989–1990. During his quarter-of-a-century-long career in journalism, Bhaumik has filed important news reports from the North East, Bangladesh, Bhutan, and Myanmar. Bhaumik has also presented over 30 papers in national and international seminars and contributed to over 20 edited anthologies. His forthcoming work, *Troubled Periphery: Crisis of India's Northeast*, is expected to be a pioneering work on security in the region.

Khatchik DerGhougassian (Argentina) defended his Doctoral thesis in International Relations in 2004 at the University of Miami in Coral Gables, Florida. He received his MA in International Relations from the Facultad Latinoamericana de Ciencias Sociales in Buenos Aires, Argentina, in 1994. He is a professor of International Relations and a researcher at the Universidad de San Andrés (Buenos Aires, Argentina). With an extensive academic experience, he has held positions as a Visiting Research Associate on the Collaborative Peace Project at the Institute for Security Studies in South Africa (1997); served as an advisor for gun control issues to the Ministry of Justice and Security for the Province of Buenos Aires (1998–1999), and as a researcher at the Partnership for the Study and Prevention of Violence at the Jackson Memorial Hospital, University of Miami (Miami, Florida, 2001–2002). He is the recipient of the Dante B. Fascell North–South Center Doctoral Fellowship (2000–2003); the Faculty Research Program on Canadian Studies 1999/2000 Award for research on Canada's gun control policy (1999); and the Ford Foundation Grant for The Southern Cone Program of Training for Civilians in Defense Policies (1998).

Adam Dolnik (Australia/Czech Republic) is the Director of Research Programmes and Senior Research Fellow at the Centre for Transnational Crime Prevention at the University of Wollongong in Australia. Previously, he has served as Chief Trainer at the International Centre for Political Violence and Terrorism Research at the Institute of Defence and Strategic Studies in Singapore, and has held research positions at the WMD Terrorism Project, Monterey Institute of International Studies in California, as well as at the United Nations Terrorism Prevention Branch in Vienna. He has published in a number of edited books and in various international journals, including *Terrorism and Political Violence, Studies in Conflict and Terrorism, International Negotiation: Journal of Theory and Practice, Perspectives: Central European Review of International Affairs*, and *Yaderny Kontrol*. Dolnik is also the author of *Understanding Terrorist Innovation: Technology, Tactics, and Global Trends* (2007) and *Negotiating Hostage Crises with the New Terrorists* (2007).

Amos N. Guiora (Israel/USA) is Professor of Law S.J. at the Quinney College of Law in the University of Utah. He has served for 19 years in the Israel Defense Forces (IDF), and held senior command positions in the Judge Advocate General's Corps, including that of Legal Advisor to the Gaza Strip, Judge Advocate for the Navy and Home Front Commands, and Commander IDF School of Military Law. The contributor would like to thank former research fellow for the Institute for Global Security Law and Policy, Rebecca Slazinski for her invaluable contribution in researching and editing the chapter.

Ramani Hariharan (India) is a retired colonel of the Indian army's Intelligence Corps, and has served in the army for nearly three decades. During his career he was a Military Intelligence specialist on Bangladesh, Burma, and Sri Lanka, with special focus on insurgency and terrorism. He participated in the Indo–Pak war in Kutch (1965) and in the Liberation of Bangladesh (1971). Col. Hariharan has taken part in counter insurgency operations in Assam, Manipur, Mizoram, Nagaland, Punjab, and Tripura. He served as the Head of Intelligence of the Indian Peace Keeping Force in Sri Lanka (1987–1990). He was awarded the Vishisht Sewa Medal by the President of India for distinguished service in Sri Lanka. He is a member of the Delhi-based intelligence think tank, South Asia Analysis Group, and has contributed chapters to *Conflict Resolution and Peace Building in Sri Lanka* (2005), *Sri Lanka: Peace Without Process* (2006) and *Peace Process in Sri Lanka: Challenges and Opportunities* (2007). Col. Hariharan was awarded the Konrad Adenauer Medal for the leadership he provided to the joint project of Madras Management Association where he served as an Executive Director upon retirement from the army.

Florencio Domínguez Iribarren (Spain) is currently chief editor of the Press Agency Vasco Press based in Bilbao. He holds a PhD in Communications, and has authored many key titles on the Basque terrorist organization ETA. Some of them are: 'Josu Ternera: una vida en ETA' (Josu Ternera: a life in ETA), a non authorised biography of the terrorist leader at the front of the terrorist group for many years; 'Las raíces del miedo' (The roots of fear), a thorough analysis of the political and social effects of ETA's terrorism; 'Dentro de ETA' (Inside ETA), an examination of the underground lives of ETA's activists based on unprecedented access to primary sources elaborated by the terrorists themselves; and 'De la negociación a la tregua: ¿el final de ETA?' (From negotiations to the truce: the end of ETA?), a highly acclaimed study of ETA's strategy and evolution. He is a regular contributor to the Basque and Spanish media on issues related to terrorism.

Jennifer Lynn Oetken (USA) is a PhD candidate in the political science department in Indiana University, Bloomington, USA. Her academic research focuses on radical politics and violence in India and South Asia. She is currently studying Bengali at the American Institute for Indian Studies in Kolkata and is conducting her dissertation research in West Bengal, India. Oetken's co-authored article, 'Secularism, Democracy and Hindu Nationalism' was published in *Asian Security*.

Mohamed Nawab Bin Mohamed Osman (Malaysia) is an Associate Research Fellow with the Contemporary Islam Program, at the S. Rajaratnam School of International Studies, Nanyang Technological University, Singapore. He graduated with a Bachelor of Arts (Hons) in History and Political Science from the National University of Singapore (NUS) and a Master of Arts (History), NUS. He taught several modules on Asian history between 2004 and 2006. His research interest includes the history and politics of Southeast Asia and South Asia, Islamic political groups in Southeast Asia namely, the Islamic Party of Malaysia (PAS), the Justice and Prosperity Party (PKS Indonesia), Hizbut Tahrir in Southeast Asia, Jemaah Islamiyah, Jamaat-e-Islami Pakistan and India, the Gulen Movement in Southeast Asia and the international politics of Southeast Asia. He is currently working on a book on the history of Islam in South East Asia. Mohamed Nawab holds the position of secretary-general, Young Association of Muslim

Professional and is also working with members of the Liberal Islam Network in Indonesia and the Middle Eastern Graduate Association in Malaysia to establish a South East Asia Liberal Islam Forum aimed at countering extremist ideologies in the region.

Bishnu Raj Upreti (Nepal) holds a PhD in conflict management from Wageningen University, the Netherlands. He is actively engaged in conflict transformation and peace related research in South Asia. During the 26 years of his professional career, he was engaged in teaching and research at University of London, University of Surrey in the United Kingdom, and Kathmandu University. Upreti has also briefly been in government service. He has authored 10 books on conflict management, including *Armed Conflict and Peace Process in Nepal* (2006), and numerous articles in national and international journals, magazines and edited books. Currently, he is the Regional Coordinator, South Asia Coordination Office of the Swiss National Centre of Competence in Research North-South, based in Kathmandu.

INDEX

Afghan war, 82
All Tripura Tiger Force (ATTF), 149
Al-Qaeda, 154, 192
    ideology of, 207
    links with LTTE, 67
Argentina
    terrorist attacks in, 20–21
Assam
    demographic invasions in, 143
Australia
    response towards LTTE, 67
Avenging Israel's Blood (DIN), 212
Awami League, in Bangladesh, 76

Bangladesh
    emergence of, 71
    introduction of fifth amendment by
        Zia (1971), 72
    Jamaat-e-Islami (JeL), in Bangladesh,
        74
    military coup after independence
        (1975), 72
Bangladesh Nationalist Party (BNP), 73
Basque Homeland and Freedom. *See*
    Euskadi ta Askatasuna (ETA)
Bengali linguistic nationalism (1952)
    emergence of, 71
Biological terrorism, 213
Black Tigers
    of LTTE, 49

Canada
    LTTE in, 62–64
Chemical, Biological, Radiological, and
    Nuclear (CBRN) terrorism, 210–12,
    214–15
    acquisition and weaponization, of
        agents, 221–24
Chemical terrorism, 212

Chhattisgarh (India)
    Maoist insurgency in, 106
Chinese aid
    to Naga insurgent groups, 148
Cold war, xviii
    post period of, xxii
Communist Party of India (Marxist)
    CPI (M)
    origin of, 105
Communist Party of Nepal (Maoist)
    CPN (M), 93
    member of Revolutionary Inter-
        nationalist Movement (RIM),
        101
    relations with CCOMOSA, 102–03
Co-ordination Committee of Maoist
    Parties and Organizations of South
    Asia (CCOMPOSA), 102
Cuban revolution (1959)
    overthrow of Batista dictatorship, 30

Defence zone, 144
Department of Homeland Security (US)
    establishment after 9/11 attacks, 18
Doctrine of National Security, 22
Drug trafficking
    in Latin America, 36

Euskadi ta Askatasuna (ETA)
    and Northern Island, 13–16
    decline of, 3
    demand for international mediators,
        for internationalization of con-
        flict, 12
    network of contacts of, 5–7
    overlapping of activities of, 11
Extremist ideology
    of terrorist groups, 194

Fast attack craft (FAC), 49. *See also*
Liberation Tigers of Tamil Eelam
(LTTE)
Federal Bureau of Investigation (FBI), 47
Foco theory, 30
Foreign policy
of Nepal, 113
Foreign Terrorist Organizations (FTO),
19, 30, 50
France
LTTE operation from, 66
Fuerzas Armadas Revolucionarias de
Colombia (FARC). *See* Revolutionary
Armed Forces of Colombia

Gaza strip, 167–68
Guerrilla warfare, xiv
definition of, 29

Hamas, 166
supporters of, 168–70
Hizb-ul-Mujahideen (HM), 79

Imperialism
in United States, 39
internal terrorism
TWEED definition on, xx
International actors
Maoist classification of, 111–12
International Humanitarian Law (IHL),
xiv
International Islamic Charitable Organ-
ization (IICO), 77
International Islamic Front (IIF), 79
International terrorism, xiii
and Palestinian, 166–67
Inter Services Intelligence's (ISI), 67, 145
Intifada
in Palestine, 165
Irish Northern Aid Committee
(NORAID), 8
Irish Republican Army (IRA)
decline of, 3
international connections of, 7–11
Islami Bank Bangladesh Limited (IBBL),
78
Islamic Circle of North America (ICNA),
79

Islamist movement
organizational specificity, 205–07
Islamist terrorism, 155
perpetration of terrorism by, 3–4
Israel Embassy (1992)
bombing in, 20

Jagrata Muslim Janata Bangladesh
(JMJB), 78, 154
Jaish-e-Mohammed (JeM), 79
Jamaat-e-Islami (JeL), in Bangladesh
ban after Bangladesh independence,
75
collaboration with Awami League
and BNP, 76
involvement in war crimes, 77–78
origin of, 75
Jama'atul Mujahideen Bangladesh
(JMB), 78, 154
Jammu Kashmir Liberation Front
(JKLF), 119
armed struggle of, 121–25
Jemaah Islamiyah (JI), 183–88
and al-qaeda
financial cooperation, 183–84
operational cooperation, 181–82
sharing of facilities, 182–83
connection with Afghanistan, 180–81
history of, 177–79
ideology, 179
origin of, 175–77

Kashmir accession to Pakistan
and Hizb-ul-Mujaheedin, 125–29

Lashkar-e-Toiba (LeT), 118
Latin America
terrorism in, 28–34, 41
after 9/11 terrorist attacks, 34–41
League of Nations, 29
Liberation Tigers of Tamil Eelam (LTTE),
21, 47
army strength of, 48
ban by India on, 50
black tigers (*see* Black Tigers, of
LTTE)

building of, international support
network of, 50, 67–69
in Canada (*see* Canada, LTTE in)
FBI statement on, 47
links with islamic terrorist groups, 67
naval arm, 49
origin of, 50–51
Pape's analysis on, 170
Prabhakaran vision, 50
in Sri Lanka, 34
terror tactics of, 48
United Kingdom (UK) ban on,
64–65
women soliders by, use of, 49–50

Manipur
annexation by India, 144
Maoist Communist Centre (MCC), 105
Maoist insurgency, in Nepal, 94, 104–08
causes of, 94–95
development of, external link by
maoist
expansion of base, 109
gaining, of publicity, 109–10
generation of, resources, 110
ending of insurgency after Comprehensive Peace Agreement
(CPA), 98–99
external actors interest on, 112–13
ideological and political dimensions
of, 100–01
Nepalese diaspora in, role of, 103–04
tactics used by Maoist, 96–98
Maoist movement
in India, 106
Memorial Institute for the Prevention of
Terrorism (MIPT), xvii, xviii
Minnesota Patriots Council (MPC), 213
Mumbai attack, 231–33
Muslim immigration
from Middle-East, 39
Muslim United Liberation Tigers of
Assam (MULTA), 78, 79

Naga insurgency, 147
Narcoguerrilla, 20, 36
Narcoterrorism, 20
Narcotic policy(ies)
during Clinton administration, 37

National Socialist Council of Nagalim
(NSCN), xiv, 146
Naxalite movement
in India, 104–08
Non-state actors
vs. terrorist, xv
Northern Ireland Civil Rights Association,
15
Nuclear terrorism, 214

Organization of Islamic countries (OIC),
73

Pakistan
support to terrorist groups, 145
Palestinian Authority (PA). *See* Palestinian
Liberation Organization (PLO)
Palestinian Liberation Organization
(PLO), 30, 161–62, 165
Hamas engagement with, 166
origin of, 163–64
People's Liberation Guerrilla Army, 107
People War Group (PWG), 105
Plan Colombia, 37
Popular Front for the Liberation of
Palestine (PFLP), 7
Proxy war, 144
in South Asia, 145

Racial profiling approach, 143
Radiological terrorism, 214
Reagan–Gorbachov summit (1987), 35
Red Fort
Islamic militants attack on, 118
Religion
and terrorism, 172–73
Revival of Islamic Heritage Society
(RIHS)
blame for bomb explosion, in
Bangladesh, 81
Revolutionary Armed Forces of
Colombia, 10

Salafi movement
in Pakistan, 146
South Asia
ideal condition for sponsored insurgency, 145

Sri Lanka government
    signing of ceasefire agreement with
        LTTE, 68
Students' Islamic Movement of India
    (SIMI), 79
Suicide bomber(s)
    motivation of, 170–72

Tamil diaspora
    in Sri Lanka, 51–52
Tamil nationalism
    rise of, 52–53
Tamil Tigers. *See* Liberation Tigers of
    Tamil Eelam
Terrorism, xiii, xvii, 193
    challenge to international community,
        192
    database on, xvii
    definition of, xx
    vs. guerrilla warfare, xiv
    infliction by ETA and IRA groups, 4
    internationalization of, xx, 22–28,
        120–21, 192
        Kashmir experience, 119–20
    in Jammu and Kashmir, 118–19
    in Latin America (*see* Latin America,
        terrorism in)
    vs. non-state actors (*see* Non-state
        actors *vs.* terrorist)
    political motivation of, xiv
    and religion (*see* Religion and
        terrorism)
    transnational Islamic, 129–34
    used by drug cartels, 36
Terrorism in Western Europe Events
    Dataset (TWEED), xx
Terrorism knowledge base, xvii
Terrorist group(s)
    advantages of, 193

contemporary assessment of, 224–27
    Jaish-e-Mohammad (JeM), xiv
    Lashkar-e-Toiba (LeT), xiv, 79
Third wave terrorism
    in Latin America, 28–34
Transnational Islamism
    and local Islamist national groups,
        194–98
    and protest against past ideologies,
        198–200
Treaty of Yandaboo, 141
Tripura
    demographic invasions in, 143

United Liberation Front of Asom (ULFA),
    xiv, 108, 143, 150–58
United Nations Security Council (UNSC),
    xvi
United States (US)
    action towards LTTE, 65–66
    imperialism in (*see* Imperialism, in
        United States)
    9/11 terrorist attack on, xvii
UN Office of the High Commissioner for
    Human Rights (UNOHCHR), 104
Unrepresented Peoples' Organization,
    148
USA Patriot Act, 18

Women soldiers
    used by LTTE, 49–50
World Assembly of Muslim Youth
    (WAMY), 77
World People's Resistance Movement
    (WPRM), 101–02
11 September 2001, 4, 18
    terrorism, in Latin America after,
        34–41
    terrorist attack on US on, xvii